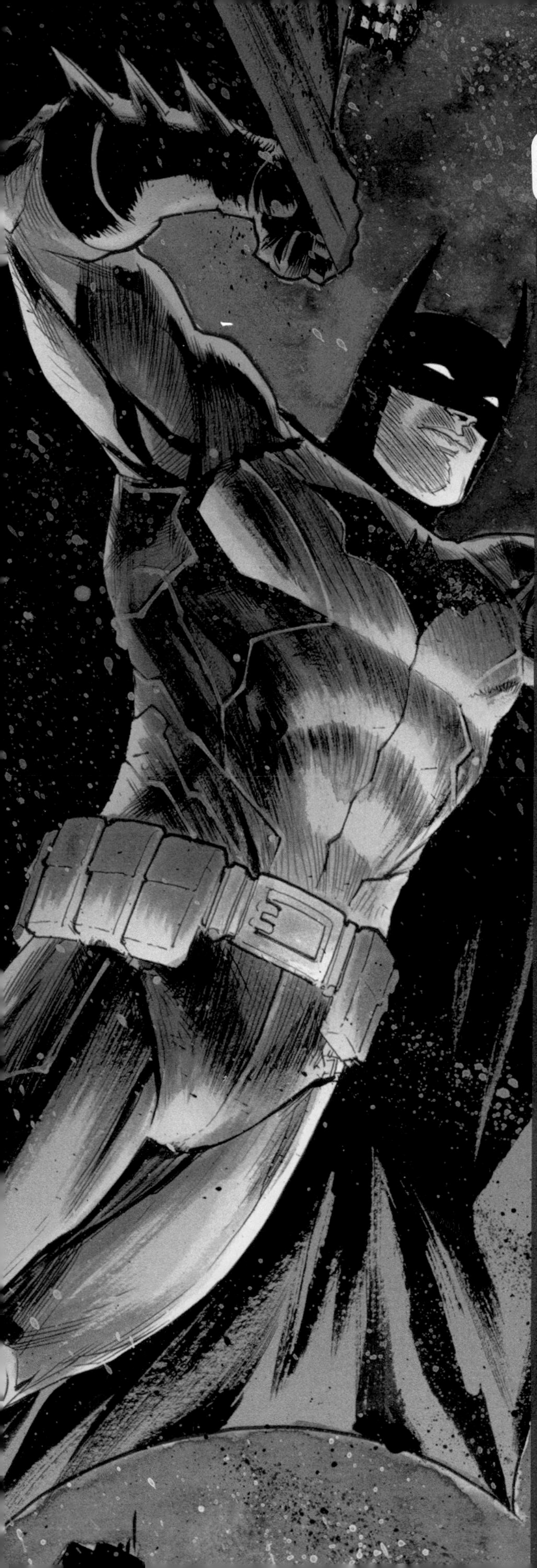

VOLUME 7
ANARKY

BATMAN - DETECTIVE COMICS

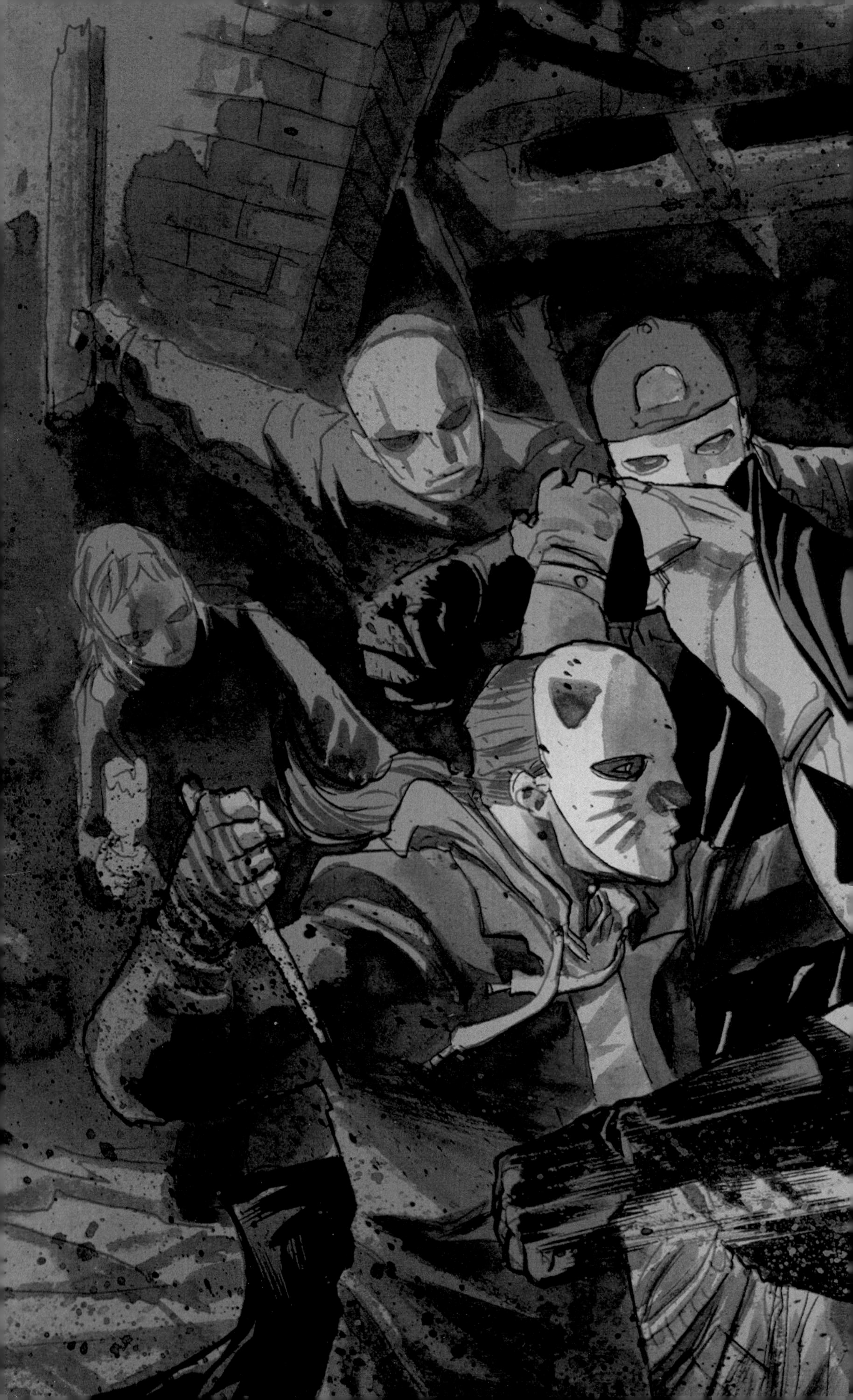

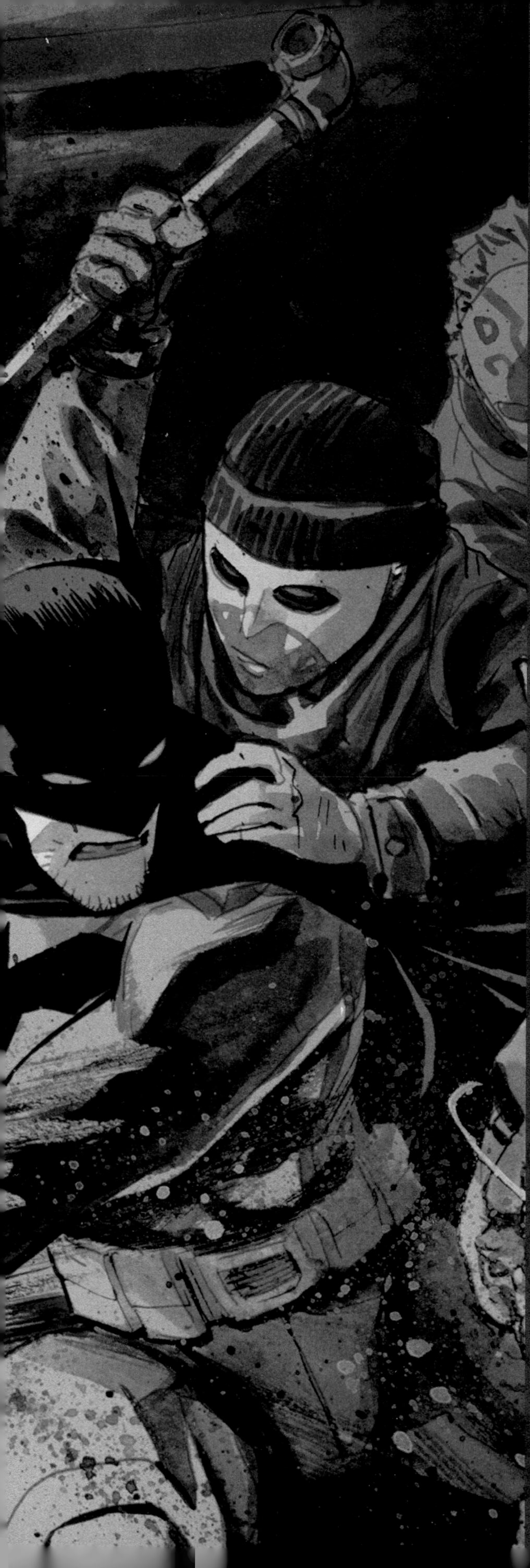

BATMAN – DETECTIVE COMICS

VOLUME 7
ANARKY

WRITTEN BY
BRIAN BUCCELLATO
FRANCIS MANAPUL
BENJAMIN PERCY

ART BY
FRANCIS MANAPUL
JOHN PAUL LEON
ROGE ANTONIO
RONAN CLIQUET
SCOTT HEPBURN
CLIFF RICHARDS
FABRIZIO FIORENTINO

COLOR BY
BRIAN BUCCELLATO
NICK FILARDI
LEE LOUGHRIDGE
DAVE STEWART
JOHN PAUL LEON

LETTERS BY
JARED K. FLETCHER
DAVE SHARPE
DEZI SIENTY

COLLECTION COVER ART BY
FRANCIS MANAPUL
& BRIAN BUCCELLATO

BATMAN CREATED BY
BOB KANE WITH **BILL FINGER**

RACHEL GLUCKSTERN Editor – Original Series
DAVE WIELGOSZ Assistant Editor – Original Series
JEB WOODARD Group Editor – Collected Editions
STEVE COOK Design Director – Books
DAMIAN RYLAND Publication Design

BOB HARRAS Senior VP – Editor-in-Chief, DC Comics

DIANE NELSON President
DAN DIDIO and JIM LEE Co-Publishers
GEOFF JOHNS Chief Creative Officer
AMIT DESAI Senior VP – Marketing & Global Franchise Management
NAIRI GARDINER Senior VP – Finance
SAM ADES VP – Digital Marketing
BOBBIE CHASE VP – Talent Development
MARK CHIARELLO Senior VP – Art, Design & Collected Editions
JOHN CUNNINGHAM VP – Content Strategy
ANNE DEPIES VP – Strategy Planning & Reporting
DON FALLETTI VP – Manufacturing Operations
LAWRENCE GANEM VP – Editorial Administration & Talent Relations
ALISON GILL Senior VP – Manufacturing & Operations
HANK KANALZ Senior VP – Editorial Strategy & Administration
JAY KOGAN VP – Legal Affairs
DEREK MADDALENA Senior VP – Sales & Business Development
JACK MAHAN VP – Business Affairs
DAN MIRON VP – Sales Planning & Trade Development
NICK NAPOLITANO VP – Manufacturing Administration
CAROL ROEDER VP – Marketing
EDDIE SCANNELL VP – Mass Account & Digital Sales
COURTNEY SIMMONS Senior VP – Publicity & Communications
JIM (SKI) SOKOLOWSKI VP – Comic Book Specialty & Newsstand Sales
SANDY YI Senior VP – Global Franchise Management

BATMAN – DETECTIVE COMICS VOLUME 7: ANARKY

DC Comics, 2900 West Alameda Ave., Burbank, CA 91505
Printed by RR Donnelley, Owensville, MO, USA. 6/24/16. First Printing.
ISBN: 978-1-4012-6354-6

Library of Congress Cataloging-in-Publication Data

Buccellato, Brian.
Batman/Detective Comics. Volume 7, Anarky / Brian Buccellato, Francis Manapul.
pages cm. — (The New 52!)
ISBN 978-1-4012-6354-6
1. Graphic novels. I. Manapul, Francis, illustrator. II. Title. III. Title: Anarky.
PN6728.B36B84 2016
741.5'973—dc23
2015033153

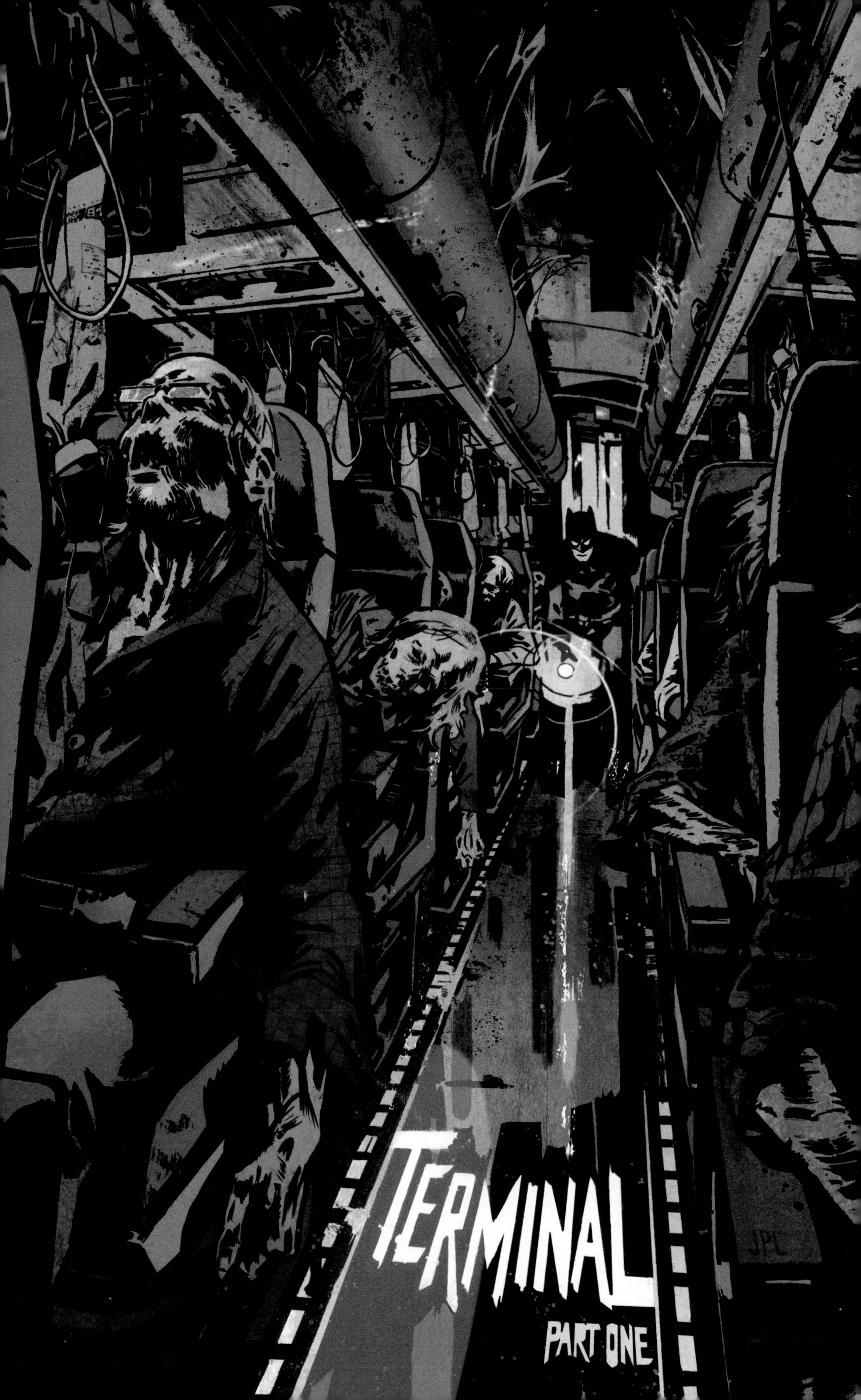
TERMINAL
PART ONE
JPL

BENJAMIN PERCY writer JOHN PAUL LEON artist DAVE STEWART colorist JARED K. FLETCHER letterer cover by JOHN PAUL LEON

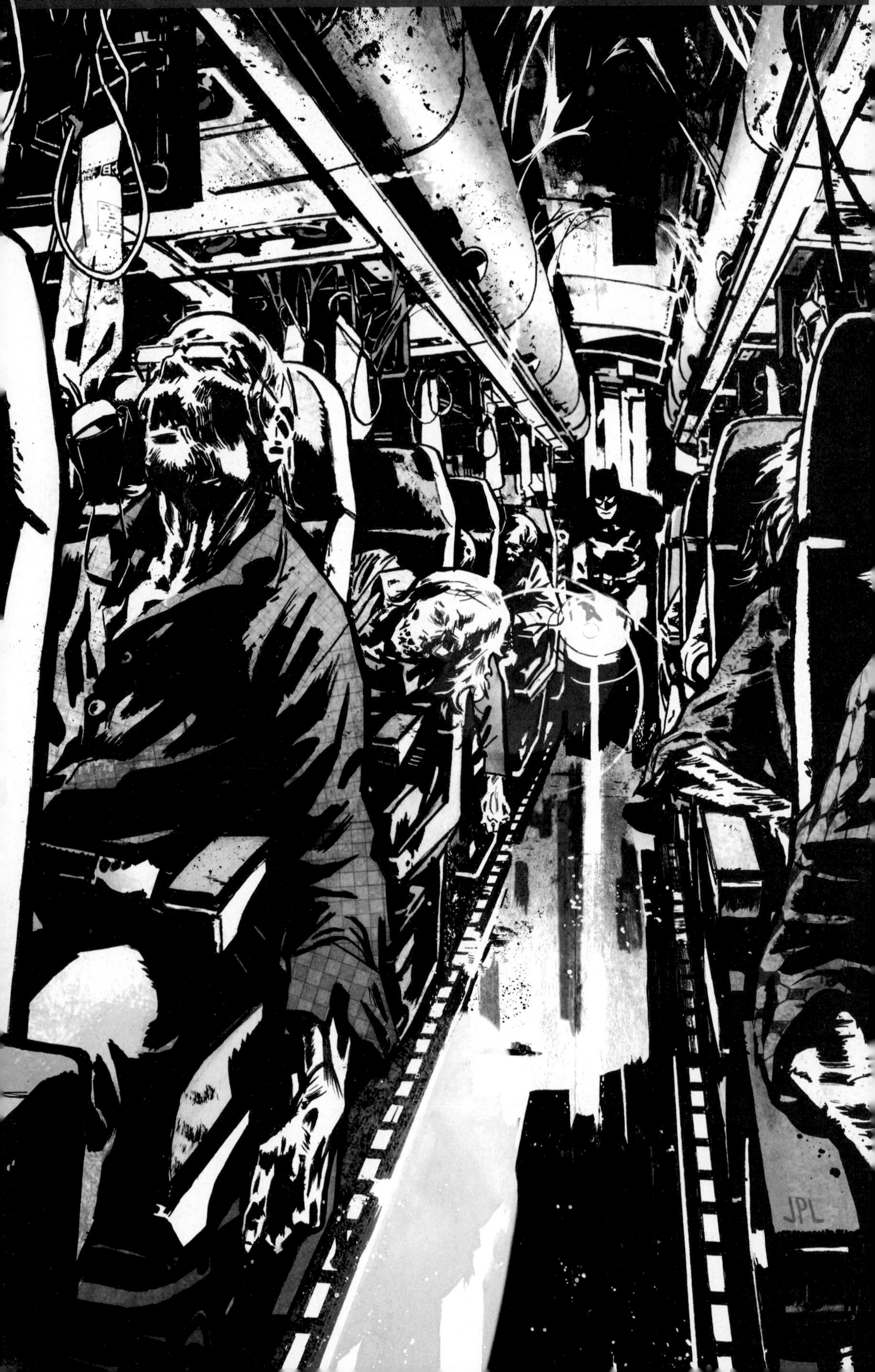
JPL

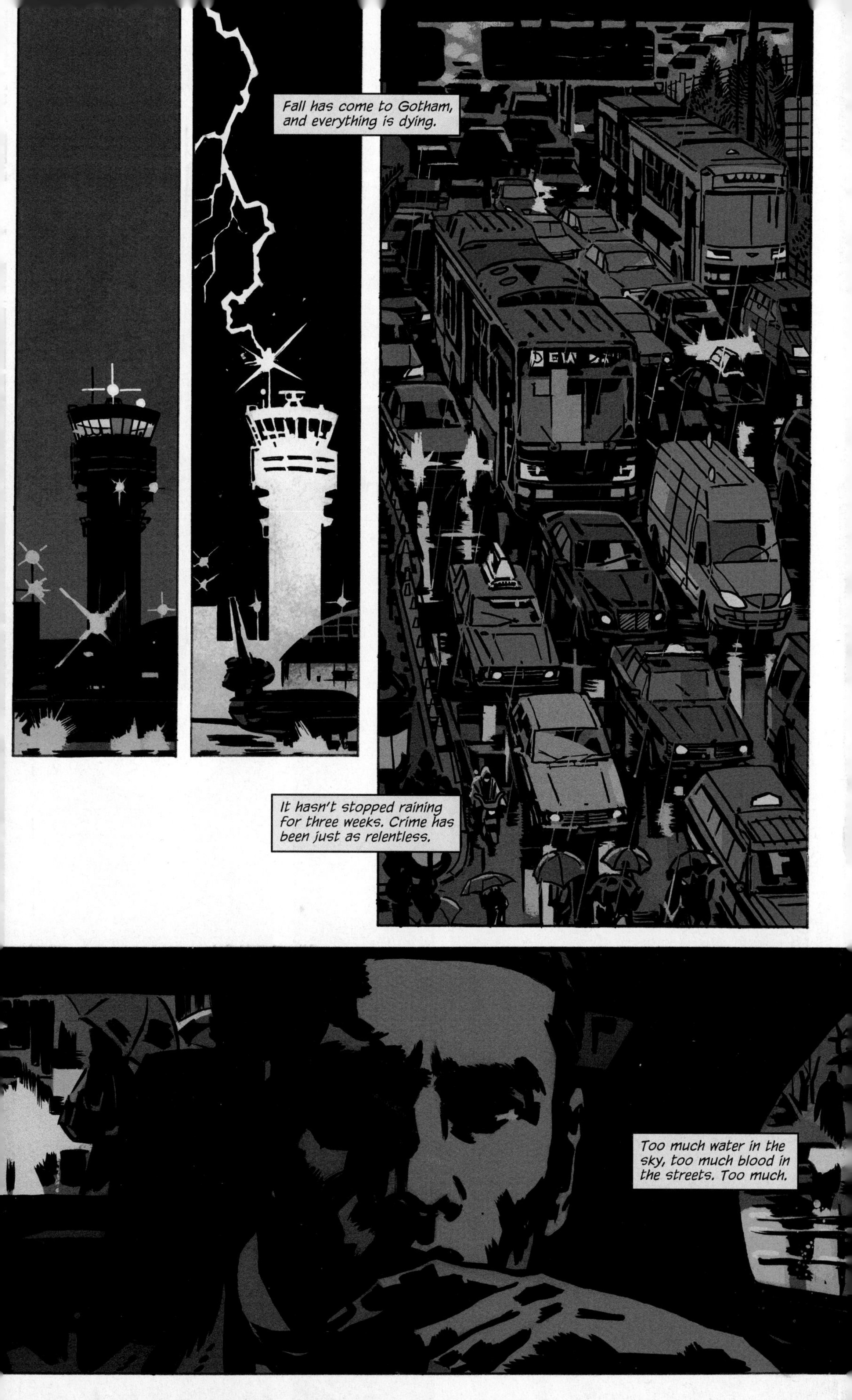
Fall has come to Gotham, and everything is dying.
It hasn't stopped raining for three weeks. Crime has been just as relentless.
Too much water in the sky, too much blood in the streets. Too much.

Terminal 1

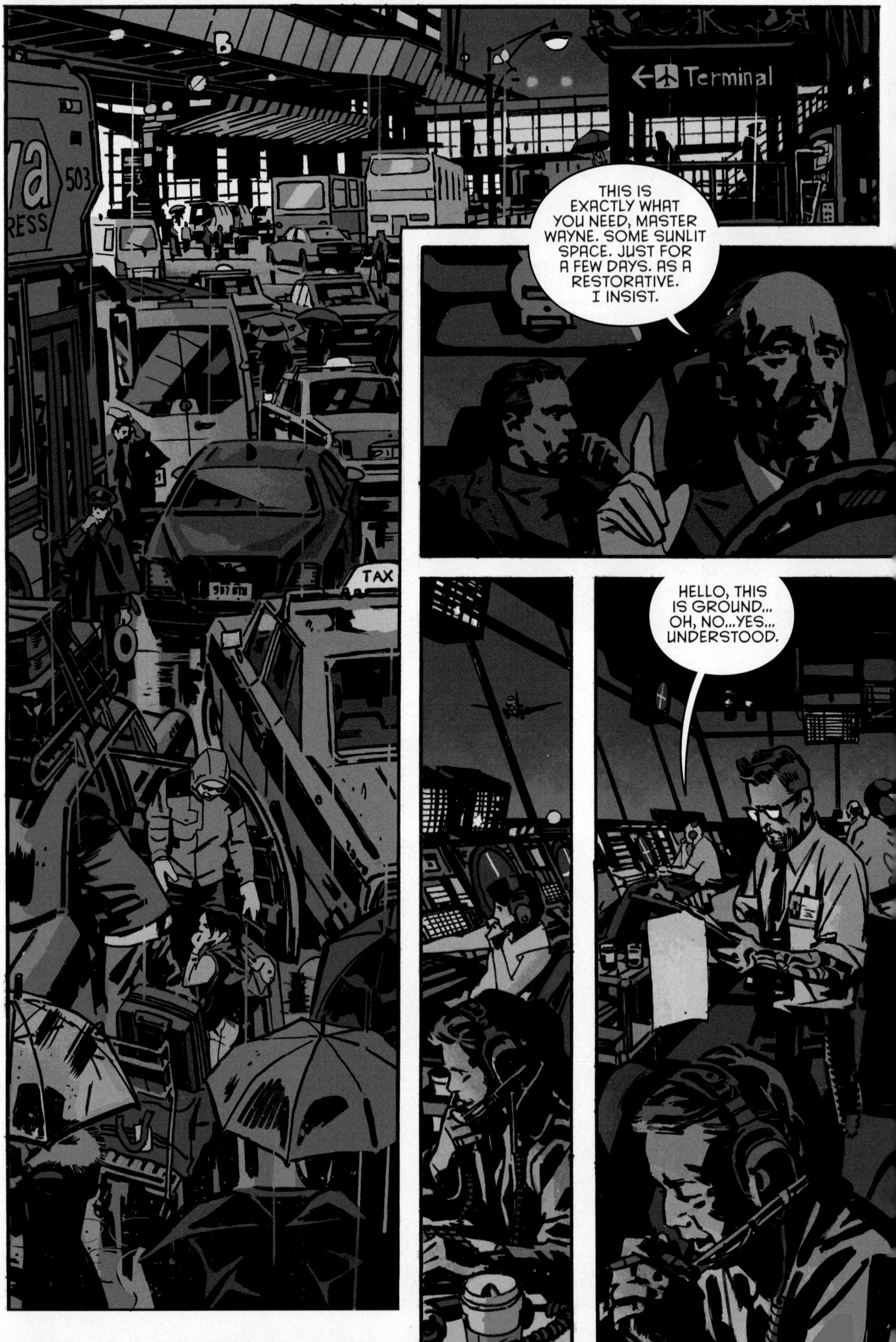

← Terminal
TAX
THIS IS EXACTLY WHAT YOU NEED, MASTER WAYNE. SOME SUNLIT SPACE. JUST FOR A FEW DAYS. AS A RESTORATIVE. I INSIST.
HELLO, THIS IS GROUND... OH, NO...YES... UNDERSTOOD.

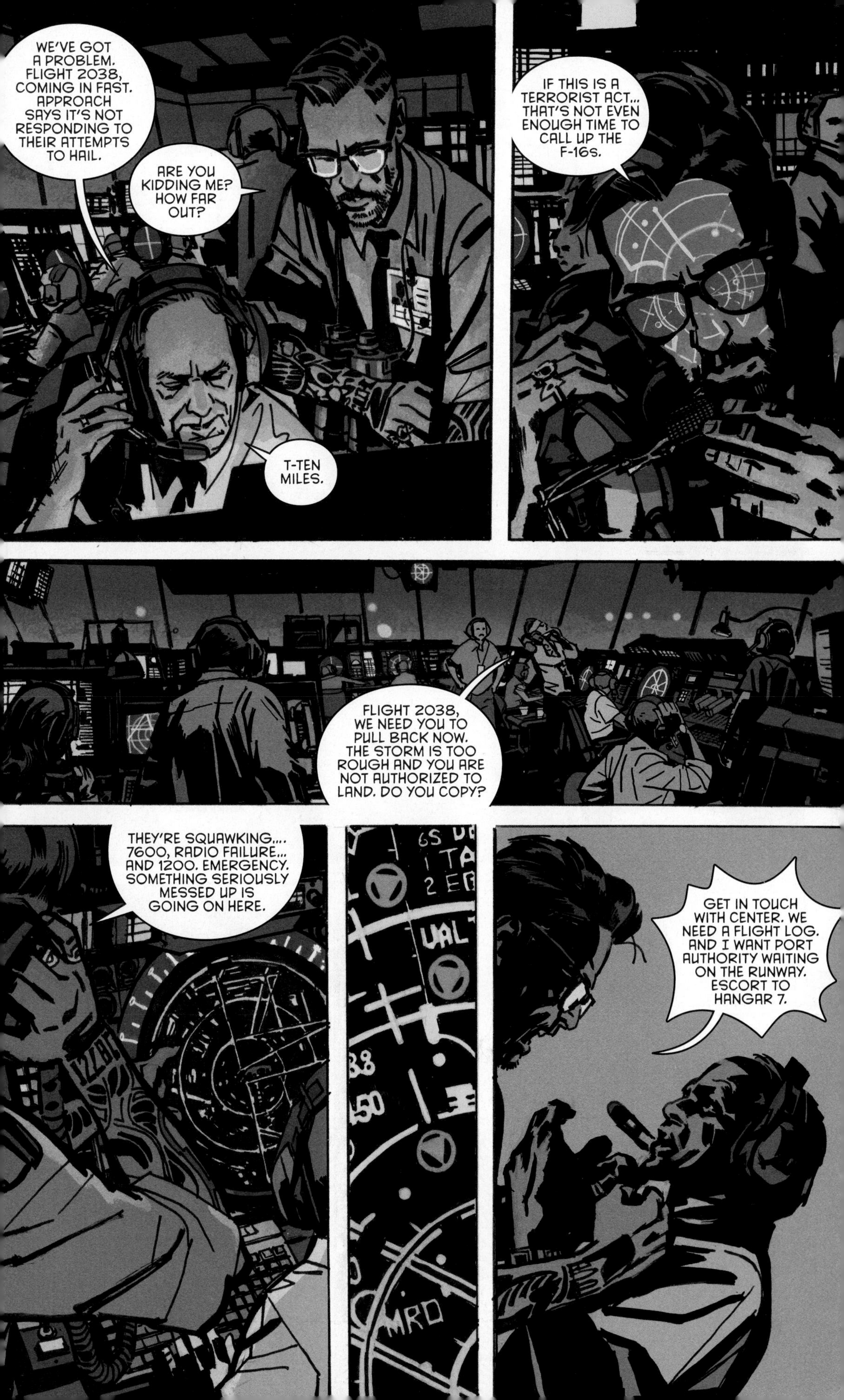
WE'VE GOT A PROBLEM. FLIGHT 2038, COMING IN FAST. APPROACH SAYS IT'S NOT RESPONDING TO THEIR ATTEMPTS TO HAIL.
ARE YOU KIDDING ME? HOW FAR OUT?
T-TEN MILES.
IF THIS IS A TERRORIST ACT... THAT'S NOT EVEN ENOUGH TIME TO CALL UP THE F-16s.
FLIGHT 2038, WE NEED YOU TO PULL BACK NOW. THE STORM IS TOO ROUGH AND YOU ARE NOT AUTHORIZED TO LAND. DO YOU COPY?
THEY'RE SQUAWKING.... 7600, RADIO FAILURE... AND 1200. EMERGENCY. SOMETHING SERIOUSLY MESSED UP IS GOING ON HERE.
GET IN TOUCH WITH CENTER. WE NEED A FLIGHT LOG. AND I WANT PORT AUTHORITY WAITING ON THE RUNWAY. ESCORT TO HANGAR 7.

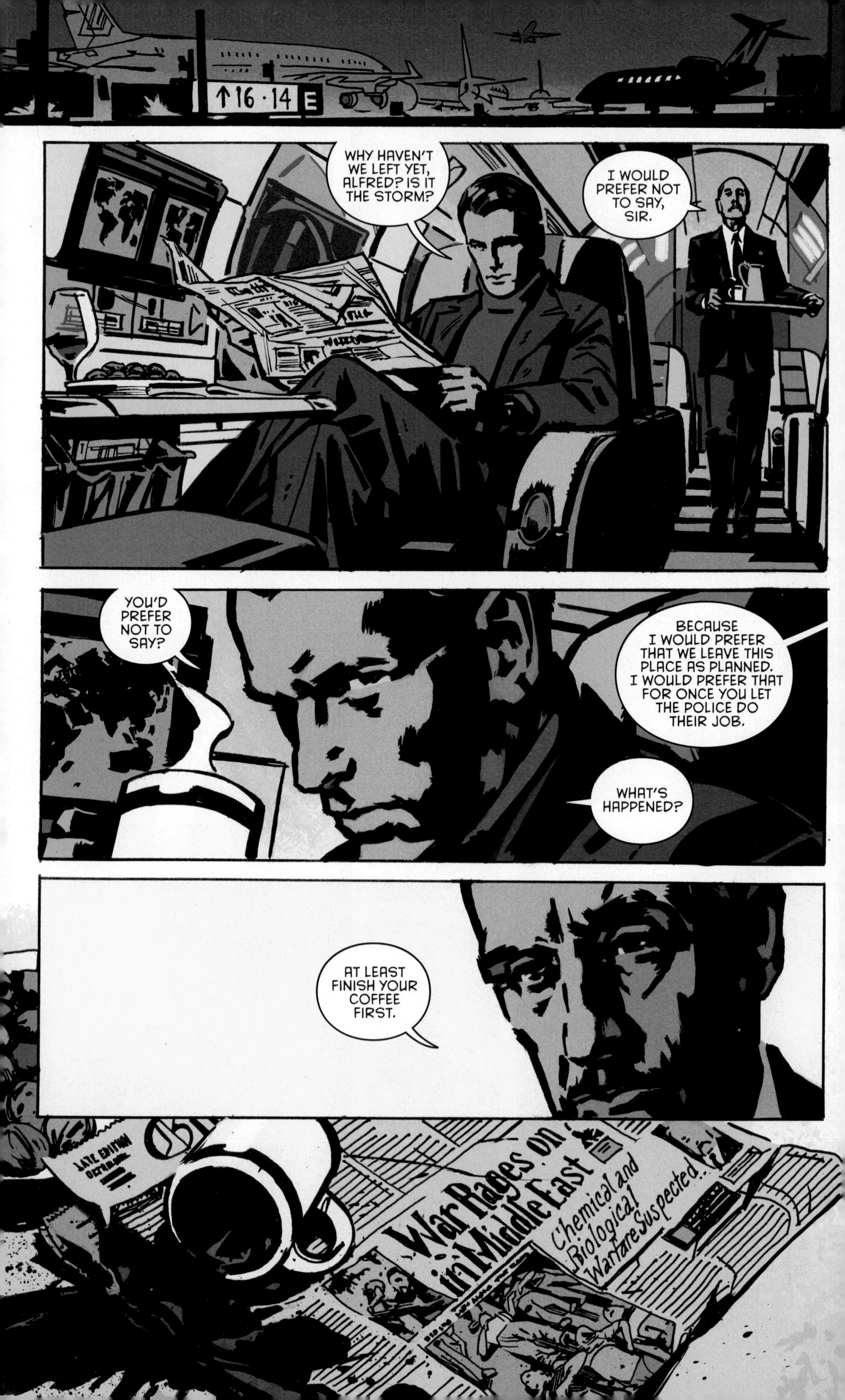
↑16 · 14 E
WHY HAVEN'T WE LEFT YET, ALFRED? IS IT THE STORM?
I WOULD PREFER NOT TO SAY, SIR.
YOU'D PREFER NOT TO SAY?
BECAUSE I WOULD PREFER THAT WE LEAVE THIS PLACE AS PLANNED. I WOULD PREFER THAT FOR ONCE YOU LET THE POLICE DO THEIR JOB.
WHAT'S HAPPENED?
AT LEAST FINISH YOUR COFFEE FIRST.
LATE EDITION
War Rages on in Middle East
Chemical and Biological Warfare Suspected...

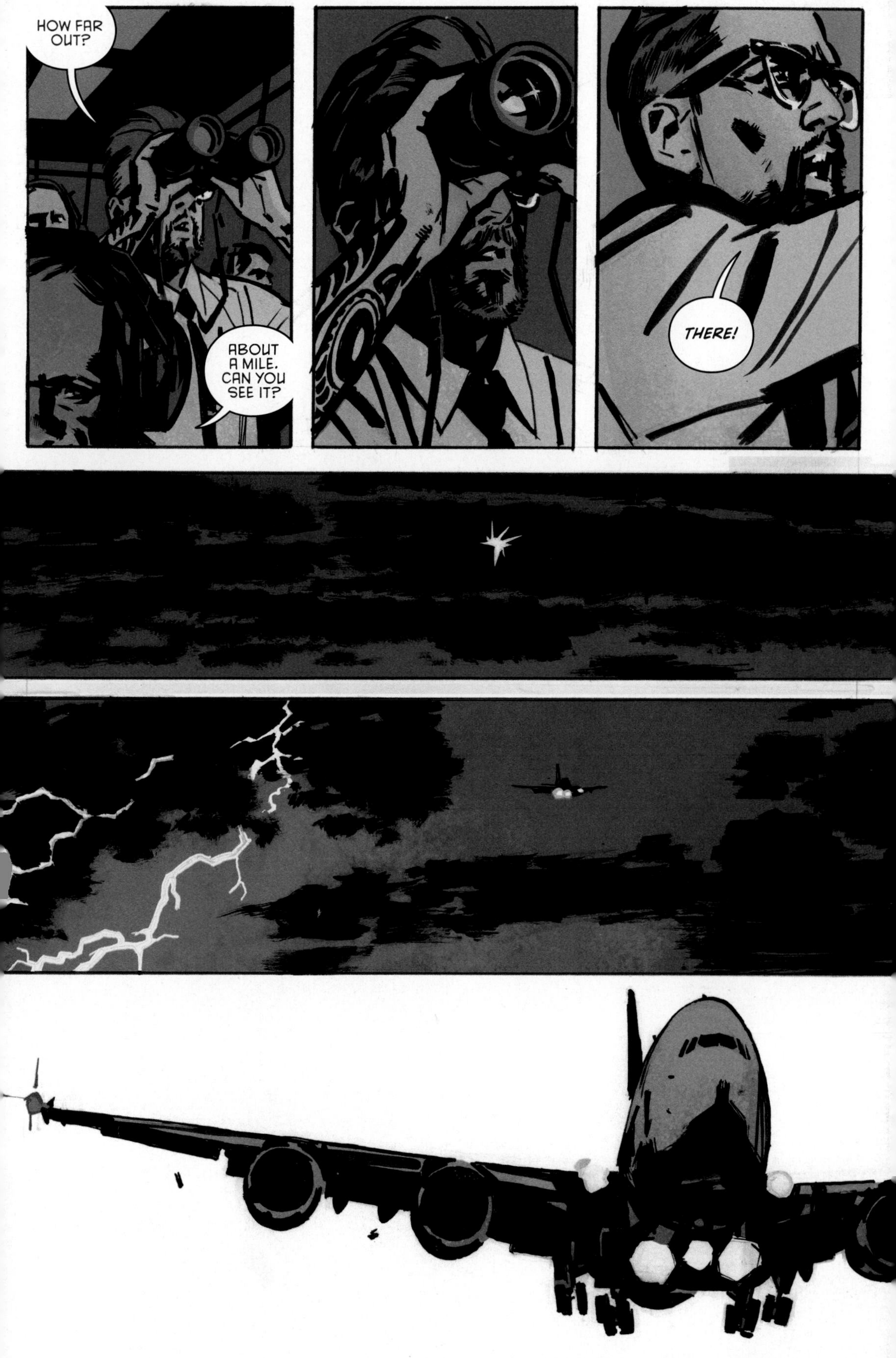
HOW FAR OUT?
ABOUT A MILE. CAN YOU SEE IT?
THERE!

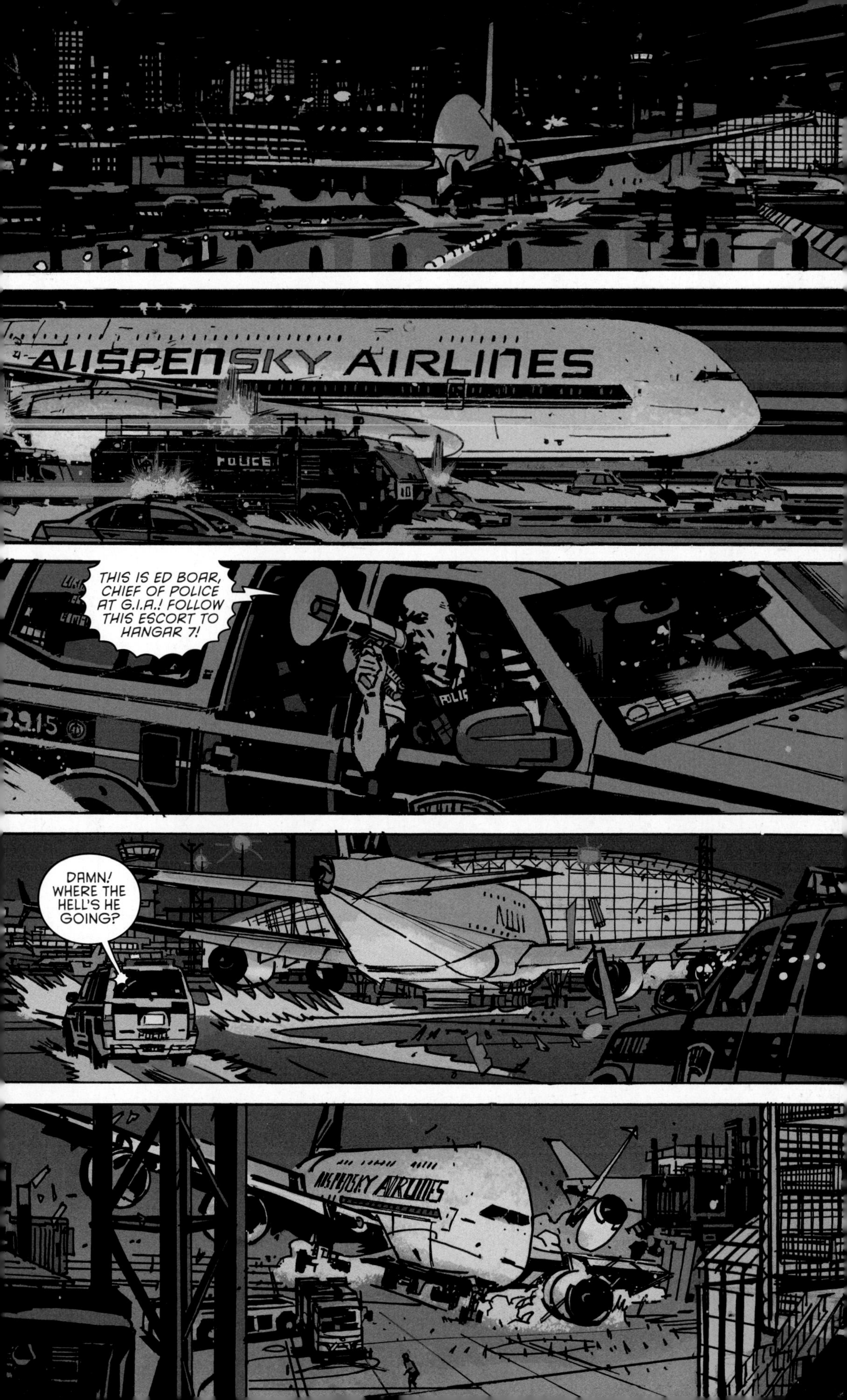
AUSPENSKY AIRLINES
POLICE
THIS IS ED BOAR, CHIEF OF POLICE AT G.I.A.! FOLLOW THIS ESCORT TO HANGAR 7!
DAMN! WHERE THE HELL'S HE GOING?

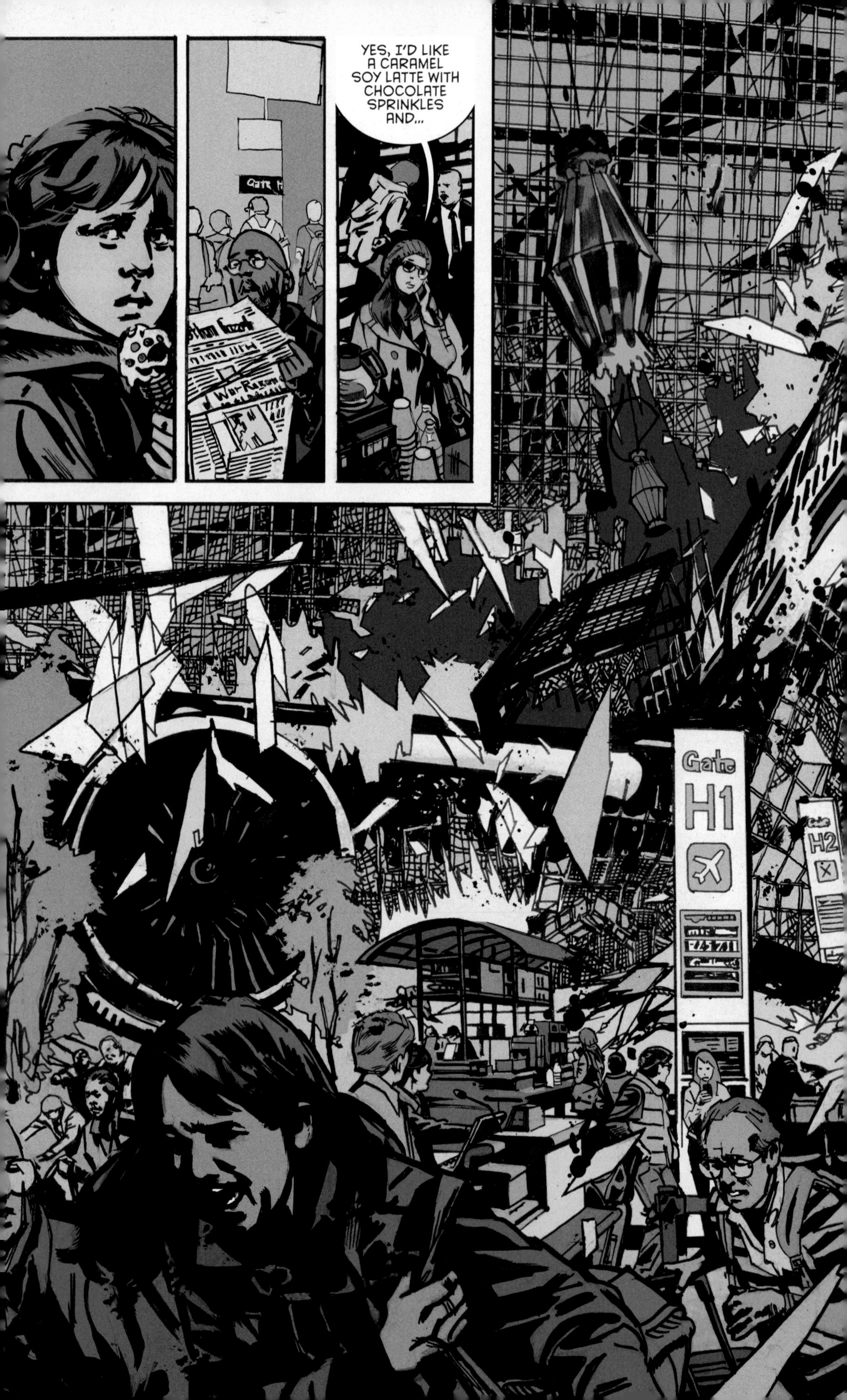
YES, I'D LIKE A CARAMEL SOY LATTE WITH CHOCOLATE SPRINKLES AND...
Gate H1
H2

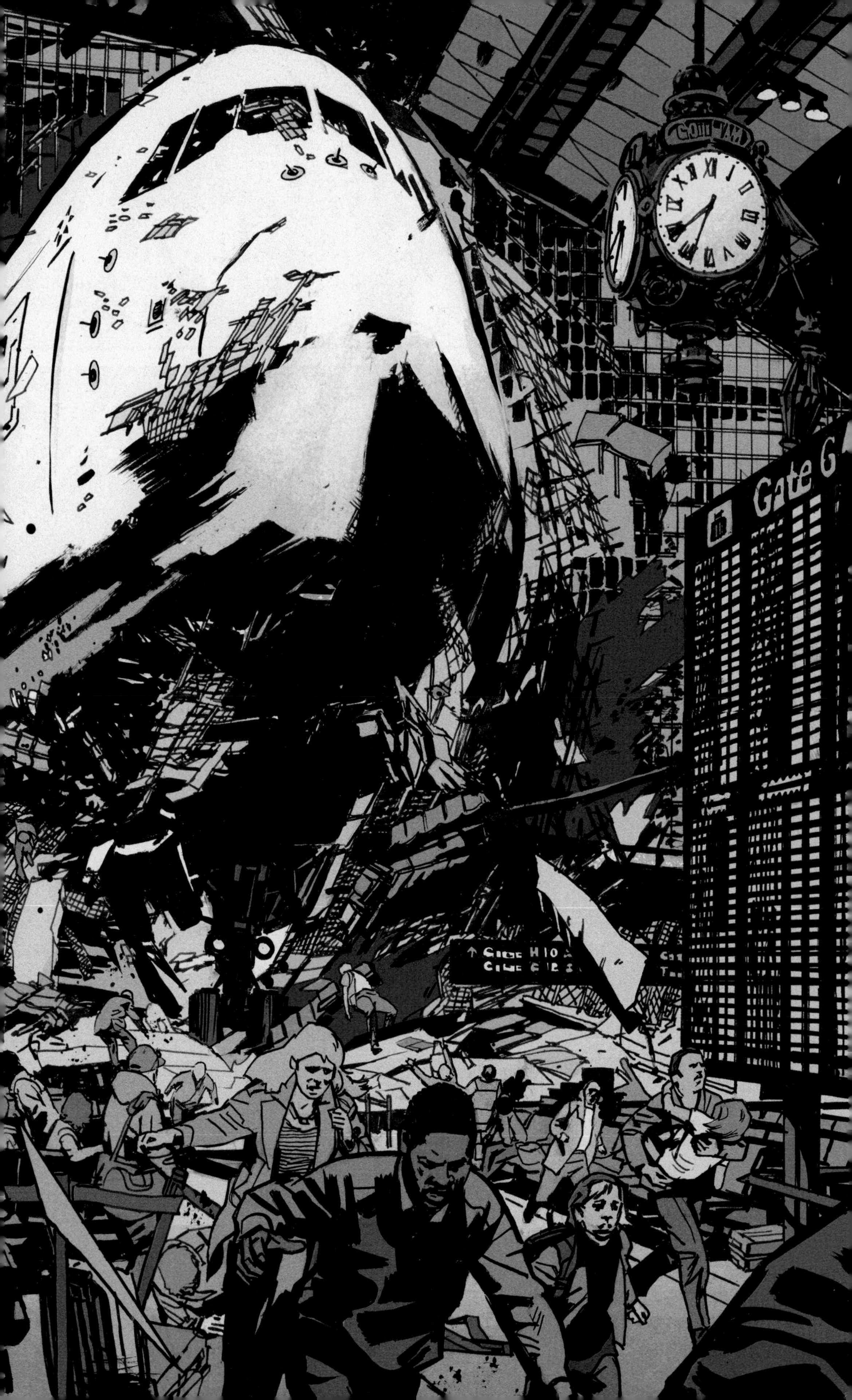
Gate G

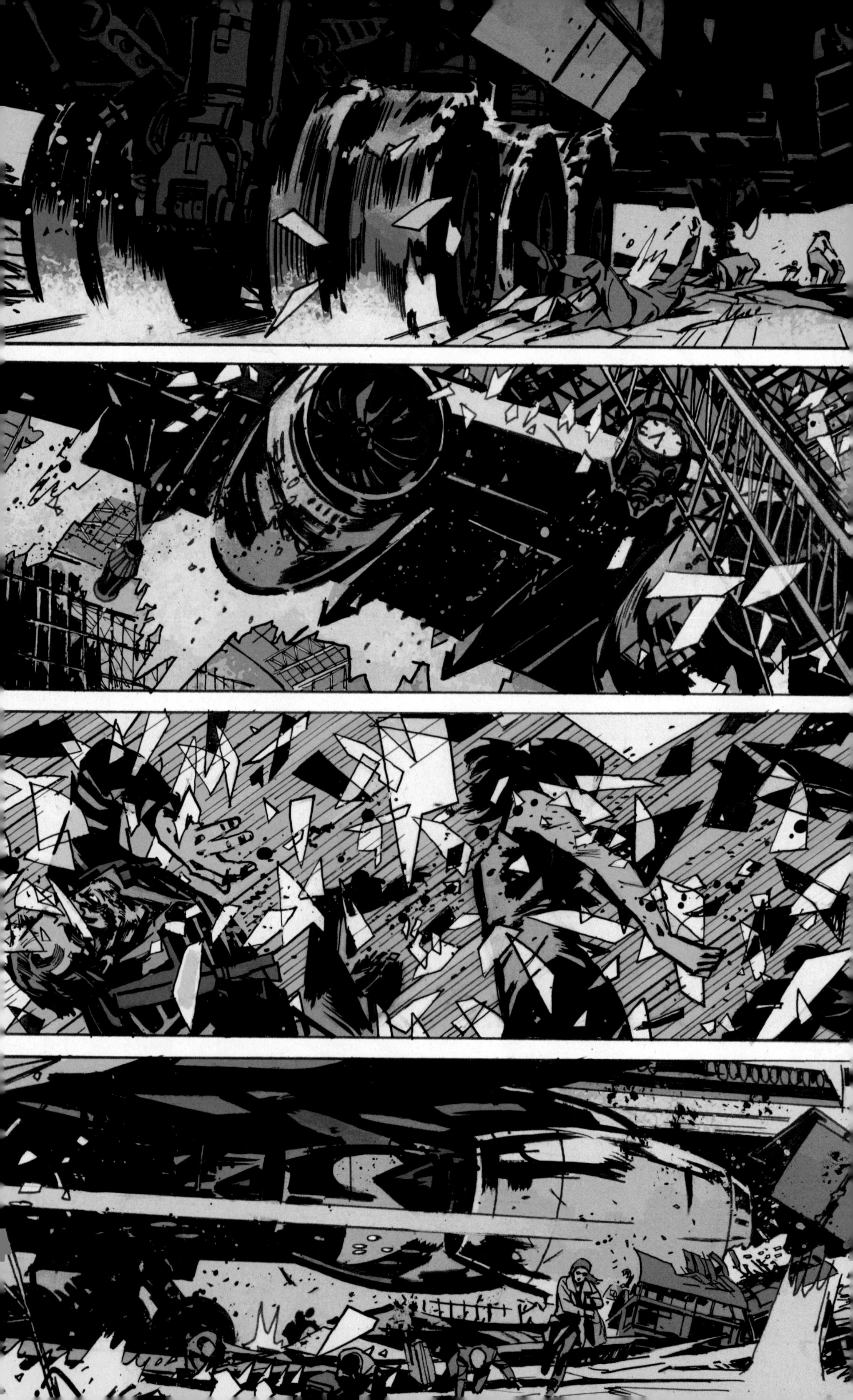

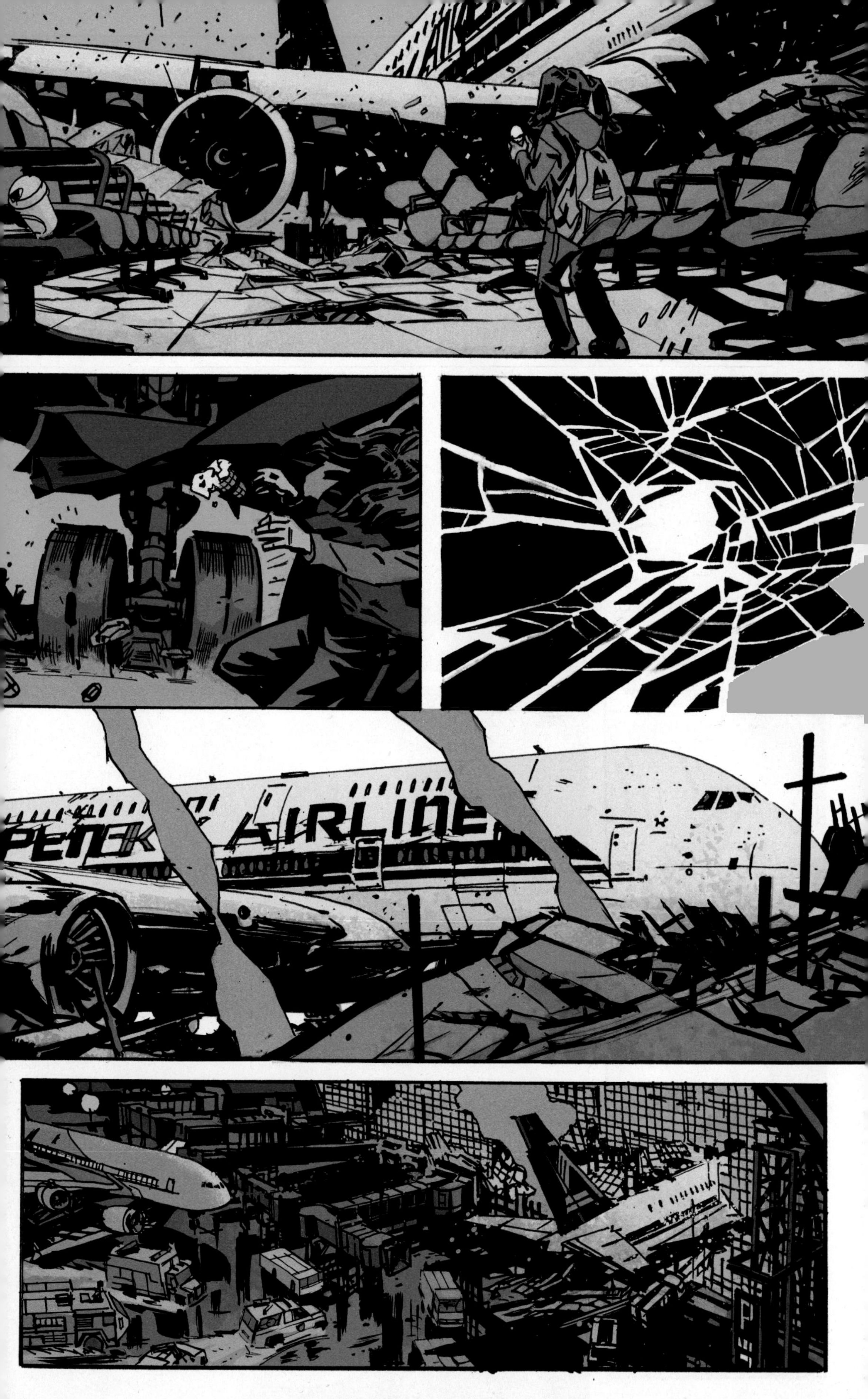

AIRLINE

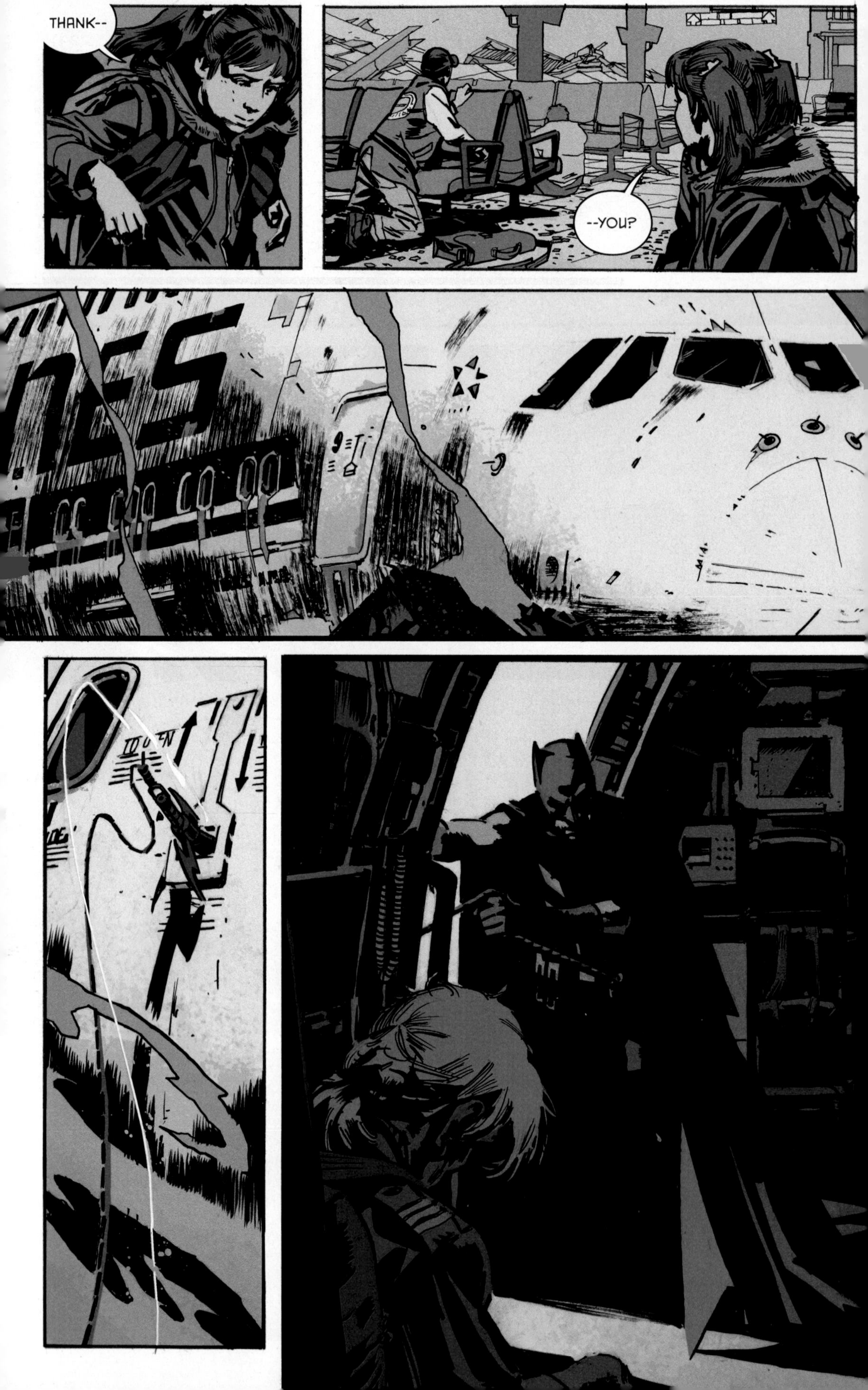
THANK--
--YOU?

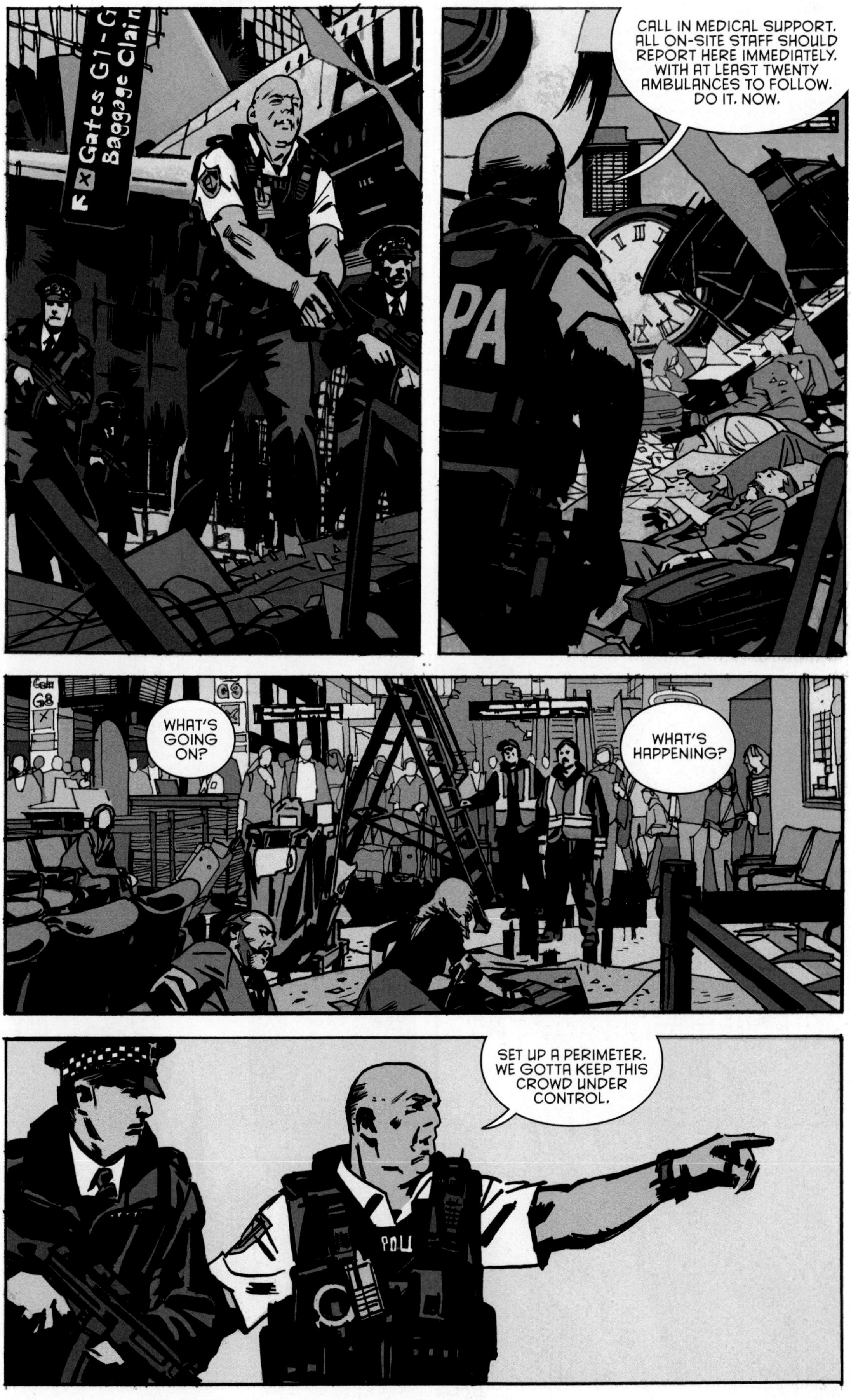
CALL IN MEDICAL SUPPORT. ALL ON-SITE STAFF SHOULD REPORT HERE IMMEDIATELY. WITH AT LEAST TWENTY AMBULANCES TO FOLLOW. DO IT. NOW.
WHAT'S GOING ON?
WHAT'S HAPPENING?
SET UP A PERIMETER. WE GOTTA KEEP THIS CROWD UNDER CONTROL.

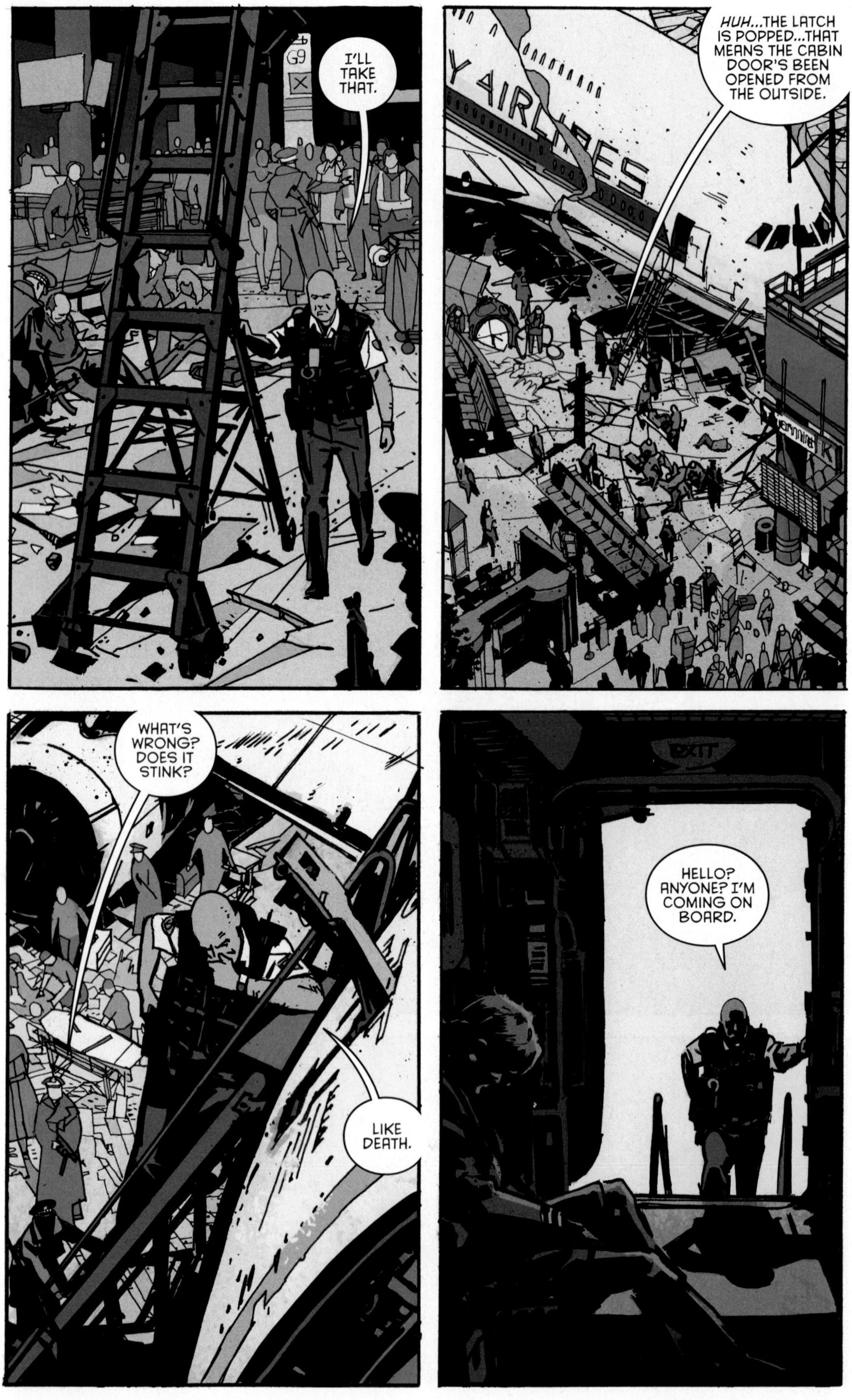
G9
I'LL TAKE THAT.
HUH...THE LATCH IS POPPED...THAT MEANS THE CABIN DOOR'S BEEN OPENED FROM THE OUTSIDE.
WHAT'S WRONG? DOES IT STINK?
LIKE DEATH.
EXIT
HELLO? ANYONE? I'M COMING ON BOARD.

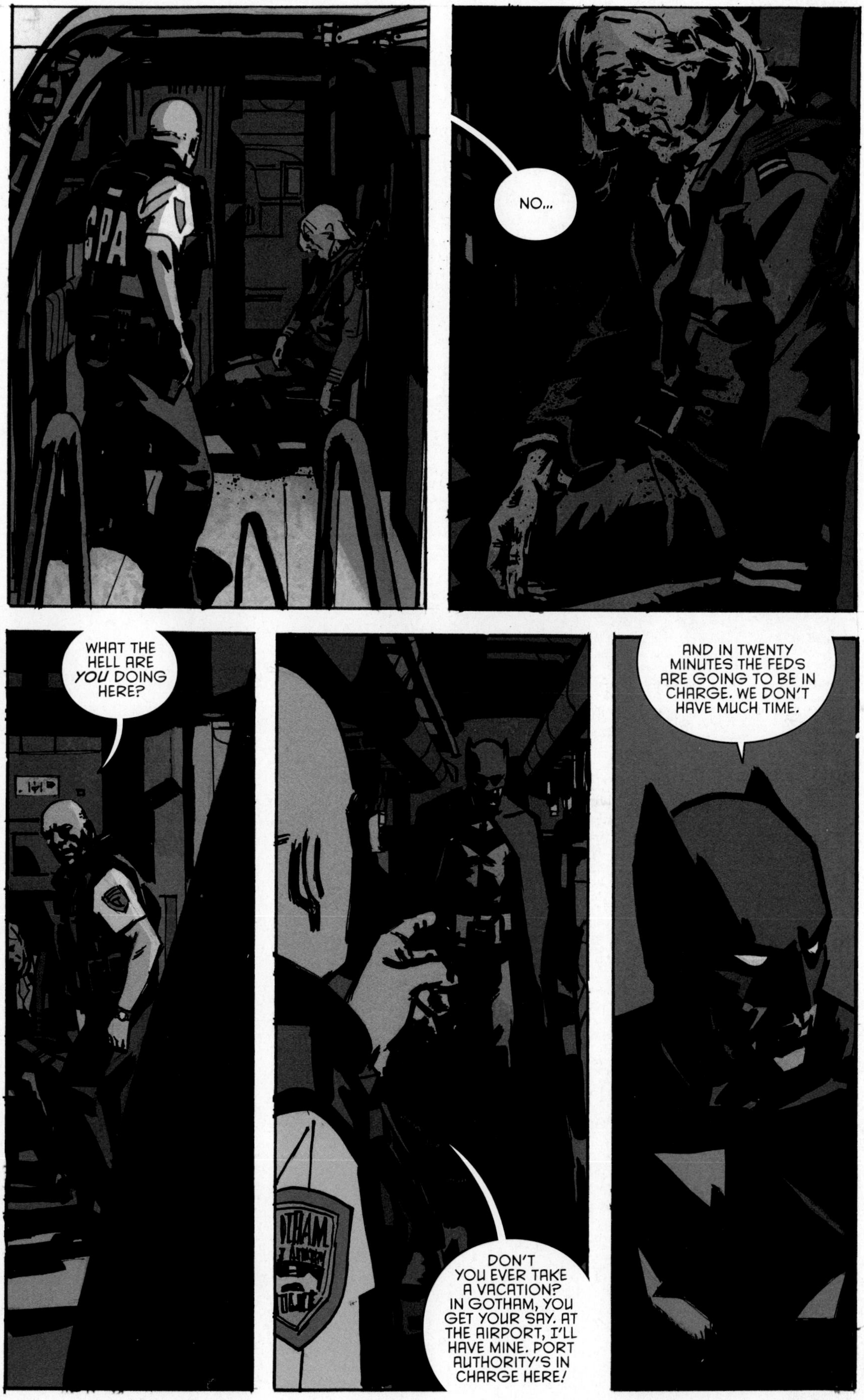
NO...
WHAT THE HELL ARE *YOU* DOING HERE?
DON'T YOU EVER TAKE A VACATION? IN GOTHAM, YOU GET YOUR SAY. AT THE AIRPORT, I'LL HAVE MINE. PORT AUTHORITY'S IN CHARGE HERE!
AND IN TWENTY MINUTES THE FEDS ARE GOING TO BE IN CHARGE. WE DON'T HAVE MUCH TIME.

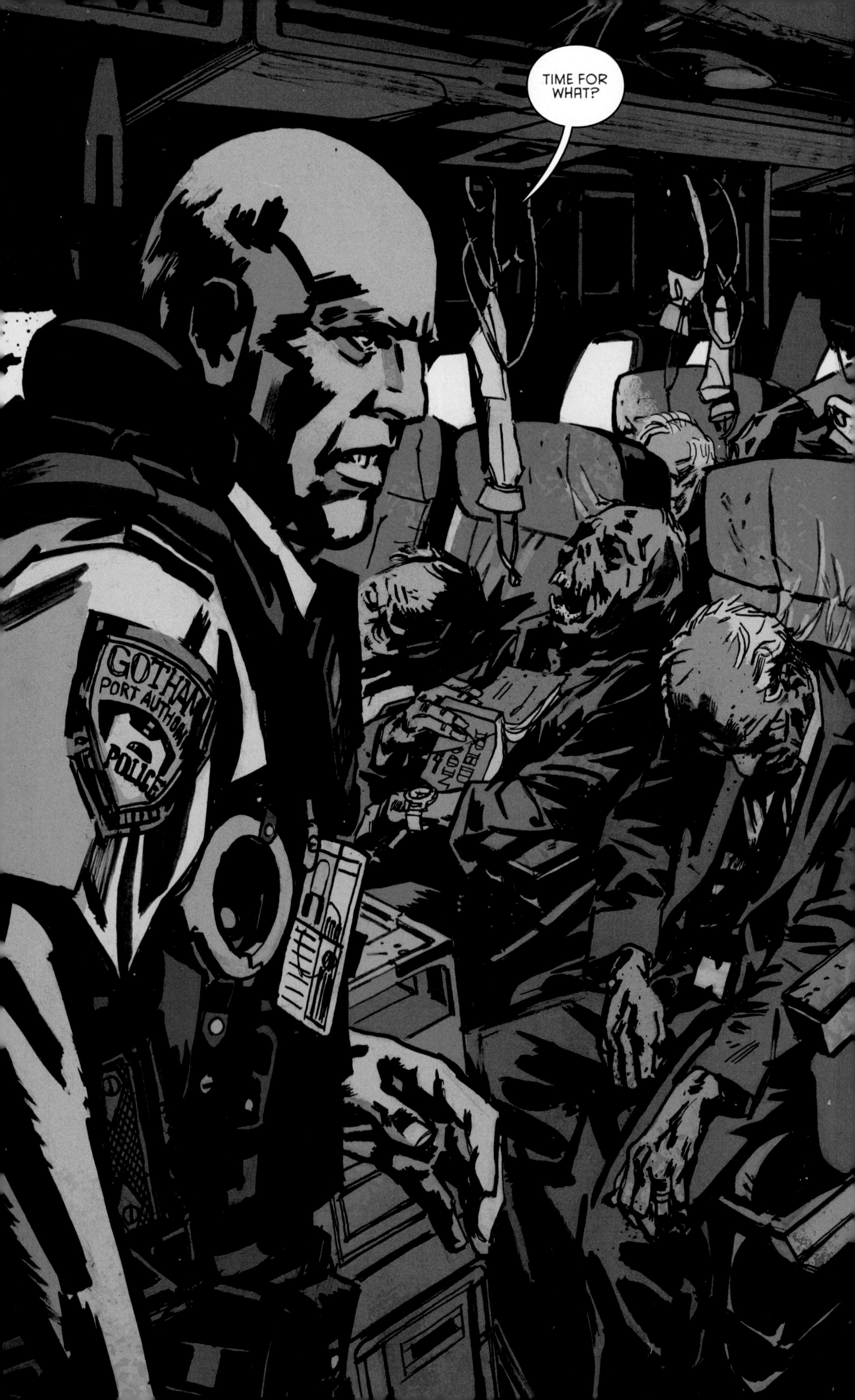
TIME FOR WHAT?
GOTHAM
PORT AUTHORITY
POLICE

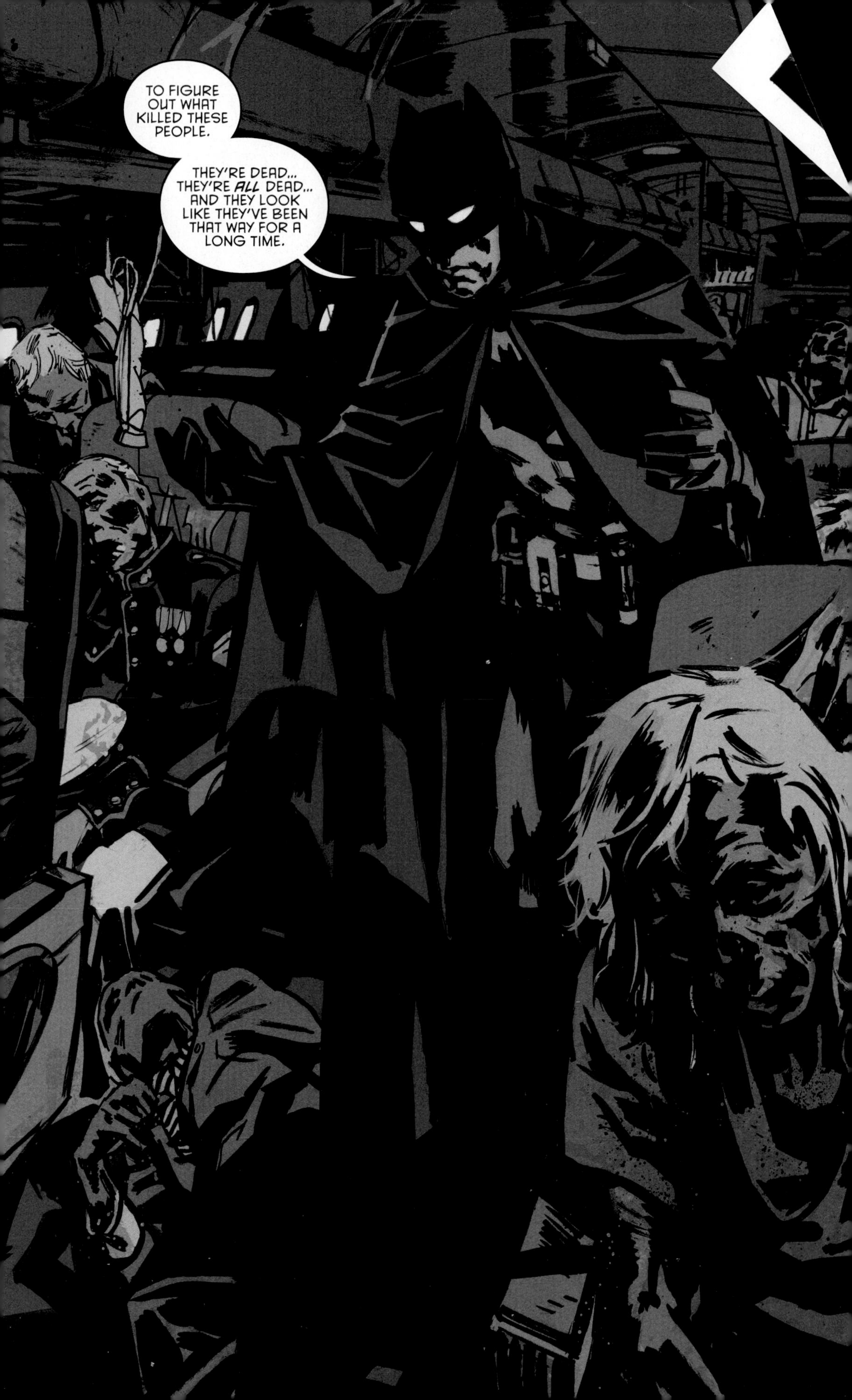
TO FIGURE OUT WHAT KILLED THESE PEOPLE.
THEY'RE DEAD... THEY'RE *ALL* DEAD... AND THEY LOOK LIKE THEY'VE BEEN THAT WAY FOR A LONG TIME.

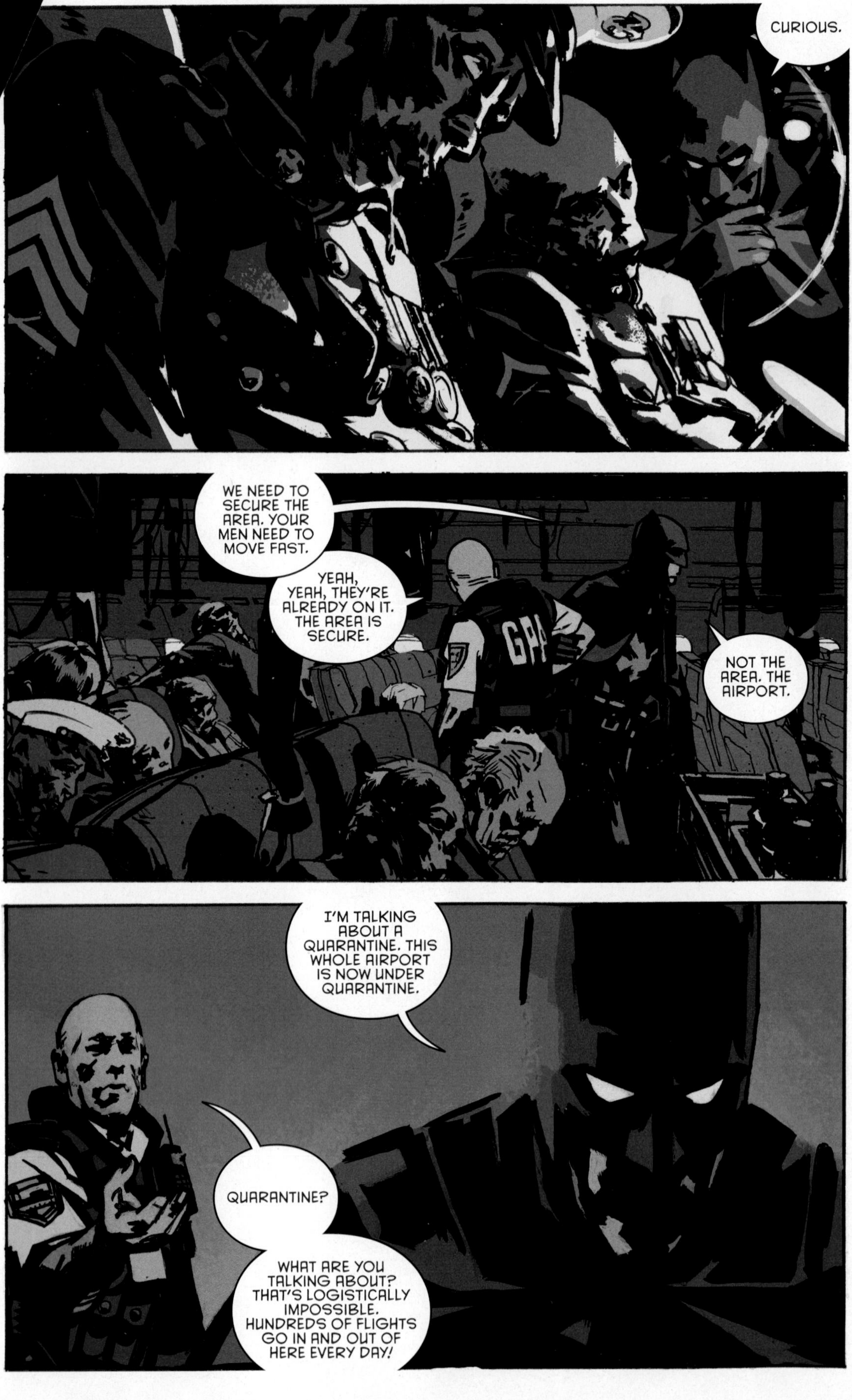
CURIOUS.
WE NEED TO SECURE THE AREA. YOUR MEN NEED TO MOVE FAST.
YEAH, YEAH, THEY'RE ALREADY ON IT. THE AREA IS SECURE.
NOT THE AREA. THE AIRPORT.
I'M TALKING ABOUT A QUARANTINE. THIS WHOLE AIRPORT IS NOW UNDER QUARANTINE.
QUARANTINE?
WHAT ARE YOU TALKING ABOUT? THAT'S LOGISTICALLY IMPOSSIBLE. HUNDREDS OF FLIGHTS GO IN AND OUT OF HERE EVERY DAY!
GPA

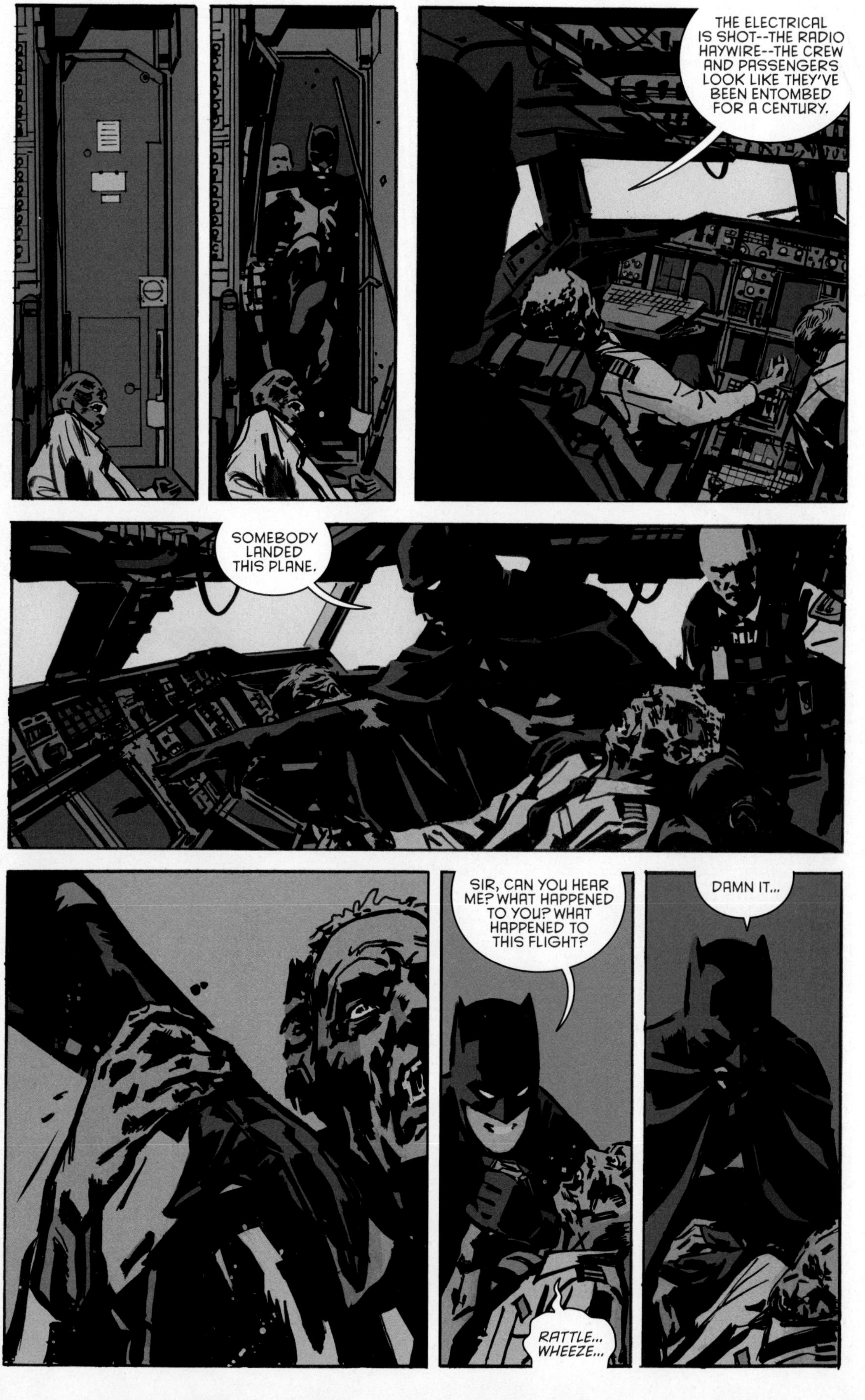
THE ELECTRICAL IS SHOT--THE RADIO HAYWIRE--THE CREW AND PASSENGERS LOOK LIKE THEY'VE BEEN ENTOMBED FOR A CENTURY.
SOMEBODY LANDED THIS PLANE.
SIR, CAN YOU HEAR ME? WHAT HAPPENED TO YOU? WHAT HAPPENED TO THIS FLIGHT?
RATTLE... WHEEZE...
DAMN IT...

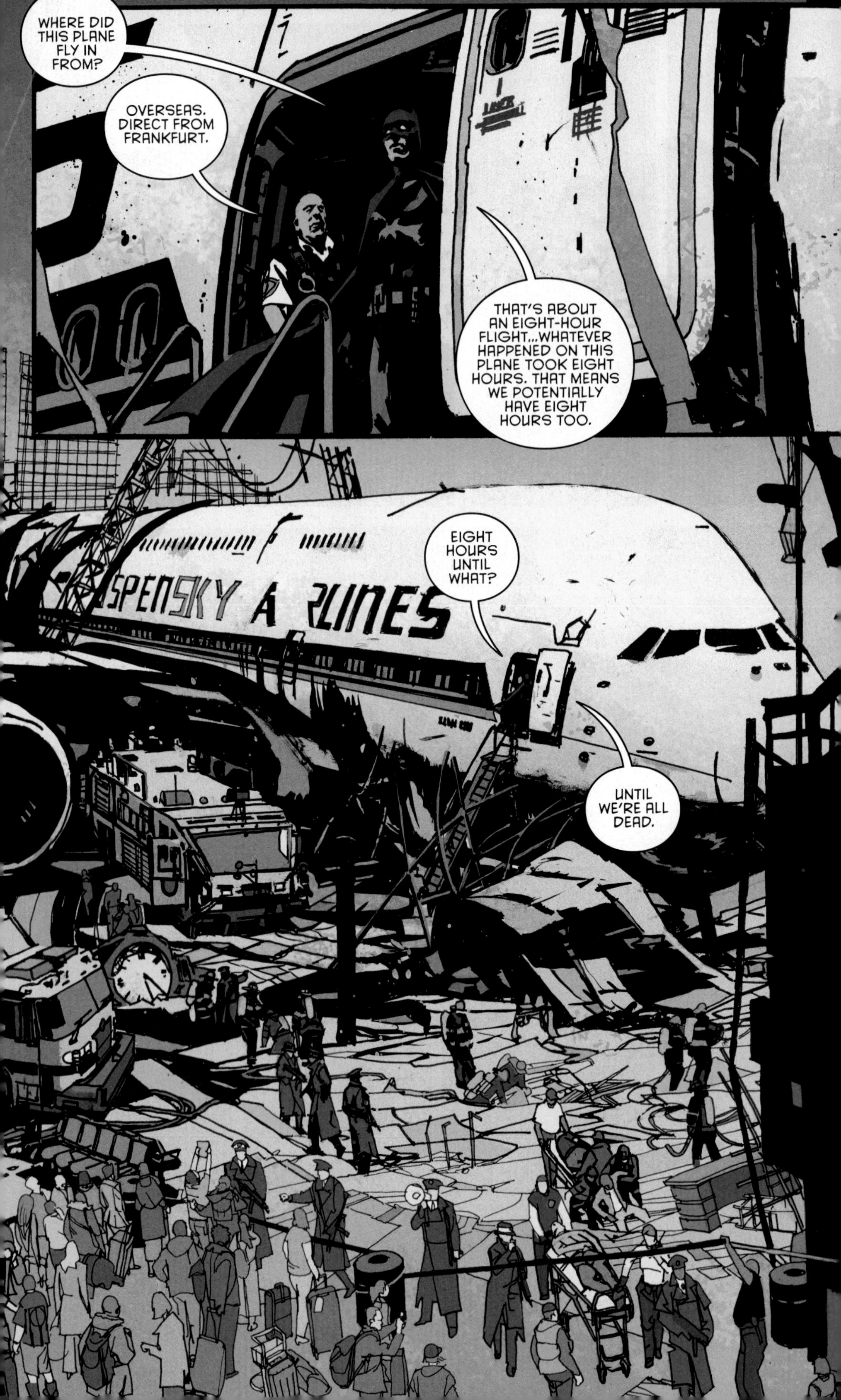
WHERE DID THIS PLANE FLY IN FROM?
OVERSEAS. DIRECT FROM FRANKFURT.
THAT'S ABOUT AN EIGHT-HOUR FLIGHT...WHATEVER HAPPENED ON THIS PLANE TOOK EIGHT HOURS. THAT MEANS WE POTENTIALLY HAVE EIGHT HOURS TOO.
SPENSKY A RLINES
EIGHT HOURS UNTIL WHAT?
UNTIL WE'RE ALL DEAD.

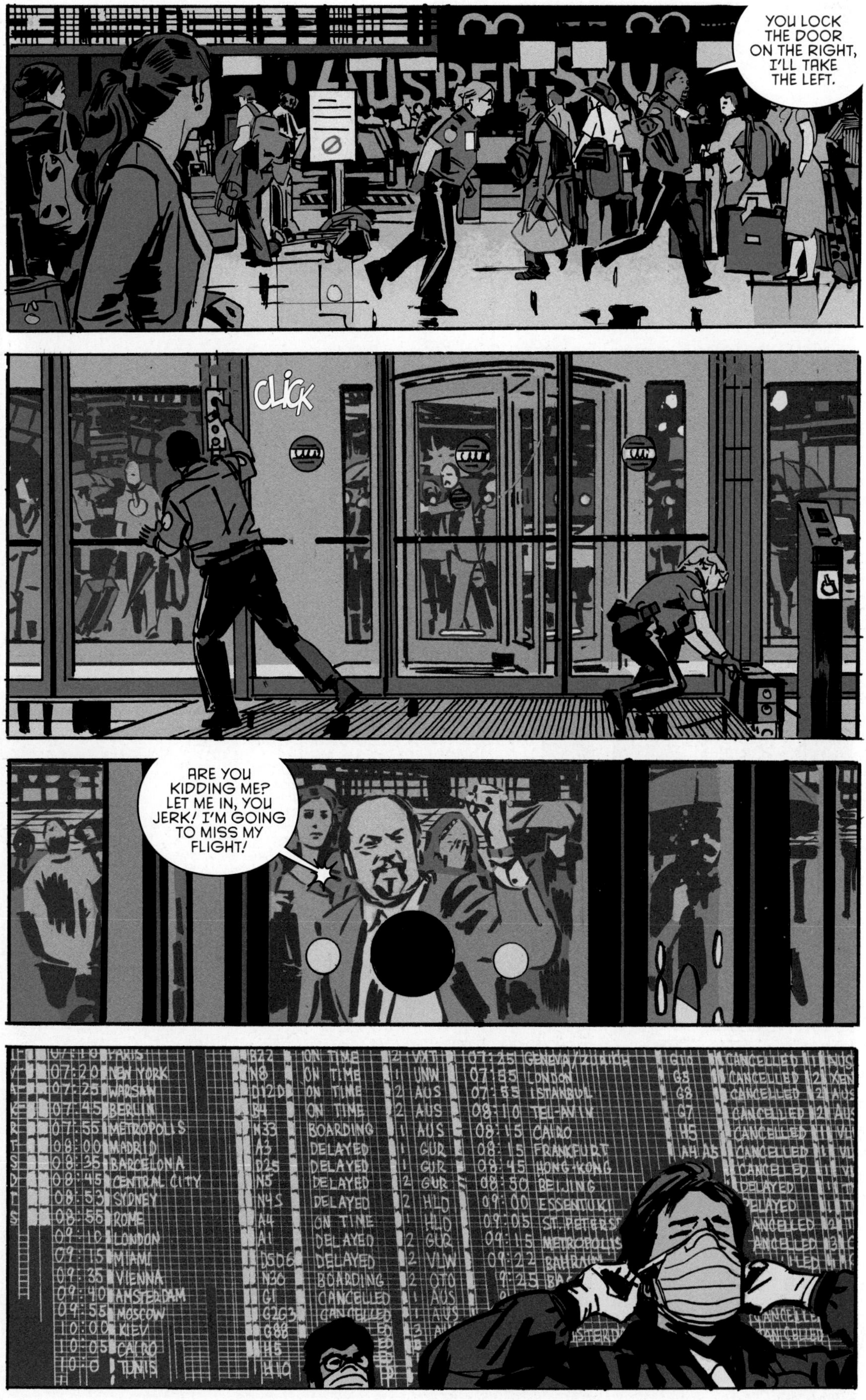
YOU LOCK THE DOOR ON THE RIGHT, I'LL TAKE THE LEFT.
CLICK
ARE YOU KIDDING ME? LET ME IN, YOU JERK! I'M GOING TO MISS MY FLIGHT!

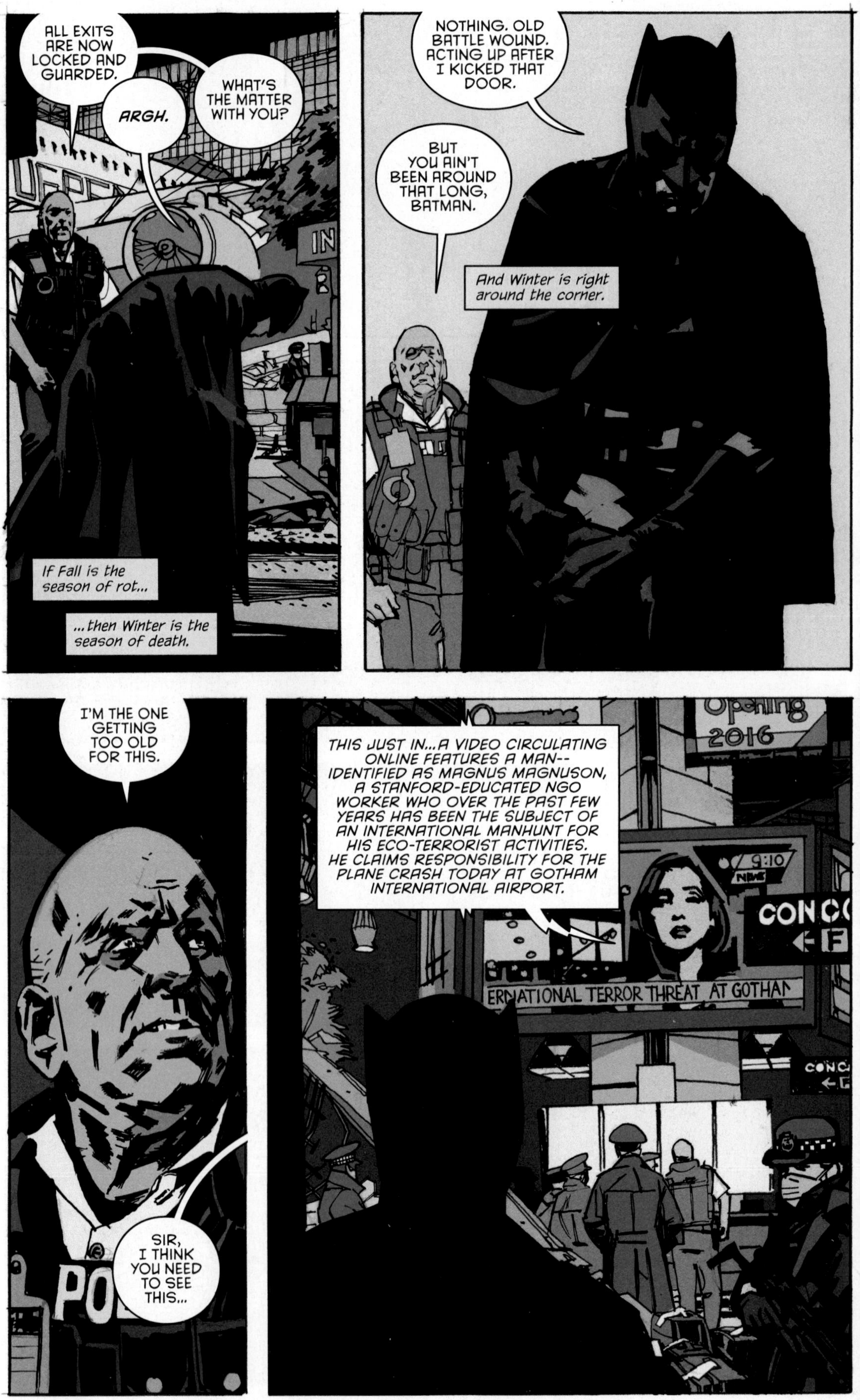
ALL EXITS ARE NOW LOCKED AND GUARDED.
ARGH.
WHAT'S THE MATTER WITH YOU?
If Fall is the season of rot...
...then Winter is the season of death.
NOTHING. OLD BATTLE WOUND. ACTING UP AFTER I KICKED THAT DOOR.
BUT YOU AIN'T BEEN AROUND THAT LONG, BATMAN.
And Winter is right around the corner.
I'M THE ONE GETTING TOO OLD FOR THIS.
SIR, I THINK YOU NEED TO SEE THIS...
Opening 2016
THIS JUST IN...A VIDEO CIRCULATING ONLINE FEATURES A MAN--IDENTIFIED AS MAGNUS MAGNUSON, A STANFORD-EDUCATED NGO WORKER WHO OVER THE PAST FEW YEARS HAS BEEN THE SUBJECT OF AN INTERNATIONAL MANHUNT FOR HIS ECO-TERRORIST ACTIVITIES. HE CLAIMS RESPONSIBILITY FOR THE PLANE CRASH TODAY AT GOTHAM INTERNATIONAL AIRPORT.
9:10
ERNATIONAL TERROR THREAT AT GOTHAM

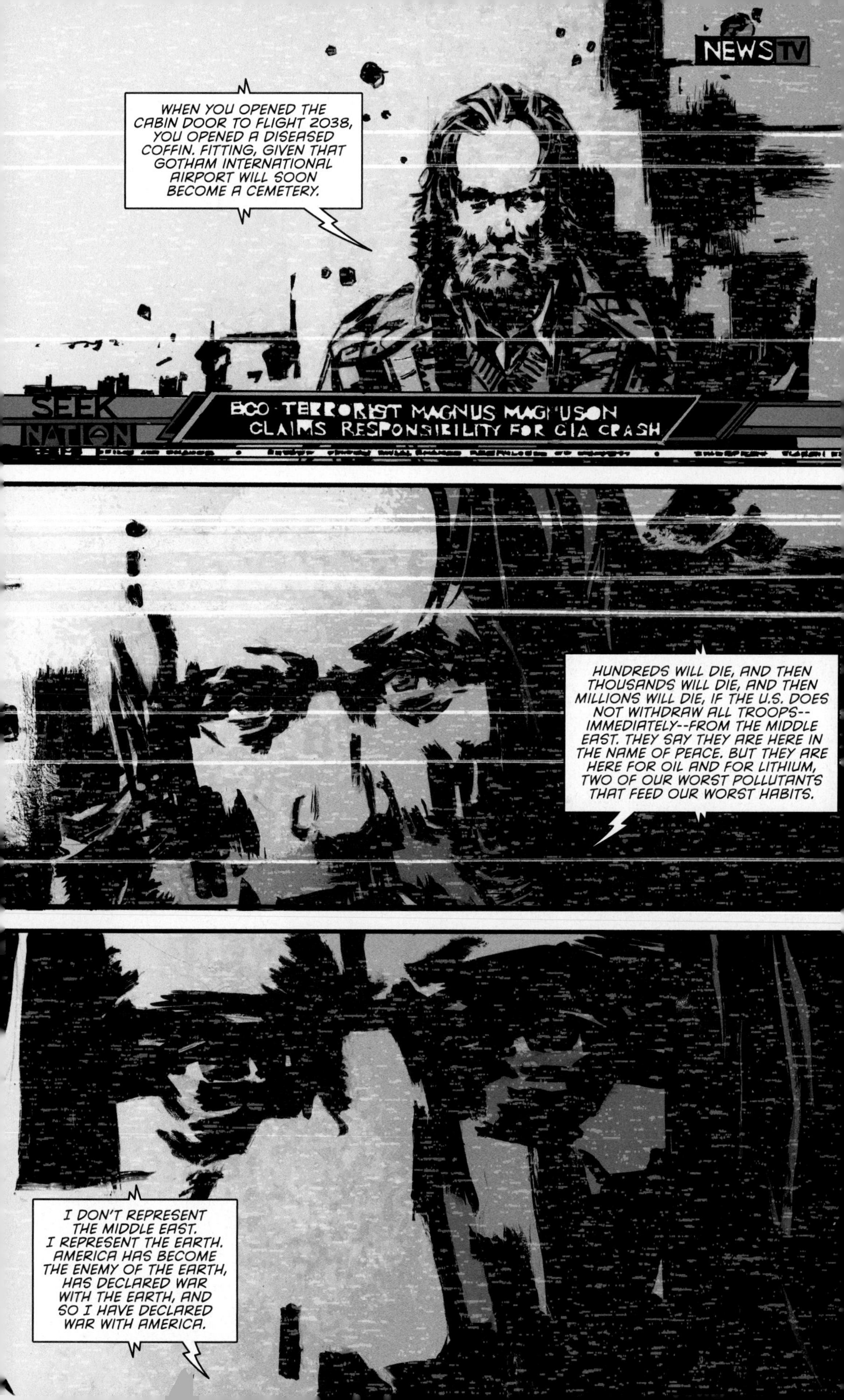
NEWS TV
WHEN YOU OPENED THE CABIN DOOR TO FLIGHT 2038, YOU OPENED A DISEASED COFFIN. FITTING, GIVEN THAT GOTHAM INTERNATIONAL AIRPORT WILL SOON BECOME A CEMETERY.
SEEK NATION
ECO-TERRORIST MAGNUS MAGNUSON CLAIMS RESPONSIBILITY FOR GIA CRASH
HUNDREDS WILL DIE, AND THEN THOUSANDS WILL DIE, AND THEN MILLIONS WILL DIE, IF THE U.S. DOES NOT WITHDRAW ALL TROOPS--IMMEDIATELY--FROM THE MIDDLE EAST. THEY SAY THEY ARE HERE IN THE NAME OF PEACE. BUT THEY ARE HERE FOR OIL AND FOR LITHIUM, TWO OF OUR WORST POLLUTANTS THAT FEED OUR WORST HABITS.
I DON'T REPRESENT THE MIDDLE EAST. I REPRESENT THE EARTH. AMERICA HAS BECOME THE ENEMY OF THE EARTH, HAS DECLARED WAR WITH THE EARTH, AND SO I HAVE DECLARED WAR WITH AMERICA.

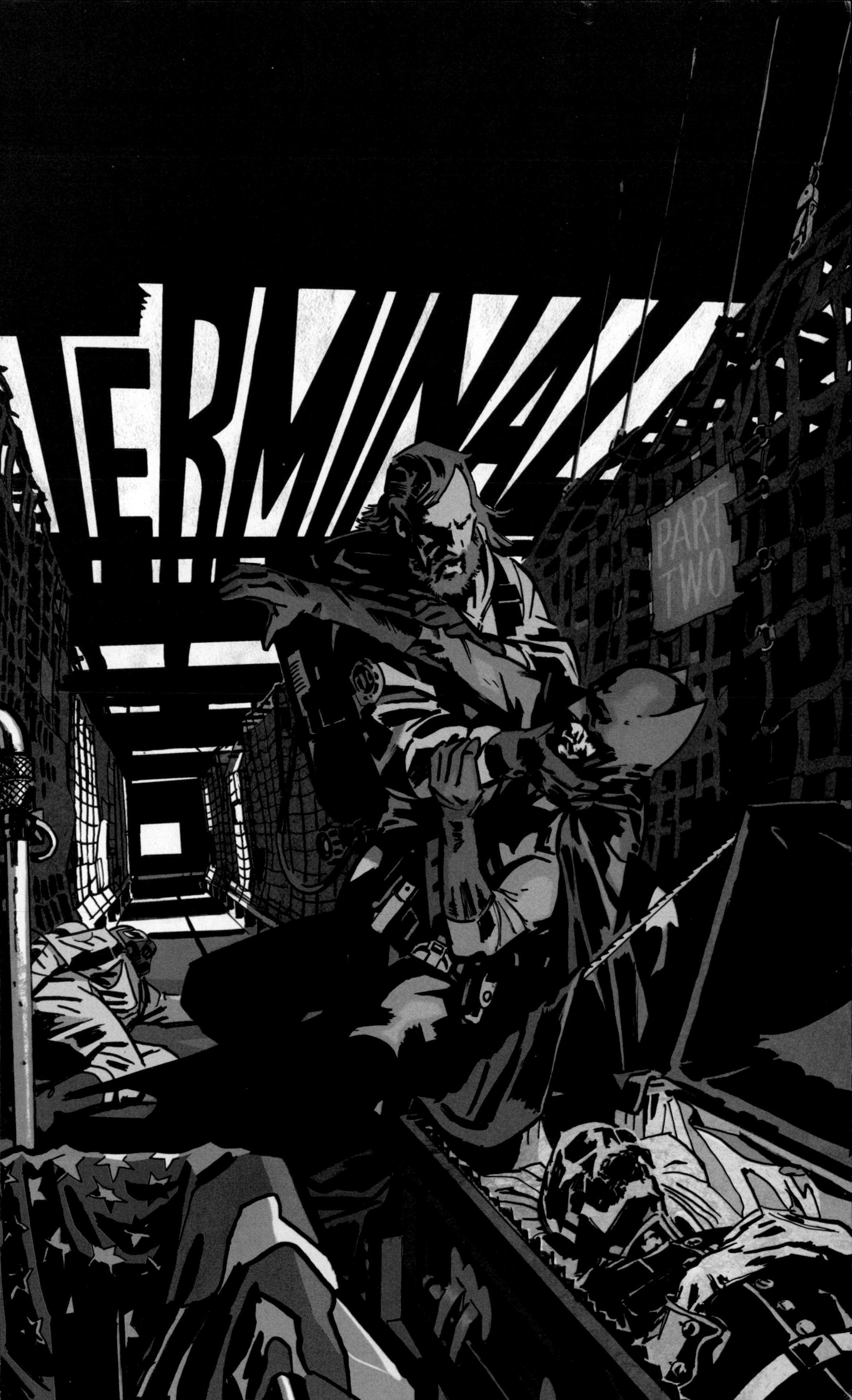
PART
TWO

BENJAMIN PERCY writer **JOHN PAUL LEON** artist **DAVE STEWART & JOHN PAUL LEON** colorists **JARED K. FLETCHER** letterer cover by **JOHN PAUL LEON**

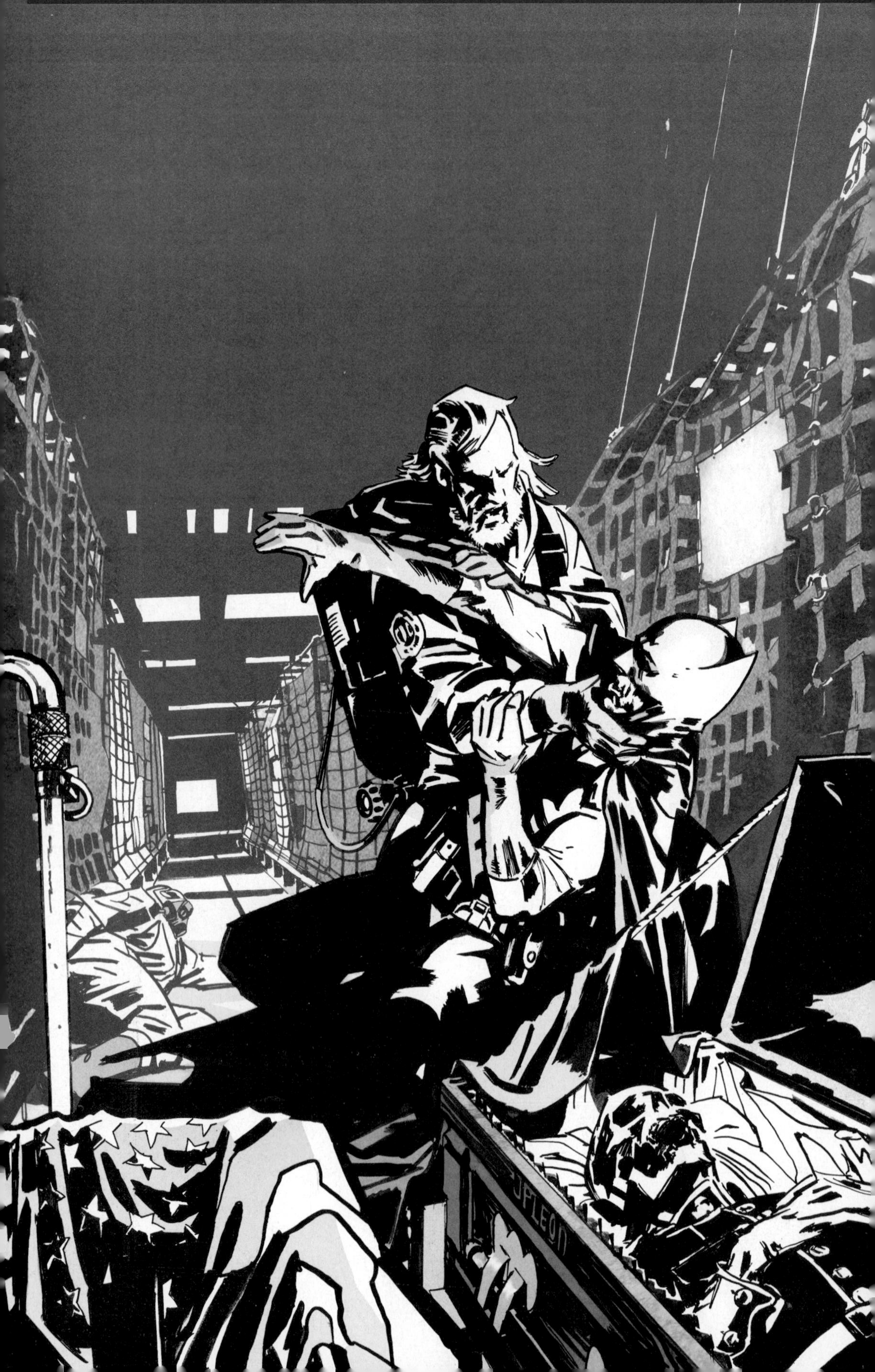
JPLEON

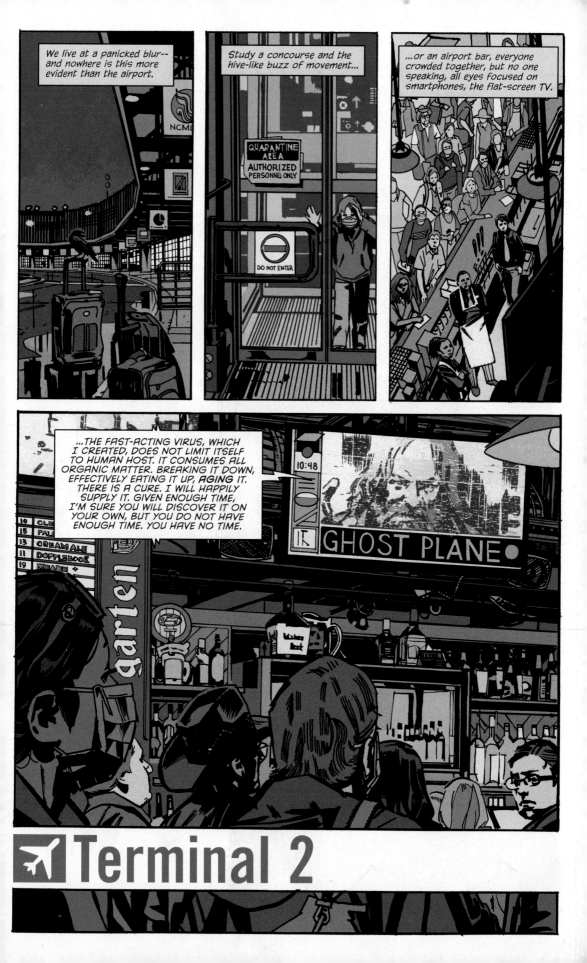

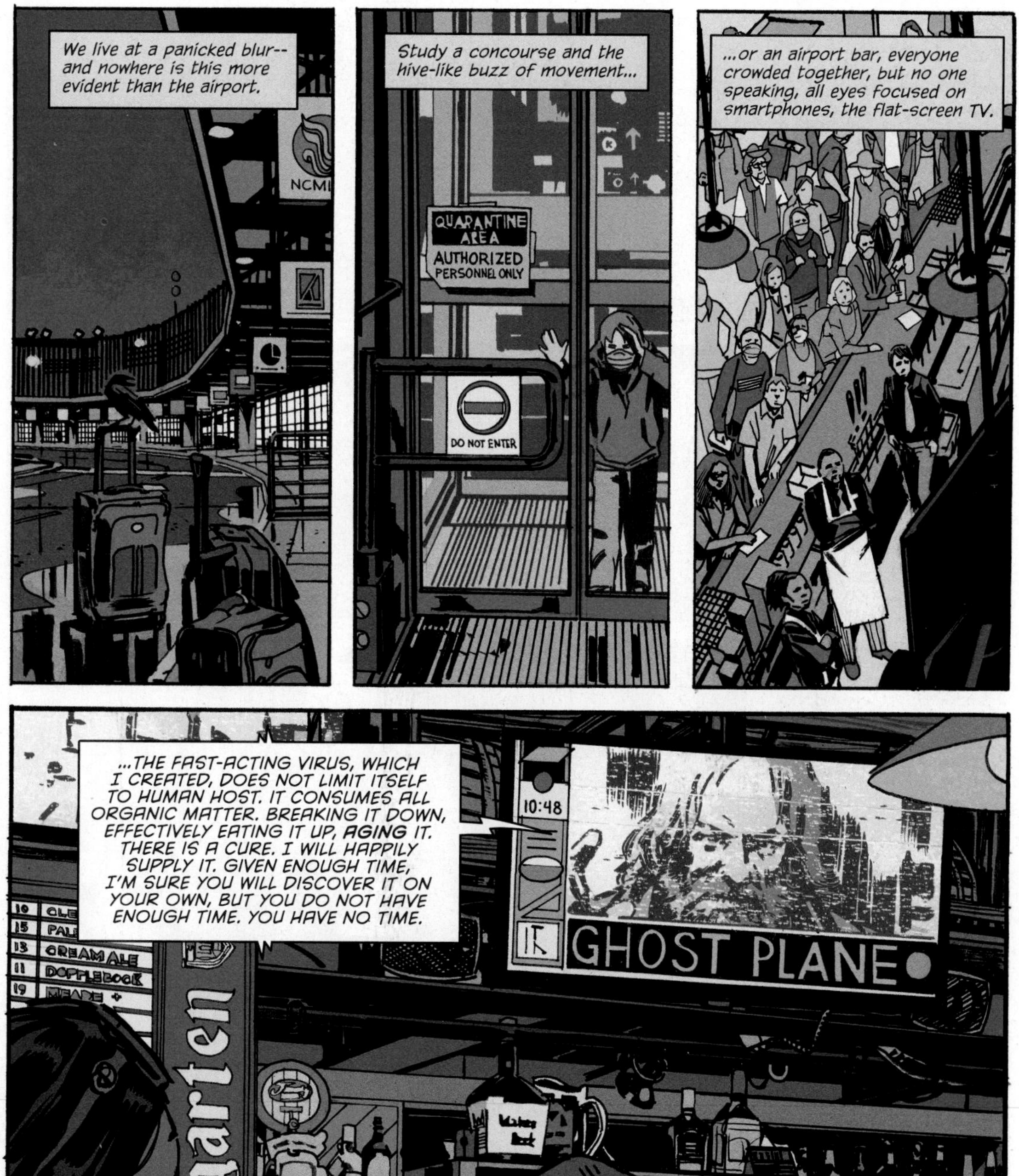
We live at a panicked blur--and nowhere is this more evident than the airport.
NCMI
Study a concourse and the hive-like buzz of movement...
QUARANTINE AREA
AUTHORIZED PERSONNEL ONLY
DO NOT ENTER
...or an airport bar, everyone crowded together, but no one speaking, all eyes focused on smartphones, the flat-screen TV.
...THE FAST-ACTING VIRUS, WHICH I CREATED, DOES NOT LIMIT ITSELF TO HUMAN HOST. IT CONSUMES ALL ORGANIC MATTER. BREAKING IT DOWN, EFFECTIVELY EATING IT UP, **AGING** IT. THERE IS A CURE. I WILL HAPPILY SUPPLY IT. GIVEN ENOUGH TIME, I'M SURE YOU WILL DISCOVER IT ON YOUR OWN, BUT YOU DO NOT HAVE ENOUGH TIME. YOU HAVE NO TIME.
10:48
GHOST PLANE
13 CREAM ALE
11 DOPPLEBOCK
garten

Terminal 2

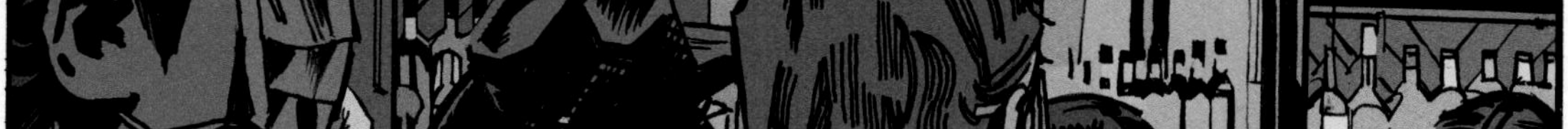

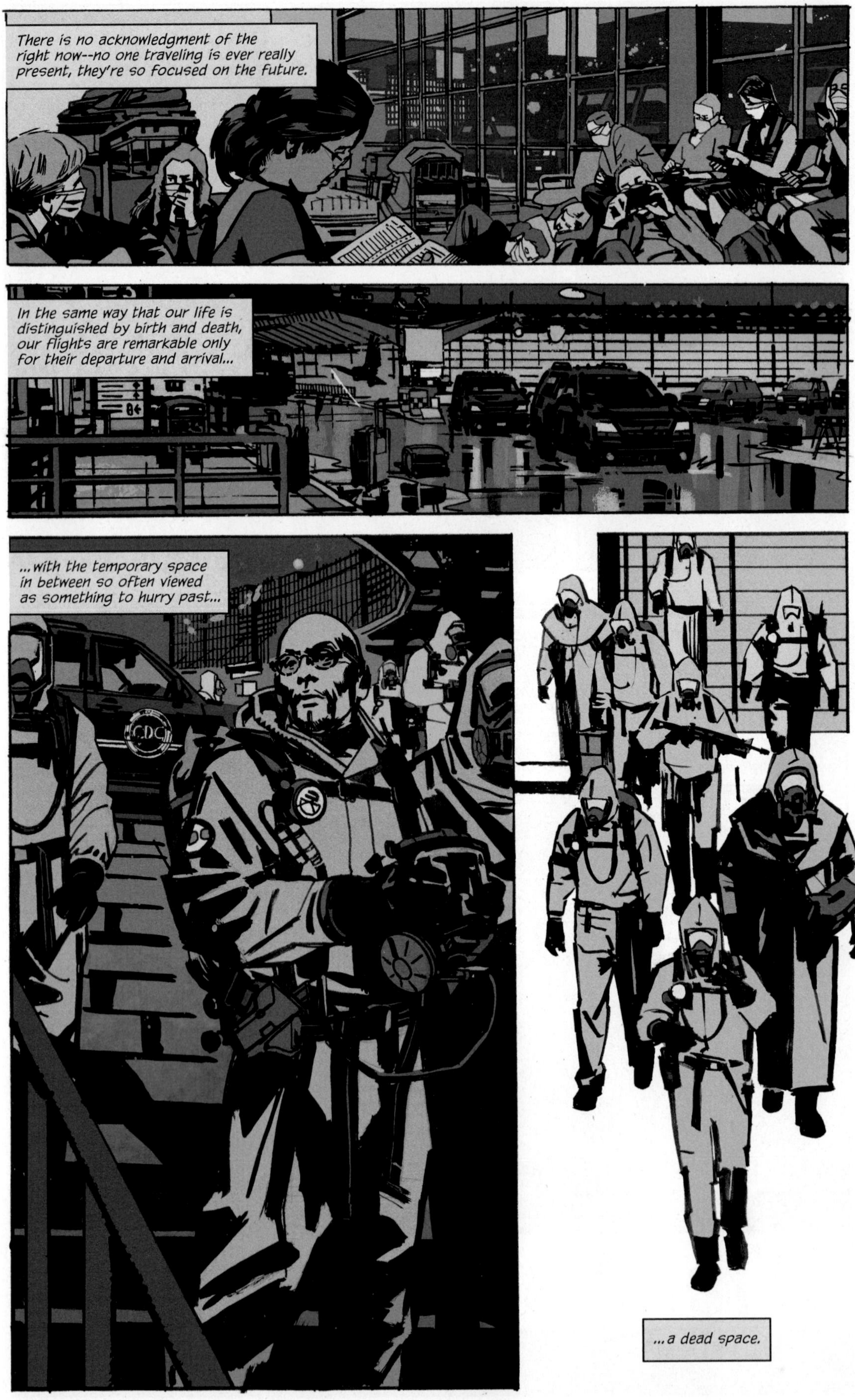
There is no acknowledgment of the right now--no one traveling is ever really present, they're so focused on the future.
In the same way that our life is distinguished by birth and death, our flights are remarkable only for their departure and arrival...
...with the temporary space in between so often viewed as something to hurry past...
...a dead space.

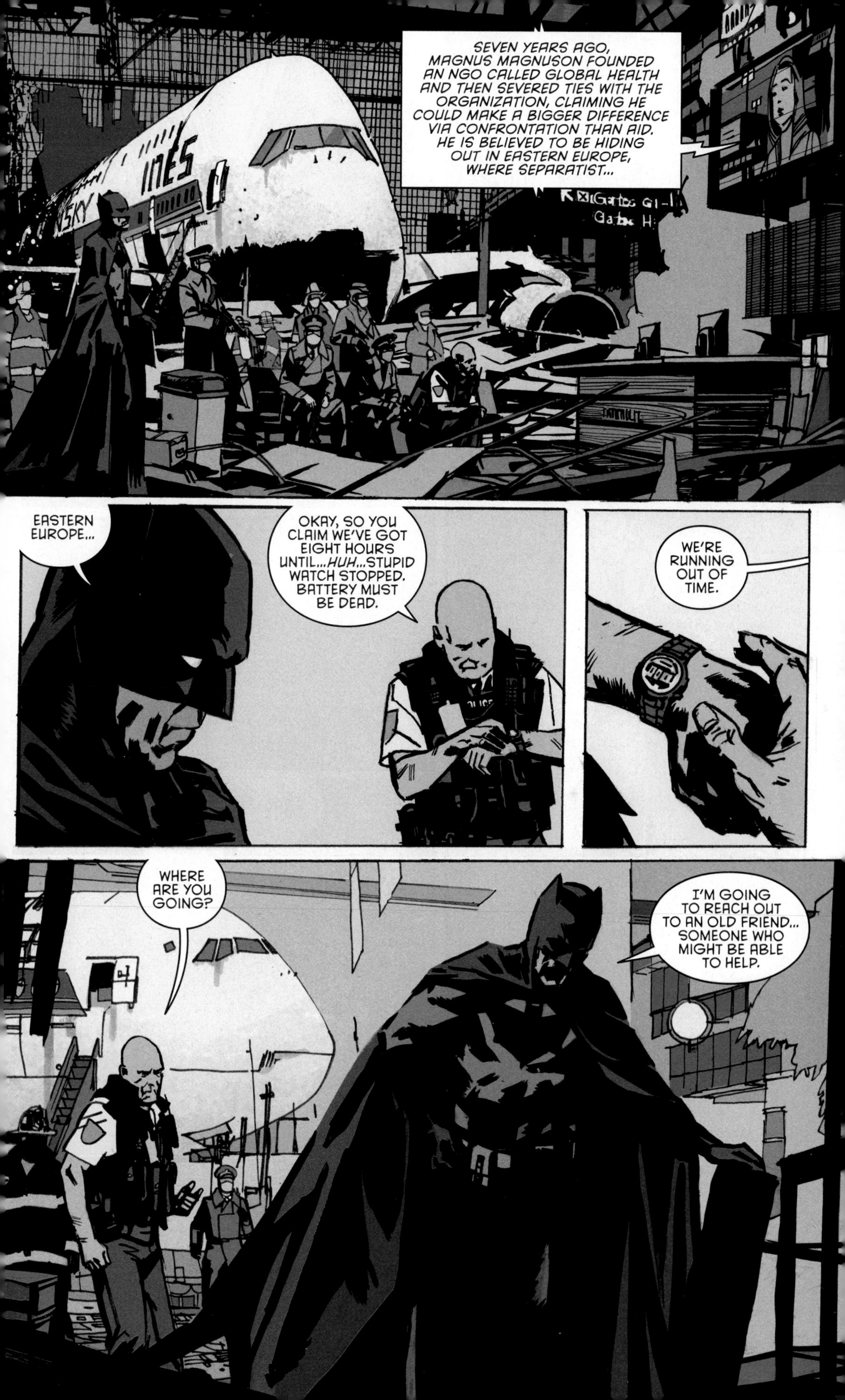

SEVEN YEARS AGO, MAGNUS MAGNUSON FOUNDED AN NGO CALLED GLOBAL HEALTH AND THEN SEVERED TIES WITH THE ORGANIZATION, CLAIMING HE COULD MAKE A BIGGER DIFFERENCE VIA CONFRONTATION THAN AID. HE IS BELIEVED TO BE HIDING OUT IN EASTERN EUROPE, WHERE SEPARATIST...
EASTERN EUROPE...
OKAY, SO YOU CLAIM WE'VE GOT EIGHT HOURS UNTIL...HUH...STUPID WATCH STOPPED. BATTERY MUST BE DEAD.
WE'RE RUNNING OUT OF TIME.
WHERE ARE YOU GOING?
I'M GOING TO REACH OUT TO AN OLD FRIEND... SOMEONE WHO MIGHT BE ABLE TO HELP.

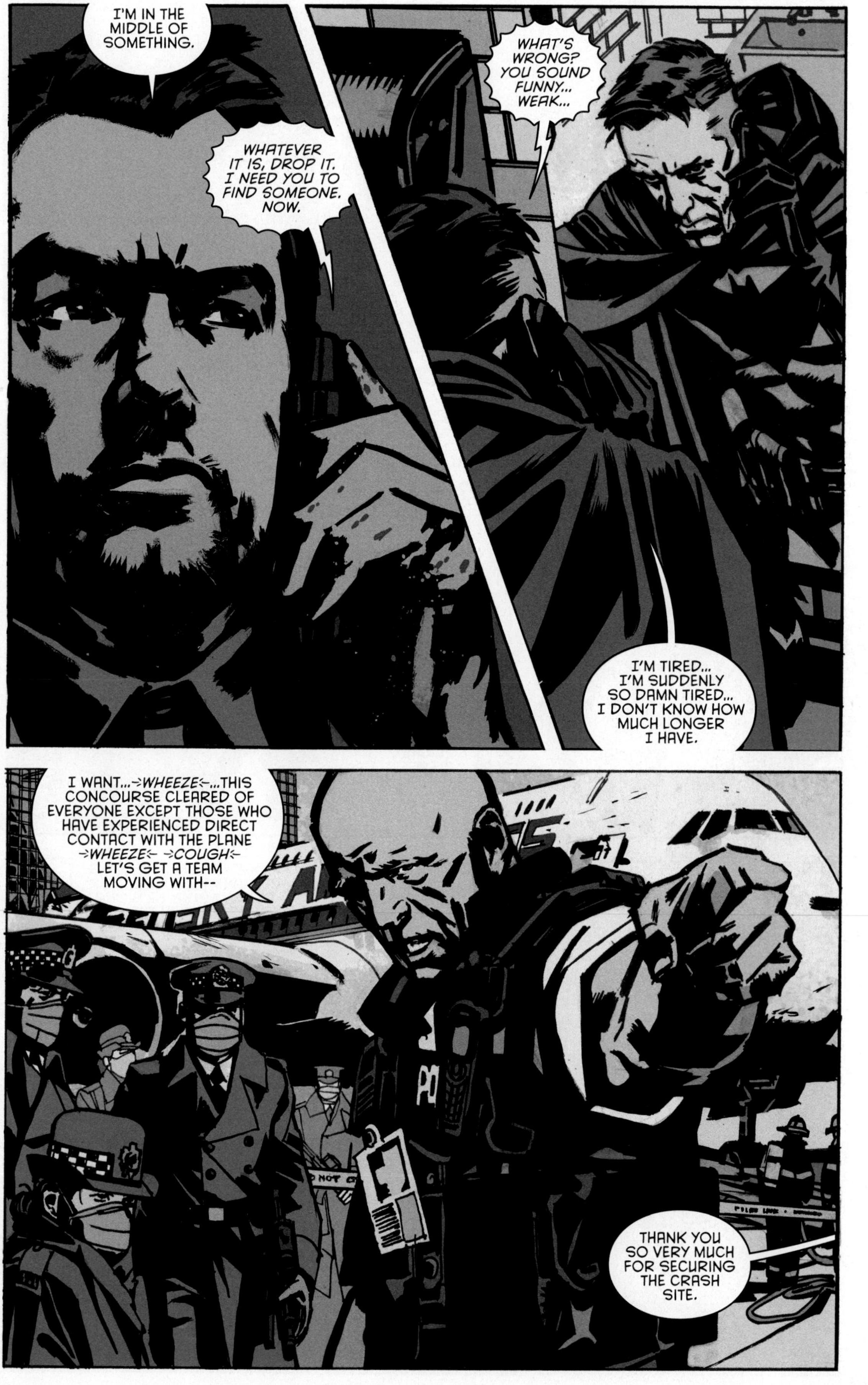
I'M IN THE MIDDLE OF SOMETHING.
WHAT'S WRONG? YOU SOUND FUNNY... WEAK...
WHATEVER IT IS, DROP IT. I NEED YOU TO FIND SOMEONE. NOW.
I'M TIRED... I'M SUDDENLY SO DAMN TIRED... I DON'T KNOW HOW MUCH LONGER I HAVE.
I WANT... >WHEEZE<...THIS CONCOURSE CLEARED OF EVERYONE EXCEPT THOSE WHO HAVE EXPERIENCED DIRECT CONTACT WITH THE PLANE >WHEEZE< >COUGH< LET'S GET A TEAM MOVING WITH--
THANK YOU SO VERY MUCH FOR SECURING THE CRASH SITE.

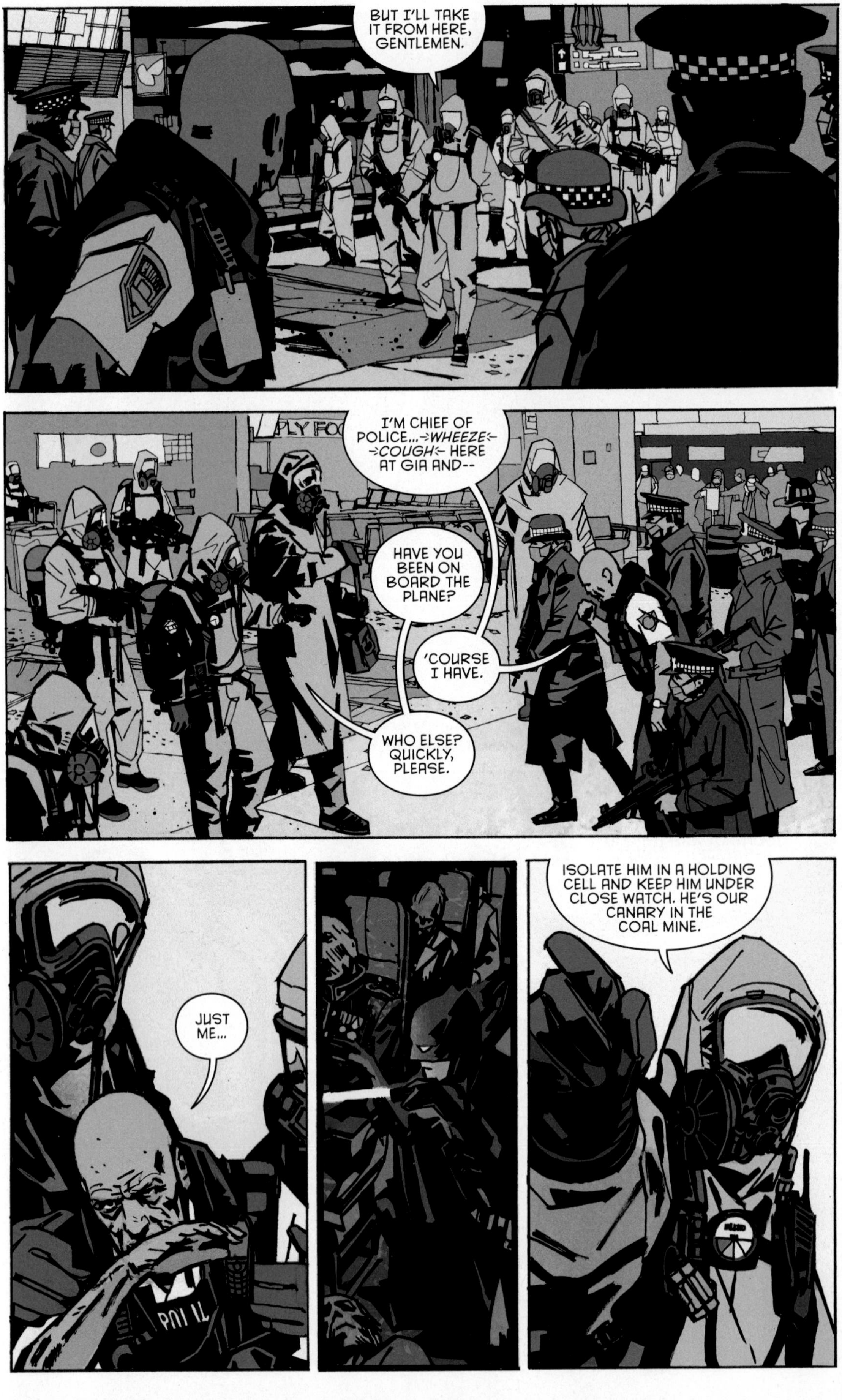

BUT I'LL TAKE IT FROM HERE, GENTLEMEN.
I'M CHIEF OF POLICE... ⇒WHEEZE⇐ ⇒COUGH⇐ HERE AT GIA AND--
HAVE YOU BEEN ON BOARD THE PLANE?
'COURSE I HAVE.
WHO ELSE? QUICKLY, PLEASE.
JUST ME...
ISOLATE HIM IN A HOLDING CELL AND KEEP HIM UNDER CLOSE WATCH. HE'S OUR CANARY IN THE COAL MINE.

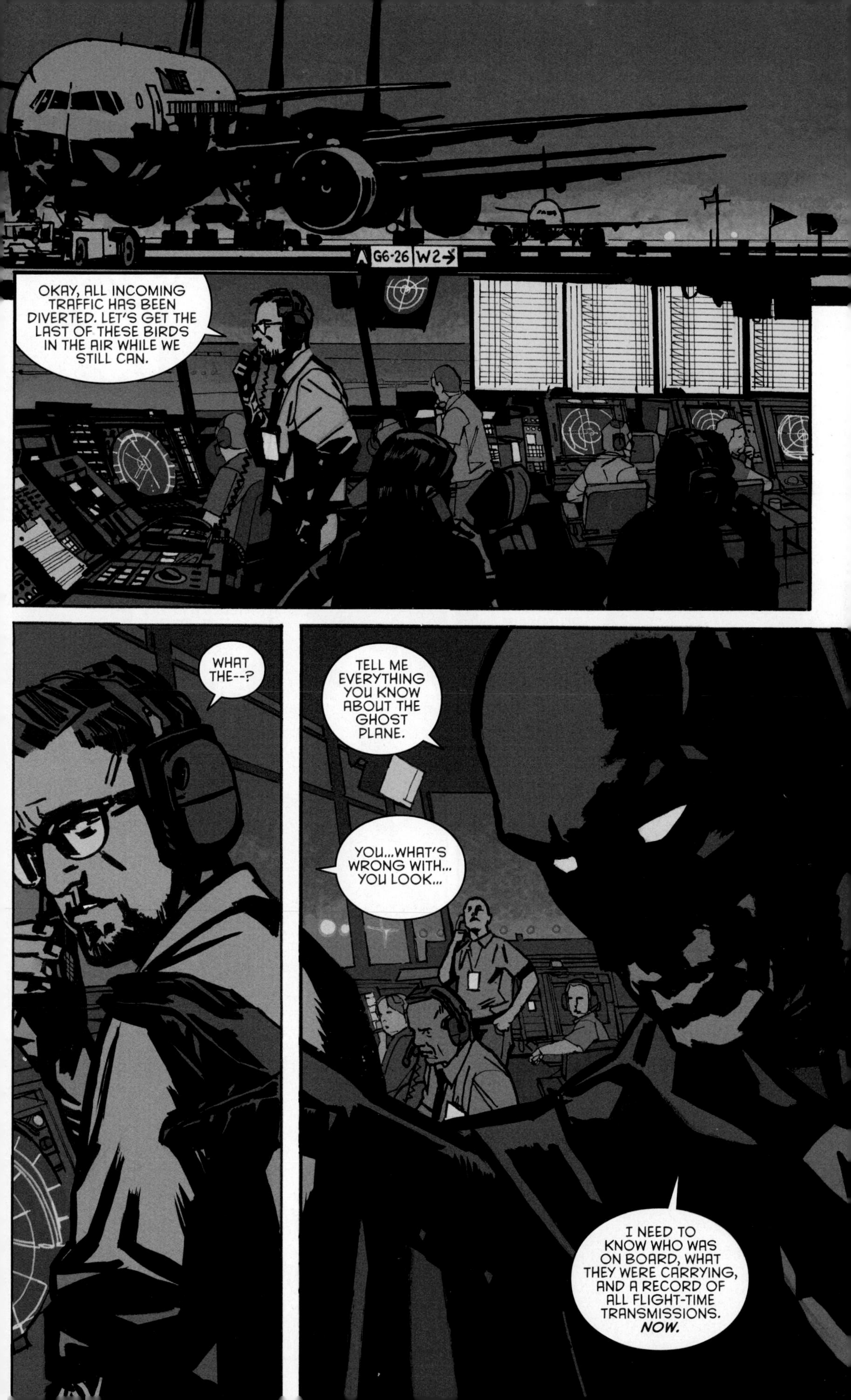
A G6-26 W2
OKAY, ALL INCOMING TRAFFIC HAS BEEN DIVERTED. LET'S GET THE LAST OF THESE BIRDS IN THE AIR WHILE WE STILL CAN.
WHAT THE--?
TELL ME EVERYTHING YOU KNOW ABOUT THE GHOST PLANE.
YOU...WHAT'S WRONG WITH... YOU LOOK...
I NEED TO KNOW WHO WAS ON BOARD, WHAT THEY WERE CARRYING, AND A RECORD OF ALL FLIGHT-TIME TRANSMISSIONS. *NOW.*

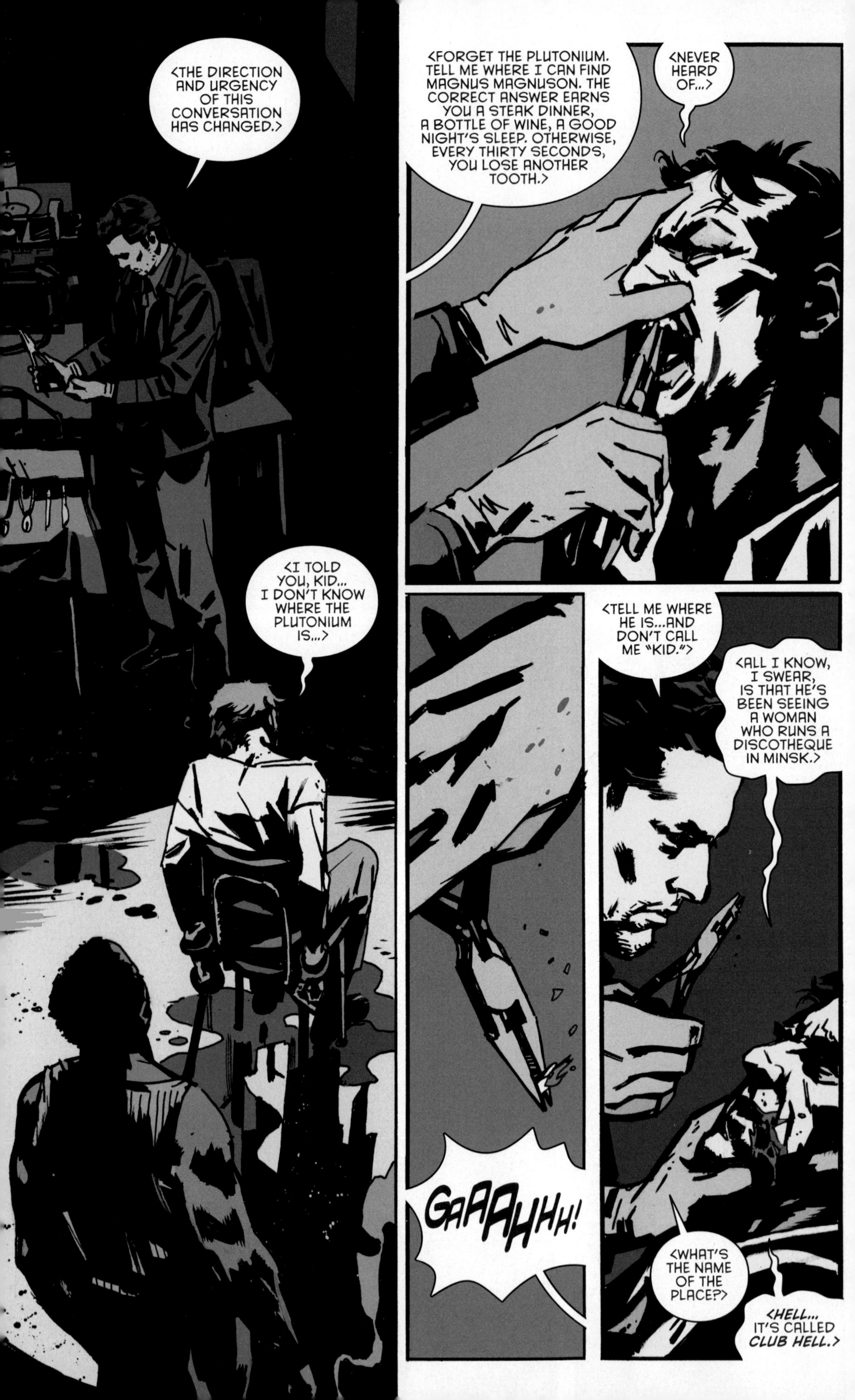

<THE DIRECTION AND URGENCY OF THIS CONVERSATION HAS CHANGED.>
<I TOLD YOU, KID... I DON'T KNOW WHERE THE PLUTONIUM IS...>
<FORGET THE PLUTONIUM. TELL ME WHERE I CAN FIND MAGNUS MAGNUSON. THE CORRECT ANSWER EARNS YOU A STEAK DINNER, A BOTTLE OF WINE, A GOOD NIGHT'S SLEEP. OTHERWISE, EVERY THIRTY SECONDS, YOU LOSE ANOTHER TOOTH.>
<NEVER HEARD OF...>
GAAAHHH!
<TELL ME WHERE HE IS...AND DON'T CALL ME "KID.">
<ALL I KNOW, I SWEAR, IS THAT HE'S BEEN SEEING A WOMAN WHO RUNS A DISCOTHEQUE IN MINSK.>
<WHAT'S THE NAME OF THE PLACE?>
<HELL... IT'S CALLED CLUB HELL.>

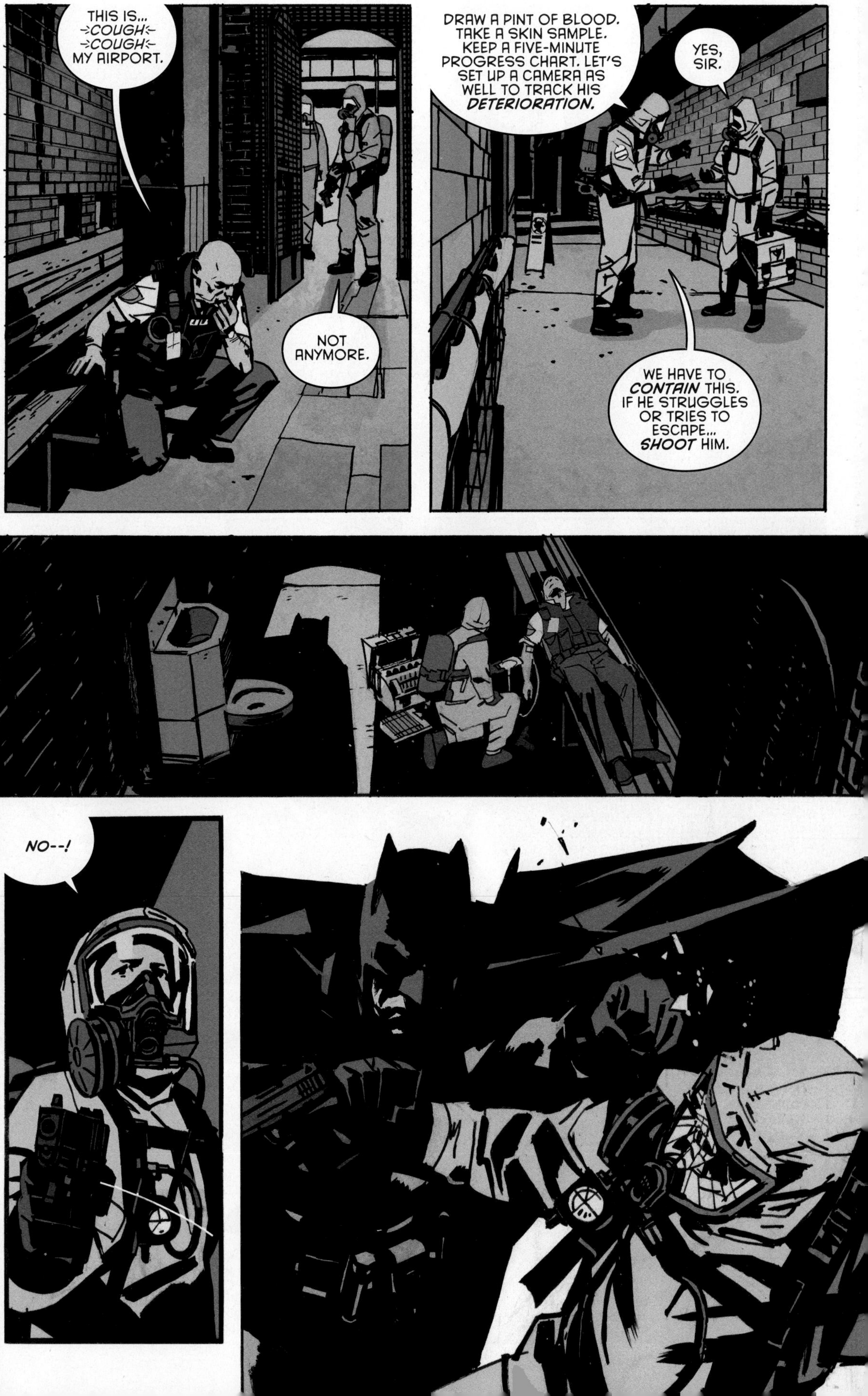
THIS IS... ~COUGH~ ~COUGH~ MY AIRPORT.
NOT ANYMORE.
DRAW A PINT OF BLOOD. TAKE A SKIN SAMPLE. KEEP A FIVE-MINUTE PROGRESS CHART. LET'S SET UP A CAMERA AS WELL TO TRACK HIS DETERIORATION.
YES, SIR.
WE HAVE TO CONTAIN THIS. IF HE STRUGGLES OR TRIES TO ESCAPE... SHOOT HIM.
NO--!

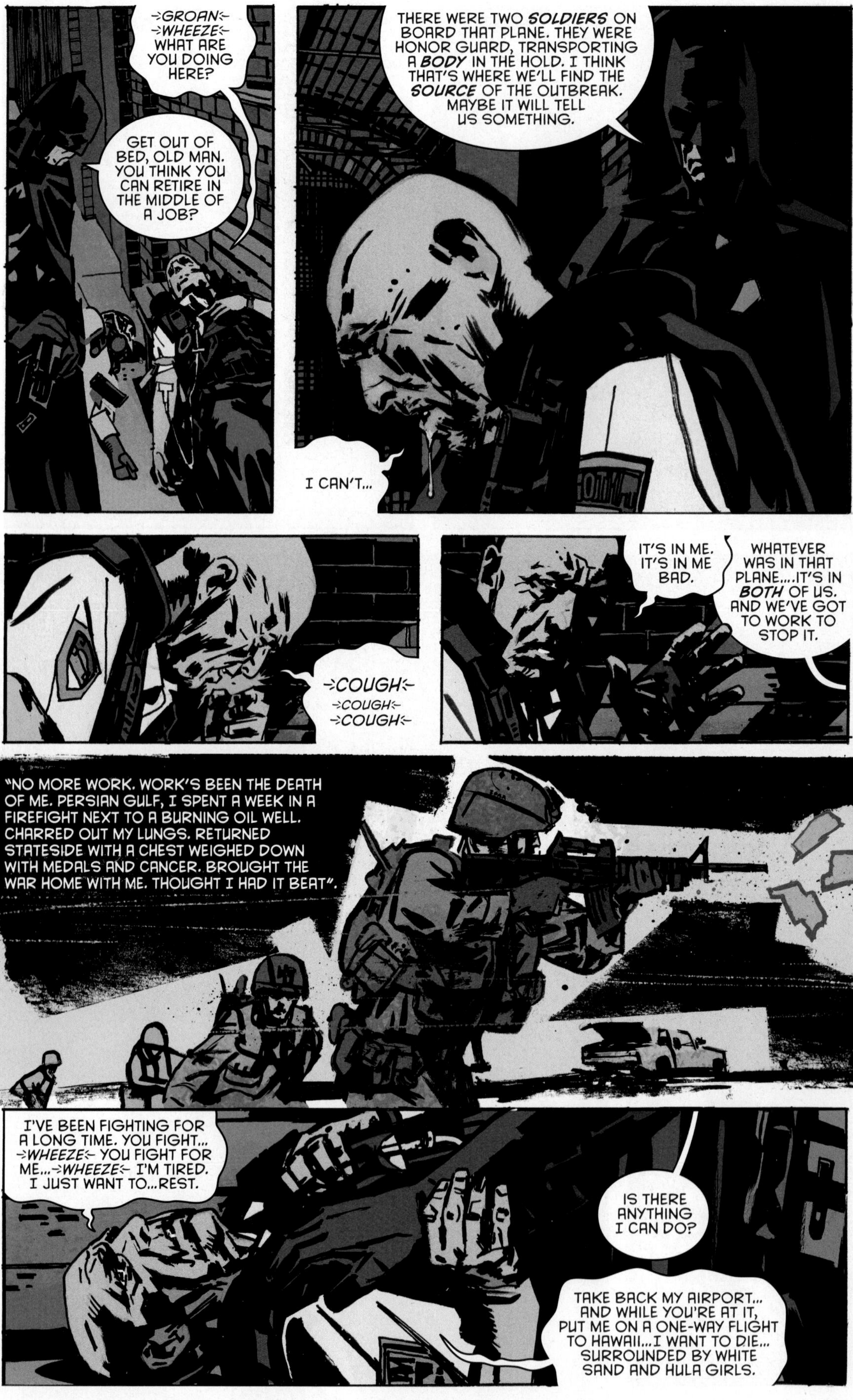

→GROAN← →WHEEZE← WHAT ARE YOU DOING HERE?
GET OUT OF BED, OLD MAN. YOU THINK YOU CAN RETIRE IN THE MIDDLE OF A JOB?
THERE WERE TWO SOLDIERS ON BOARD THAT PLANE. THEY WERE HONOR GUARD, TRANSPORTING A BODY IN THE HOLD. I THINK THAT'S WHERE WE'LL FIND THE SOURCE OF THE OUTBREAK. MAYBE IT WILL TELL US SOMETHING.
I CAN'T...
→COUGH← →COUGH← →COUGH←
IT'S IN ME. IT'S IN ME BAD.
WHATEVER WAS IN THAT PLANE....IT'S IN BOTH OF US. AND WE'VE GOT TO WORK TO STOP IT.
"NO MORE WORK. WORK'S BEEN THE DEATH OF ME. PERSIAN GULF, I SPENT A WEEK IN A FIREFIGHT NEXT TO A BURNING OIL WELL. CHARRED OUT MY LUNGS. RETURNED STATESIDE WITH A CHEST WEIGHED DOWN WITH MEDALS AND CANCER. BROUGHT THE WAR HOME WITH ME. THOUGHT I HAD IT BEAT".
I'VE BEEN FIGHTING FOR A LONG TIME. YOU FIGHT... →WHEEZE← YOU FIGHT FOR ME...→WHEEZE← I'M TIRED. I JUST WANT TO...REST.
IS THERE ANYTHING I CAN DO?
TAKE BACK MY AIRPORT... AND WHILE YOU'RE AT IT, PUT ME ON A ONE-WAY FLIGHT TO HAWAII...I WANT TO DIE... SURROUNDED BY WHITE SAND AND HULA GIRLS.

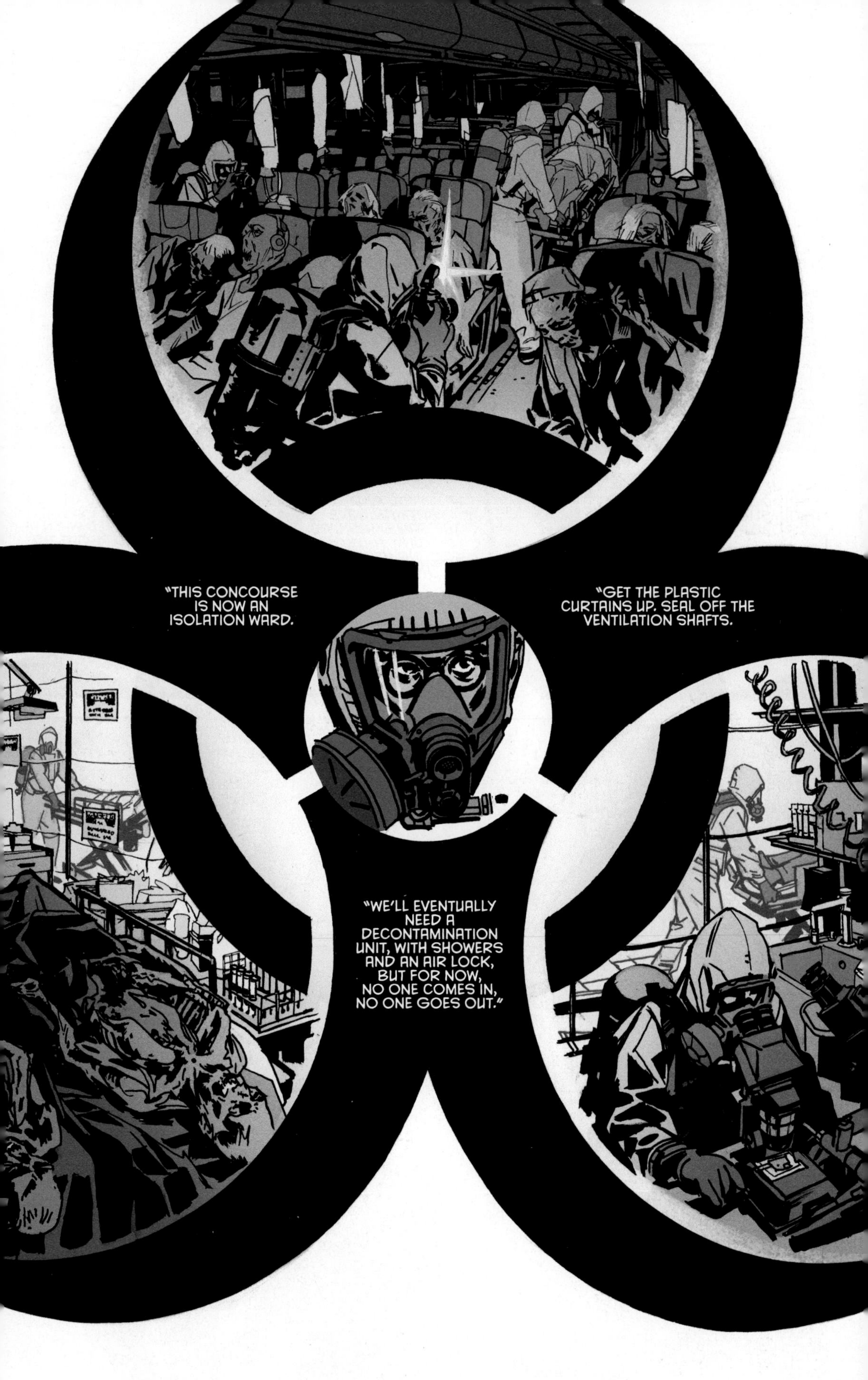
"THIS CONCOURSE IS NOW AN ISOLATION WARD.
"GET THE PLASTIC CURTAINS UP. SEAL OFF THE VENTILATION SHAFTS.
"WE'LL EVENTUALLY NEED A DECONTAMINATION UNIT, WITH SHOWERS AND AN AIR LOCK, BUT FOR NOW, NO ONE COMES IN, NO ONE GOES OUT."

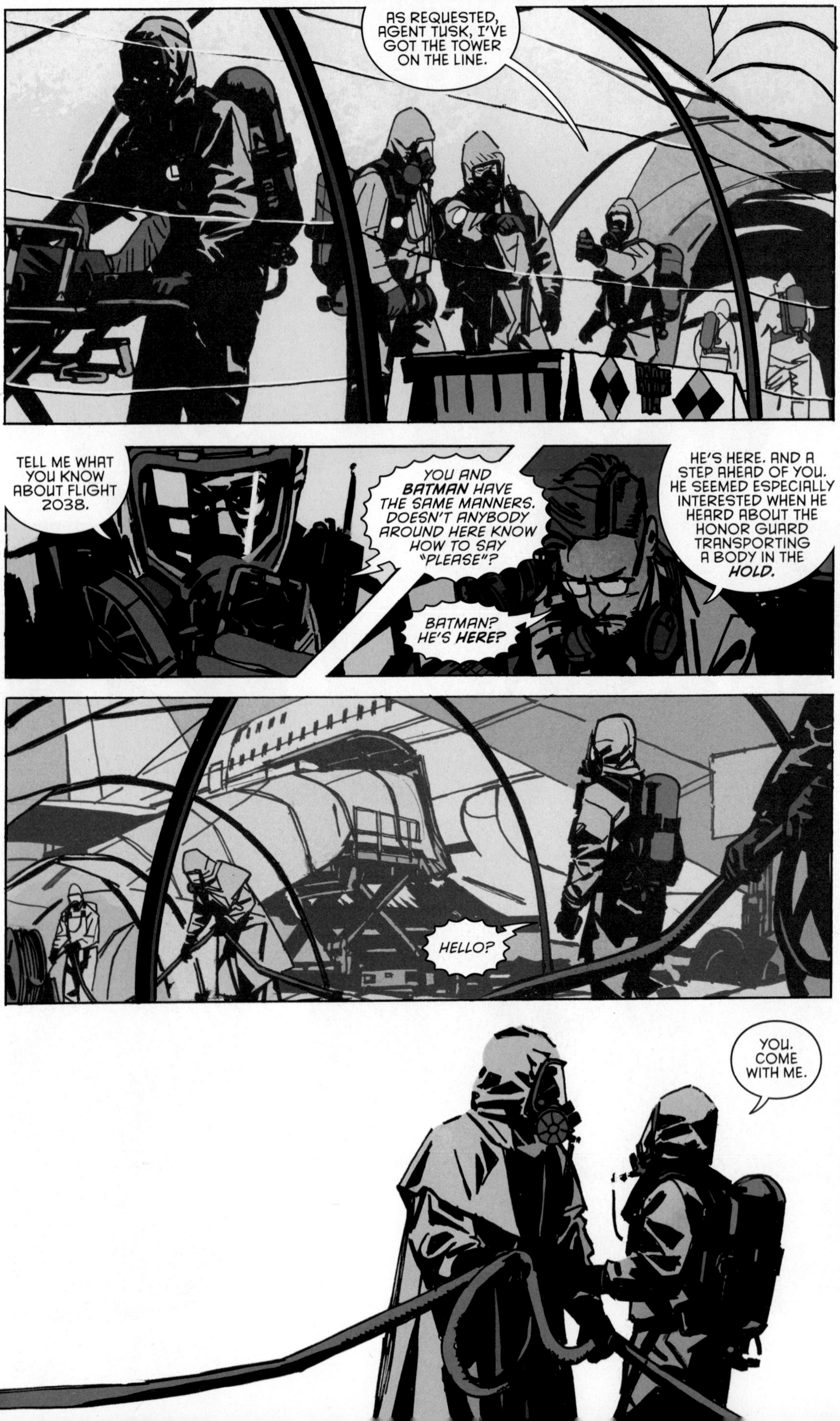
AS REQUESTED, AGENT TUSK, I'VE GOT THE TOWER ON THE LINE.
TELL ME WHAT YOU KNOW ABOUT FLIGHT 2038.
YOU AND BATMAN HAVE THE SAME MANNERS. DOESN'T ANYBODY AROUND HERE KNOW HOW TO SAY "PLEASE"?
BATMAN? HE'S HERE?
HE'S HERE. AND A STEP AHEAD OF YOU. HE SEEMED ESPECIALLY INTERESTED WHEN HE HEARD ABOUT THE HONOR GUARD TRANSPORTING A BODY IN THE HOLD.
HELLO?
YOU. COME WITH ME.

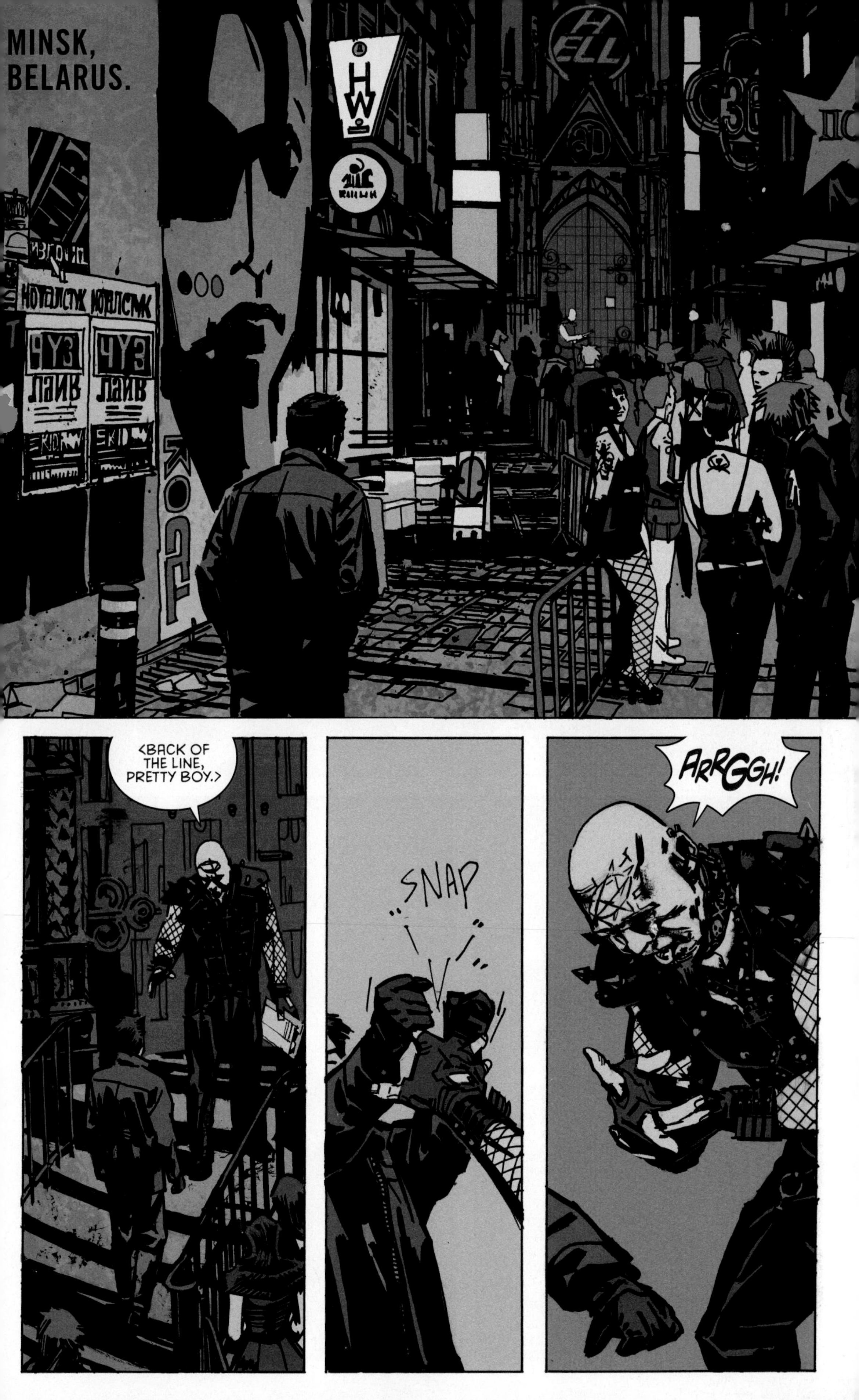
MINSK, BELARUS.
<BACK OF THE LINE, PRETTY BOY.>
SNAP
ARRGGH!

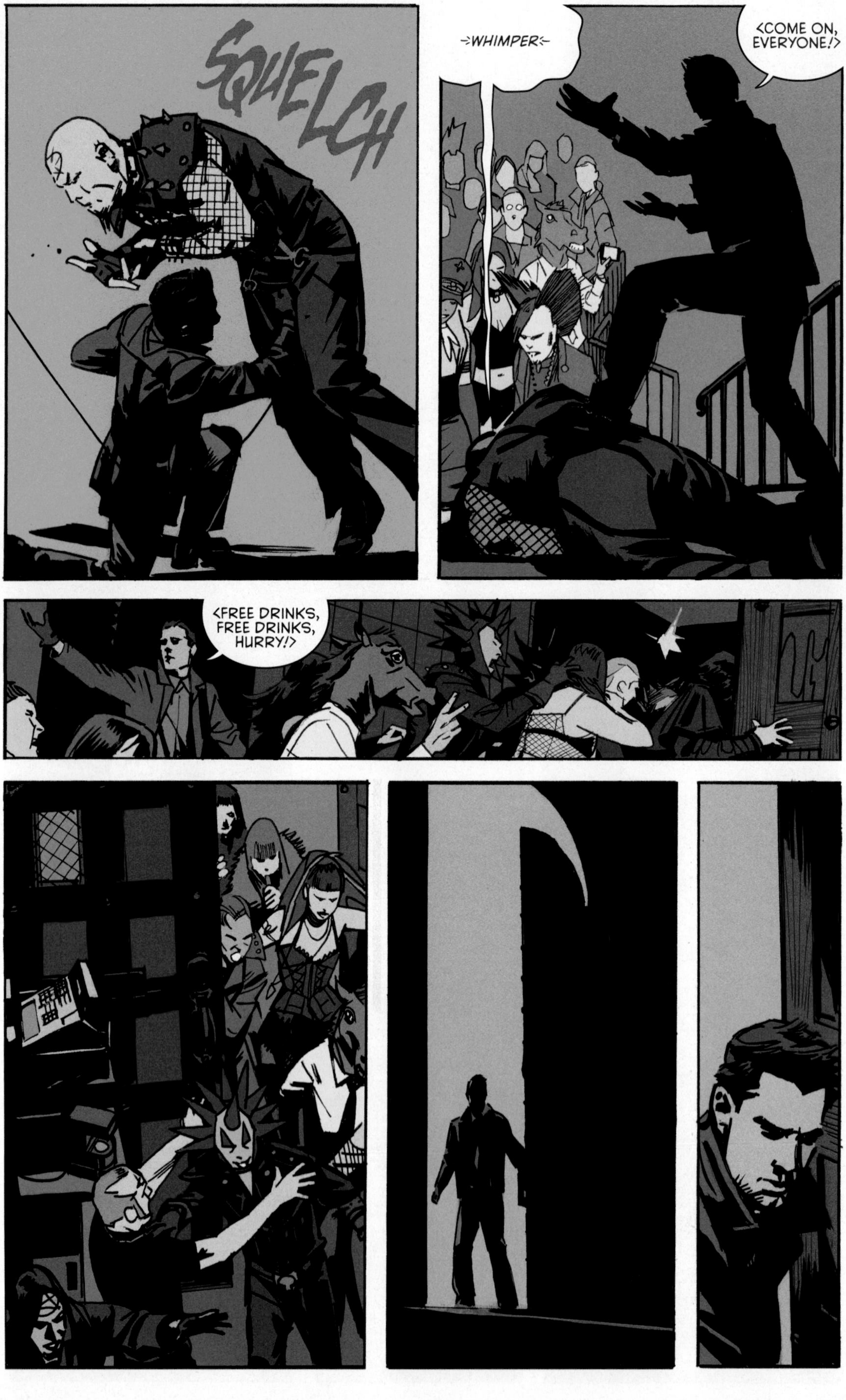
SQUELCH
-WHIMPER-
<COME ON, EVERYONE!>
<FREE DRINKS, FREE DRINKS, HURRY!>

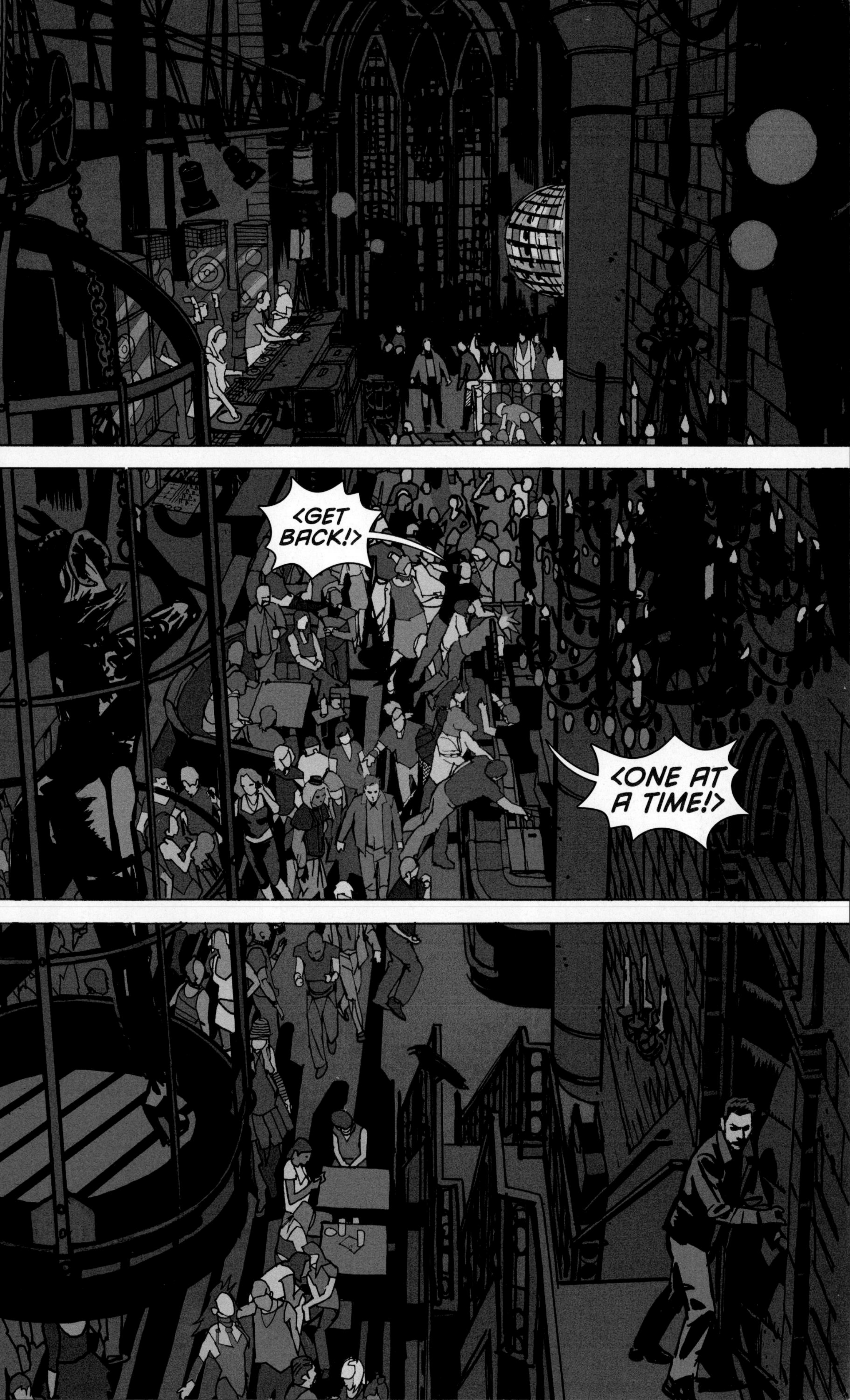
<GET BACK!>
<ONE AT A TIME!>

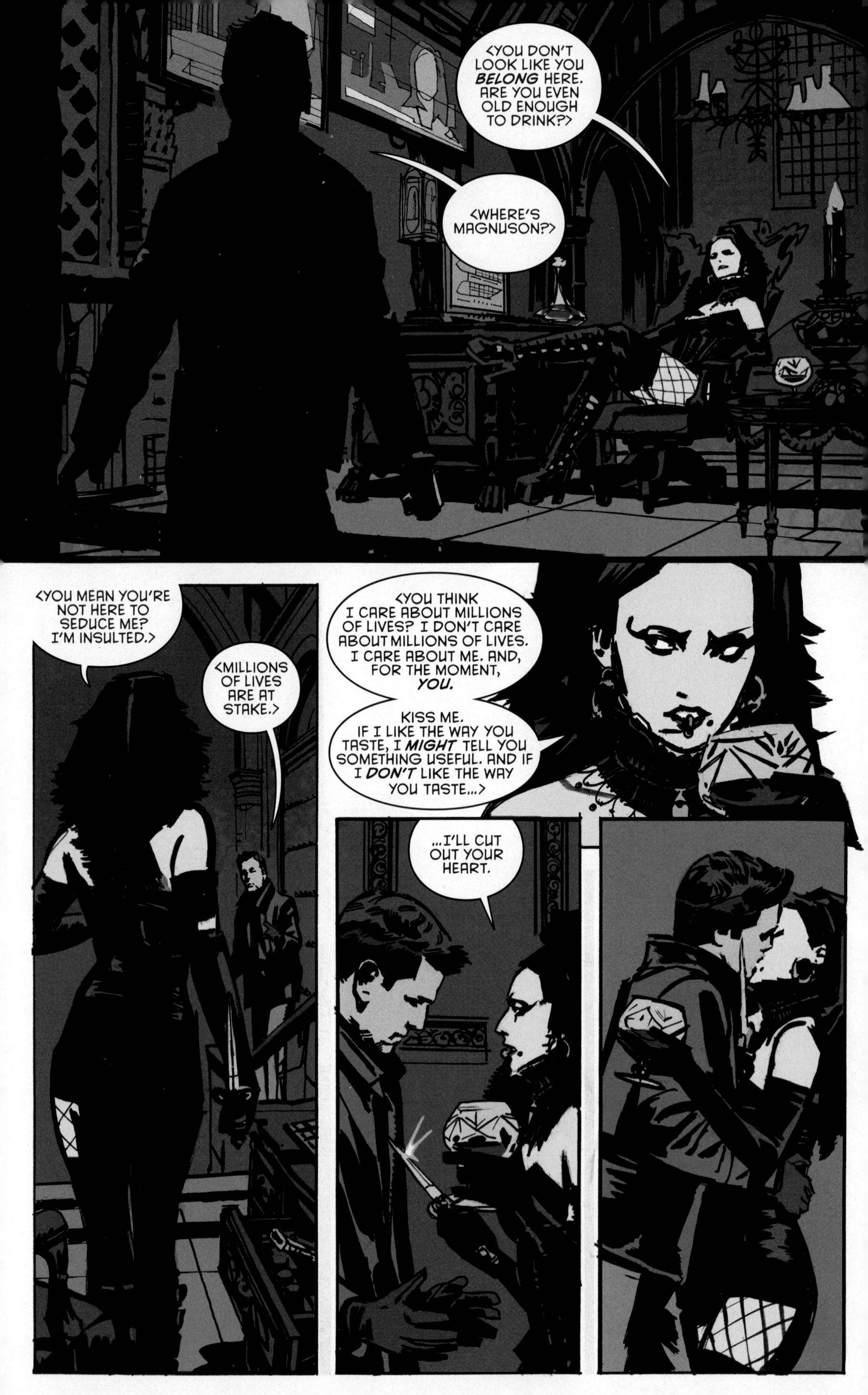
<YOU DON'T LOOK LIKE YOU **BELONG** HERE. ARE YOU EVEN OLD ENOUGH TO DRINK?>
<WHERE'S MAGNUSON?>
<YOU MEAN YOU'RE NOT HERE TO SEDUCE ME? I'M INSULTED.>
<MILLIONS OF LIVES ARE AT STAKE.>
<YOU THINK I CARE ABOUT MILLIONS OF LIVES? I DON'T CARE ABOUT MILLIONS OF LIVES. I CARE ABOUT ME. AND, FOR THE MOMENT, ***YOU.***
KISS ME. IF I LIKE THE WAY YOU TASTE, I ***MIGHT*** TELL YOU SOMETHING USEFUL. AND IF I ***DON'T*** LIKE THE WAY YOU TASTE...>
...I'LL CUT OUT YOUR HEART.

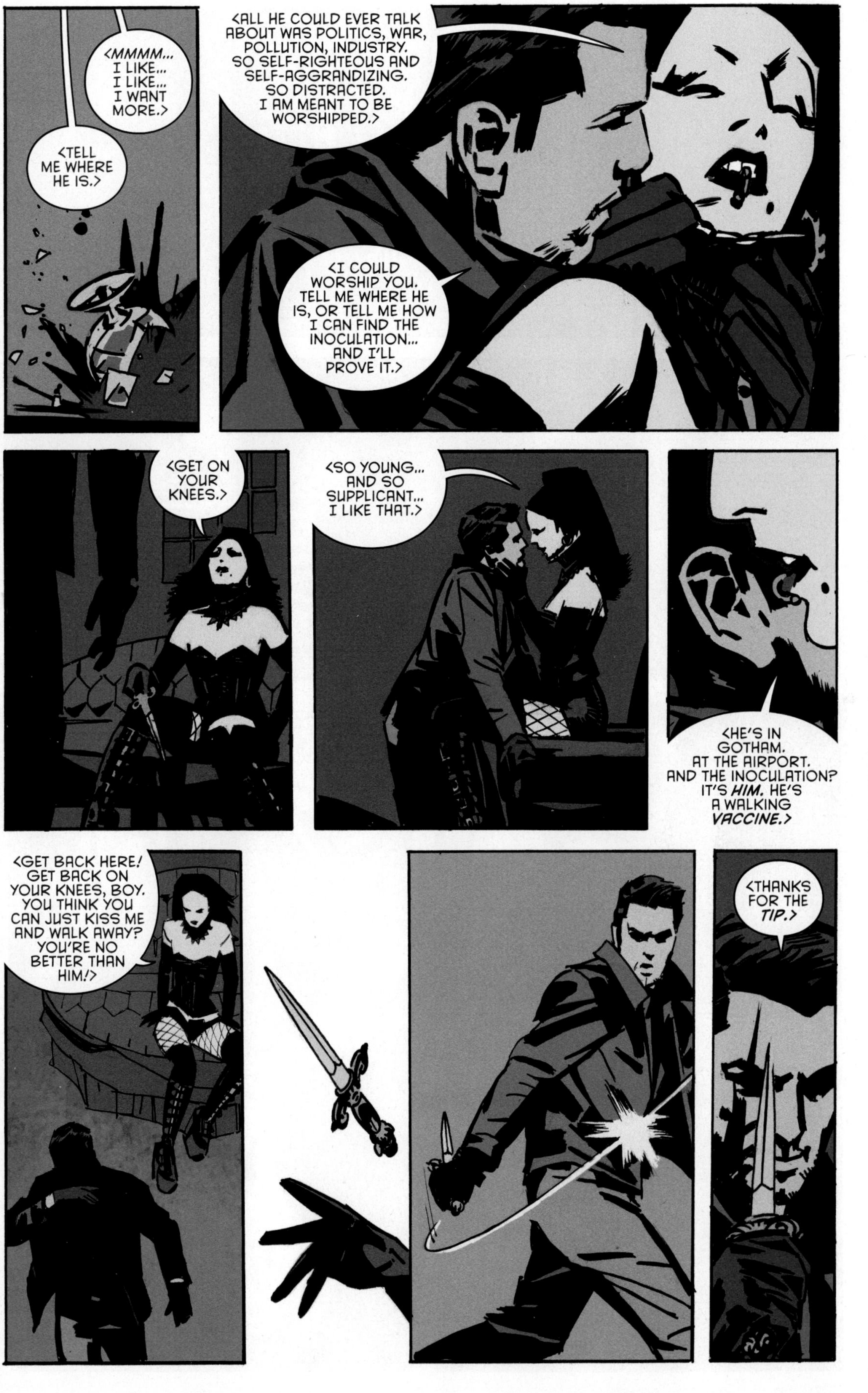
<MMMM... I LIKE... I LIKE... I WANT MORE.>
<TELL ME WHERE HE IS.>
<ALL HE COULD EVER TALK ABOUT WAS POLITICS, WAR, POLLUTION, INDUSTRY. SO SELF-RIGHTEOUS AND SELF-AGGRANDIZING. SO DISTRACTED. I AM MEANT TO BE WORSHIPPED.>
<I COULD WORSHIP YOU. TELL ME WHERE HE IS, OR TELL ME HOW I CAN FIND THE INOCULATION... AND I'LL PROVE IT.>
<GET ON YOUR KNEES.>
<SO YOUNG... AND SO SUPPLICANT... I LIKE THAT.>
<HE'S IN GOTHAM. AT THE AIRPORT. AND THE INOCULATION? IT'S *HIM.* HE'S A WALKING *VACCINE.*>
<GET BACK HERE! GET BACK ON YOUR KNEES, BOY. YOU THINK YOU CAN JUST KISS ME AND WALK AWAY? YOU'RE NO BETTER THAN HIM!>
<THANKS FOR THE *TIP.*>

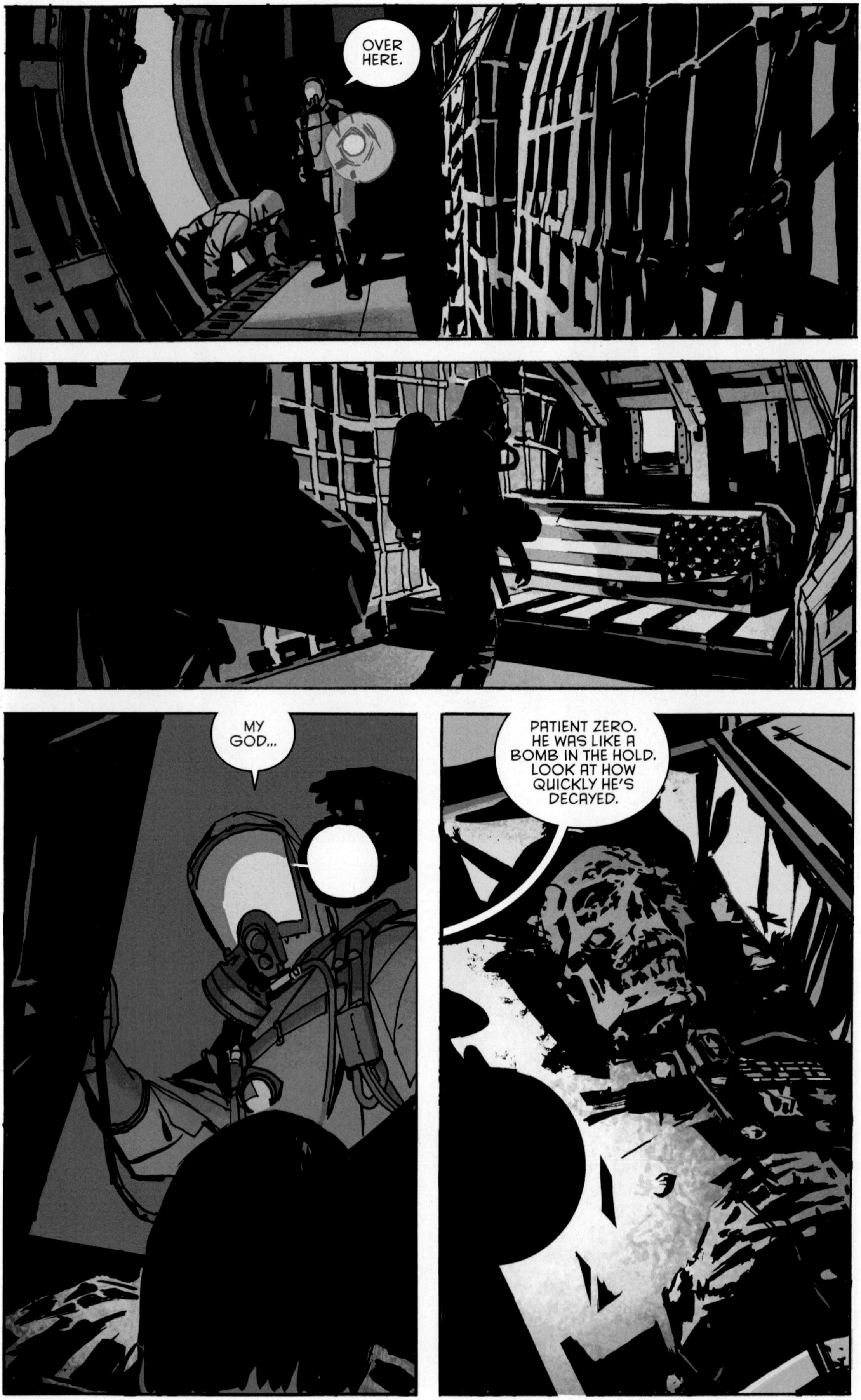
OVER HERE.
MY GOD...
PATIENT ZERO. HE WAS LIKE A BOMB IN THE HOLD. LOOK AT HOW QUICKLY HE'S DECAYED.

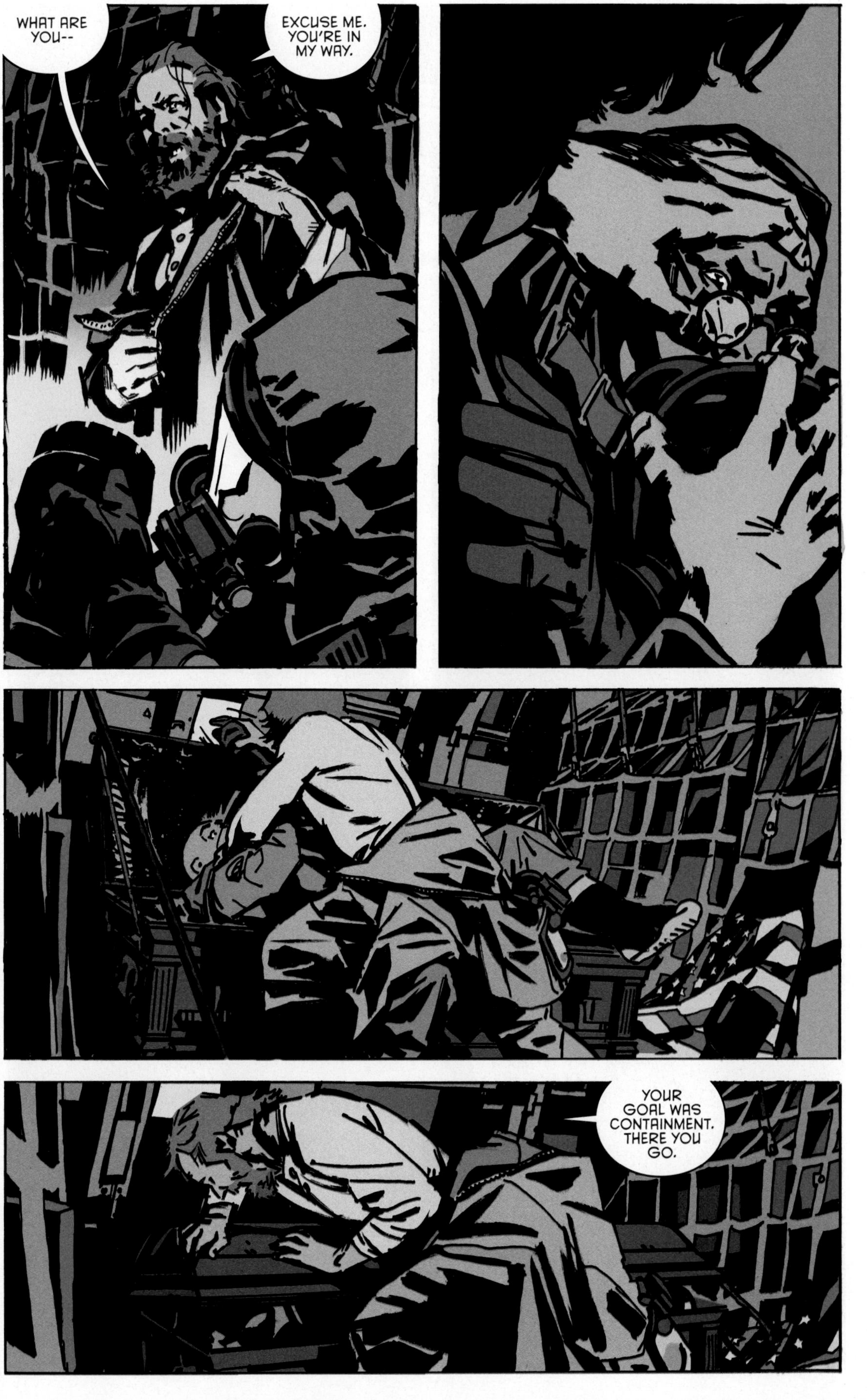
WHAT ARE YOU--
EXCUSE ME. YOU'RE IN MY WAY.
YOUR GOAL WAS CONTAINMENT. THERE YOU GO.

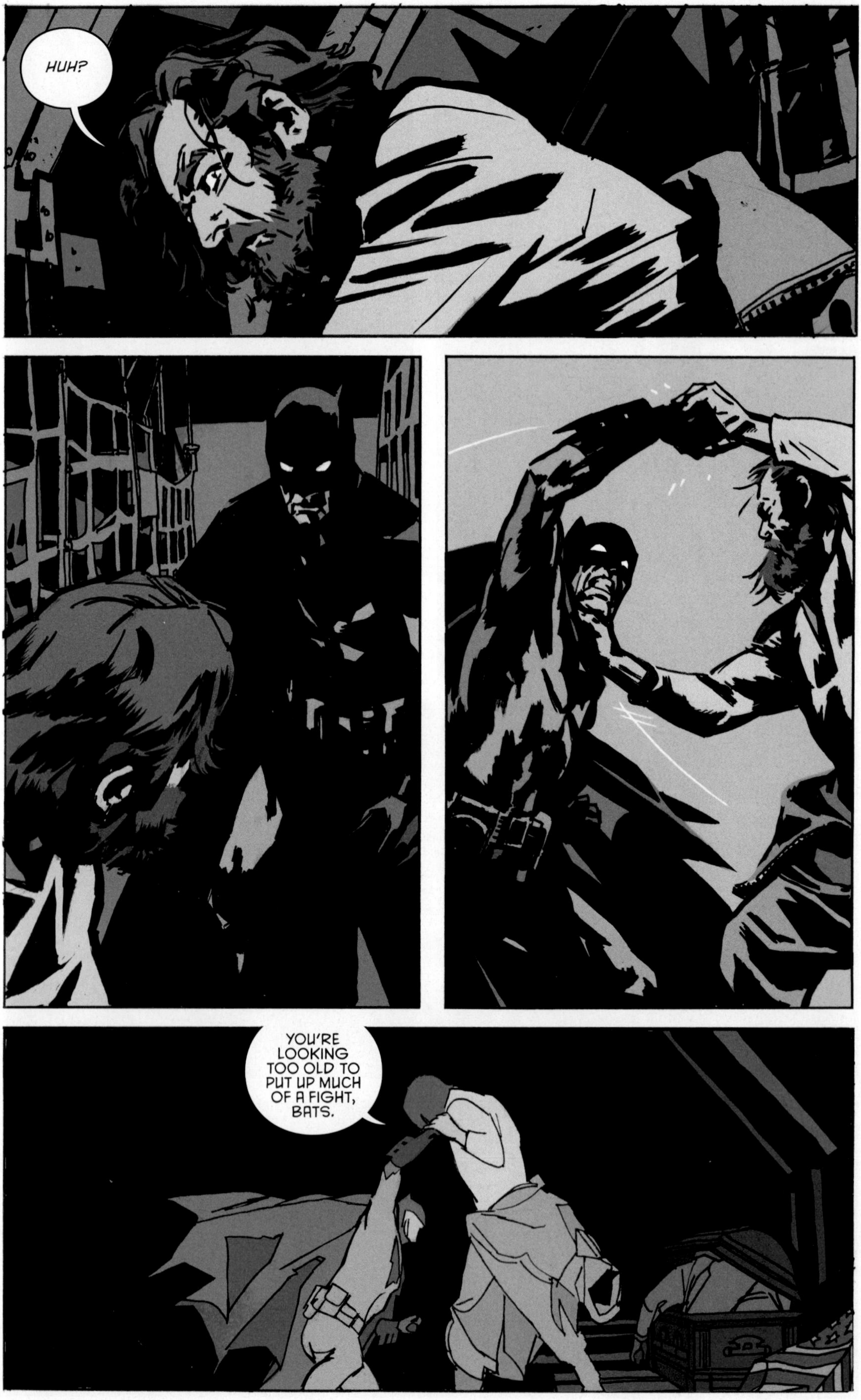
HUH?
YOU'RE LOOKING TOO OLD TO PUT UP MUCH OF A FIGHT, BATS.

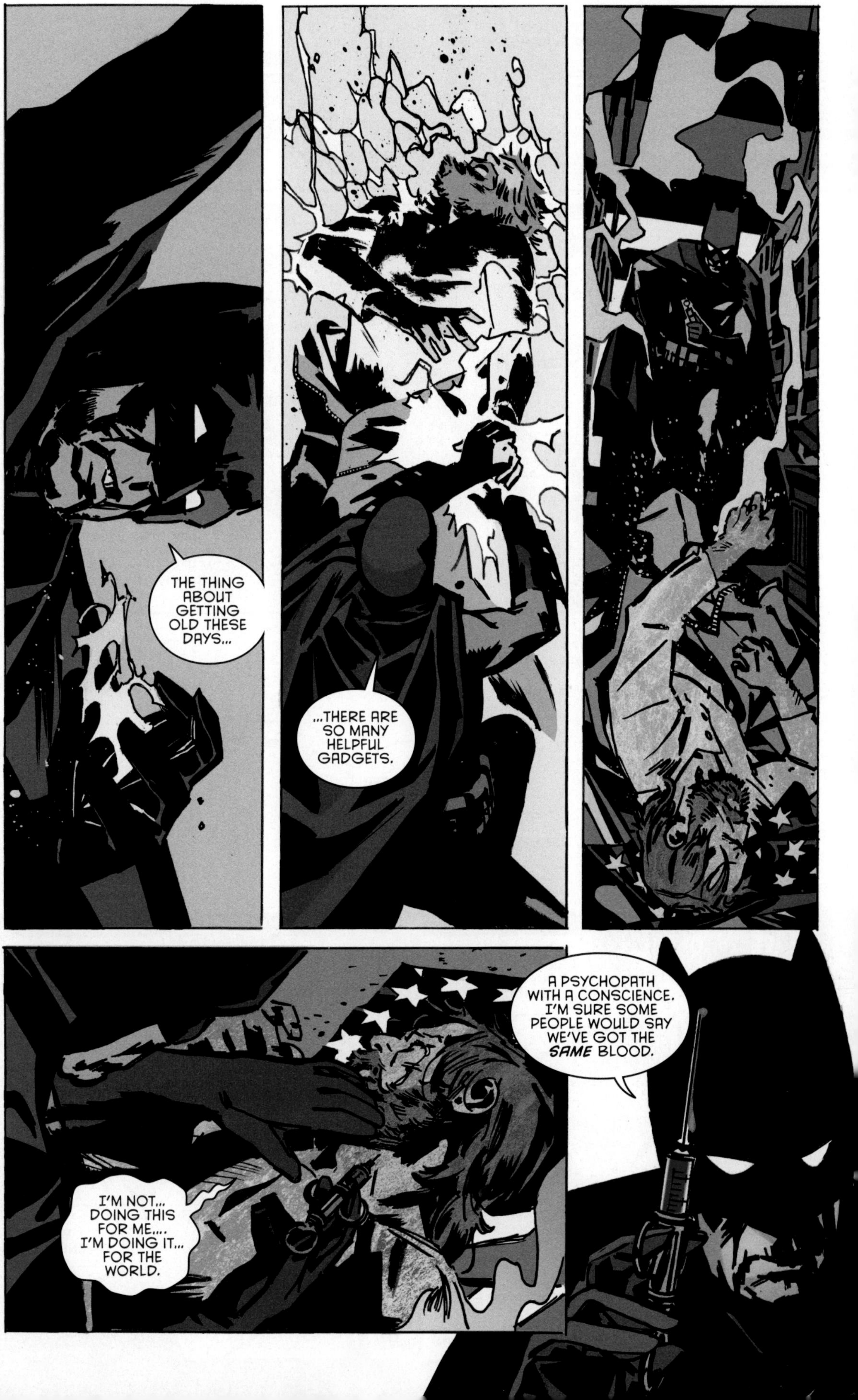
THE THING ABOUT GETTING OLD THESE DAYS...
...THERE ARE SO MANY HELPFUL GADGETS.
A PSYCHOPATH WITH A CONSCIENCE. I'M SURE SOME PEOPLE WOULD SAY WE'VE GOT THE *SAME* BLOOD.
I'M NOT... DOING THIS FOR ME.... I'M DOING IT... FOR THE WORLD.

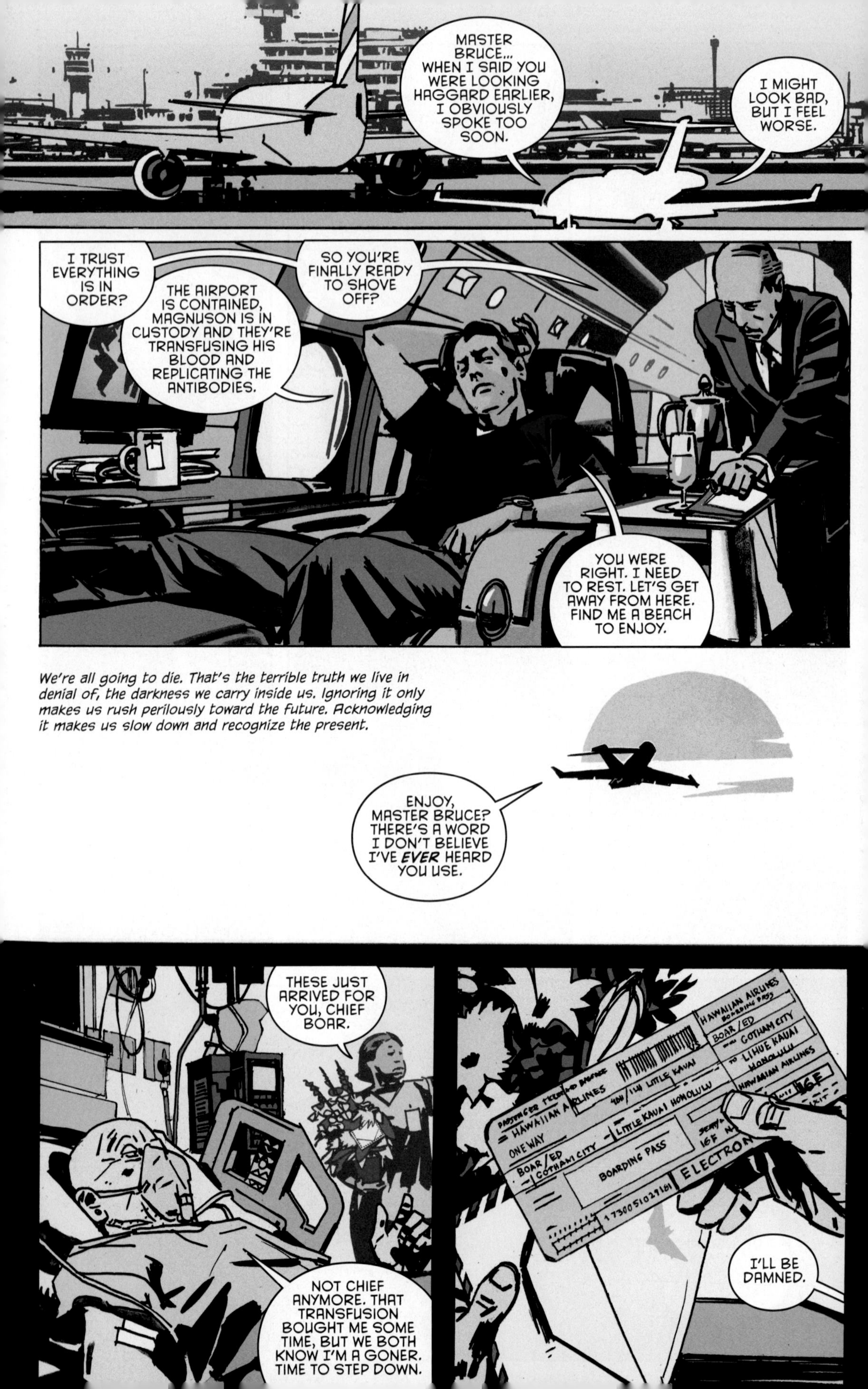
MASTER BRUCE... WHEN I SAID YOU WERE LOOKING HAGGARD EARLIER, I OBVIOUSLY SPOKE TOO SOON.
I MIGHT LOOK BAD, BUT I FEEL WORSE.
I TRUST EVERYTHING IS IN ORDER?
THE AIRPORT IS CONTAINED, MAGNUSON IS IN CUSTODY AND THEY'RE TRANSFUSING HIS BLOOD AND REPLICATING THE ANTIBODIES.
SO YOU'RE FINALLY READY TO SHOVE OFF?
YOU WERE RIGHT. I NEED TO REST. LET'S GET AWAY FROM HERE. FIND ME A BEACH TO ENJOY.
We're all going to die. That's the terrible truth we live in denial of, the darkness we carry inside us. Ignoring it only makes us rush perilously toward the future. Acknowledging it makes us slow down and recognize the present.
ENJOY, MASTER BRUCE? THERE'S A WORD I DON'T BELIEVE I'VE EVER HEARD YOU USE.
THESE JUST ARRIVED FOR YOU, CHIEF BOAR.
NOT CHIEF ANYMORE. THAT TRANSFUSION BOUGHT ME SOME TIME, BUT WE BOTH KNOW I'M A GONER. TIME TO STEP DOWN.
HAWAIIAN AIRLINES
BOARDING PASS
BOAR / ED
GOTHAM CITY
LIHUE KAUAI
I'LL BE DAMNED.

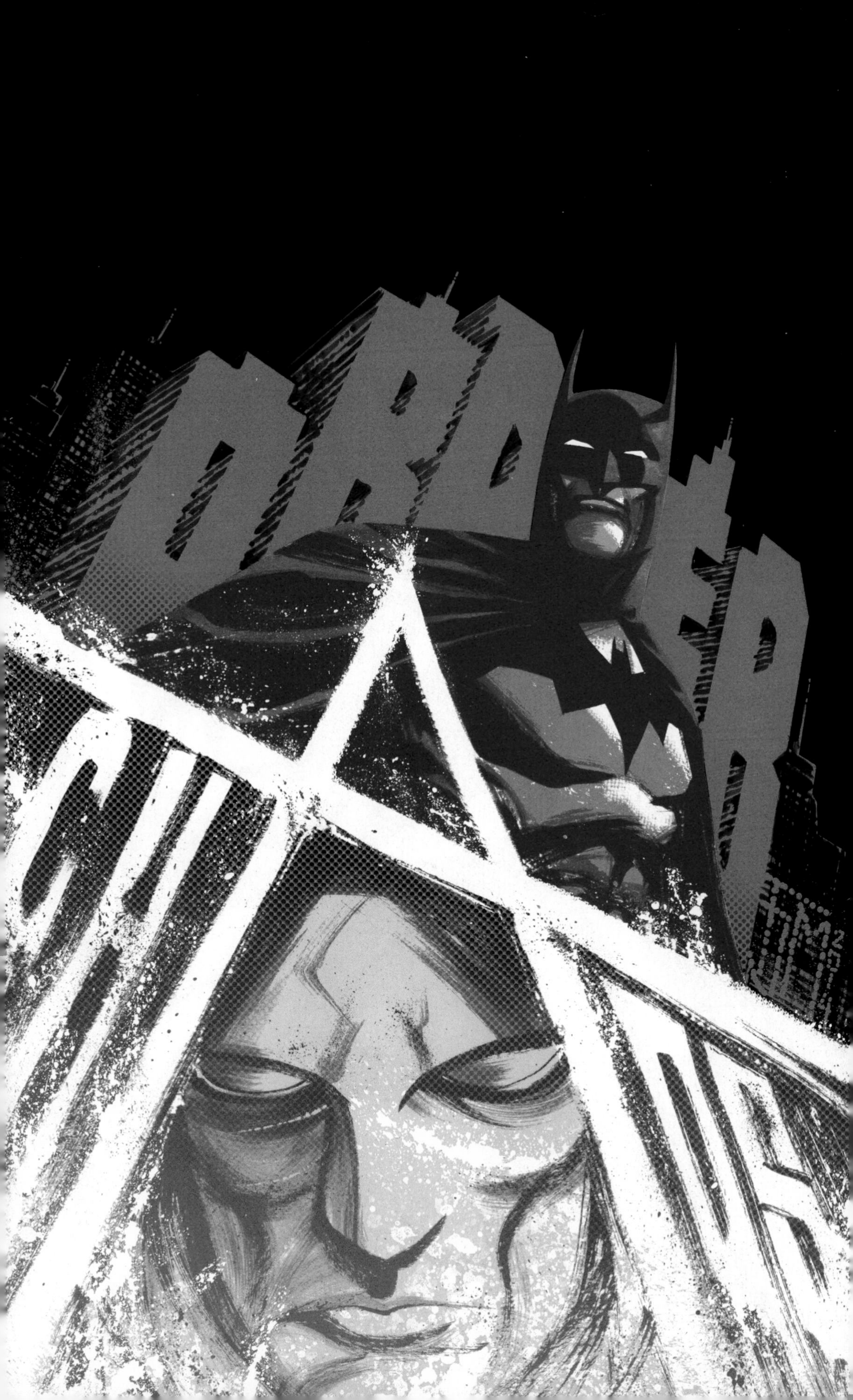

ANARKY PART 1

FRANCIS MANAPUL & BRIAN BUCCELLATO writers FRANCIS MANAPUL artist BRIAN BUCCELLATO colorist JARED K. FLETCHER letterer cover by FRANCIS MANAPUL

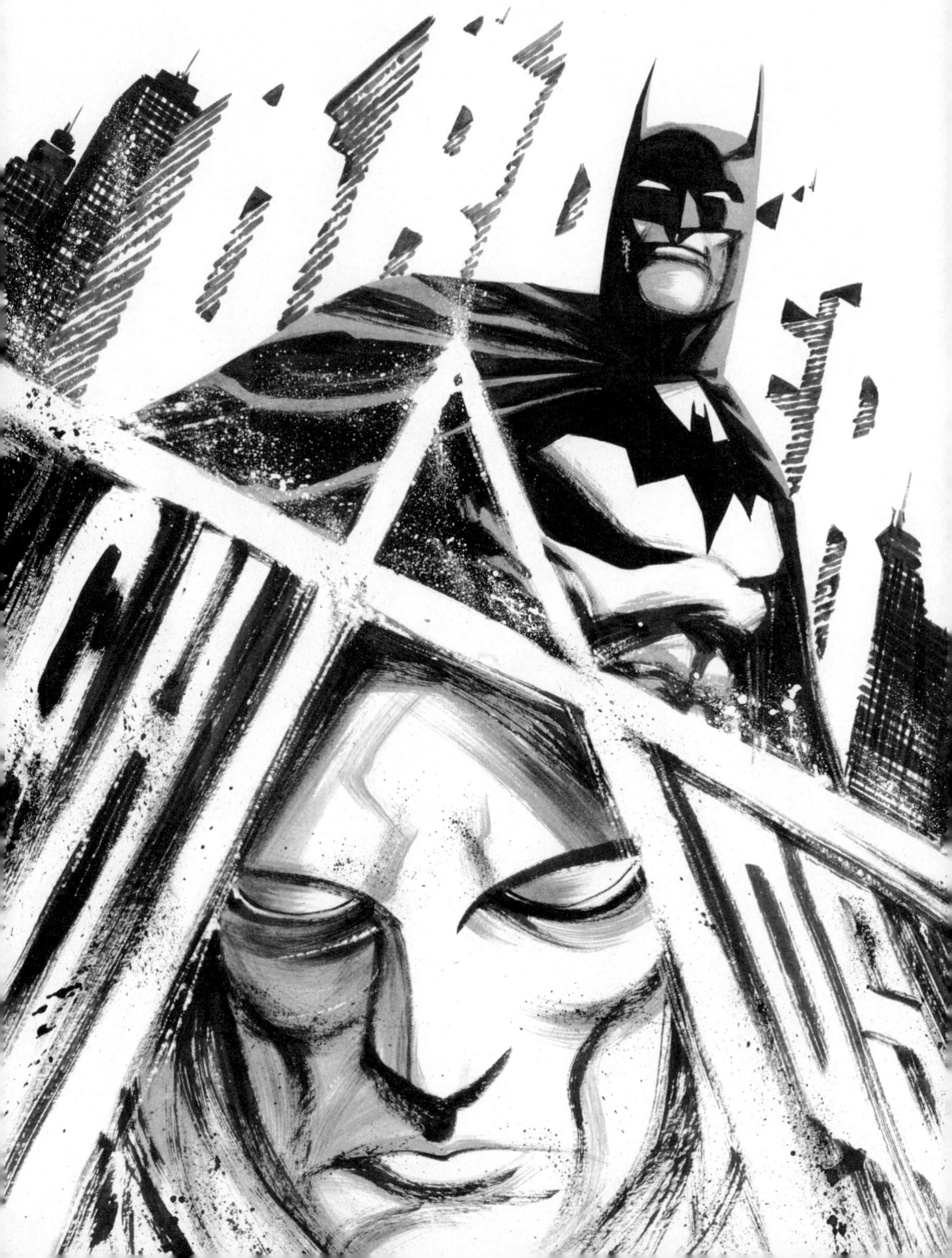

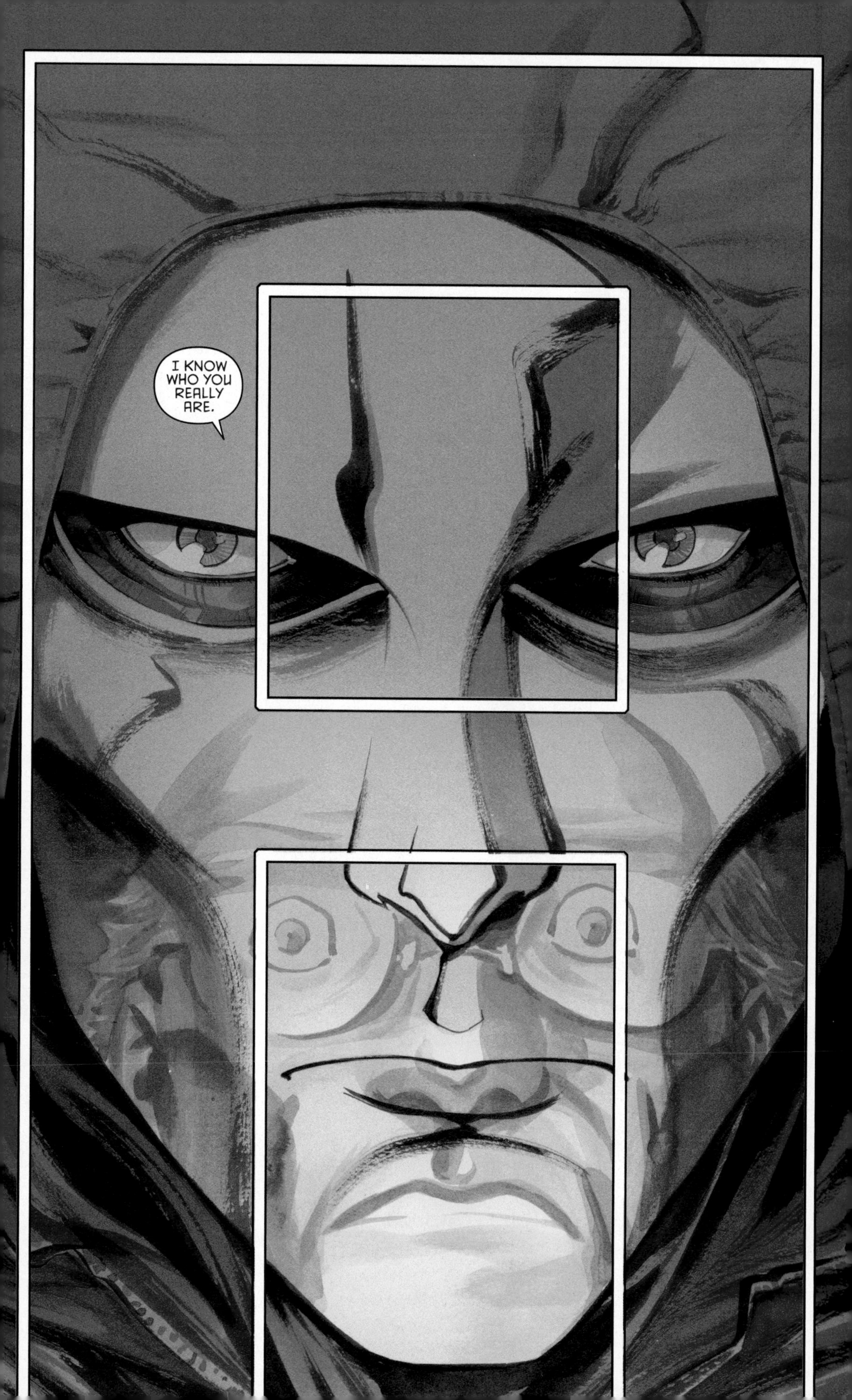
I KNOW WHO YOU REALLY ARE.

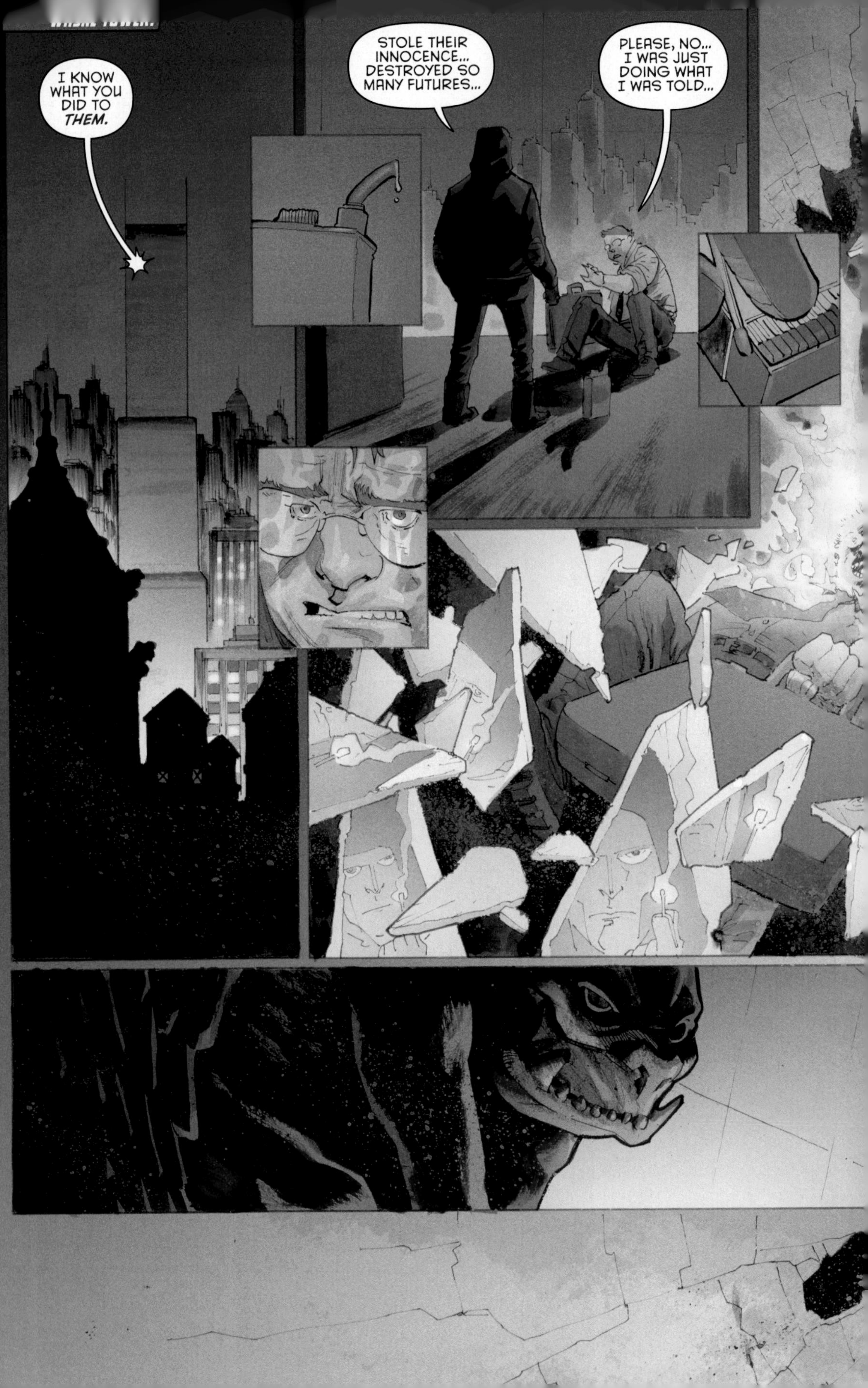
I KNOW WHAT YOU DID TO *THEM.*
STOLE THEIR INNOCENCE... DESTROYED SO MANY FUTURES...
PLEASE, NO... I WAS JUST DOING WHAT I WAS TOLD...

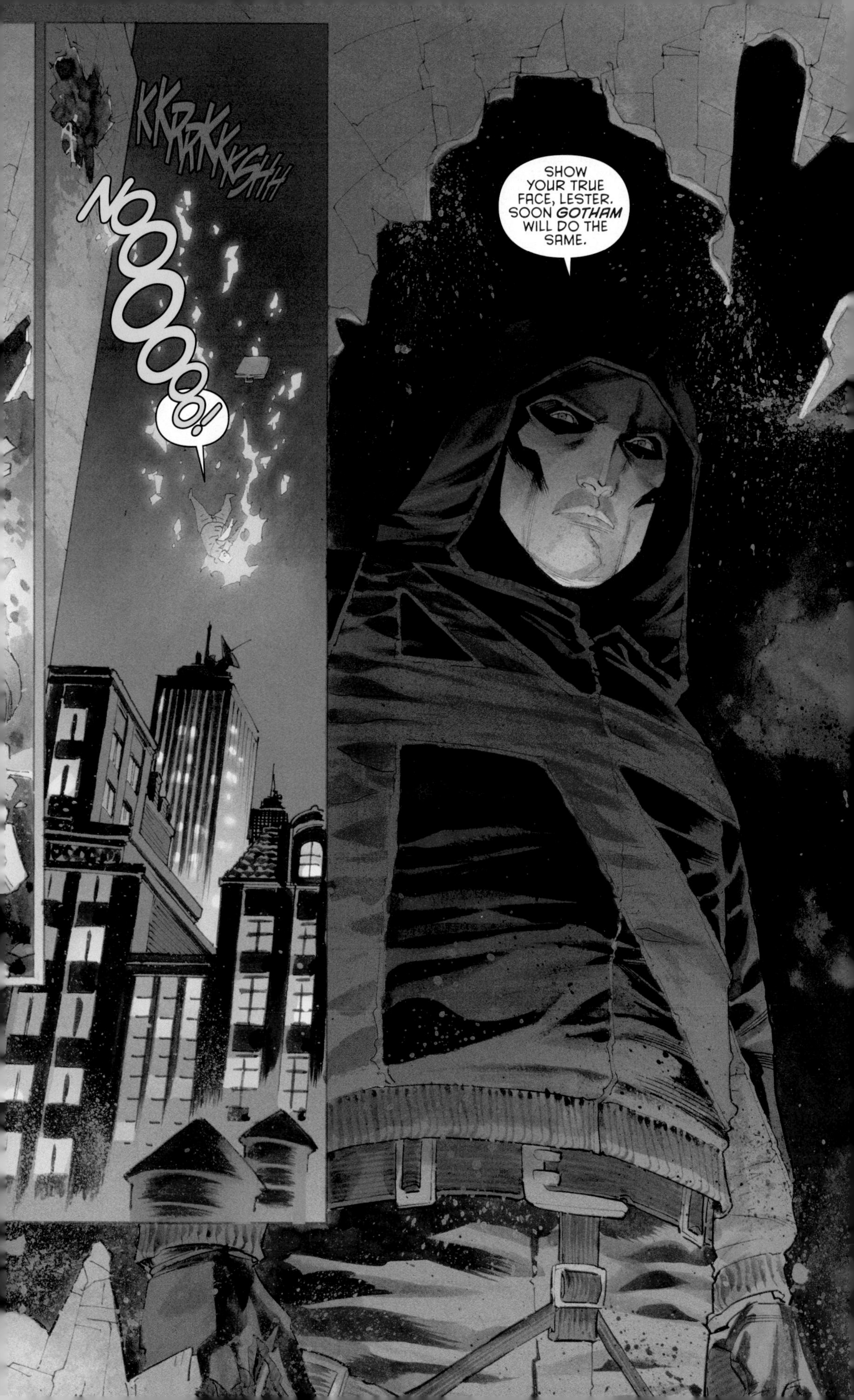

KKRRKKKSHH
NOOOOOO!
SHOW YOUR TRUE FACE, LESTER. SOON *GOTHAM* WILL DO THE SAME.

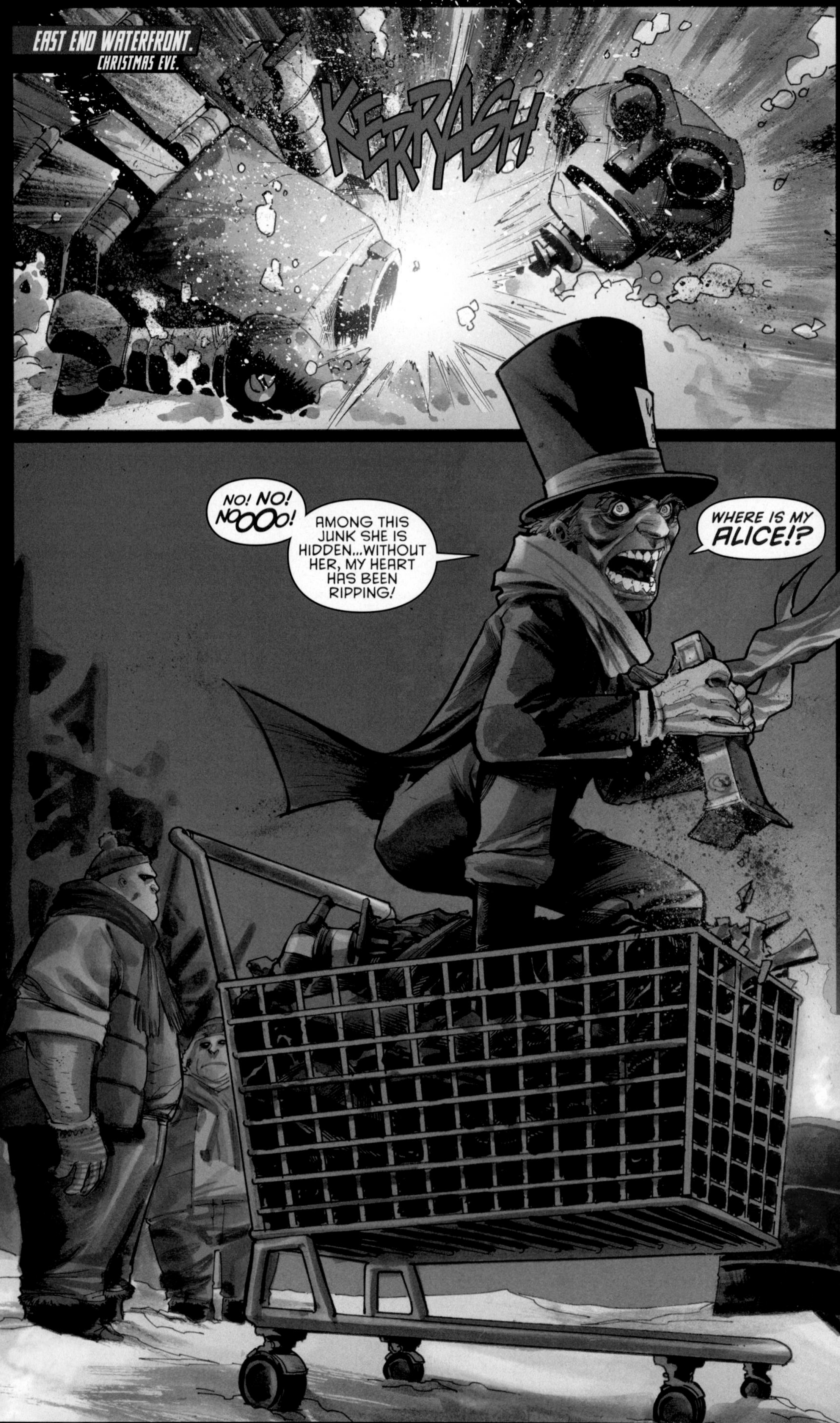
EAST END WATERFRONT.
CHRISTMAS EVE.
KERRASH
NO! NO! NOOOO!
AMONG THIS JUNK SHE IS HIDDEN...WITHOUT HER, MY HEART HAS BEEN RIPPING!
WHERE IS MY ALICE!?

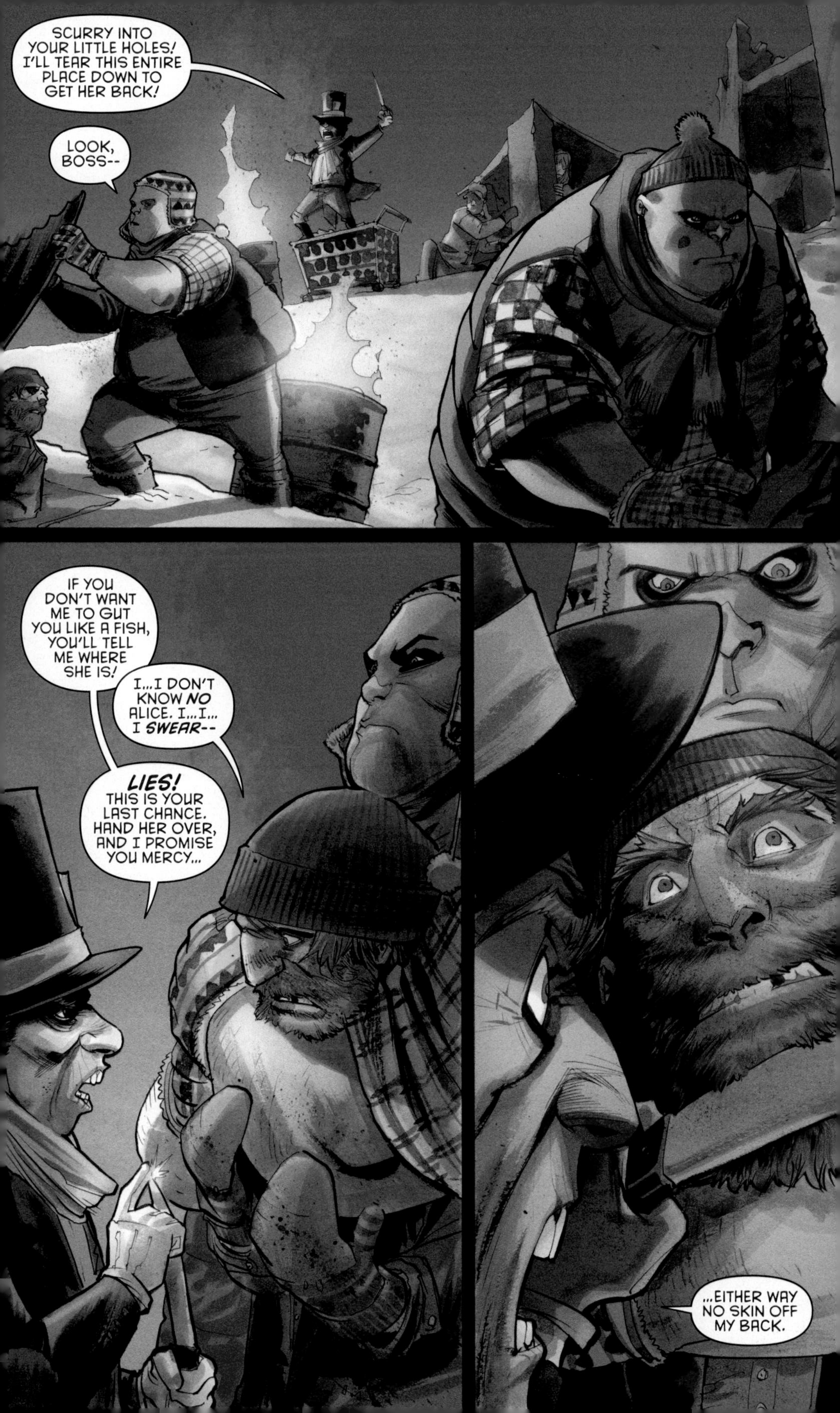
SCURRY INTO YOUR LITTLE HOLES! I'LL TEAR THIS ENTIRE PLACE DOWN TO GET HER BACK!
LOOK, BOSS--
IF YOU DON'T WANT ME TO GUT YOU LIKE A FISH, YOU'LL TELL ME WHERE SHE IS!
I...I DON'T KNOW NO ALICE. I...I... I SWEAR--
LIES! THIS IS YOUR LAST CHANCE. HAND HER OVER, AND I PROMISE YOU MERCY...
...EITHER WAY NO SKIN OFF MY BACK.

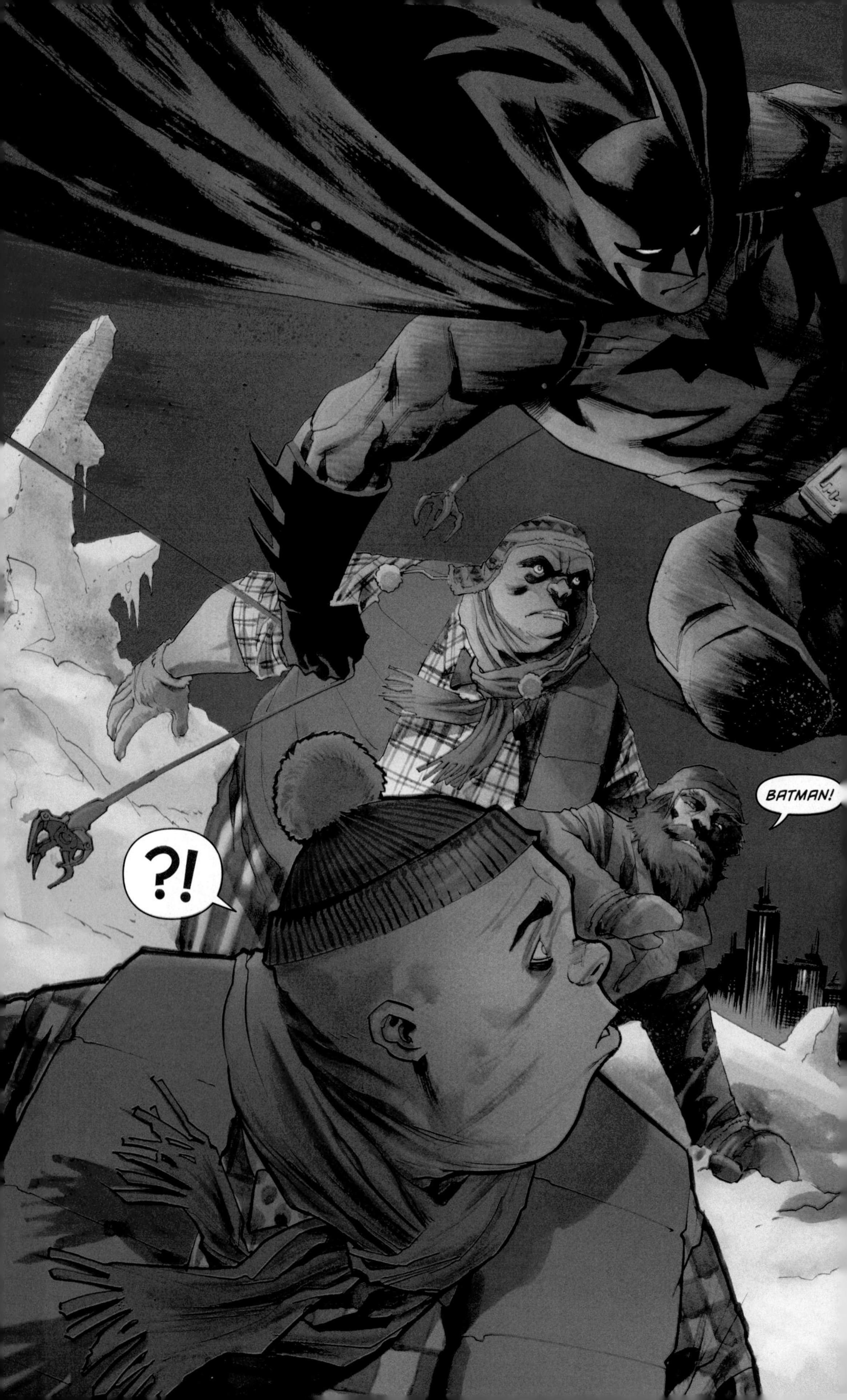
BATMAN!
?!

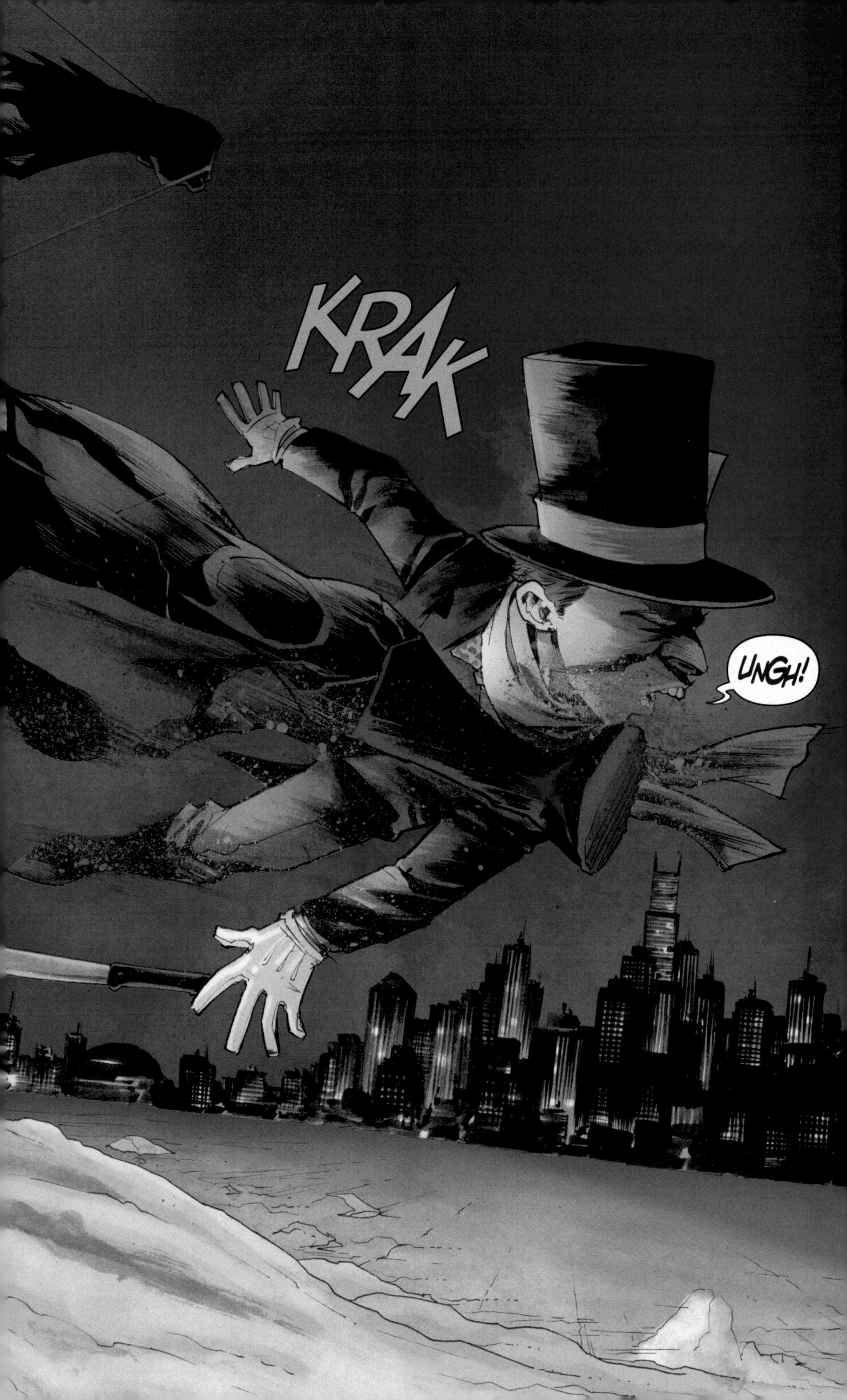
KRAK
UNGH!

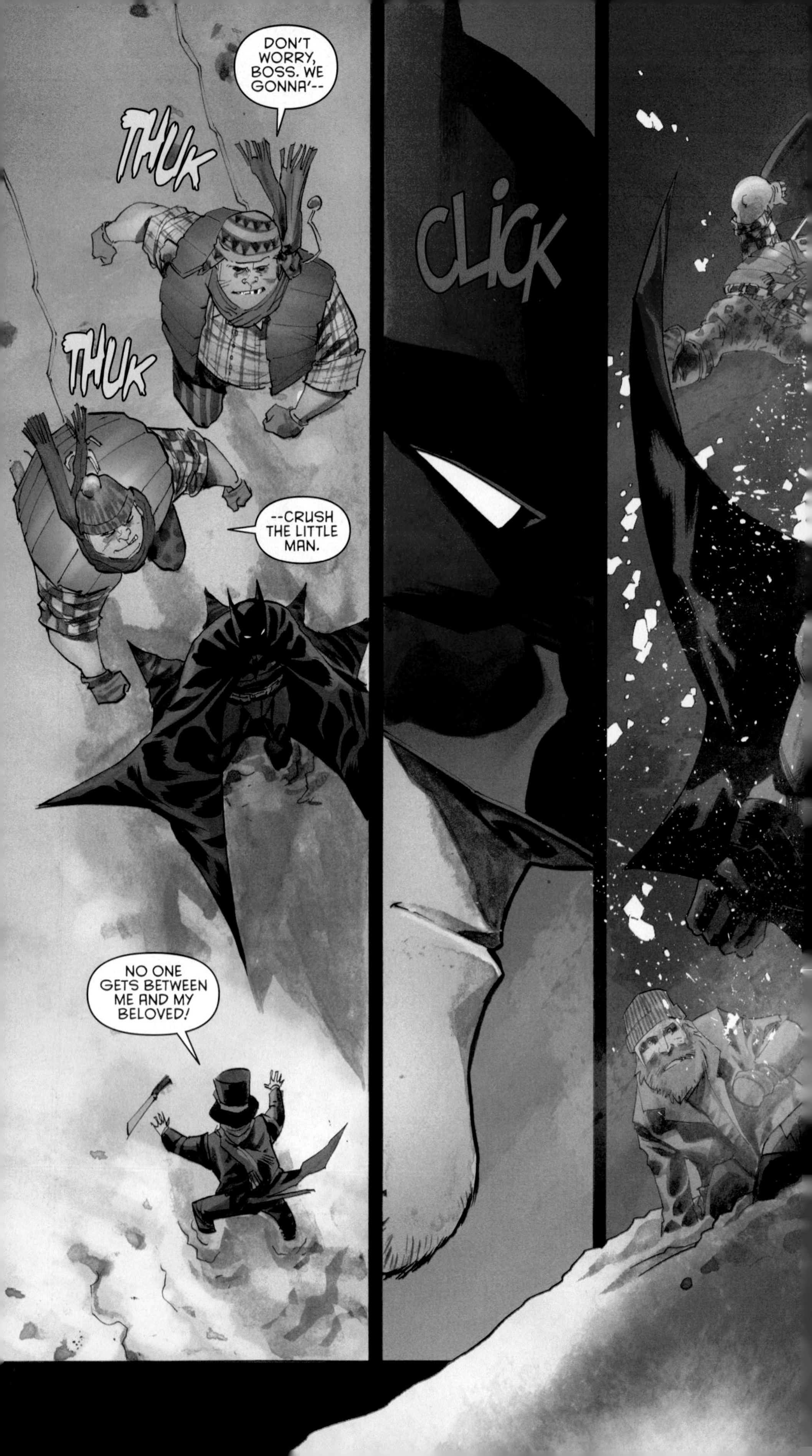
DON'T WORRY, BOSS. WE GONNA'--
THUK
THUK
--CRUSH THE LITTLE MAN.
NO ONE GETS BETWEEN ME AND MY BELOVED!
CLICK

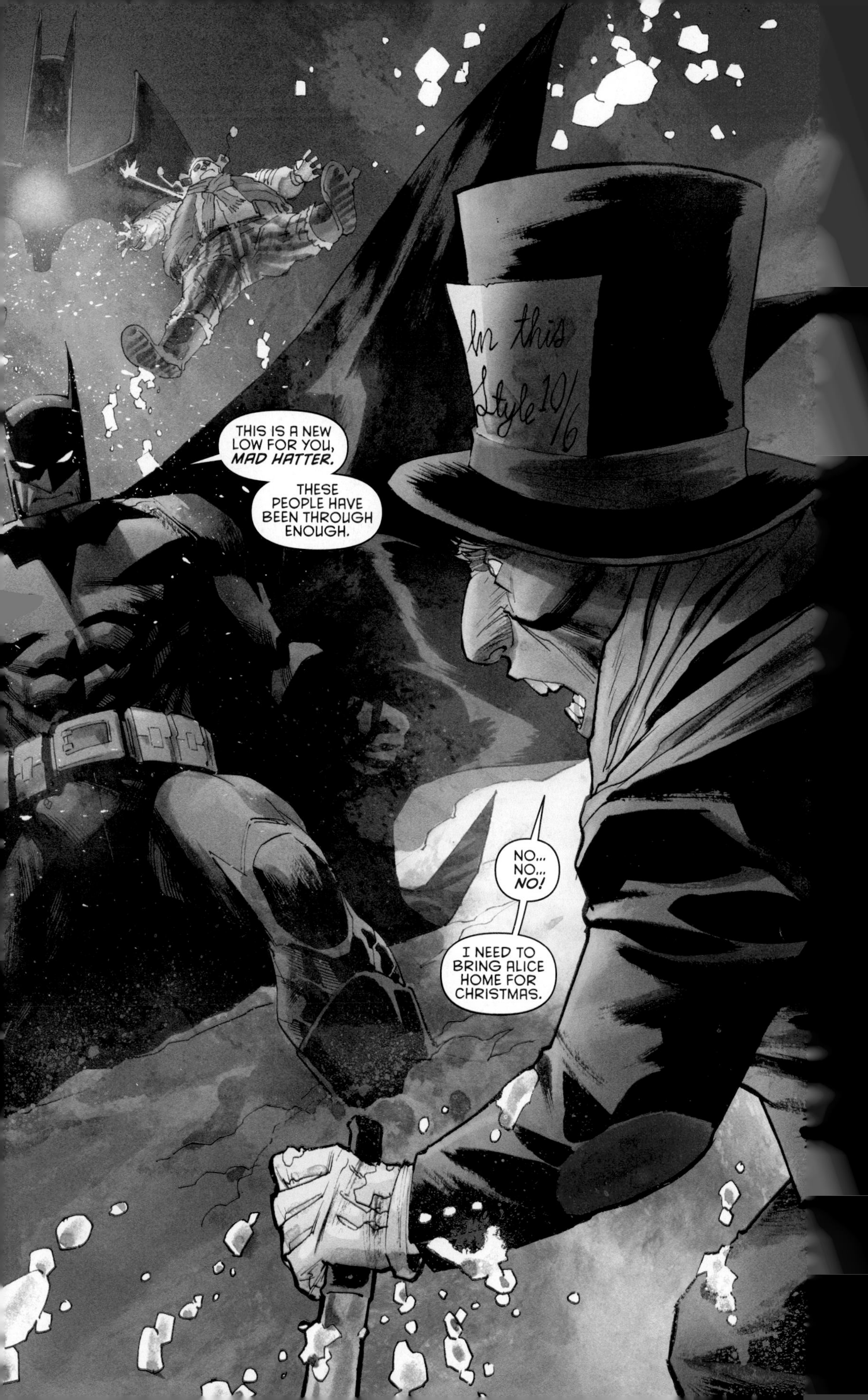
In this Style 10/6
THIS IS A NEW LOW FOR YOU, *MAD HATTER.*
THESE PEOPLE HAVE BEEN THROUGH ENOUGH.
NO... NO... *NO!*
I NEED TO BRING ALICE HOME FOR CHRISTMAS.

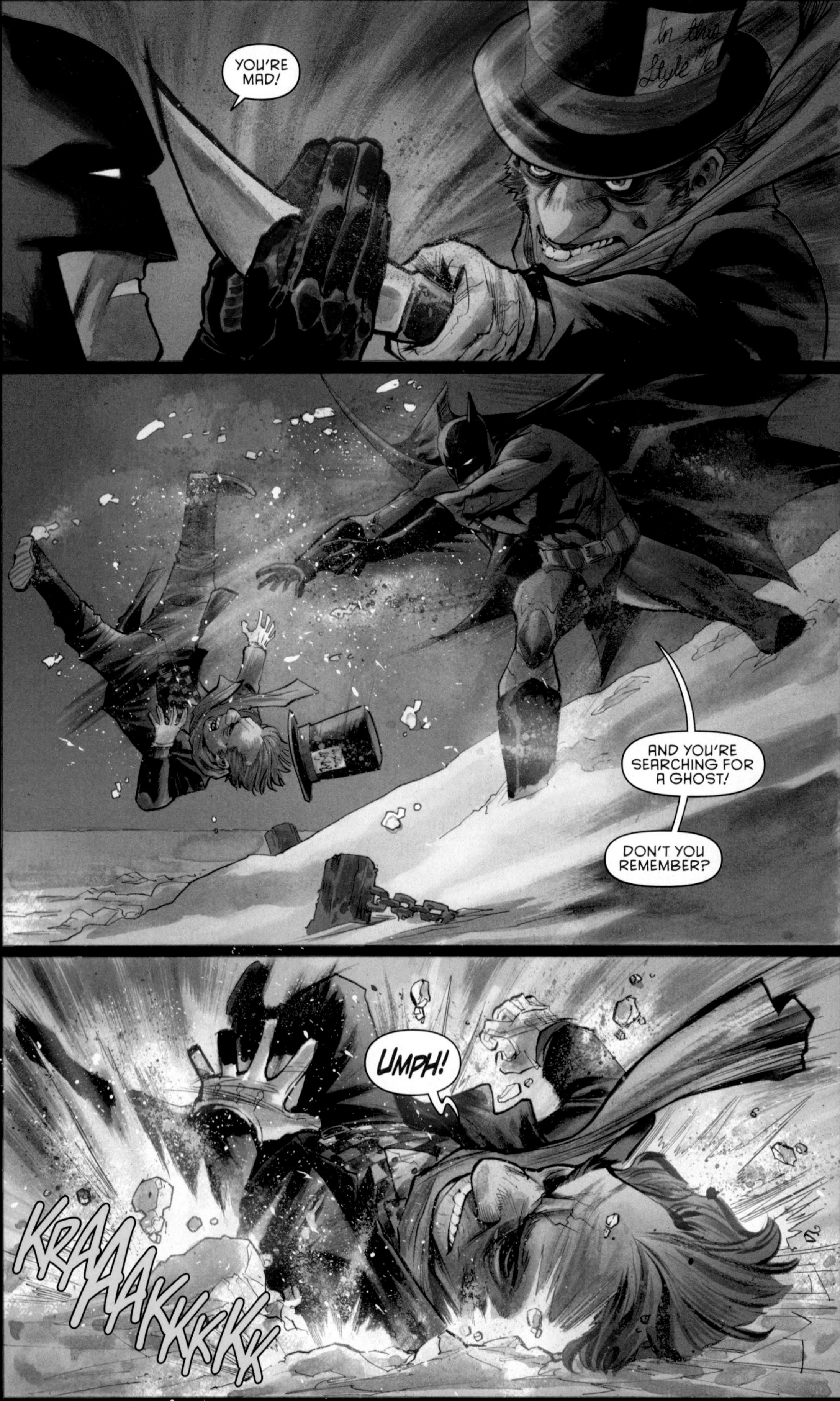
YOU'RE MAD!
AND YOU'RE SEARCHING FOR A GHOST!
DON'T YOU REMEMBER?
UMPH!
KRAAAAKKKKKK

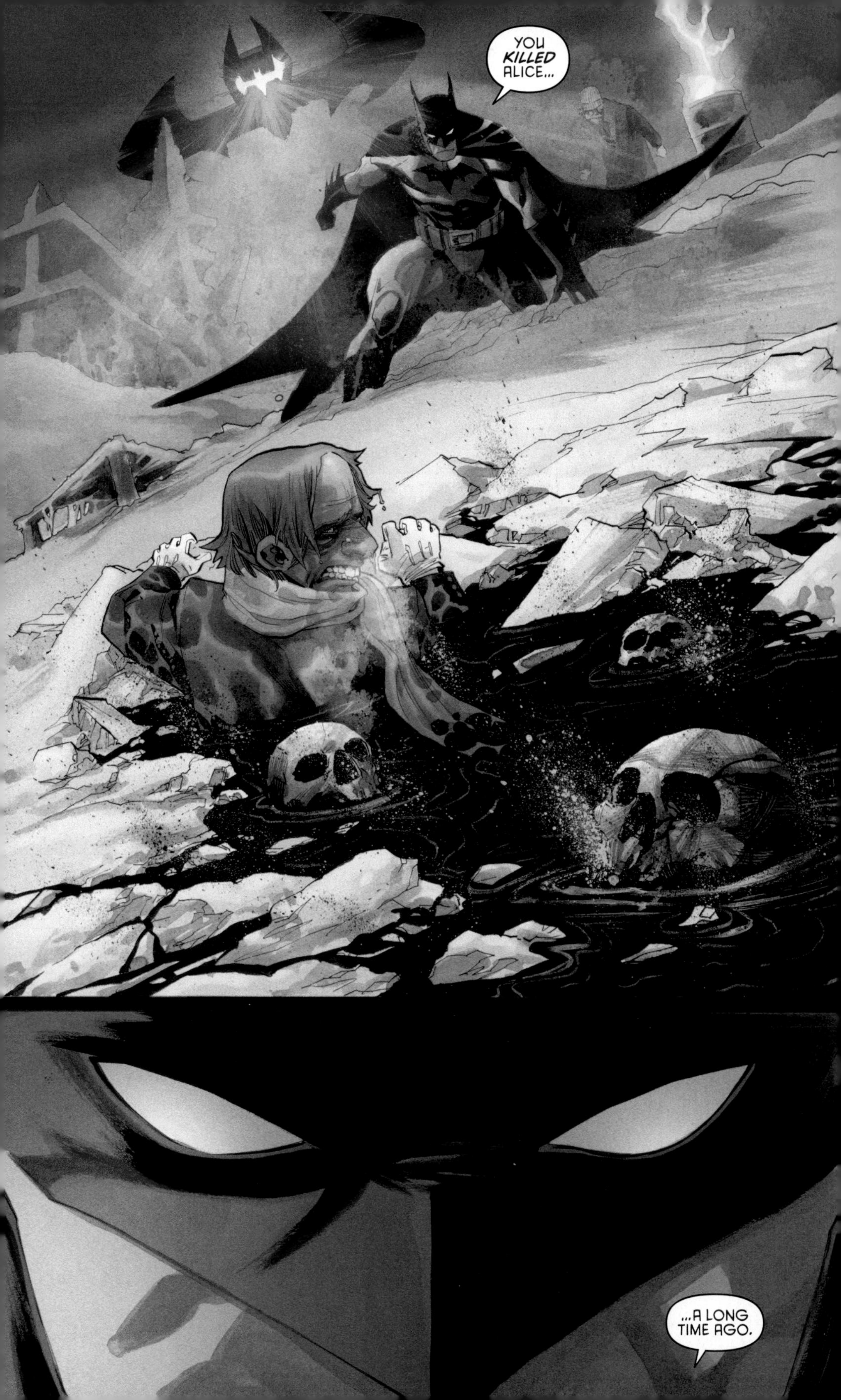
YOU *KILLED* ALICE...
...A LONG TIME AGO.

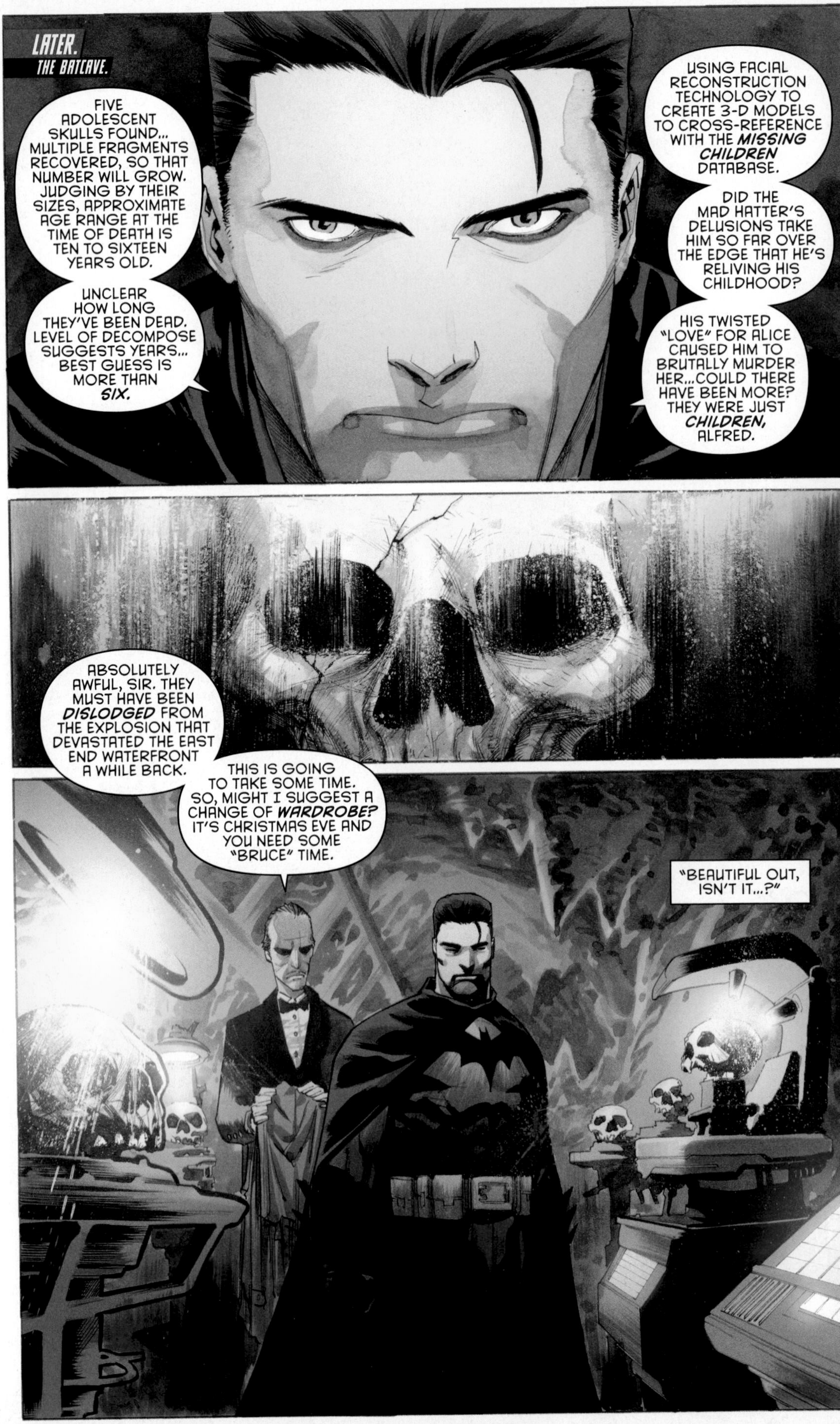
LATER.
THE BATCAVE.
FIVE ADOLESCENT SKULLS FOUND... MULTIPLE FRAGMENTS RECOVERED, SO THAT NUMBER WILL GROW. JUDGING BY THEIR SIZES, APPROXIMATE AGE RANGE AT THE TIME OF DEATH IS TEN TO SIXTEEN YEARS OLD.
UNCLEAR HOW LONG THEY'VE BEEN DEAD. LEVEL OF DECOMPOSE SUGGESTS YEARS... BEST GUESS IS MORE THAN SIX.
USING FACIAL RECONSTRUCTION TECHNOLOGY TO CREATE 3-D MODELS TO CROSS-REFERENCE WITH THE MISSING CHILDREN DATABASE.
DID THE MAD HATTER'S DELUSIONS TAKE HIM SO FAR OVER THE EDGE THAT HE'S RELIVING HIS CHILDHOOD?
HIS TWISTED "LOVE" FOR ALICE CAUSED HIM TO BRUTALLY MURDER HER...COULD THERE HAVE BEEN MORE? THEY WERE JUST CHILDREN, ALFRED.
ABSOLUTELY AWFUL, SIR. THEY MUST HAVE BEEN DISLODGED FROM THE EXPLOSION THAT DEVASTATED THE EAST END WATERFRONT A WHILE BACK.
THIS IS GOING TO TAKE SOME TIME. SO, MIGHT I SUGGEST A CHANGE OF WARDROBE? IT'S CHRISTMAS EVE AND YOU NEED SOME "BRUCE" TIME.
"BEAUTIFUL OUT, ISN'T IT...?"

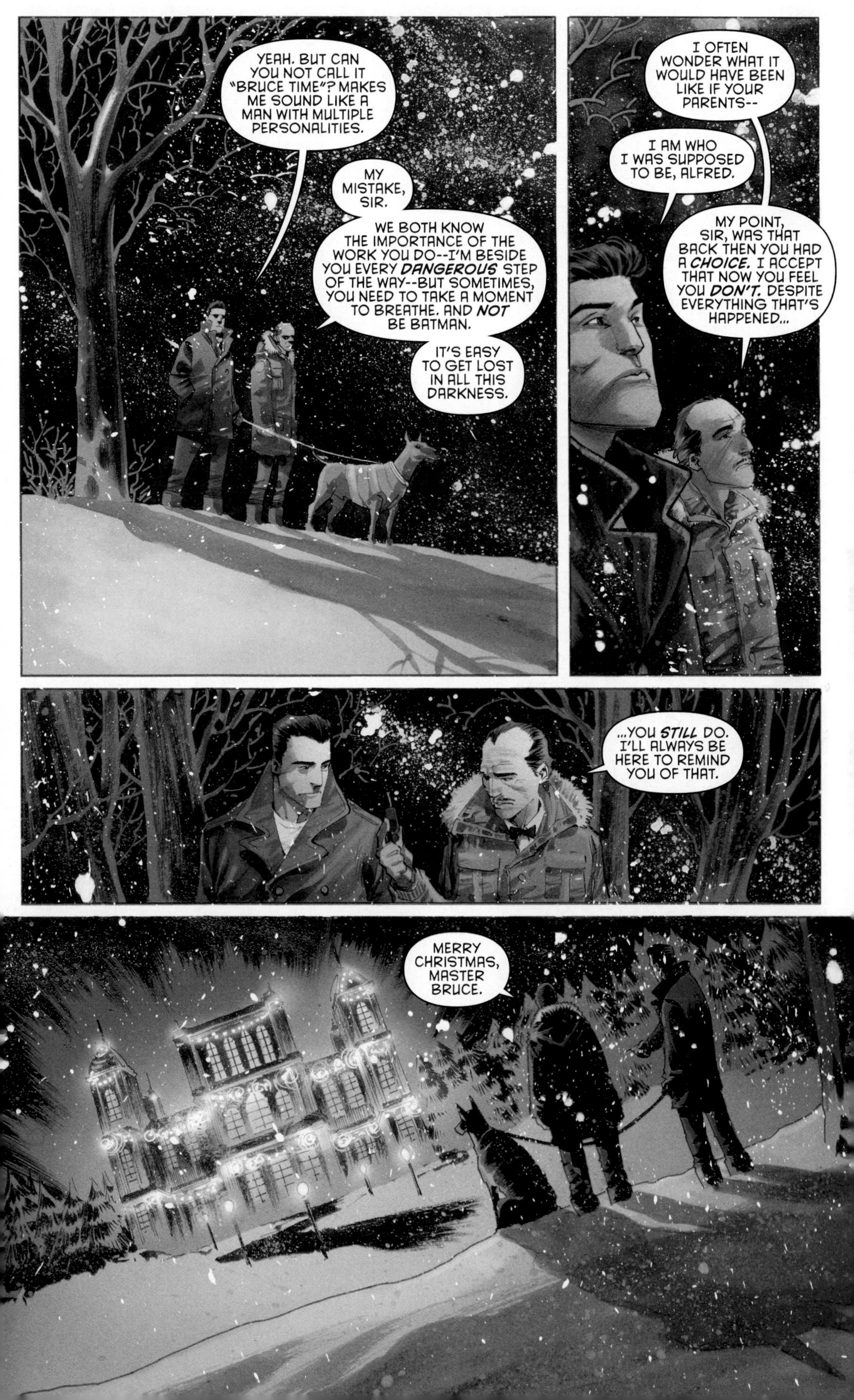

YEAH. BUT CAN YOU NOT CALL IT "BRUCE TIME"? MAKES ME SOUND LIKE A MAN WITH MULTIPLE PERSONALITIES.
MY MISTAKE, SIR.
WE BOTH KNOW THE IMPORTANCE OF THE WORK YOU DO--I'M BESIDE YOU EVERY *DANGEROUS* STEP OF THE WAY--BUT SOMETIMES, YOU NEED TO TAKE A MOMENT TO BREATHE. AND *NOT* BE BATMAN.
IT'S EASY TO GET LOST IN ALL THIS DARKNESS.
I OFTEN WONDER WHAT IT WOULD HAVE BEEN LIKE IF YOUR PARENTS--
I AM WHO I WAS SUPPOSED TO BE, ALFRED.
MY POINT, SIR, WAS THAT BACK THEN YOU HAD A *CHOICE.* I ACCEPT THAT NOW YOU FEEL YOU *DON'T.* DESPITE EVERYTHING THAT'S HAPPENED...
...YOU *STILL* DO. I'LL ALWAYS BE HERE TO REMIND YOU OF THAT.
MERRY CHRISTMAS, MASTER BRUCE.

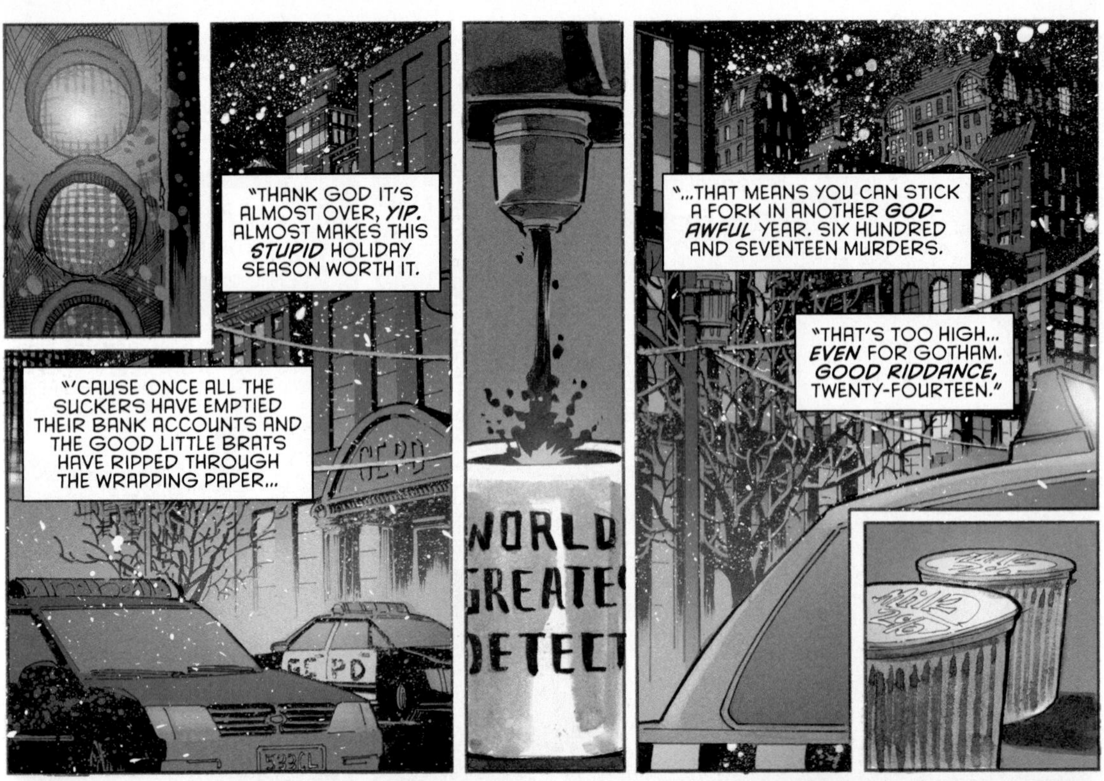

"THANK GOD IT'S ALMOST OVER, *YIP.* ALMOST MAKES THIS *STUPID* HOLIDAY SEASON WORTH IT.
"'CAUSE ONCE ALL THE SUCKERS HAVE EMPTIED THEIR BANK ACCOUNTS AND THE GOOD LITTLE BRATS HAVE RIPPED THROUGH THE WRAPPING PAPER...
GCPD
GCPD
533CL
WORLD GREATES DETECT
"...THAT MEANS YOU CAN STICK A FORK IN ANOTHER *GOD-AWFUL* YEAR. SIX HUNDRED AND SEVENTEEN MURDERS.
"THAT'S TOO HIGH... *EVEN* FOR GOTHAM. *GOOD RIDDANCE,* TWENTY-FOURTEEN."

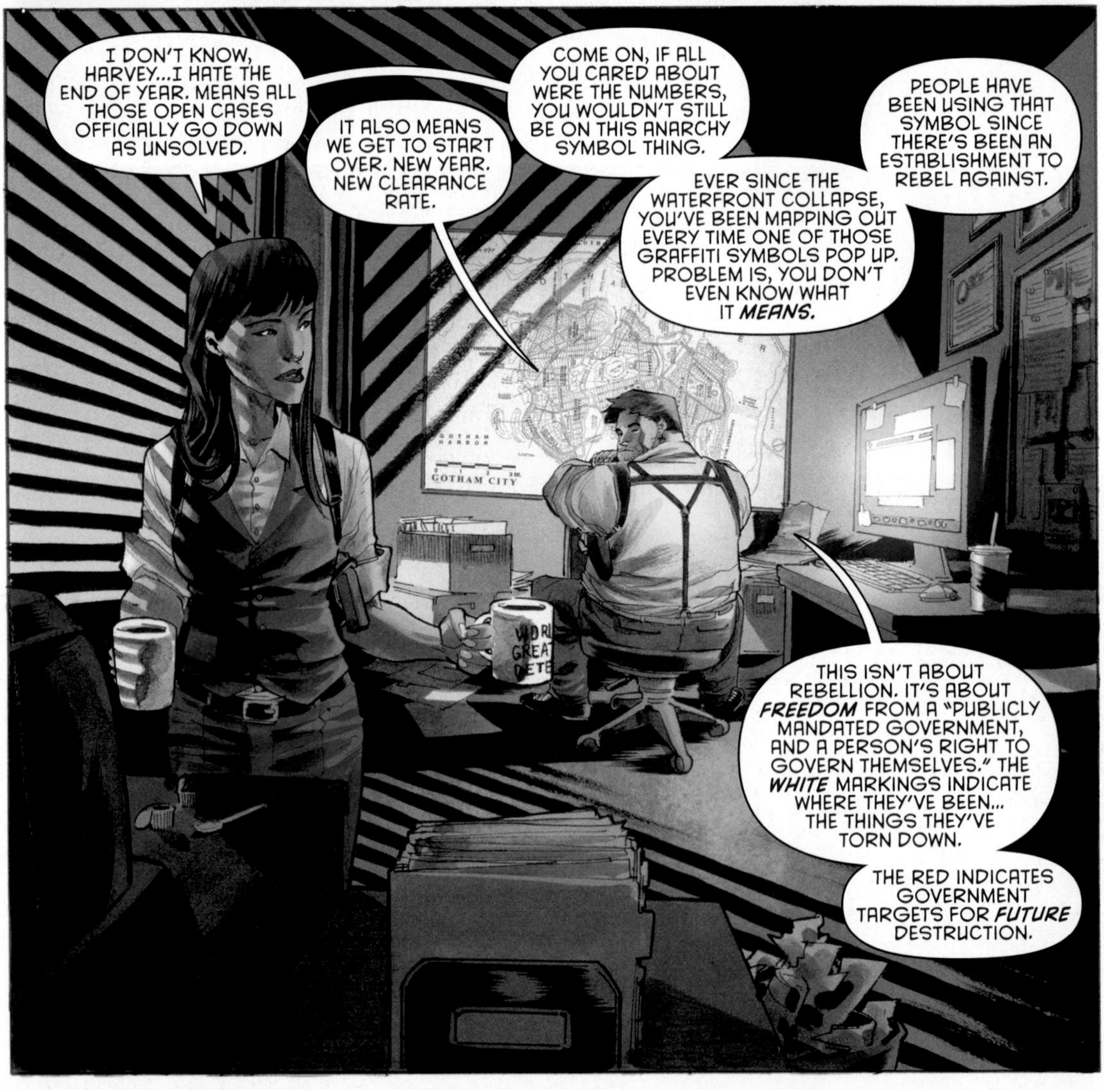

I DON'T KNOW, HARVEY...I HATE THE END OF YEAR. MEANS ALL THOSE OPEN CASES OFFICIALLY GO DOWN AS UNSOLVED.
IT ALSO MEANS WE GET TO START OVER. NEW YEAR. NEW CLEARANCE RATE.
COME ON, IF ALL YOU CARED ABOUT WERE THE NUMBERS, YOU WOULDN'T STILL BE ON THIS ANARCHY SYMBOL THING.
EVER SINCE THE WATERFRONT COLLAPSE, YOU'VE BEEN MAPPING OUT EVERY TIME ONE OF THOSE GRAFFITI SYMBOLS POP UP. PROBLEM IS, YOU DON'T EVEN KNOW WHAT IT *MEANS.*
PEOPLE HAVE BEEN USING THAT SYMBOL SINCE THERE'S BEEN AN ESTABLISHMENT TO REBEL AGAINST.
GOTHAM HARBOR
GOTHAM CITY
WORLD GREAT DETE
THIS ISN'T ABOUT REBELLION. IT'S ABOUT *FREEDOM* FROM A "PUBLICLY MANDATED GOVERNMENT, AND A PERSON'S RIGHT TO GOVERN THEMSELVES." THE *WHITE* MARKINGS INDICATE WHERE THEY'VE BEEN... THE THINGS THEY'VE TORN DOWN.
THE RED INDICATES GOVERNMENT TARGETS FOR *FUTURE* DESTRUCTION.

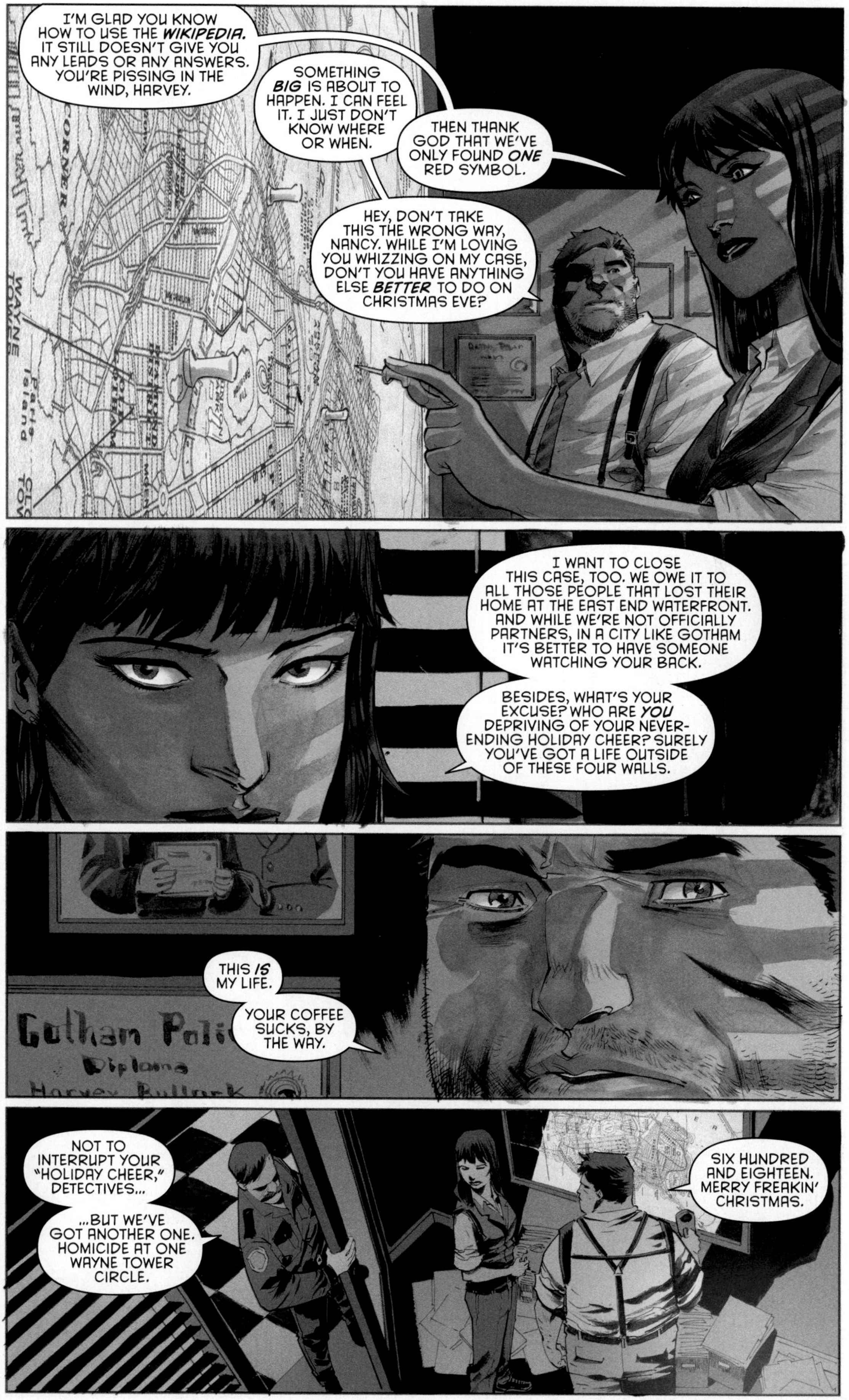
I'M GLAD YOU KNOW HOW TO USE THE *WIKIPEDIA.* IT STILL DOESN'T GIVE YOU ANY LEADS OR ANY ANSWERS. YOU'RE PISSING IN THE WIND, HARVEY.
SOMETHING *BIG* IS ABOUT TO HAPPEN. I CAN FEEL IT. I JUST DON'T KNOW WHERE OR WHEN.
THEN THANK GOD THAT WE'VE ONLY FOUND *ONE* RED SYMBOL.
HEY, DON'T TAKE THIS THE WRONG WAY, NANCY. WHILE I'M LOVING YOU WHIZZING ON MY CASE, DON'T YOU HAVE ANYTHING ELSE *BETTER* TO DO ON CHRISTMAS EVE?
I WANT TO CLOSE THIS CASE, TOO. WE OWE IT TO ALL THOSE PEOPLE THAT LOST THEIR HOME AT THE EAST END WATERFRONT. AND WHILE WE'RE NOT OFFICIALLY PARTNERS, IN A CITY LIKE GOTHAM IT'S BETTER TO HAVE SOMEONE WATCHING YOUR BACK.
BESIDES, WHAT'S YOUR EXCUSE? WHO ARE *YOU* DEPRIVING OF YOUR NEVER-ENDING HOLIDAY CHEER? SURELY YOU'VE GOT A LIFE OUTSIDE OF THESE FOUR WALLS.
THIS *IS* MY LIFE.
YOUR COFFEE SUCKS, BY THE WAY.
Diploma
NOT TO INTERRUPT YOUR "HOLIDAY CHEER," DETECTIVES...
...BUT WE'VE GOT ANOTHER ONE. HOMICIDE AT ONE WAYNE TOWER CIRCLE.
SIX HUNDRED AND EIGHTEEN. MERRY FREAKIN' CHRISTMAS.

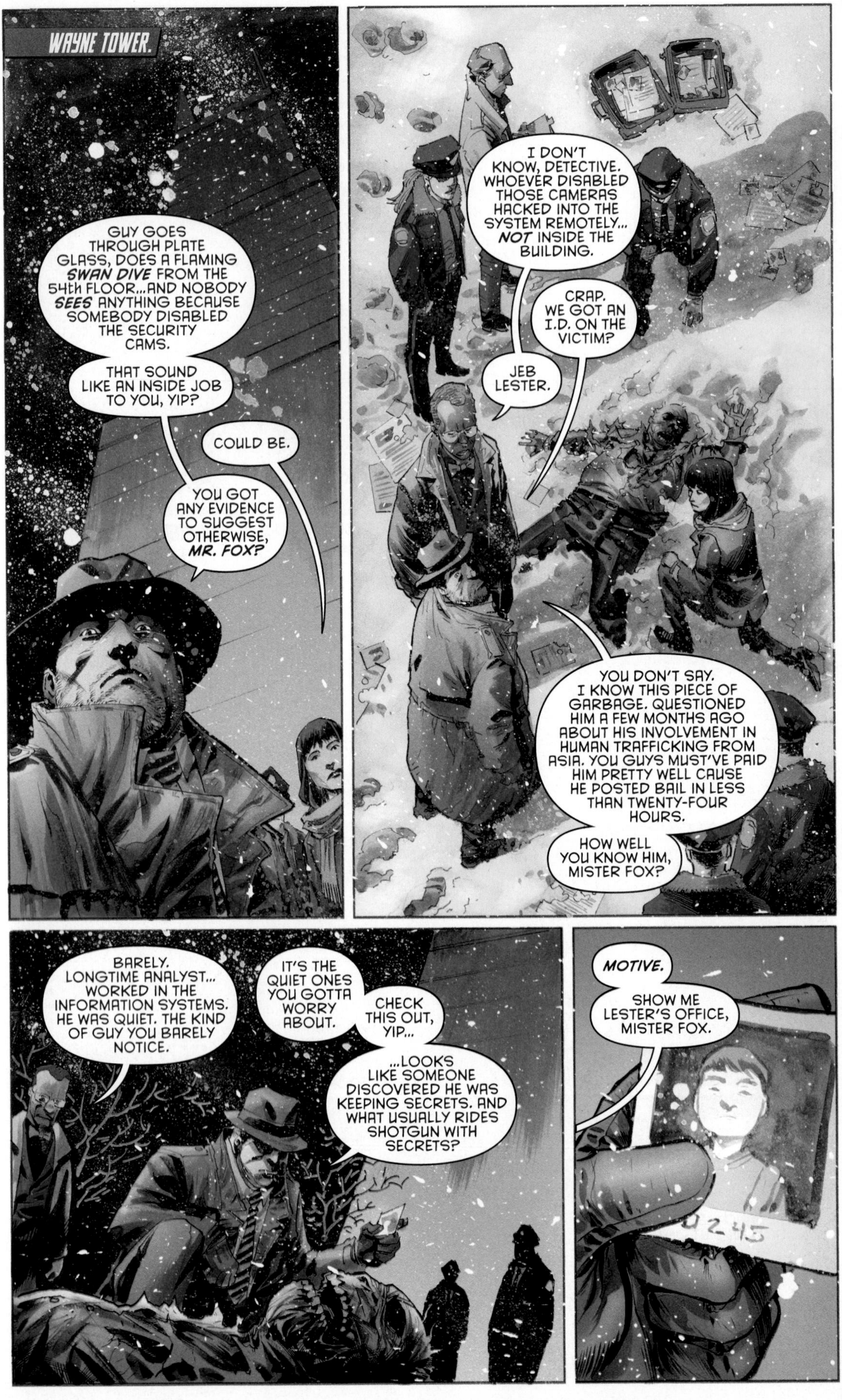
WAYNE TOWER.
GUY GOES THROUGH PLATE GLASS, DOES A FLAMING SWAN DIVE FROM THE 54th FLOOR...AND NOBODY SEES ANYTHING BECAUSE SOMEBODY DISABLED THE SECURITY CAMS.
THAT SOUND LIKE AN INSIDE JOB TO YOU, YIP?
COULD BE.
YOU GOT ANY EVIDENCE TO SUGGEST OTHERWISE, MR. FOX?
I DON'T KNOW, DETECTIVE. WHOEVER DISABLED THOSE CAMERAS HACKED INTO THE SYSTEM REMOTELY... NOT INSIDE THE BUILDING.
CRAP. WE GOT AN I.D. ON THE VICTIM?
JEB LESTER.
YOU DON'T SAY. I KNOW THIS PIECE OF GARBAGE. QUESTIONED HIM A FEW MONTHS AGO ABOUT HIS INVOLVEMENT IN HUMAN TRAFFICKING FROM ASIA. YOU GUYS MUST'VE PAID HIM PRETTY WELL CAUSE HE POSTED BAIL IN LESS THAN TWENTY-FOUR HOURS.
HOW WELL YOU KNOW HIM, MISTER FOX?
BARELY. LONGTIME ANALYST... WORKED IN THE INFORMATION SYSTEMS. HE WAS QUIET. THE KIND OF GUY YOU BARELY NOTICE.
IT'S THE QUIET ONES YOU GOTTA WORRY ABOUT.
CHECK THIS OUT, YIP...
...LOOKS LIKE SOMEONE DISCOVERED HE WAS KEEPING SECRETS. AND WHAT USUALLY RIDES SHOTGUN WITH SECRETS?
MOTIVE.
SHOW ME LESTER'S OFFICE, MISTER FOX.

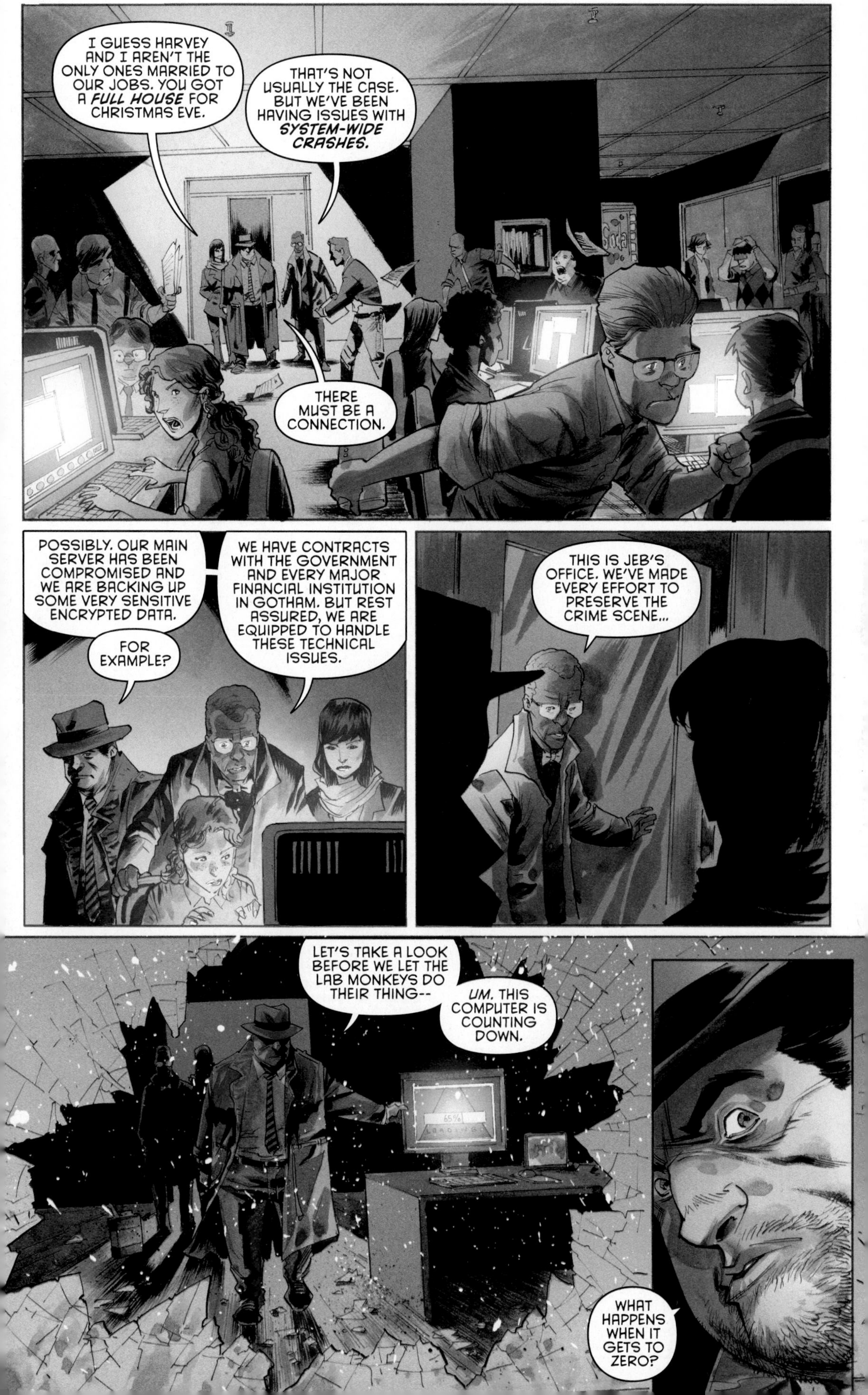
I GUESS HARVEY AND I AREN'T THE ONLY ONES MARRIED TO OUR JOBS. YOU GOT A FULL HOUSE FOR CHRISTMAS EVE.
THAT'S NOT USUALLY THE CASE. BUT WE'VE BEEN HAVING ISSUES WITH SYSTEM-WIDE CRASHES.
THERE MUST BE A CONNECTION.
POSSIBLY. OUR MAIN SERVER HAS BEEN COMPROMISED AND WE ARE BACKING UP SOME VERY SENSITIVE ENCRYPTED DATA.
FOR EXAMPLE?
WE HAVE CONTRACTS WITH THE GOVERNMENT AND EVERY MAJOR FINANCIAL INSTITUTION IN GOTHAM. BUT REST ASSURED, WE ARE EQUIPPED TO HANDLE THESE TECHNICAL ISSUES.
THIS IS JEB'S OFFICE. WE'VE MADE EVERY EFFORT TO PRESERVE THE CRIME SCENE...
LET'S TAKE A LOOK BEFORE WE LET THE LAB MONKEYS DO THEIR THING--
UM. THIS COMPUTER IS COUNTING DOWN.
65%
WHAT HAPPENS WHEN IT GETS TO ZERO?

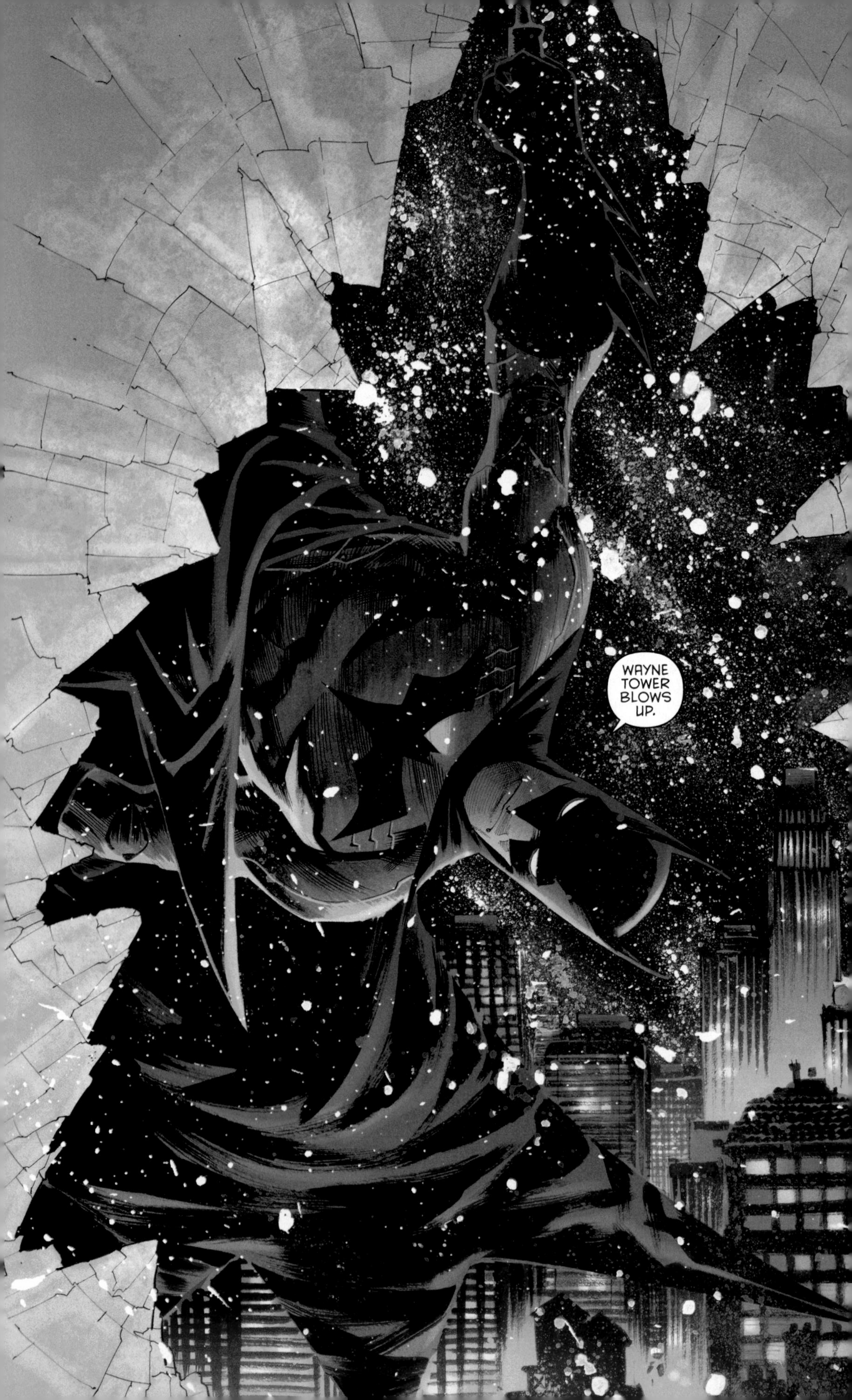
WAYNE TOWER BLOWS UP.

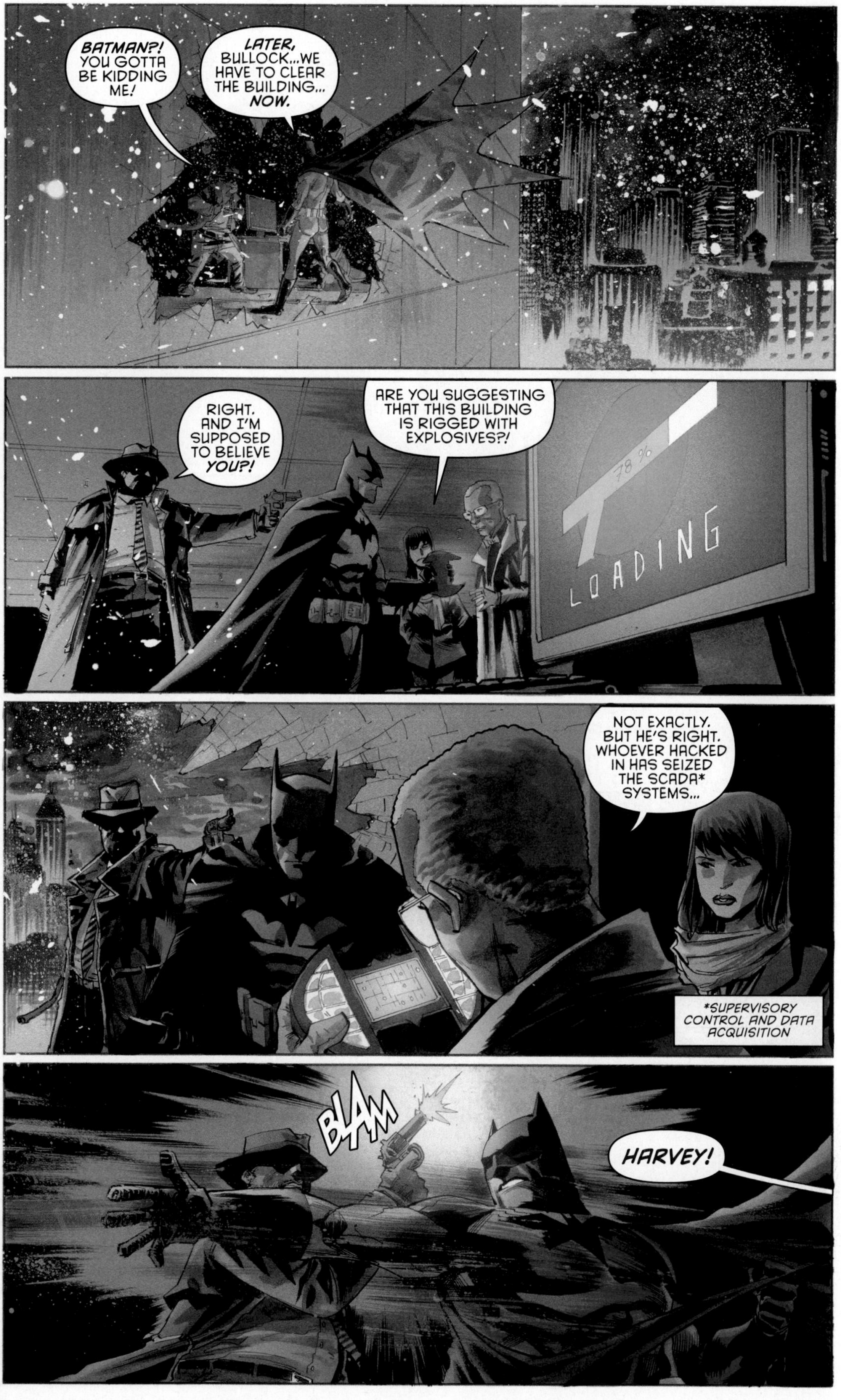

BATMAN?! YOU GOTTA BE KIDDING ME!
LATER, BULLOCK...WE HAVE TO CLEAR THE BUILDING... NOW.
RIGHT. AND I'M SUPPOSED TO BELIEVE YOU?!
ARE YOU SUGGESTING THAT THIS BUILDING IS RIGGED WITH EXPLOSIVES?!
78 %
LOADING
NOT EXACTLY. BUT HE'S RIGHT. WHOEVER HACKED IN HAS SEIZED THE SCADA* SYSTEMS...
*SUPERVISORY CONTROL AND DATA ACQUISITION
BLAM
HARVEY!

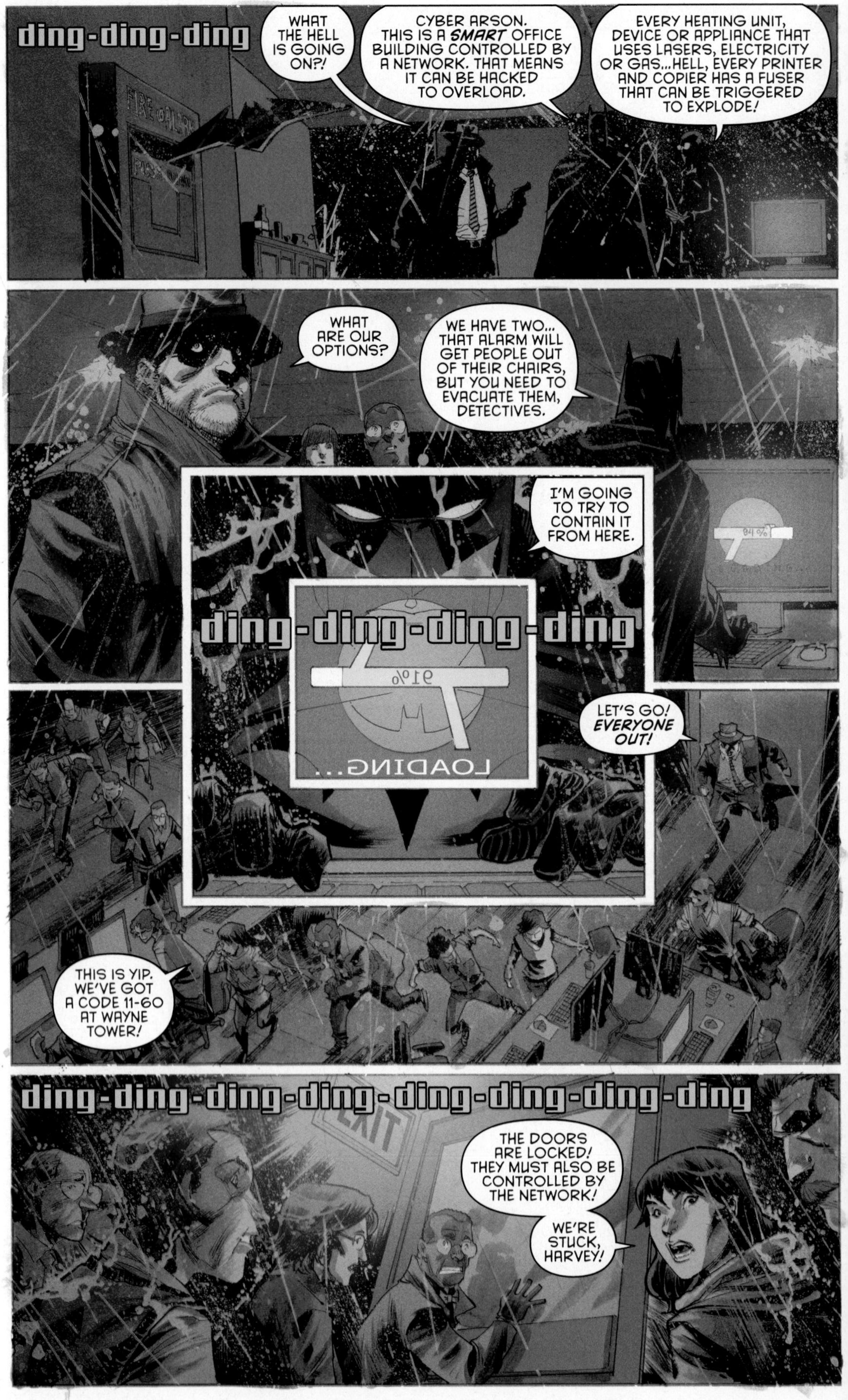
ding-ding-ding
WHAT THE HELL IS GOING ON?!
CYBER ARSON. THIS IS A *SMART* OFFICE BUILDING CONTROLLED BY A NETWORK. THAT MEANS IT CAN BE HACKED TO OVERLOAD.
EVERY HEATING UNIT, DEVICE OR APPLIANCE THAT USES LASERS, ELECTRICITY OR GAS...HELL, EVERY PRINTER AND COPIER HAS A FUSER THAT CAN BE TRIGGERED TO EXPLODE!
WHAT ARE OUR OPTIONS?
WE HAVE TWO... THAT ALARM WILL GET PEOPLE OUT OF THEIR CHAIRS, BUT YOU NEED TO EVACUATE THEM, DETECTIVES.
I'M GOING TO TRY TO CONTAIN IT FROM HERE.
84%
ding-ding-ding-ding
91%
LOADING...
LET'S GO! *EVERYONE OUT!*
THIS IS YIP. WE'VE GOT A CODE 11-60 AT WAYNE TOWER!
ding-ding-ding-ding-ding-ding-ding-ding
EXIT
THE DOORS ARE LOCKED! THEY MUST ALSO BE CONTROLLED BY THE NETWORK!
WE'RE STUCK, HARVEY!

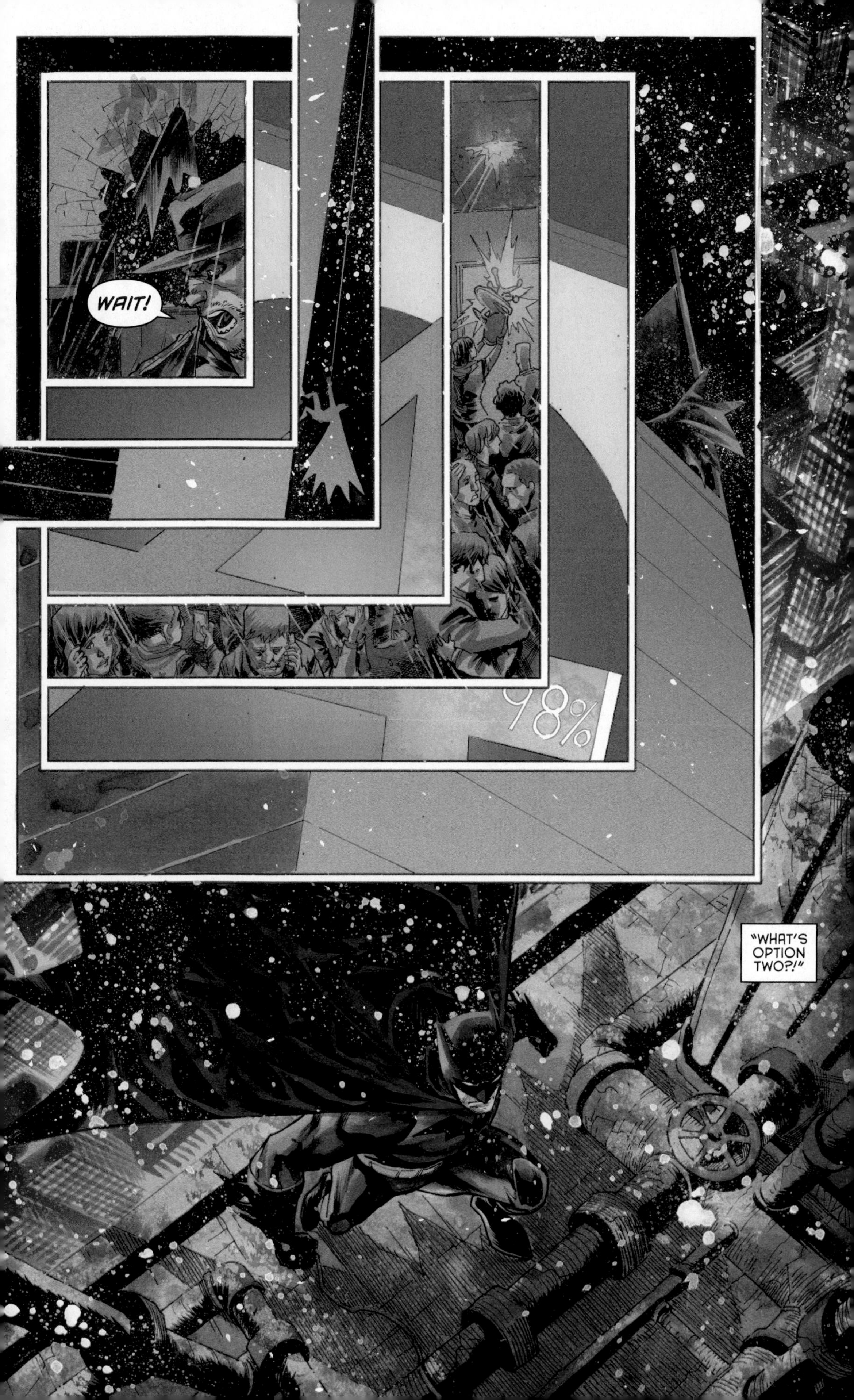
WAIT!
98%
"WHAT'S OPTION TWO?!"

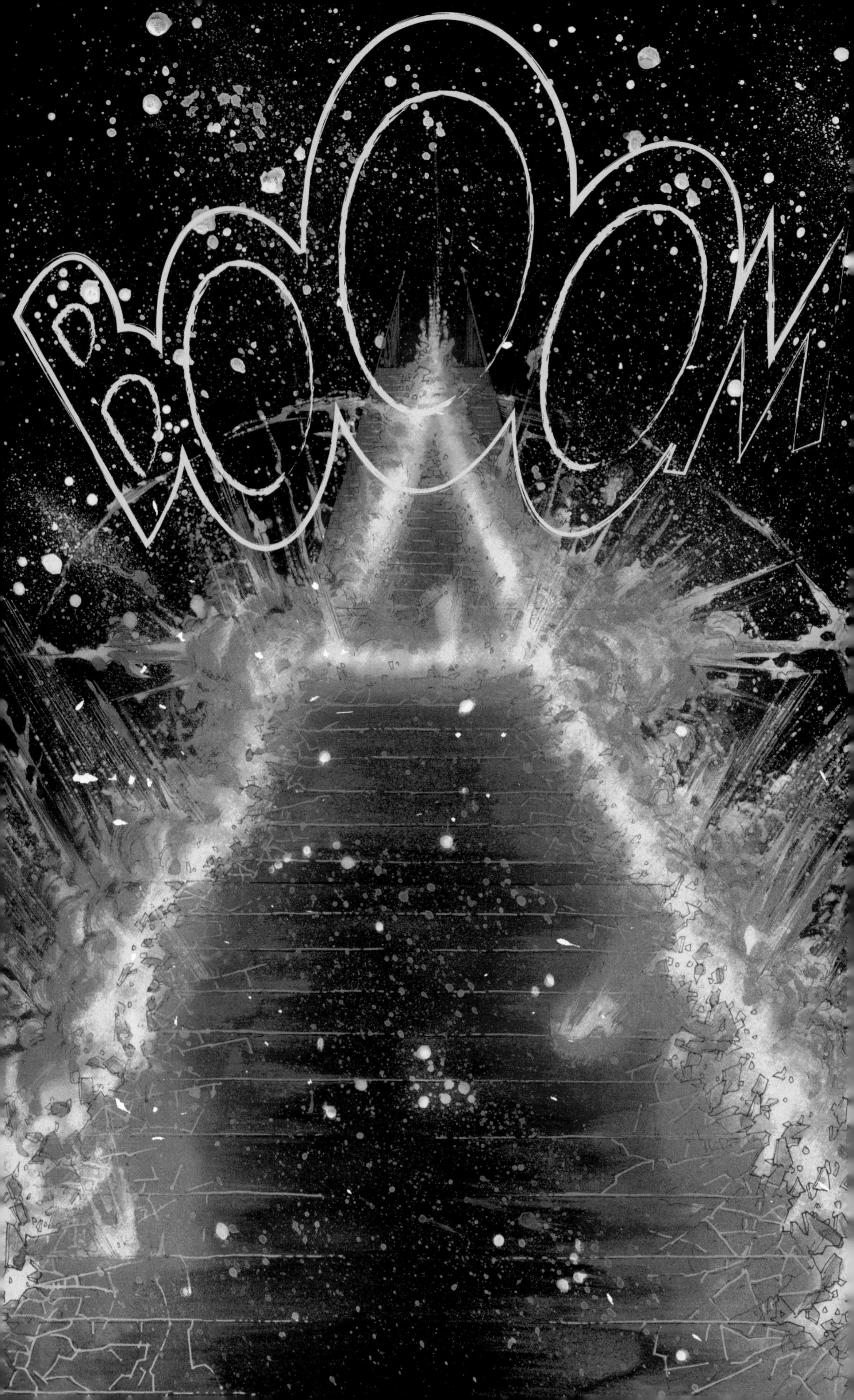
BOOOOM

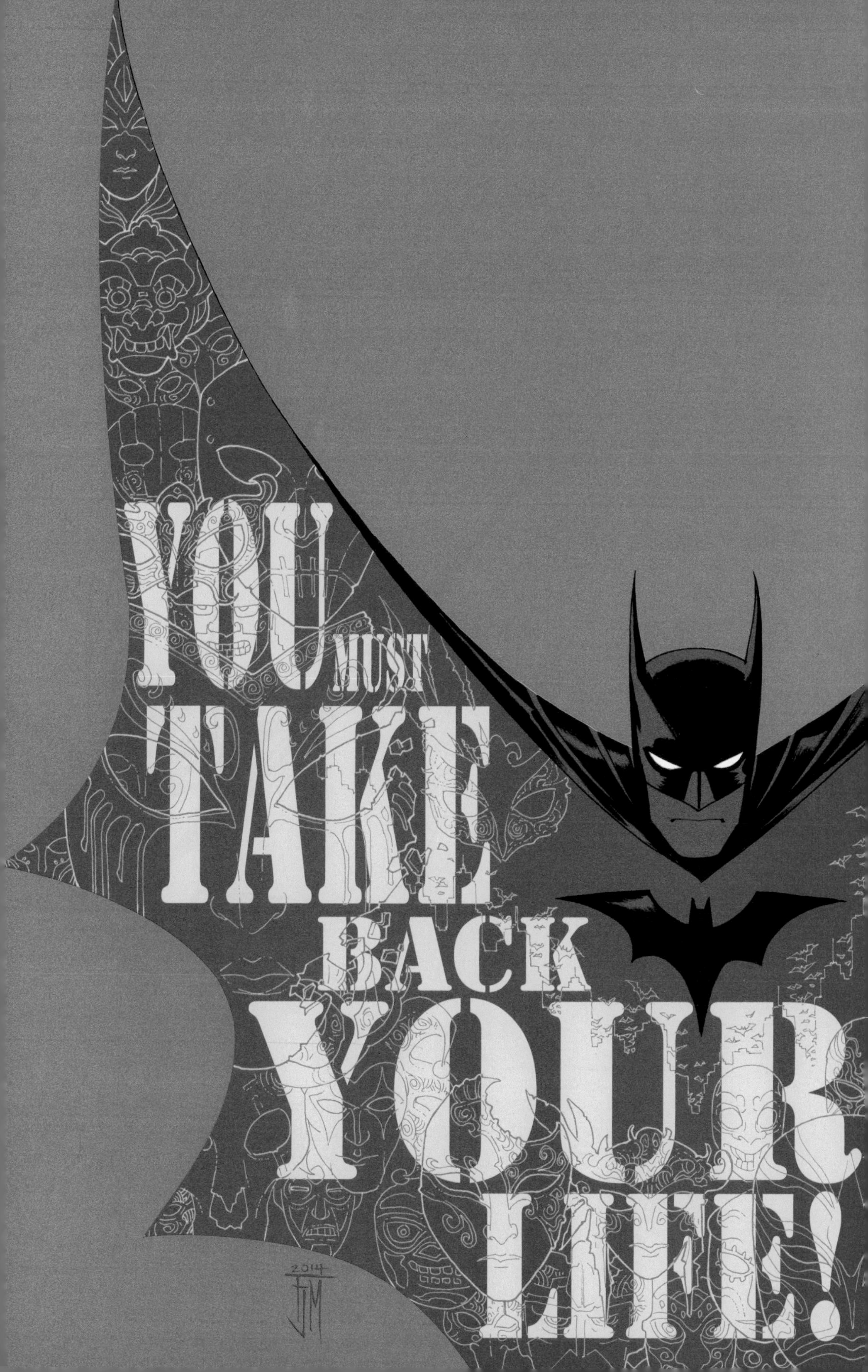
YOU MUST TAKE BACK YOUR LIFE!
2014
JIM

ANARKY PART 2

FRANCIS MANAPUL & BRIAN BUCCELLATO writers FRANCIS MANAPUL artist BRIAN BUCCELLATO colorist JARED K. FLETCHER letterer cover by FRANCIS MANAPUL

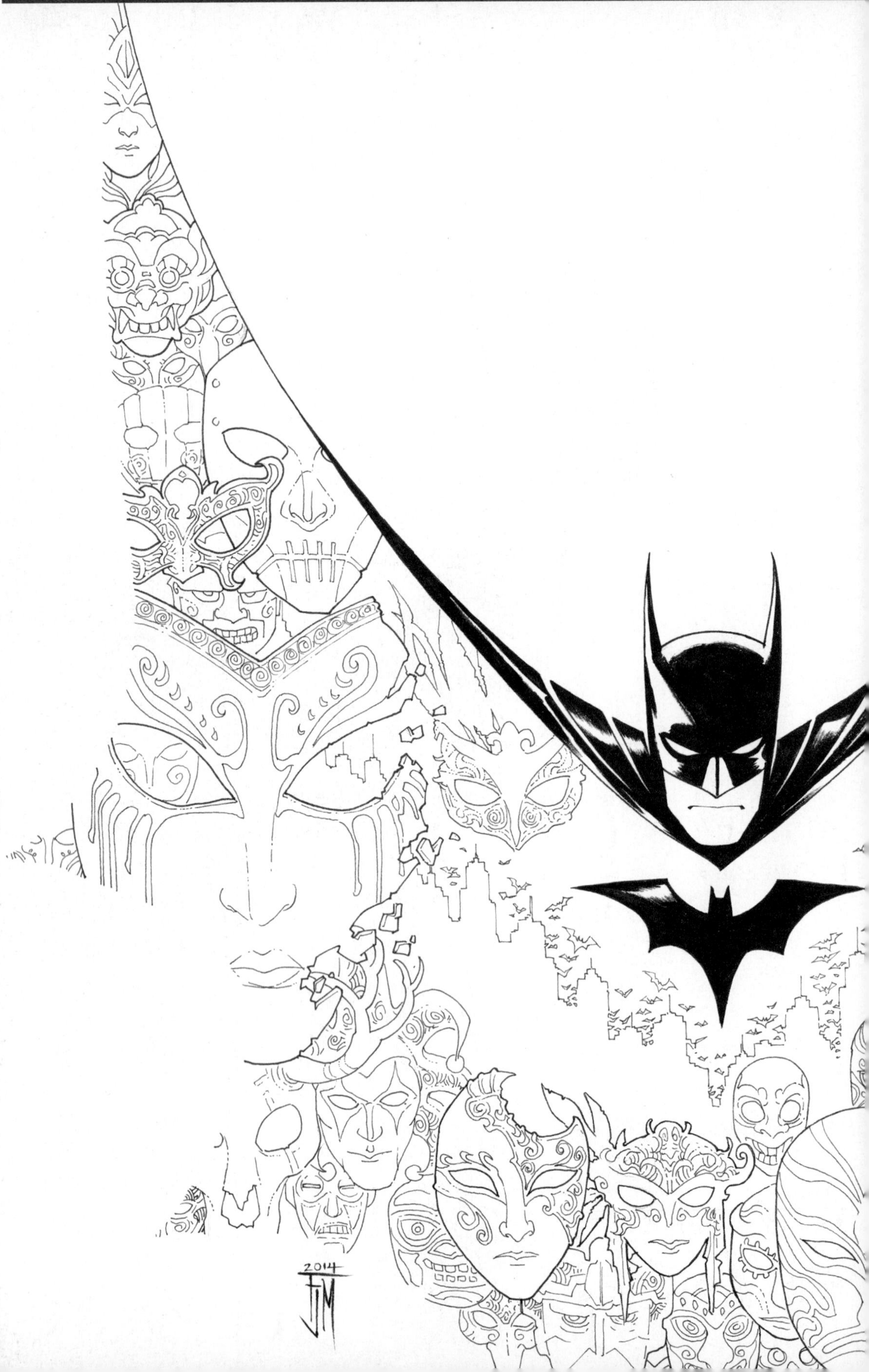
2014
FJM

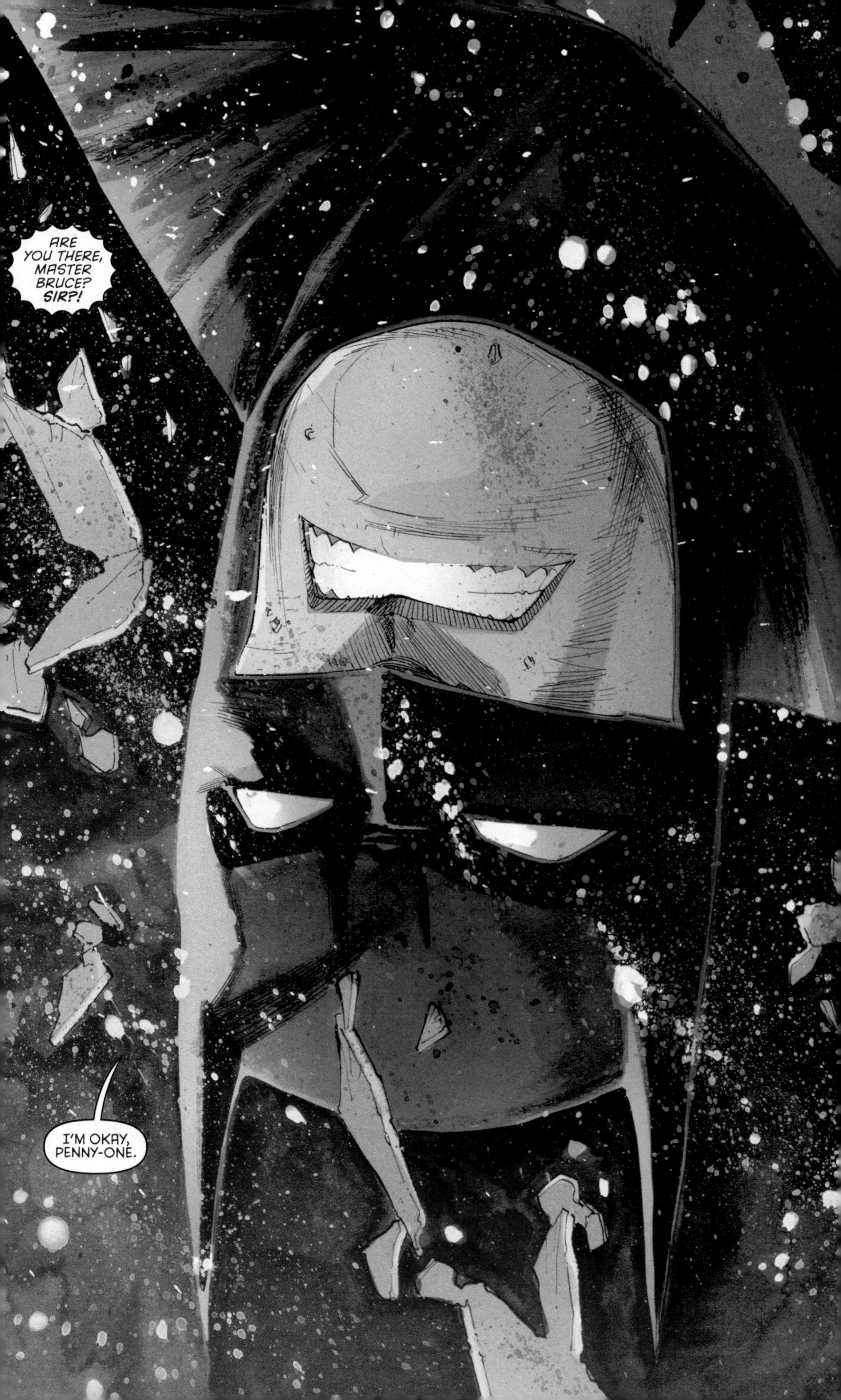
ARE YOU THERE, MASTER BRUCE? SIR?!
I'M OKAY, PENNY-ONE.

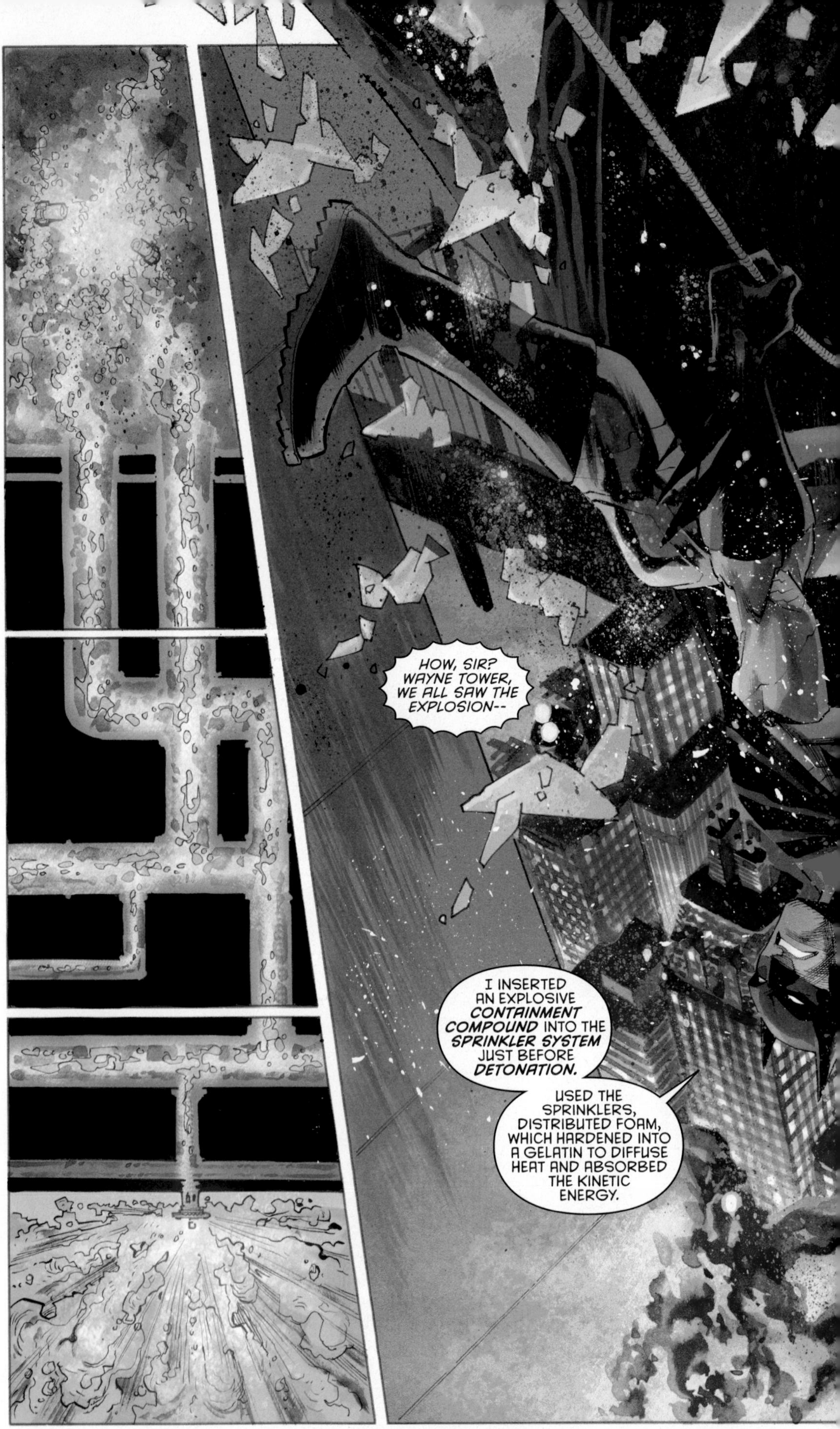

HOW, SIR? WAYNE TOWER, WE ALL SAW THE EXPLOSION--
I INSERTED AN EXPLOSIVE CONTAINMENT COMPOUND INTO THE SPRINKLER SYSTEM JUST BEFORE DETONATION.
USED THE SPRINKLERS, DISTRIBUTED FOAM, WHICH HARDENED INTO A GELATIN TO DIFFUSE HEAT AND ABSORBED THE KINETIC ENERGY.

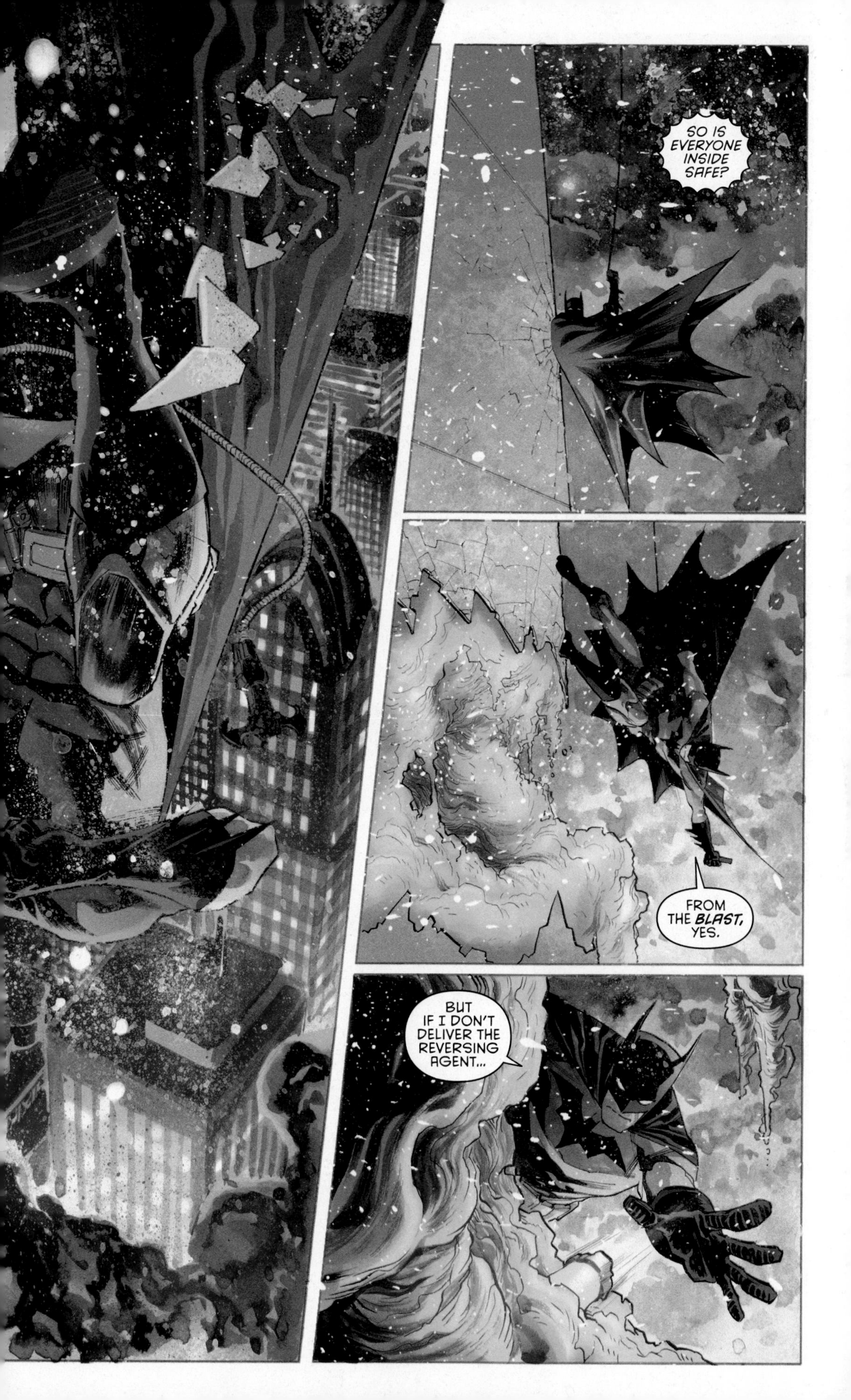
SO IS EVERYONE INSIDE SAFE?
FROM THE BLAST, YES.
BUT IF I DON'T DELIVER THE REVERSING AGENT...

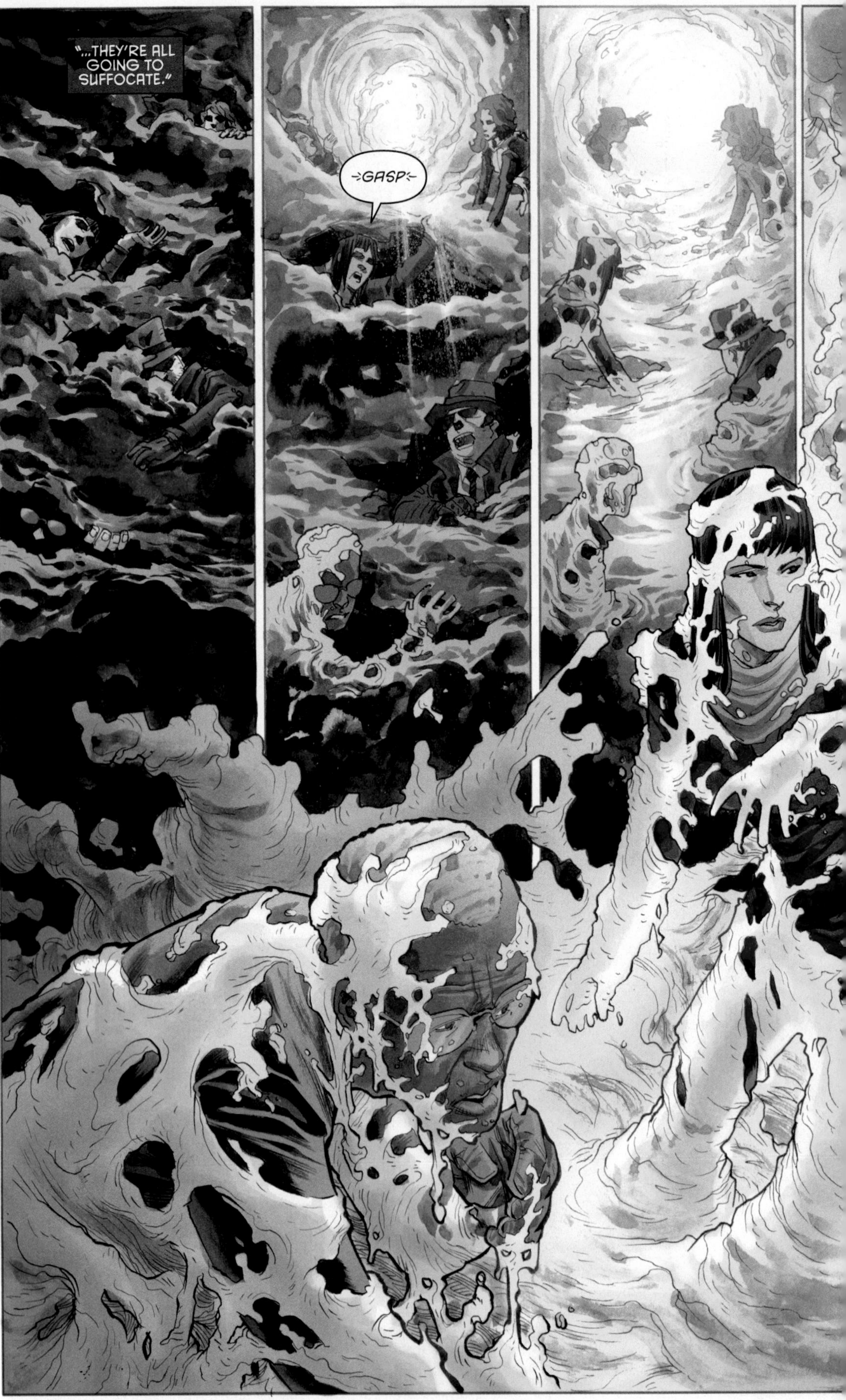
"...THEY'RE ALL GOING TO SUFFOCATE."
GASP

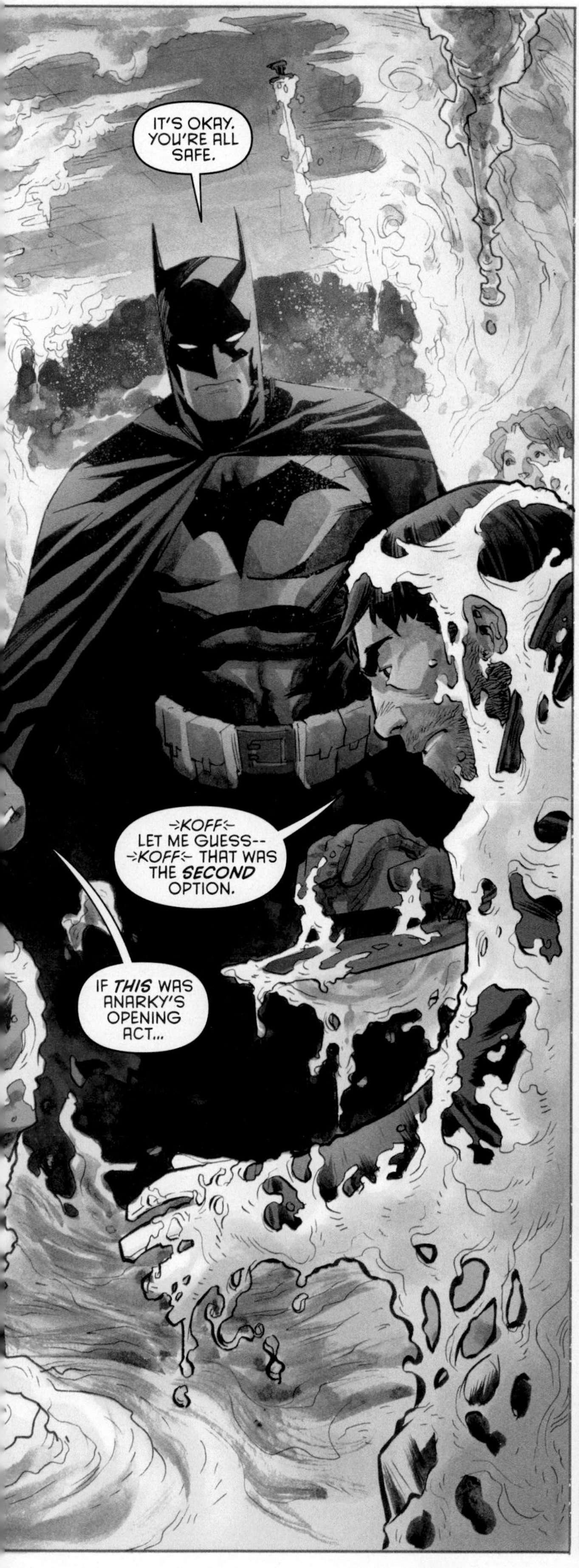
IT'S OKAY. YOU'RE ALL SAFE.
-KOFF- LET ME GUESS-- -KOFF- THAT WAS THE SECOND OPTION.
IF THIS WAS ANARKY'S OPENING ACT...

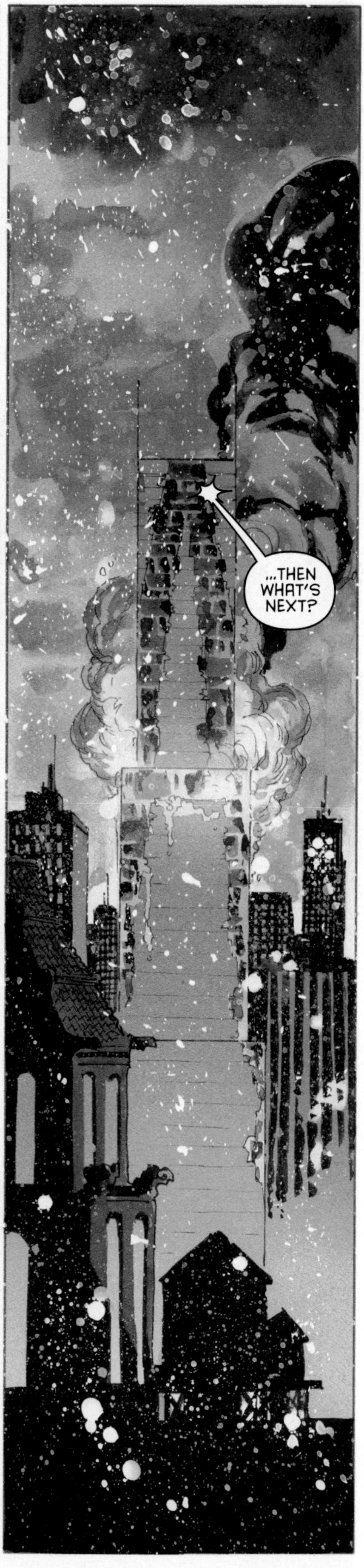
...THEN WHAT'S NEXT?

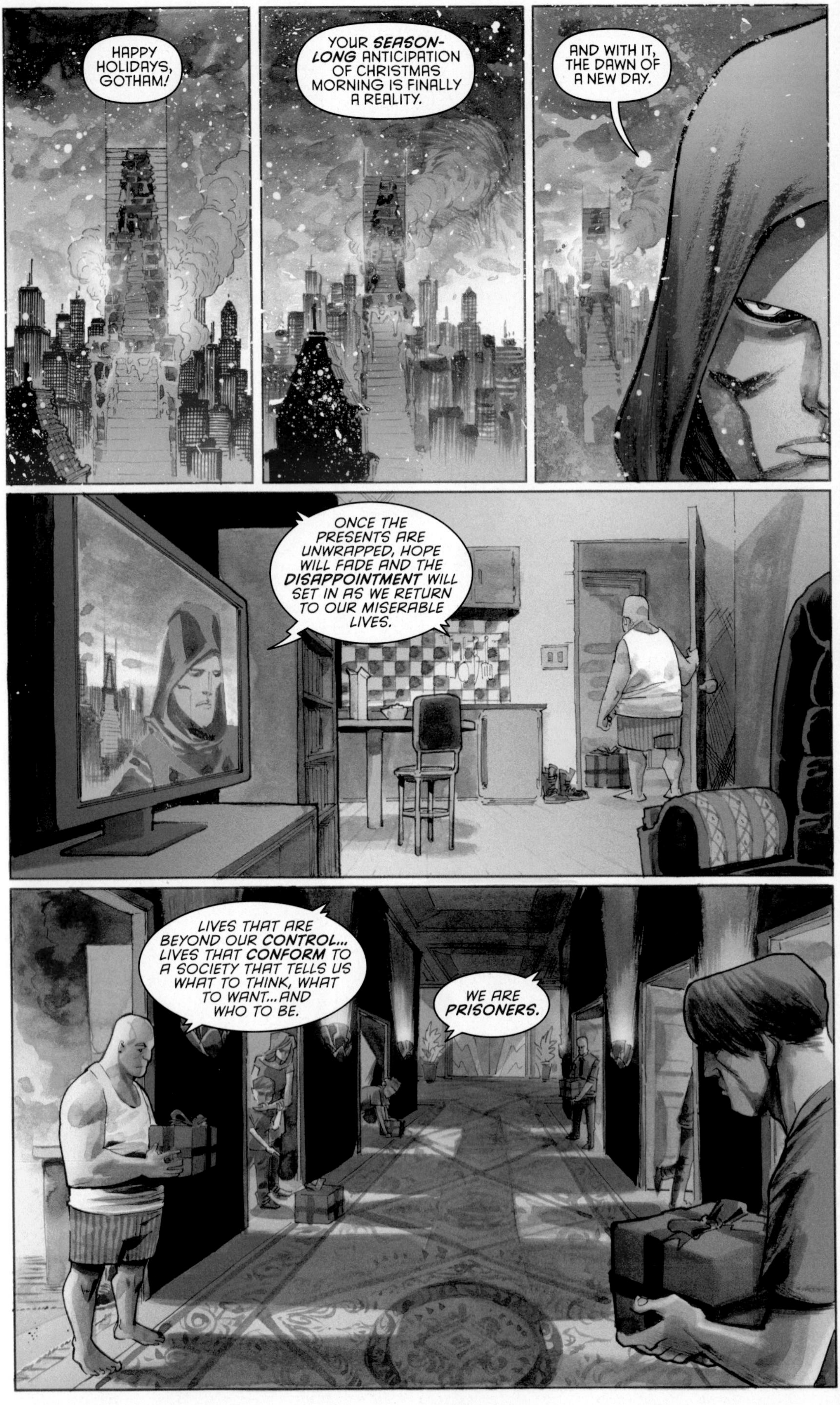
HAPPY HOLIDAYS, GOTHAM!
YOUR SEASON-LONG ANTICIPATION OF CHRISTMAS MORNING IS FINALLY A REALITY.
AND WITH IT, THE DAWN OF A NEW DAY.
ONCE THE PRESENTS ARE UNWRAPPED, HOPE WILL FADE AND THE DISAPPOINTMENT WILL SET IN AS WE RETURN TO OUR MISERABLE LIVES.
LIVES THAT ARE BEYOND OUR CONTROL... LIVES THAT CONFORM TO A SOCIETY THAT TELLS US WHAT TO THINK, WHAT TO WANT...AND WHO TO BE.
WE ARE PRISONERS.

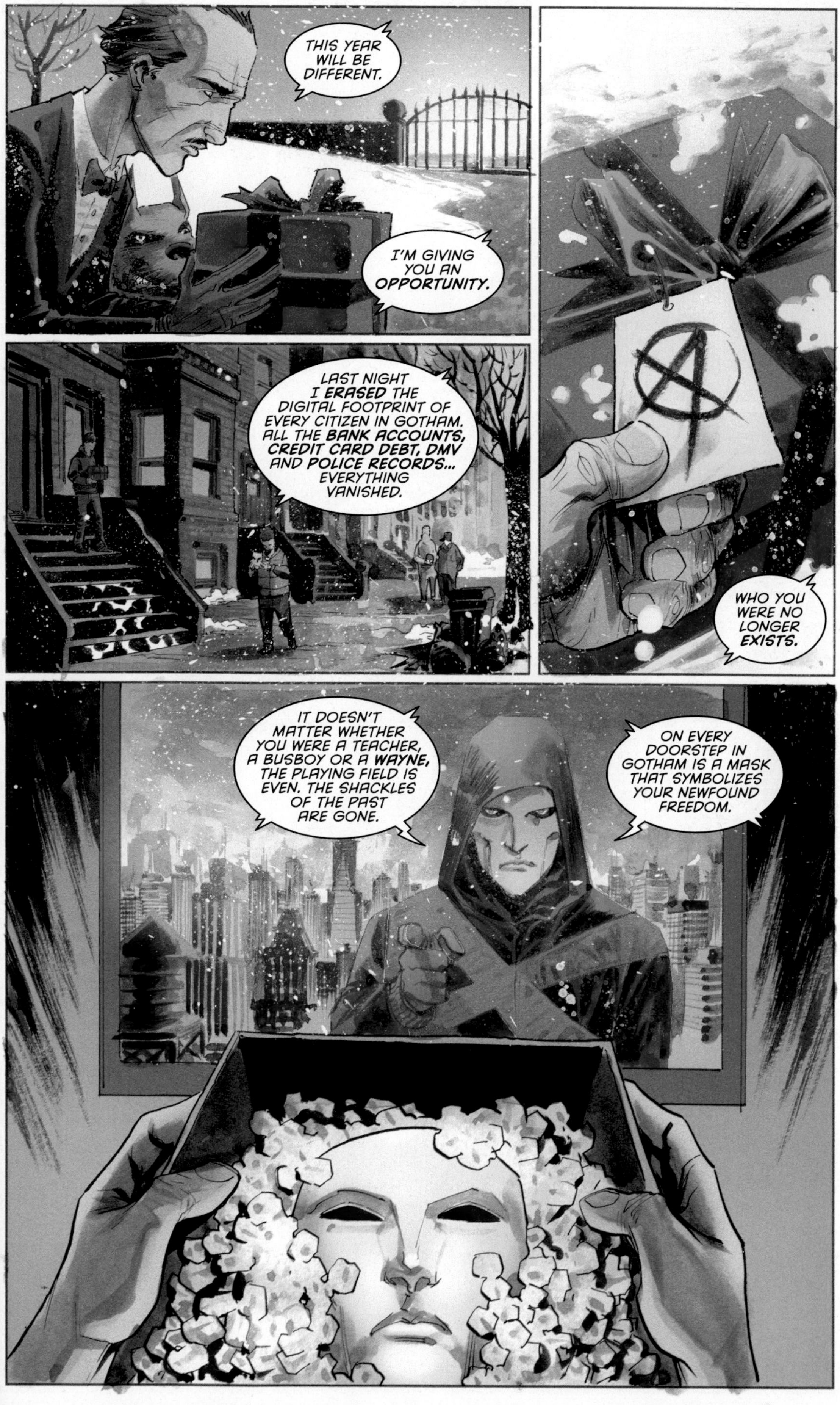
THIS YEAR WILL BE DIFFERENT.
I'M GIVING YOU AN OPPORTUNITY.
LAST NIGHT I ERASED THE DIGITAL FOOTPRINT OF EVERY CITIZEN IN GOTHAM. ALL THE BANK ACCOUNTS, CREDIT CARD DEBT, DMV AND POLICE RECORDS... EVERYTHING VANISHED.
WHO YOU WERE NO LONGER EXISTS.
IT DOESN'T MATTER WHETHER YOU WERE A TEACHER, A BUSBOY OR A WAYNE, THE PLAYING FIELD IS EVEN. THE SHACKLES OF THE PAST ARE GONE.
ON EVERY DOORSTEP IN GOTHAM IS A MASK THAT SYMBOLIZES YOUR NEWFOUND FREEDOM.

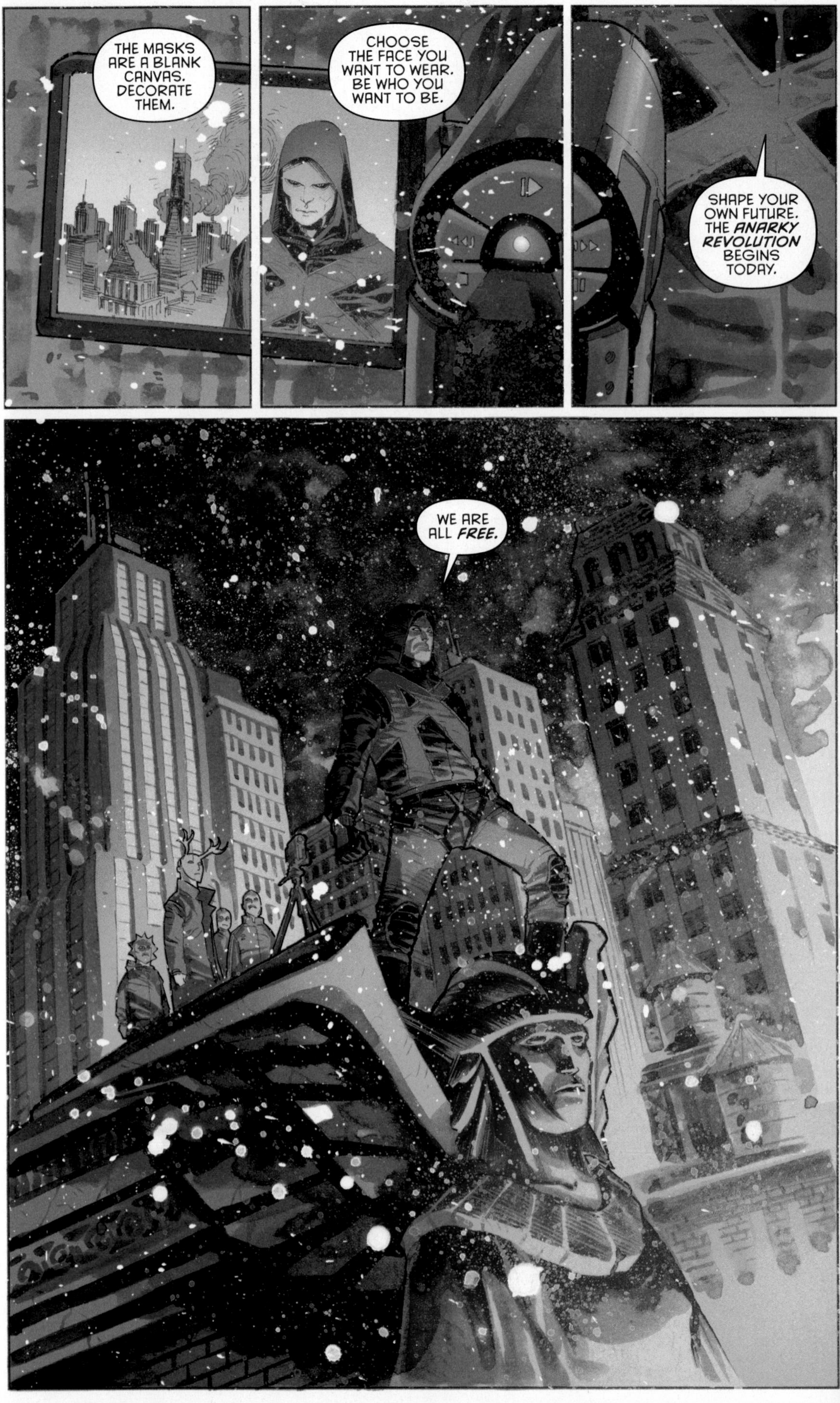
THE MASKS ARE A BLANK CANVAS. DECORATE THEM.
CHOOSE THE FACE YOU WANT TO WEAR. BE WHO YOU WANT TO BE.
SHAPE YOUR OWN FUTURE. THE *ANARKY REVOLUTION* BEGINS TODAY.
WE ARE ALL *FREE.*

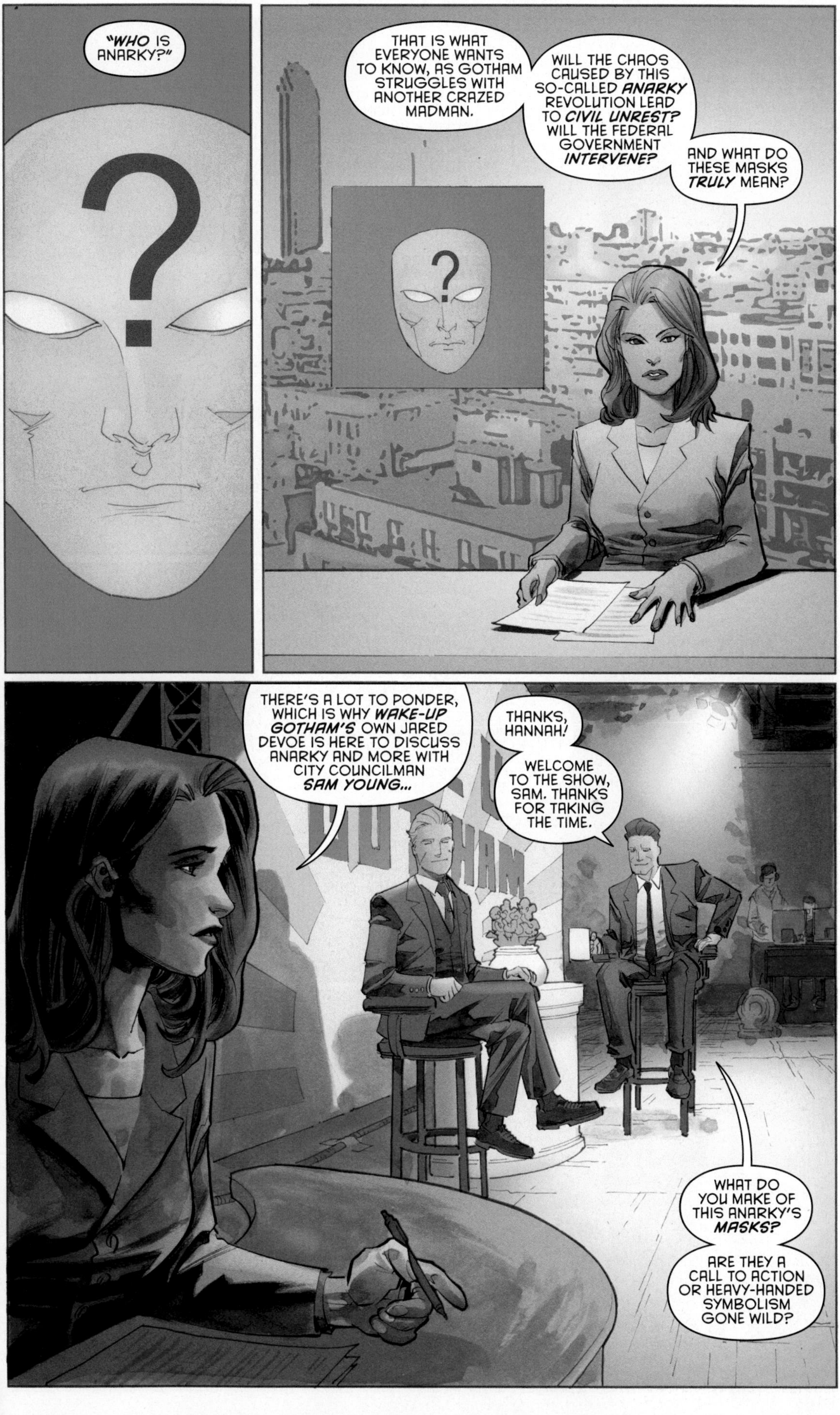
"WHO IS ANARKY?"
THAT IS WHAT EVERYONE WANTS TO KNOW, AS GOTHAM STRUGGLES WITH ANOTHER CRAZED MADMAN.
WILL THE CHAOS CAUSED BY THIS SO-CALLED ANARKY REVOLUTION LEAD TO CIVIL UNREST? WILL THE FEDERAL GOVERNMENT INTERVENE?
AND WHAT DO THESE MASKS TRULY MEAN?
THERE'S A LOT TO PONDER, WHICH IS WHY WAKE-UP GOTHAM'S OWN JARED DEVOE IS HERE TO DISCUSS ANARKY AND MORE WITH CITY COUNCILMAN SAM YOUNG...
THANKS, HANNAH!
WELCOME TO THE SHOW, SAM. THANKS FOR TAKING THE TIME.
WHAT DO YOU MAKE OF THIS ANARKY'S MASKS?
ARE THEY A CALL TO ACTION OR HEAVY-HANDED SYMBOLISM GONE WILD?

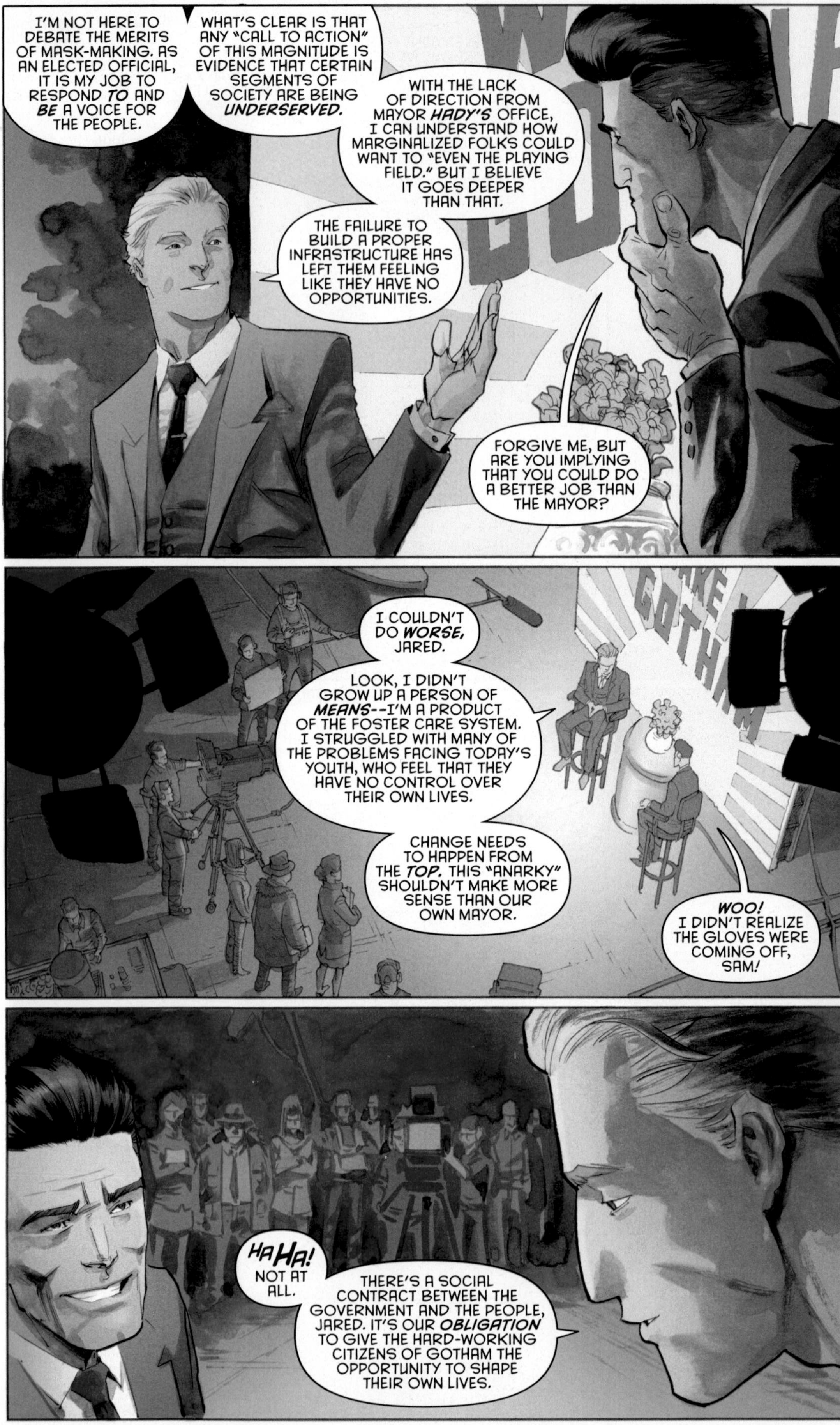
I'M NOT HERE TO DEBATE THE MERITS OF MASK-MAKING. AS AN ELECTED OFFICIAL, IT IS MY JOB TO RESPOND *TO* AND *BE* A VOICE FOR THE PEOPLE.
WHAT'S CLEAR IS THAT ANY "CALL TO ACTION" OF THIS MAGNITUDE IS EVIDENCE THAT CERTAIN SEGMENTS OF SOCIETY ARE BEING *UNDERSERVED.*
WITH THE LACK OF DIRECTION FROM MAYOR *HADY'S* OFFICE, I CAN UNDERSTAND HOW MARGINALIZED FOLKS COULD WANT TO "EVEN THE PLAYING FIELD." BUT I BELIEVE IT GOES DEEPER THAN THAT.
THE FAILURE TO BUILD A PROPER INFRASTRUCTURE HAS LEFT THEM FEELING LIKE THEY HAVE NO OPPORTUNITIES.
FORGIVE ME, BUT ARE YOU IMPLYING THAT YOU COULD DO A BETTER JOB THAN THE MAYOR?
GOTHAM
I COULDN'T DO *WORSE,* JARED.
LOOK, I DIDN'T GROW UP A PERSON OF *MEANS*--I'M A PRODUCT OF THE FOSTER CARE SYSTEM. I STRUGGLED WITH MANY OF THE PROBLEMS FACING TODAY'S YOUTH, WHO FEEL THAT THEY HAVE NO CONTROL OVER THEIR OWN LIVES.
CHANGE NEEDS TO HAPPEN FROM THE *TOP.* THIS "ANARKY" SHOULDN'T MAKE MORE SENSE THAN OUR OWN MAYOR.
WOO! I DIDN'T REALIZE THE GLOVES WERE COMING OFF, SAM!
HA HA! NOT AT ALL.
THERE'S A SOCIAL CONTRACT BETWEEN THE GOVERNMENT AND THE PEOPLE, JARED. IT'S OUR *OBLIGATION* TO GIVE THE HARD-WORKING CITIZENS OF GOTHAM THE OPPORTUNITY TO SHAPE THEIR OWN LIVES.

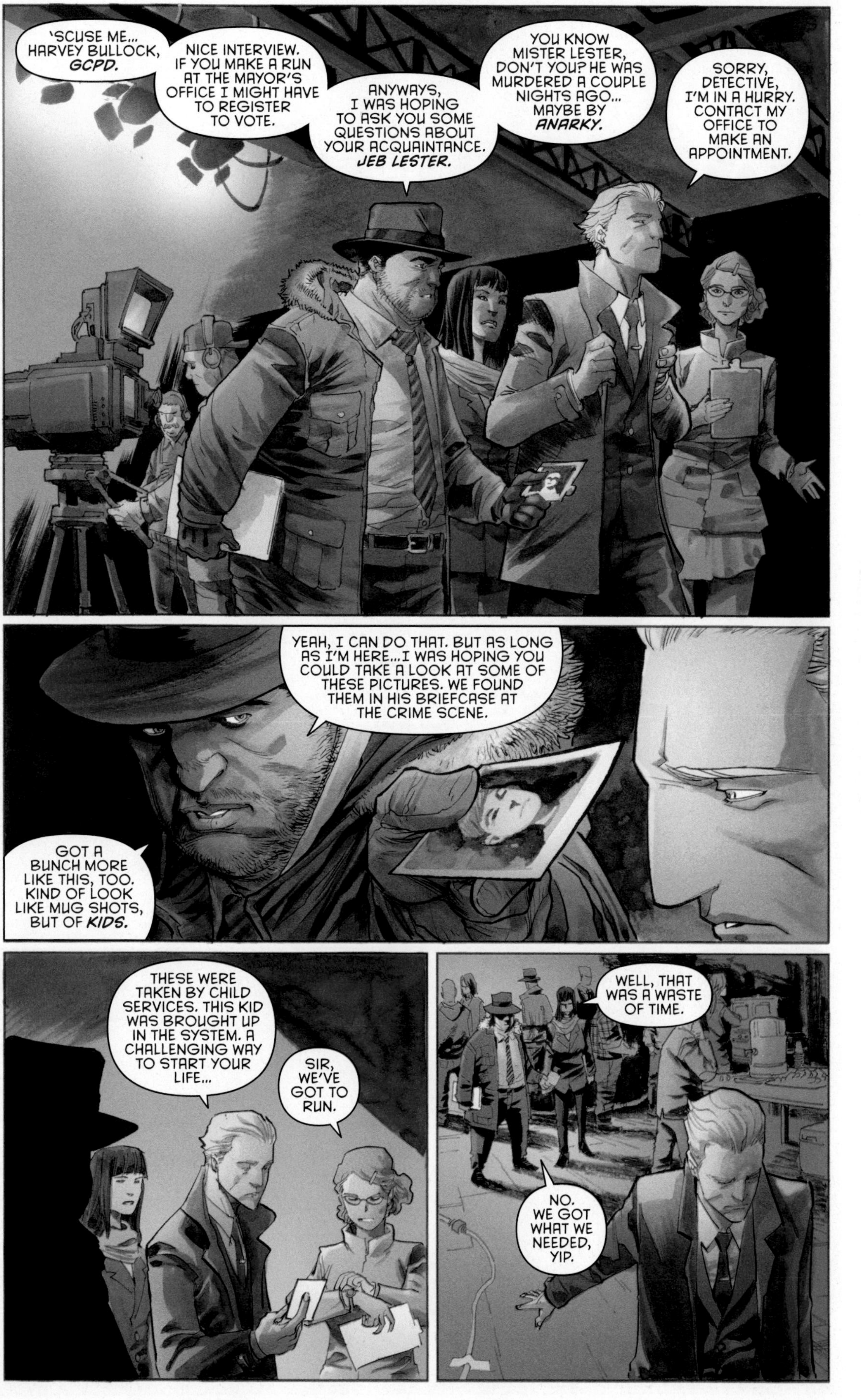
'SCUSE ME... HARVEY BULLOCK, GCPD.
NICE INTERVIEW. IF YOU MAKE A RUN AT THE MAYOR'S OFFICE I MIGHT HAVE TO REGISTER TO VOTE.
ANYWAYS, I WAS HOPING TO ASK YOU SOME QUESTIONS ABOUT YOUR ACQUAINTANCE. JEB LESTER.
YOU KNOW MISTER LESTER, DON'T YOU? HE WAS MURDERED A COUPLE NIGHTS AGO... MAYBE BY ANARKY.
SORRY, DETECTIVE, I'M IN A HURRY. CONTACT MY OFFICE TO MAKE AN APPOINTMENT.
YEAH, I CAN DO THAT. BUT AS LONG AS I'M HERE...I WAS HOPING YOU COULD TAKE A LOOK AT SOME OF THESE PICTURES. WE FOUND THEM IN HIS BRIEFCASE AT THE CRIME SCENE.
GOT A BUNCH MORE LIKE THIS, TOO. KIND OF LOOK LIKE MUG SHOTS, BUT OF KIDS.
THESE WERE TAKEN BY CHILD SERVICES. THIS KID WAS BROUGHT UP IN THE SYSTEM. A CHALLENGING WAY TO START YOUR LIFE...
SIR, WE'VE GOT TO RUN.
WELL, THAT WAS A WASTE OF TIME.
NO. WE GOT WHAT WE NEEDED, YIP.

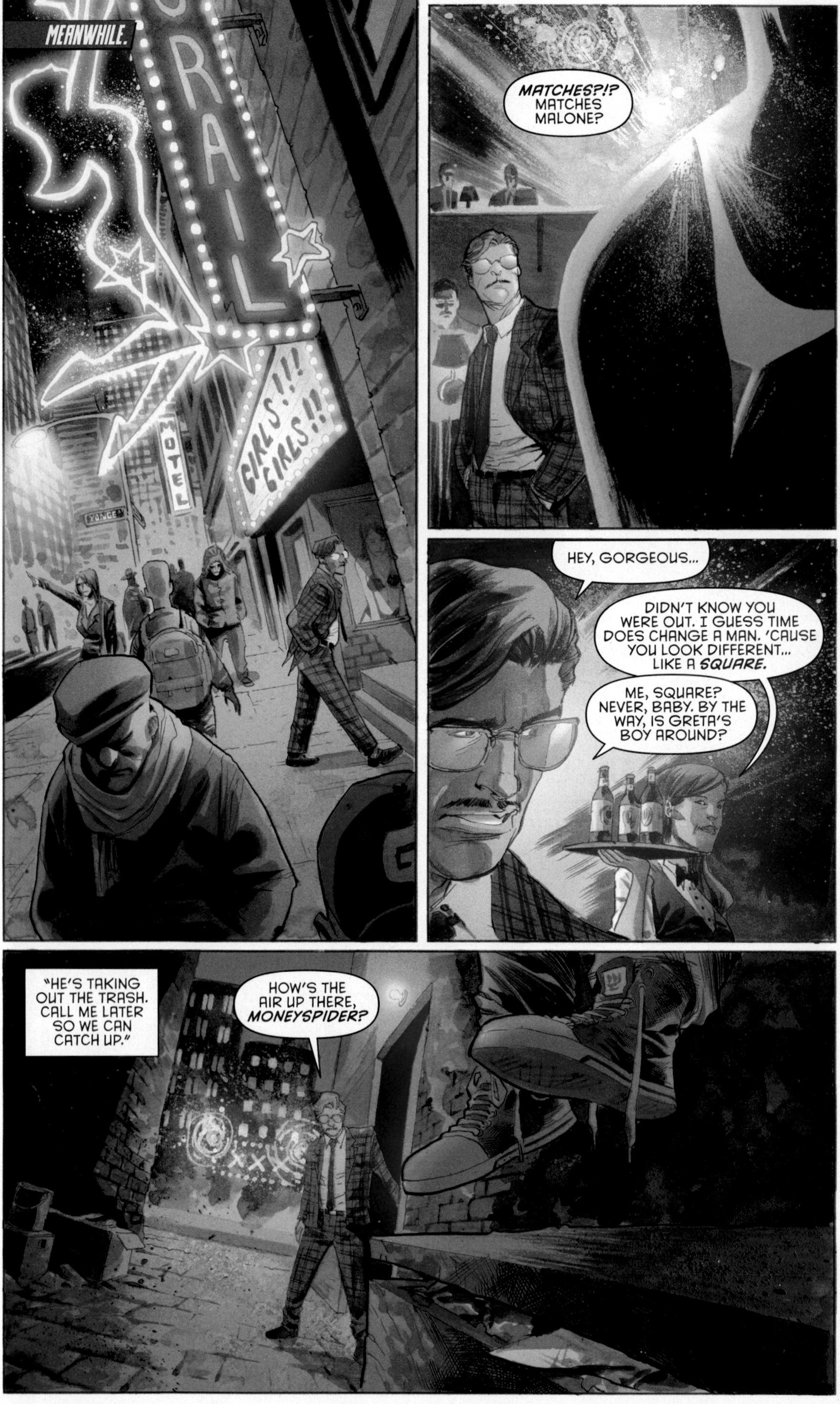
MEANWHILE.
GIRLS!!! GIRLS!!
MOTEL
YONGE
MATCHES?!? MATCHES MALONE?
HEY, GORGEOUS...
DIDN'T KNOW YOU WERE OUT. I GUESS TIME DOES CHANGE A MAN. 'CAUSE YOU LOOK DIFFERENT... LIKE A SQUARE.
ME, SQUARE? NEVER, BABY. BY THE WAY, IS GRETA'S BOY AROUND?
"HE'S TAKING OUT THE TRASH. CALL ME LATER SO WE CAN CATCH UP."
HOW'S THE AIR UP THERE, MONEYSPIDER?

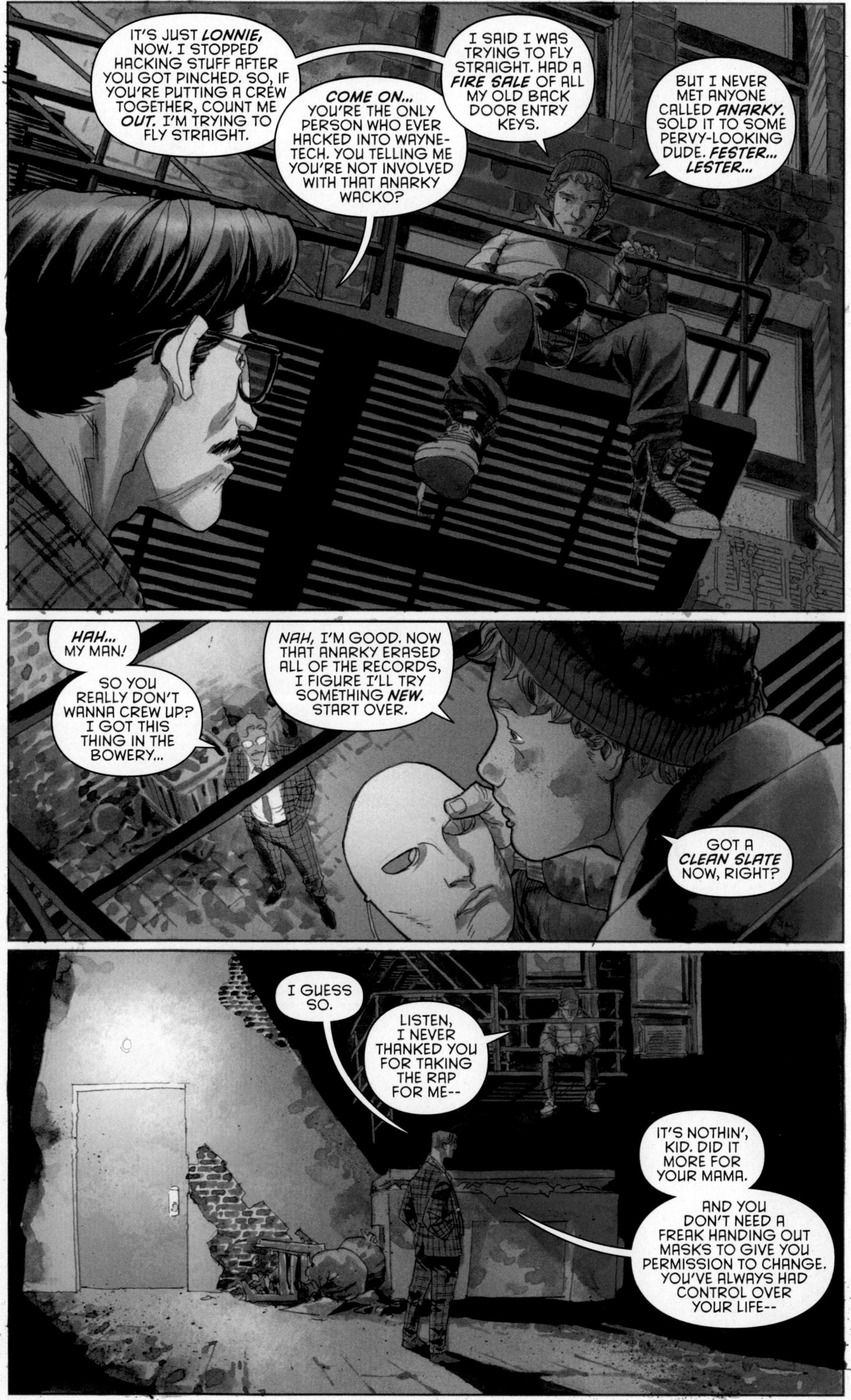
IT'S JUST LONNIE, NOW. I STOPPED HACKING STUFF AFTER YOU GOT PINCHED. SO, IF YOU'RE PUTTING A CREW TOGETHER, COUNT ME OUT. I'M TRYING TO FLY STRAIGHT.
COME ON... YOU'RE THE ONLY PERSON WHO EVER HACKED INTO WAYNE-TECH. YOU TELLING ME YOU'RE NOT INVOLVED WITH THAT ANARKY WACKO?
I SAID I WAS TRYING TO FLY STRAIGHT. HAD A FIRE SALE OF ALL MY OLD BACK DOOR ENTRY KEYS.
BUT I NEVER MET ANYONE CALLED ANARKY. SOLD IT TO SOME PERVY-LOOKING DUDE. FESTER... LESTER...
HAH... MY MAN!
SO YOU REALLY DON'T WANNA CREW UP? I GOT THIS THING IN THE BOWERY...
NAH, I'M GOOD. NOW THAT ANARKY ERASED ALL OF THE RECORDS, I FIGURE I'LL TRY SOMETHING NEW. START OVER.
GOT A CLEAN SLATE NOW, RIGHT?
I GUESS SO.
LISTEN, I NEVER THANKED YOU FOR TAKING THE RAP FOR ME--
IT'S NOTHIN', KID. DID IT MORE FOR YOUR MAMA.
AND YOU DON'T NEED A FREAK HANDING OUT MASKS TO GIVE YOU PERMISSION TO CHANGE. YOU'VE ALWAYS HAD CONTROL OVER YOUR LIFE--

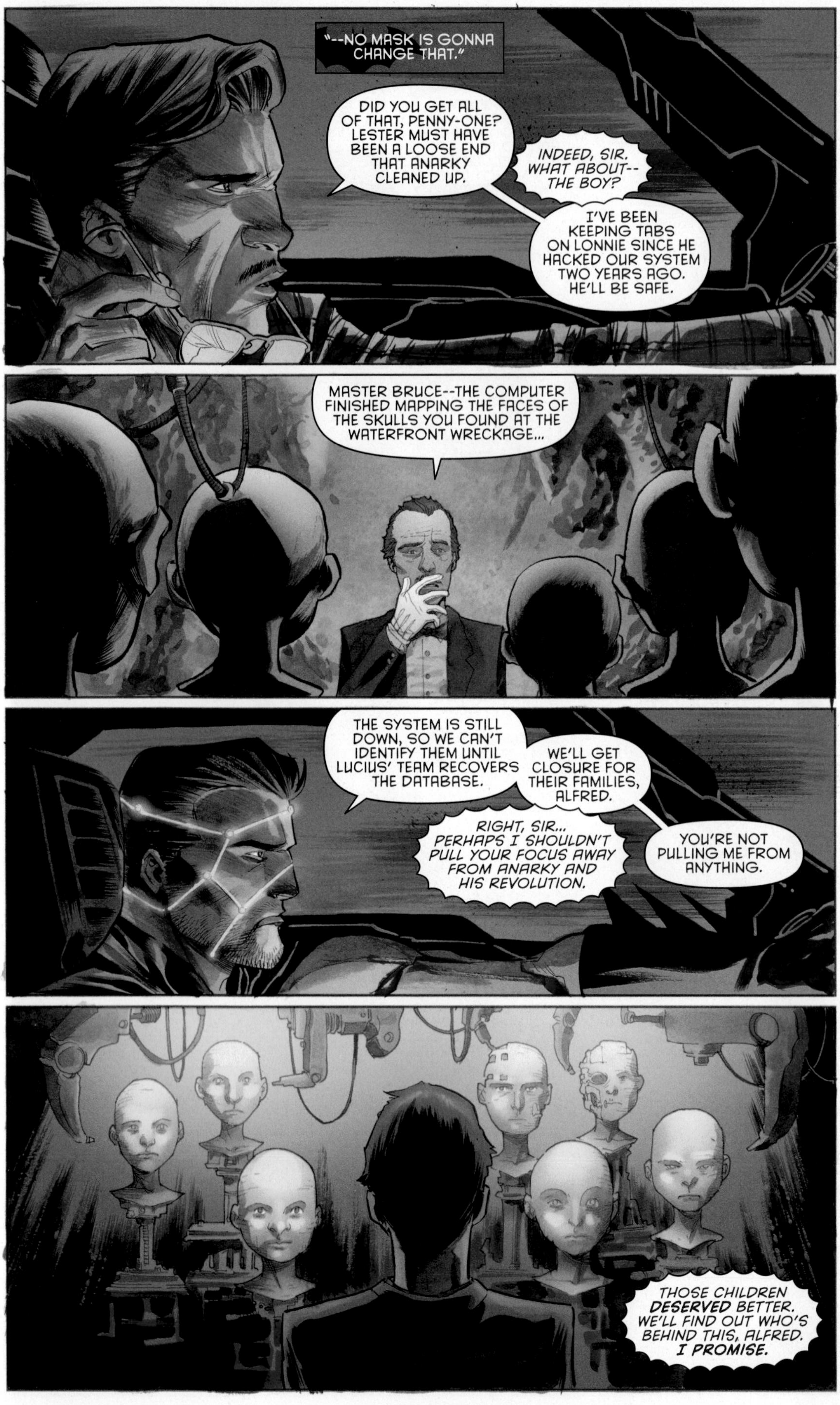
"--NO MASK IS GONNA CHANGE THAT."
DID YOU GET ALL OF THAT, PENNY-ONE? LESTER MUST HAVE BEEN A LOOSE END THAT ANARKY CLEANED UP.
INDEED, SIR. WHAT ABOUT-- THE BOY?
I'VE BEEN KEEPING TABS ON LONNIE SINCE HE HACKED OUR SYSTEM TWO YEARS AGO. HE'LL BE SAFE.
MASTER BRUCE--THE COMPUTER FINISHED MAPPING THE FACES OF THE SKULLS YOU FOUND AT THE WATERFRONT WRECKAGE...
THE SYSTEM IS STILL DOWN, SO WE CAN'T IDENTIFY THEM UNTIL LUCIUS' TEAM RECOVERS THE DATABASE.
WE'LL GET CLOSURE FOR THEIR FAMILIES, ALFRED.
RIGHT, SIR... PERHAPS I SHOULDN'T PULL YOUR FOCUS AWAY FROM ANARKY AND HIS REVOLUTION.
YOU'RE NOT PULLING ME FROM ANYTHING.
THOSE CHILDREN DESERVED BETTER. WE'LL FIND OUT WHO'S BEHIND THIS, ALFRED. I PROMISE.

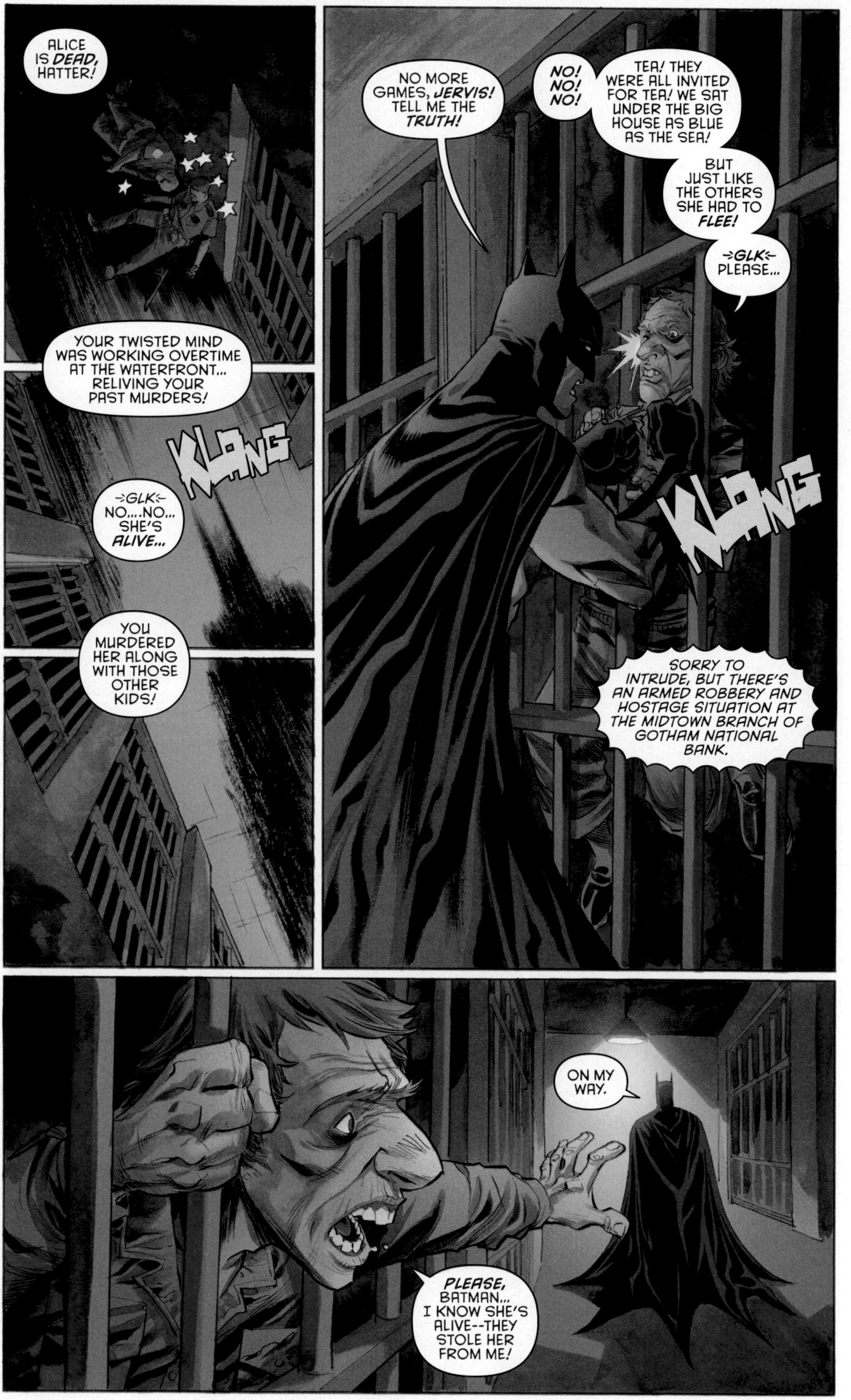
ALICE IS DEAD, HATTER!
YOUR TWISTED MIND WAS WORKING OVERTIME AT THE WATERFRONT... RELIVING YOUR PAST MURDERS!
KLANG
⇒GLK⇐ NO....NO... SHE'S ALIVE...
YOU MURDERED HER ALONG WITH THOSE OTHER KIDS!
NO MORE GAMES, JERVIS! TELL ME THE TRUTH!
NO! NO! NO!
TEA! THEY WERE ALL INVITED FOR TEA! WE SAT UNDER THE BIG HOUSE AS BLUE AS THE SEA!
BUT JUST LIKE THE OTHERS SHE HAD TO FLEE!
⇒GLK⇐ PLEASE...
KLANG
SORRY TO INTRUDE, BUT THERE'S AN ARMED ROBBERY AND HOSTAGE SITUATION AT THE MIDTOWN BRANCH OF GOTHAM NATIONAL BANK.
ON MY WAY.
PLEASE, BATMAN... I KNOW SHE'S ALIVE--THEY STOLE HER FROM ME!

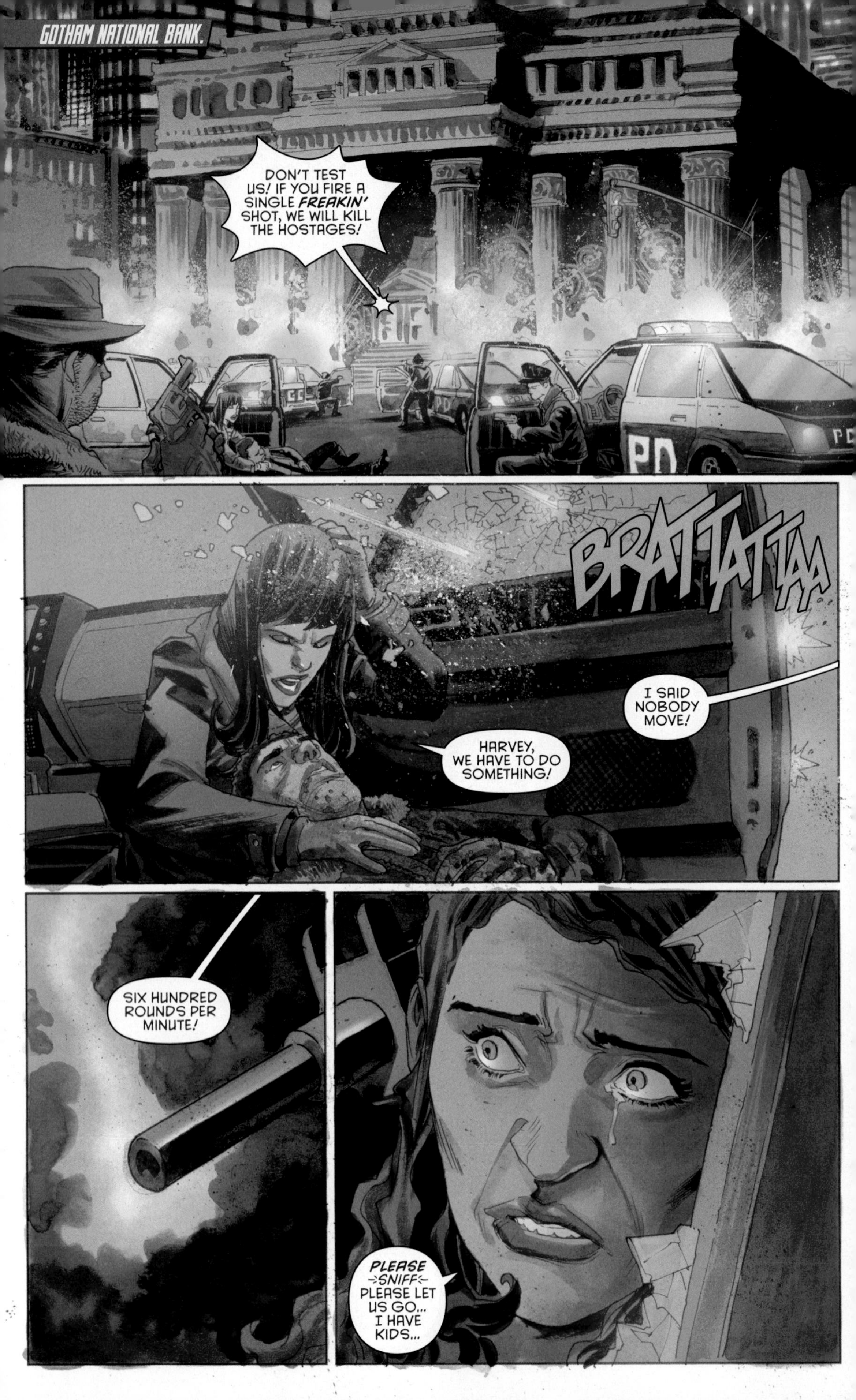
GOTHAM NATIONAL BANK.
DON'T TEST US! IF YOU FIRE A SINGLE *FREAKIN'* SHOT, WE WILL KILL THE HOSTAGES!
BRATTATTAA
I SAID NOBODY MOVE!
HARVEY, WE HAVE TO DO SOMETHING!
SIX HUNDRED ROUNDS PER MINUTE!
PLEASE -SNIFF- PLEASE LET US GO... I HAVE KIDS...

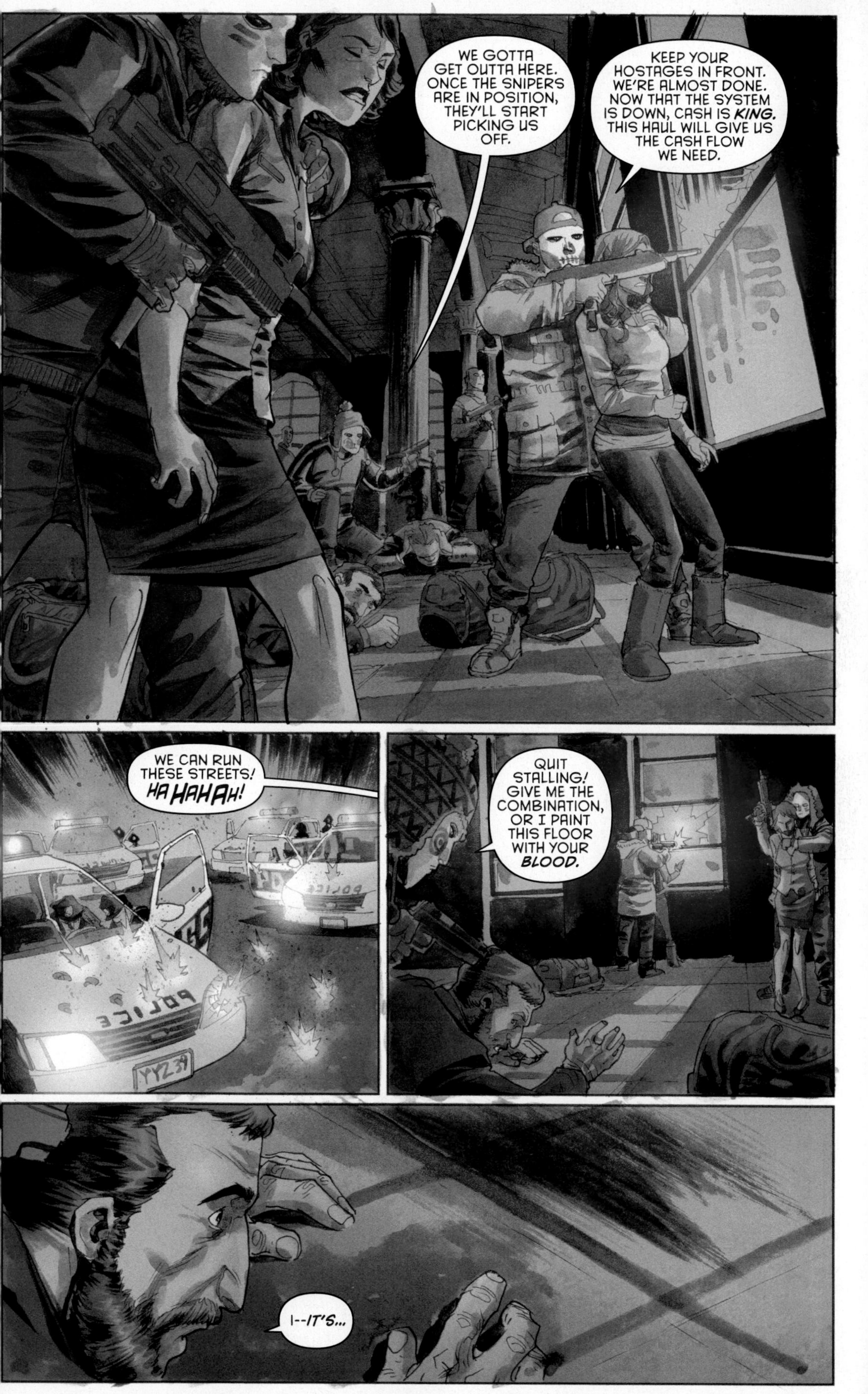
WE GOTTA GET OUTTA HERE. ONCE THE SNIPERS ARE IN POSITION, THEY'LL START PICKING US OFF.
KEEP YOUR HOSTAGES IN FRONT. WE'RE ALMOST DONE. NOW THAT THE SYSTEM IS DOWN, CASH IS KING. THIS HAUL WILL GIVE US THE CASH FLOW WE NEED.
WE CAN RUN THESE STREETS! HA HAHAH!
POLICE
YY239
QUIT STALLING! GIVE ME THE COMBINATION, OR I PAINT THIS FLOOR WITH YOUR BLOOD.
I--IT'S...

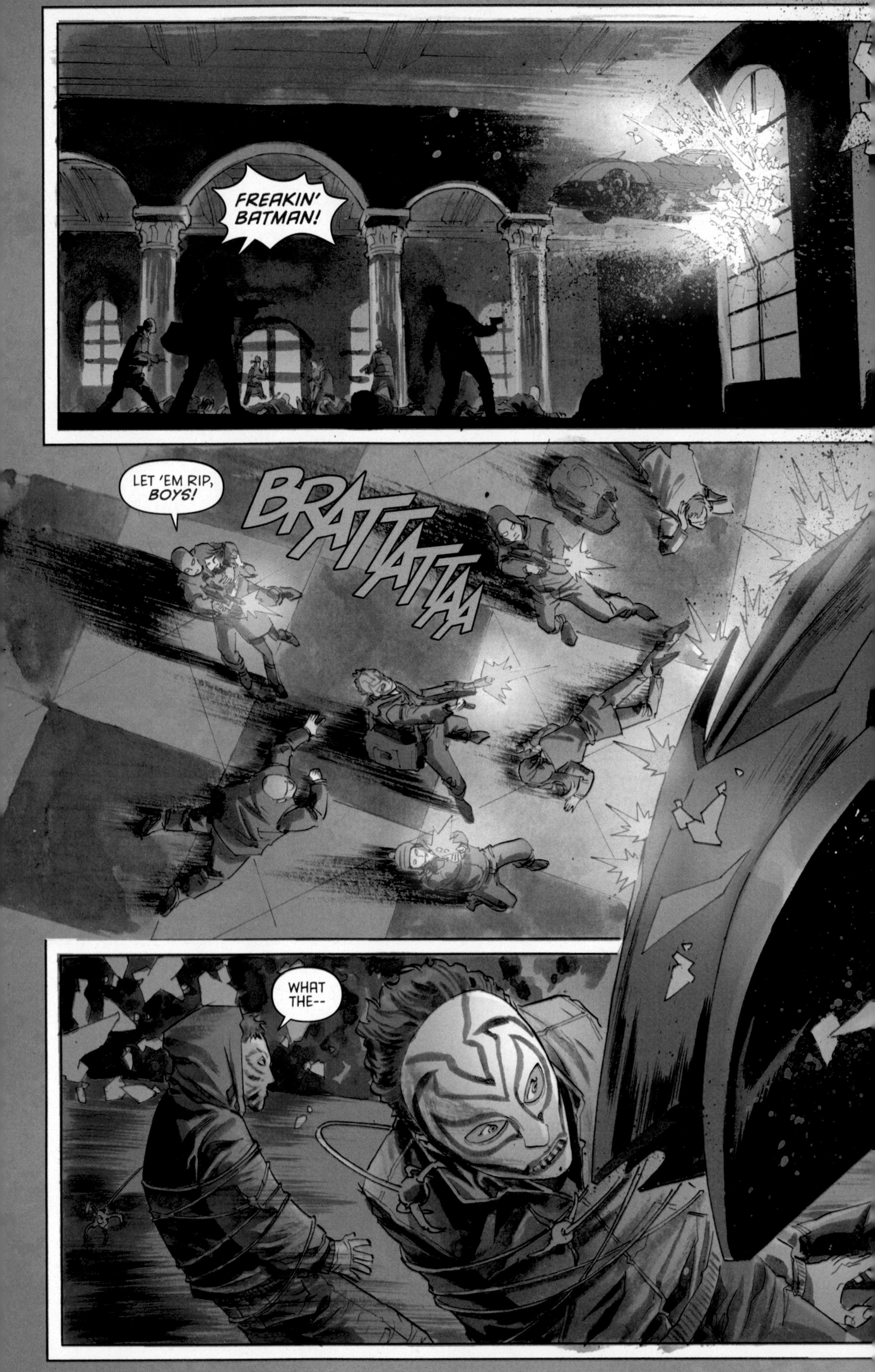
FREAKIN' BATMAN!
LET 'EM RIP, BOYS!
BRATTATTAA
WHAT THE--

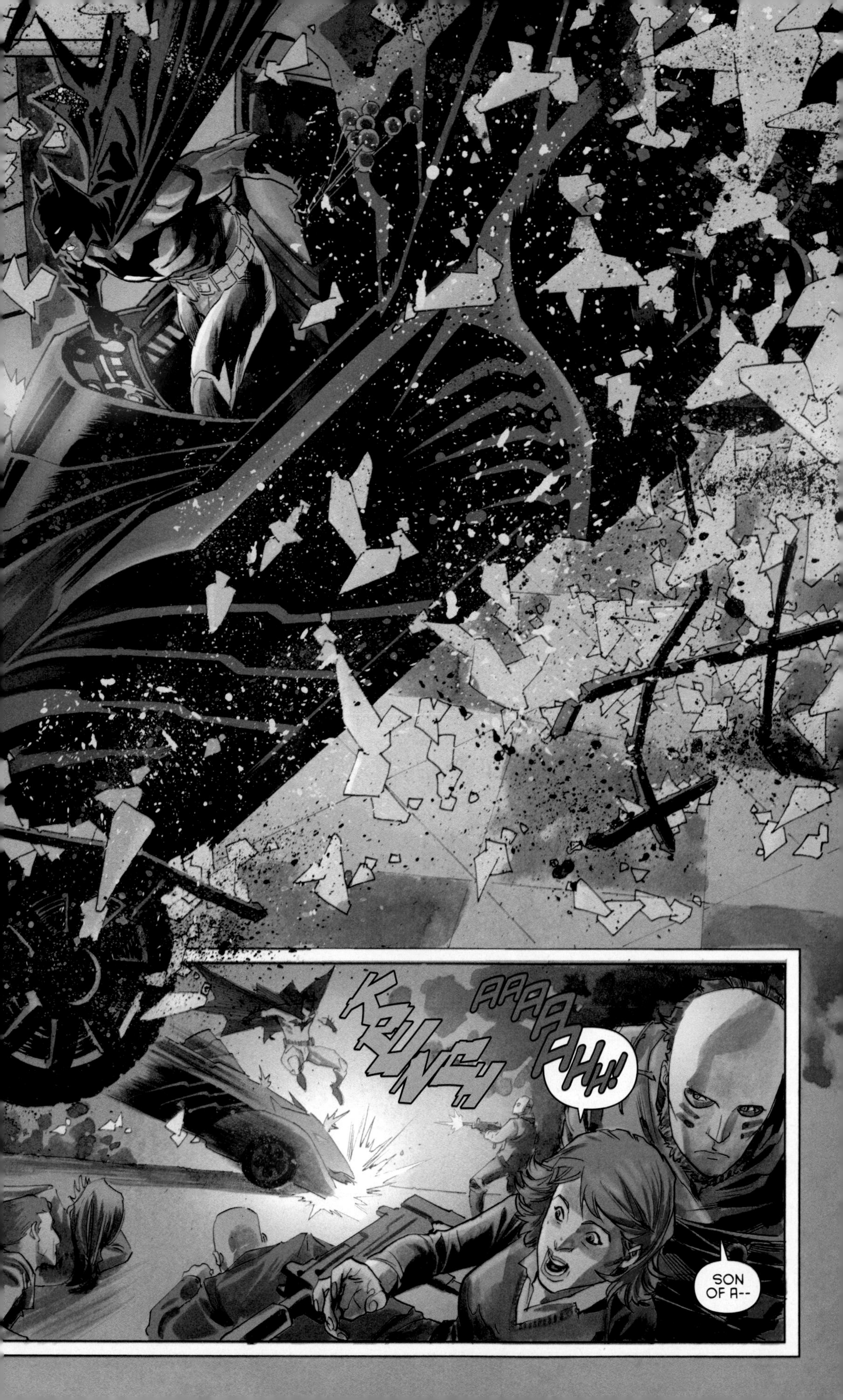

KRUNCH
AAAAAHH!
SON OF A--

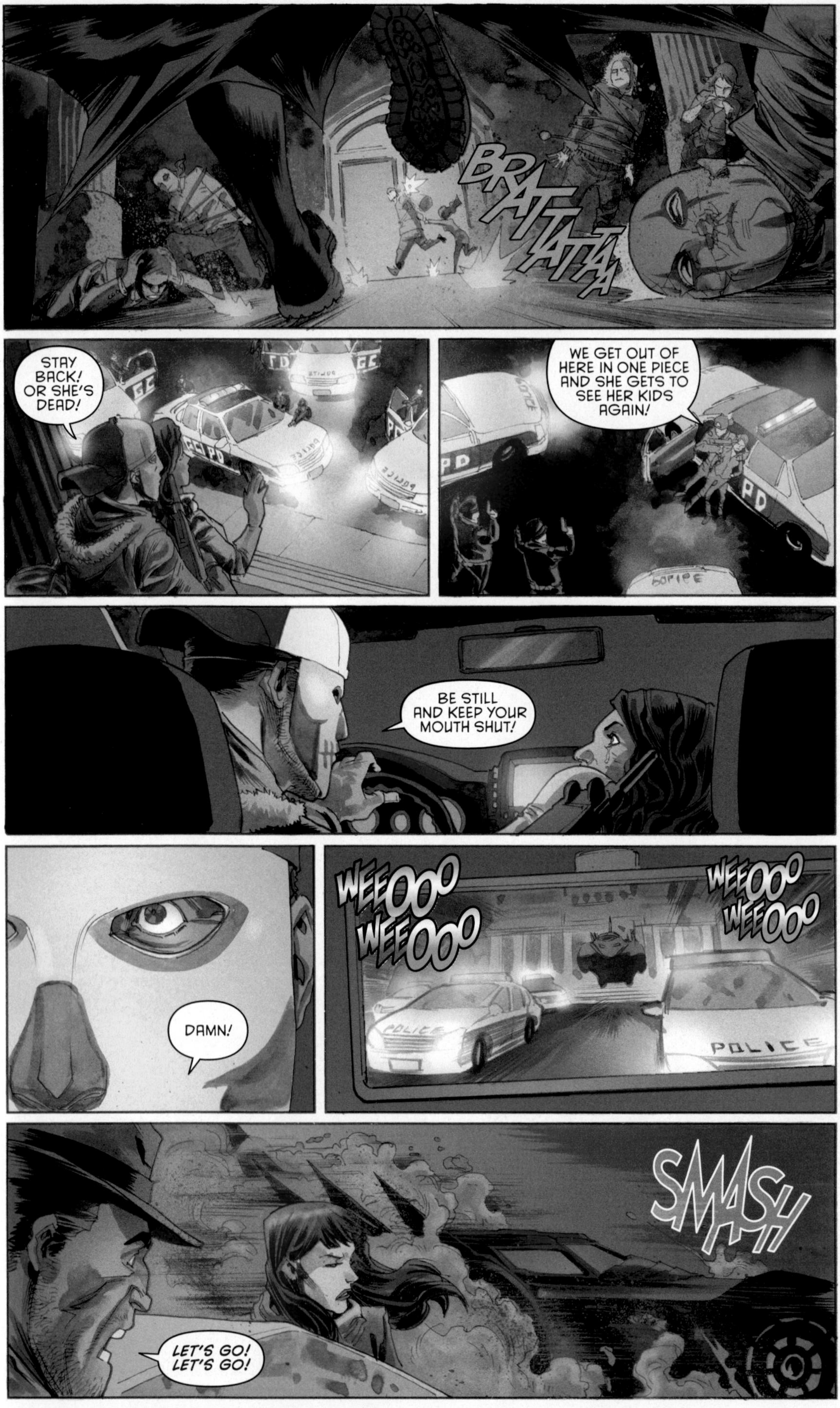
BRATTATTA
STAY BACK! OR SHE'S DEAD!
WE GET OUT OF HERE IN ONE PIECE AND SHE GETS TO SEE HER KIDS AGAIN!
BE STILL AND KEEP YOUR MOUTH SHUT!
DAMN!
WEEOOO WEEOOO
WEEOOO WEEOOO
SMASH
LET'S GO! LET'S GO!

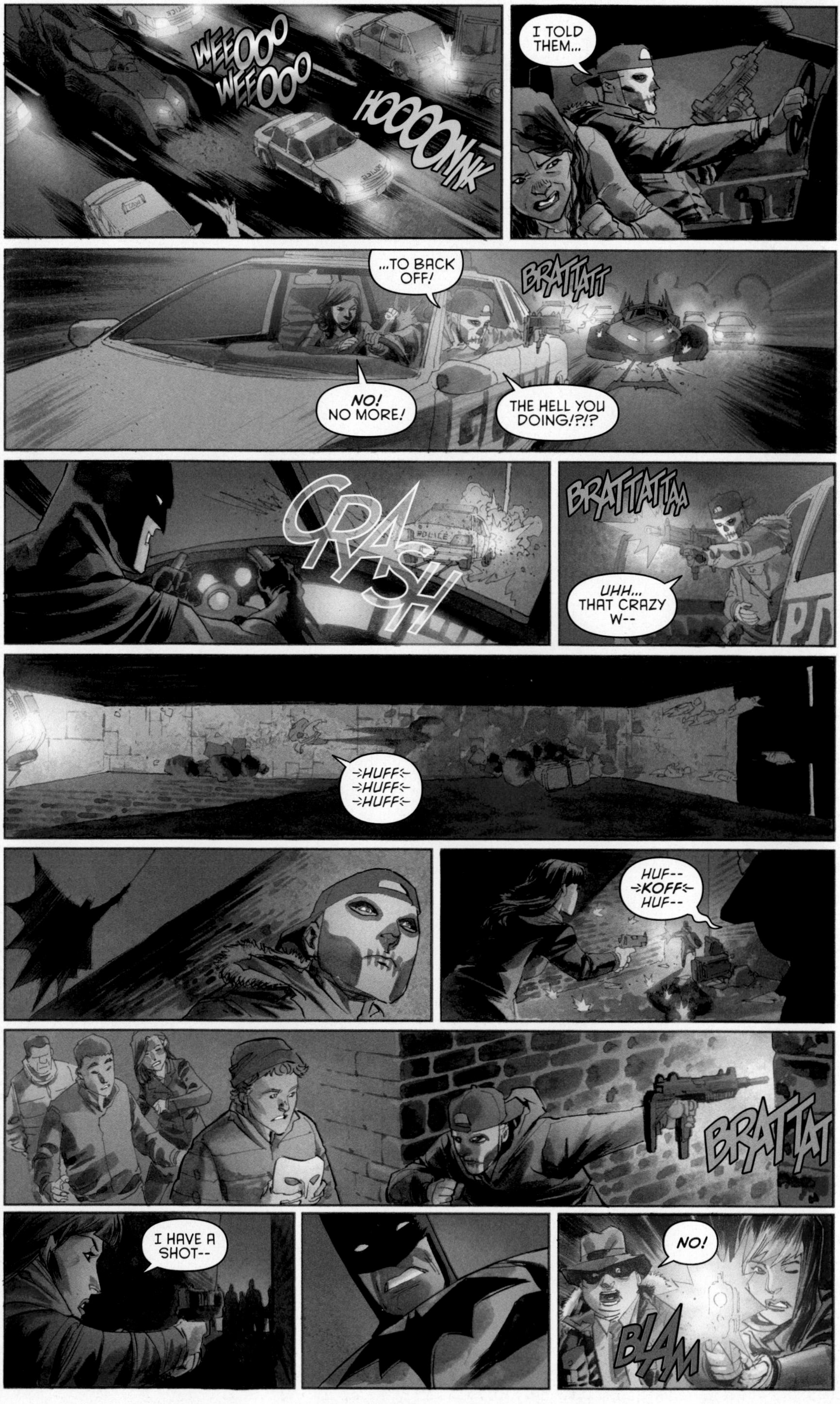
WEEOOO
WEEOOO
HOOOONNK
I TOLD THEM...
...TO BACK OFF!
BRATTATT
NO! NO MORE!
THE HELL YOU DOING!?!?
CRASH
BRATTATTAA
UHH... THAT CRAZY W--
HUFF HUFF HUFF
HUF-- KOFF HUF--
BRATTAT
I HAVE A SHOT--
NO!
BLAM

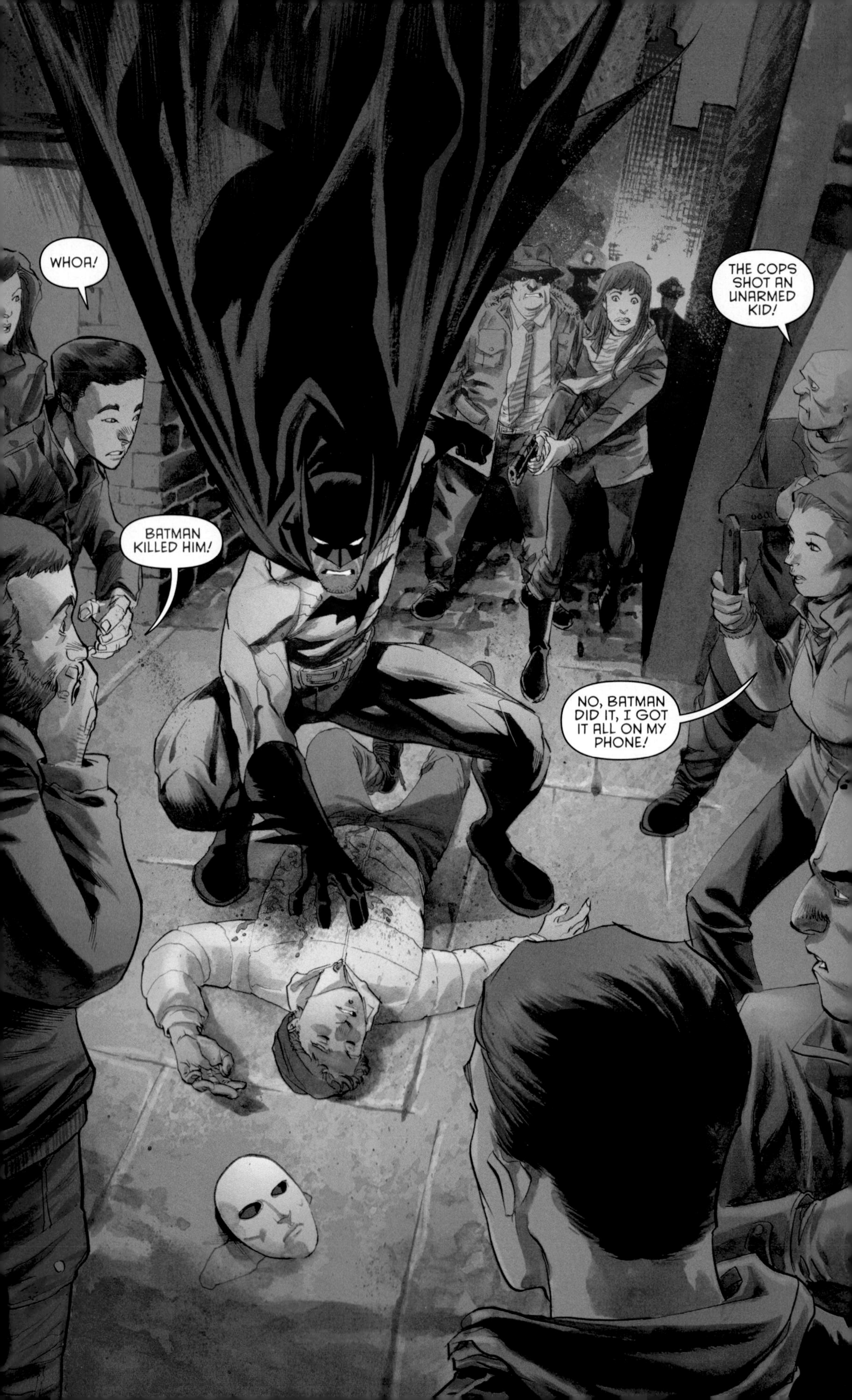
WHOA!
THE COPS SHOT AN UNARMED KID!
BATMAN KILLED HIM!
NO, BATMAN DID IT, I GOT IT ALL ON MY PHONE!

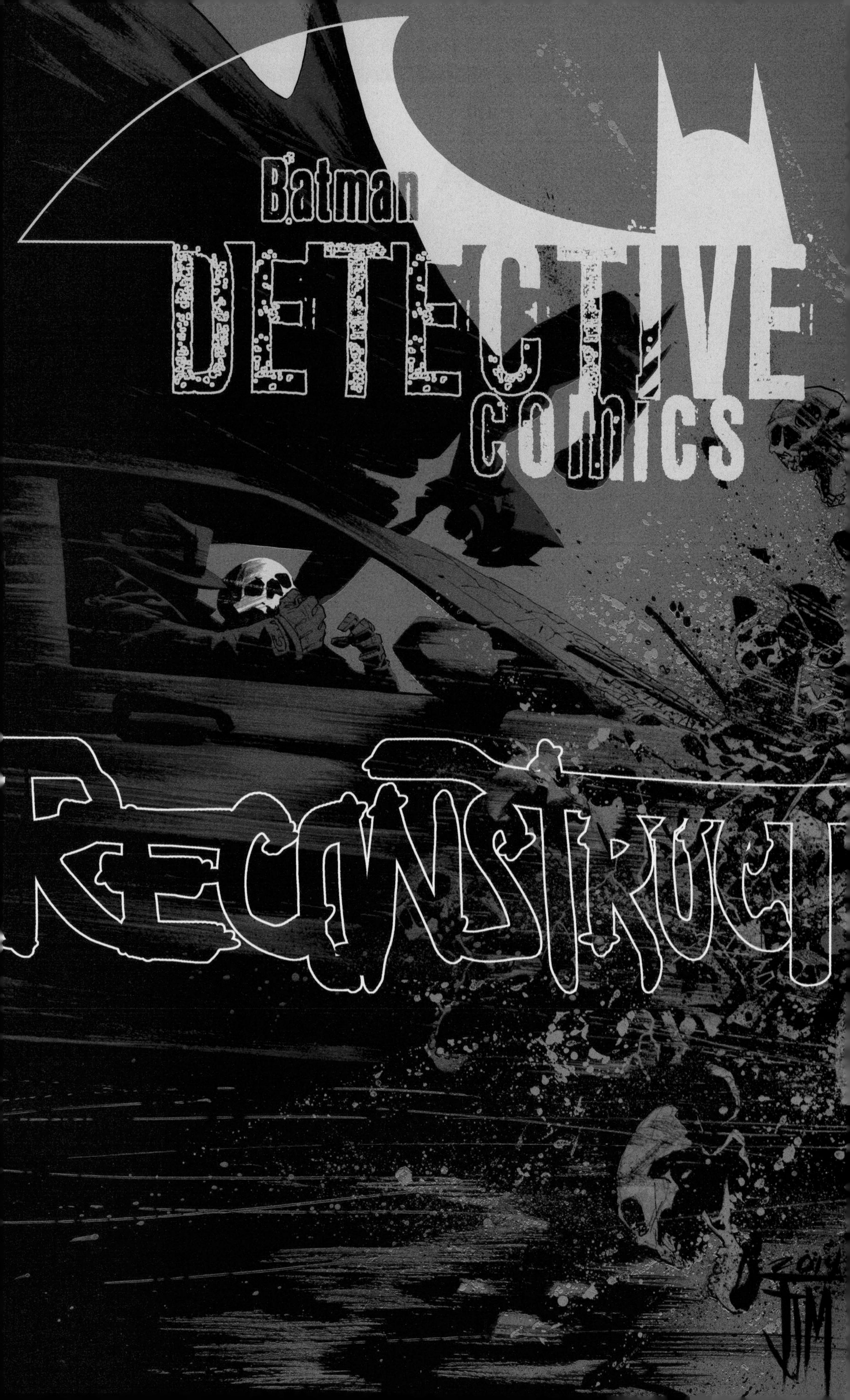

Batman
DETECTIVE
comics
RECONSTRUCT

ANARKY PART 3

FRANCIS MANAPUL & BRIAN BUCCELLATO writers FRANCIS MANAPUL artist BRIAN BUCCELLATO colorist JARED K. FLETCHER letterer cover by FRANCIS MANAPUL

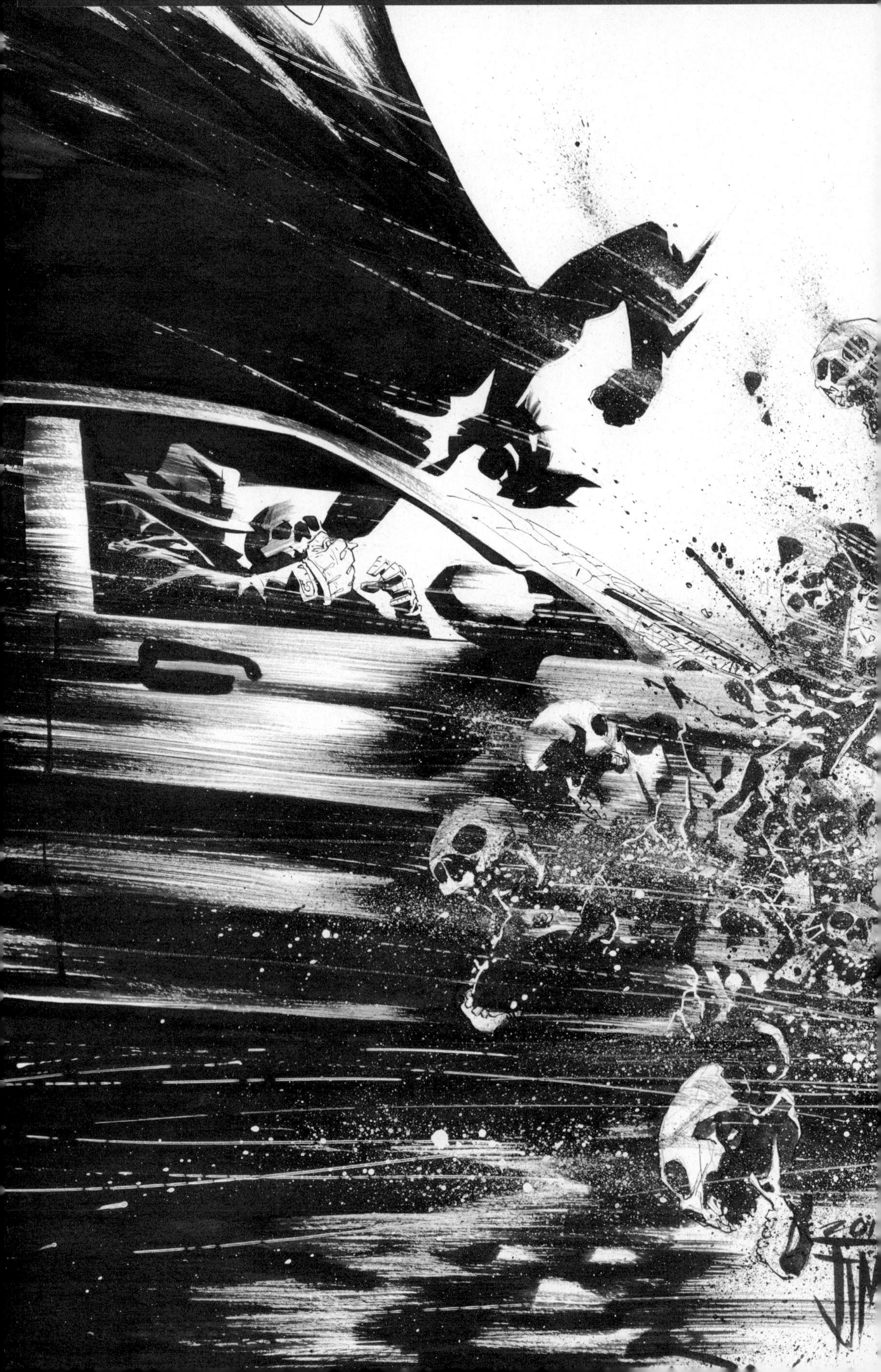

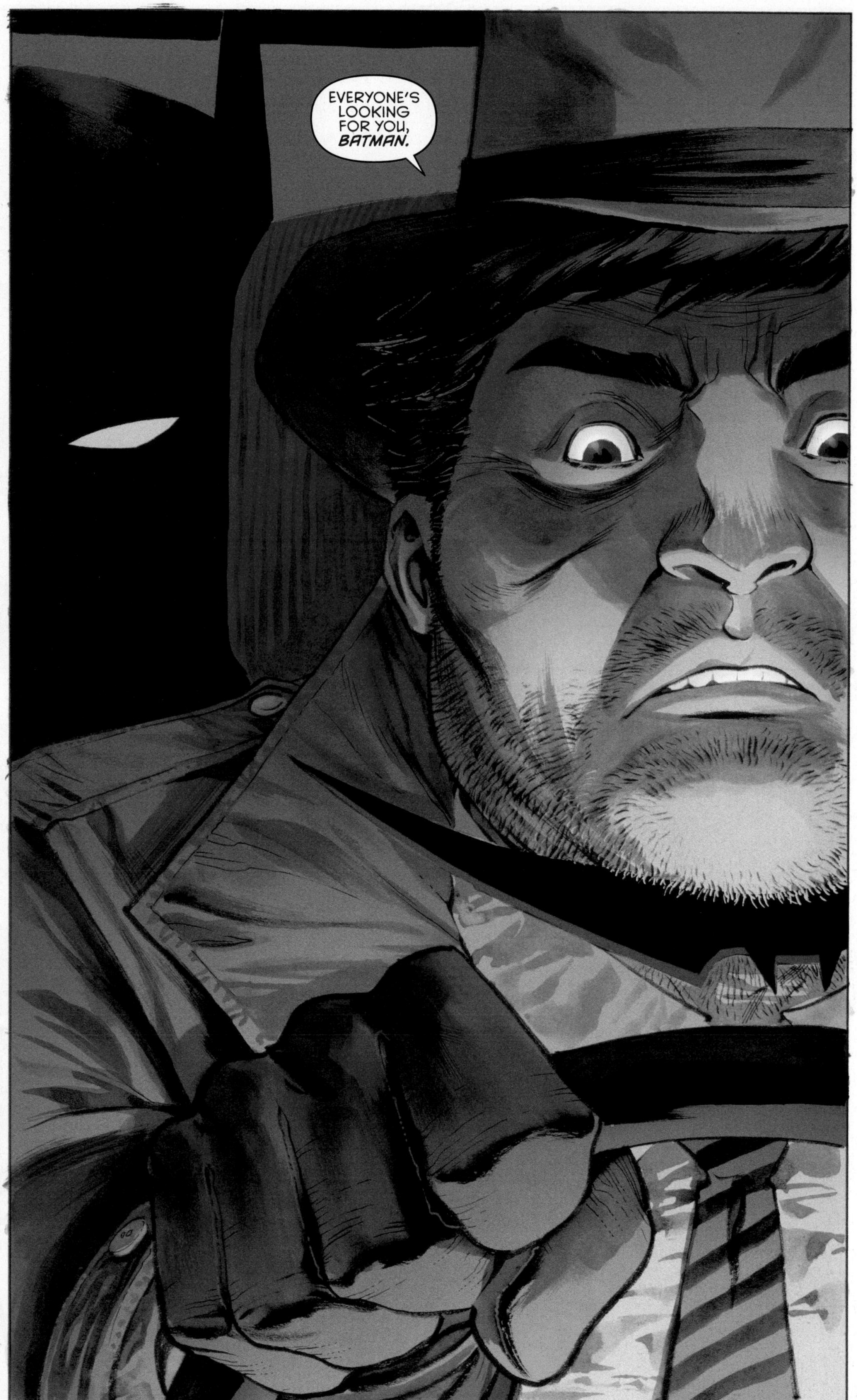
EVERYONE'S LOOKING FOR YOU, *BATMAN.*

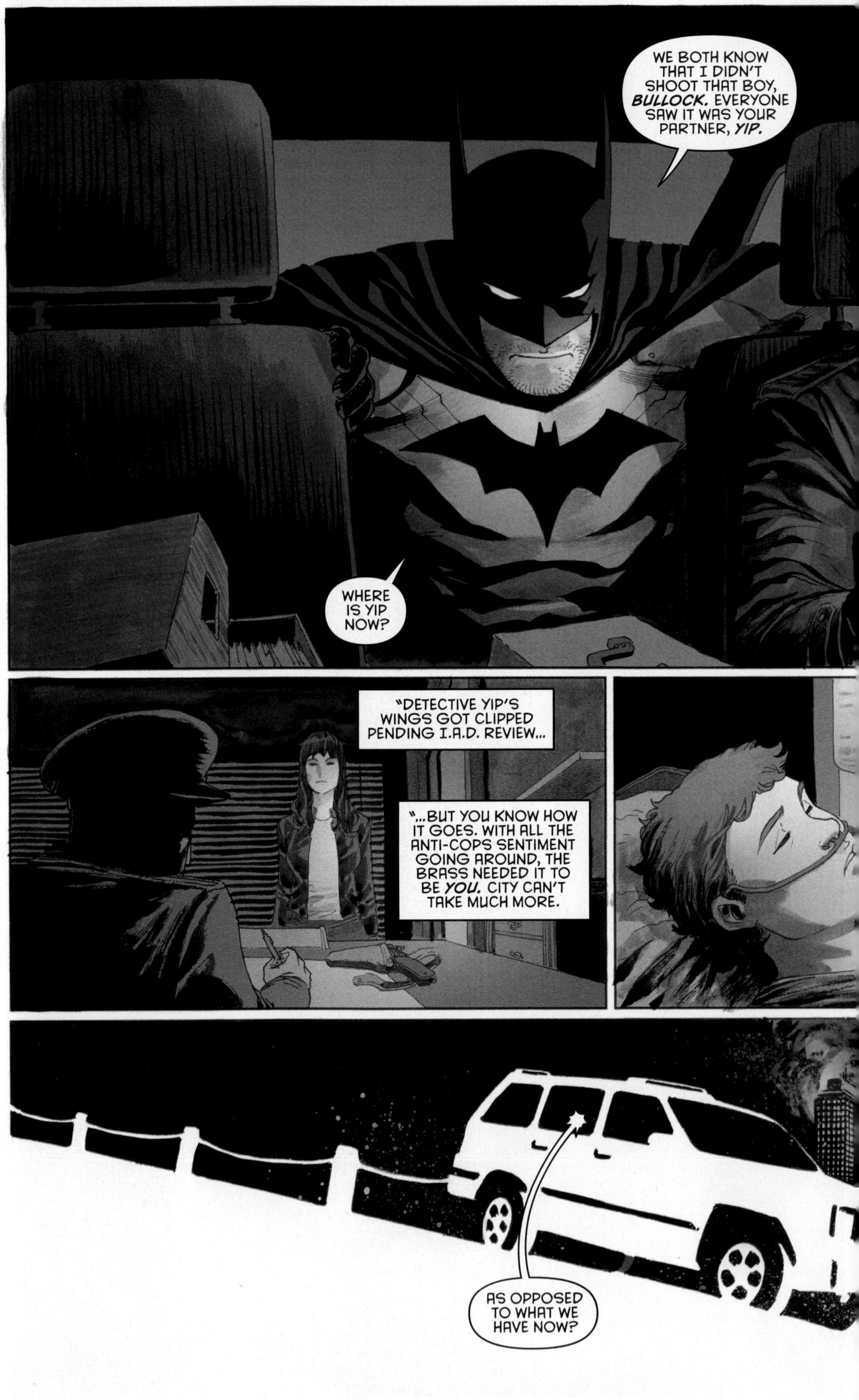
WE BOTH KNOW THAT I DIDN'T SHOOT THAT BOY, BULLOCK. EVERYONE SAW IT WAS YOUR PARTNER, YIP.
WHERE IS YIP NOW?
"DETECTIVE YIP'S WINGS GOT CLIPPED PENDING I.A.D. REVIEW...
"...BUT YOU KNOW HOW IT GOES. WITH ALL THE ANTI-COPS SENTIMENT GOING AROUND, THE BRASS NEEDED IT TO BE YOU. CITY CAN'T TAKE MUCH MORE.
AS OPPOSED TO WHAT WE HAVE NOW?

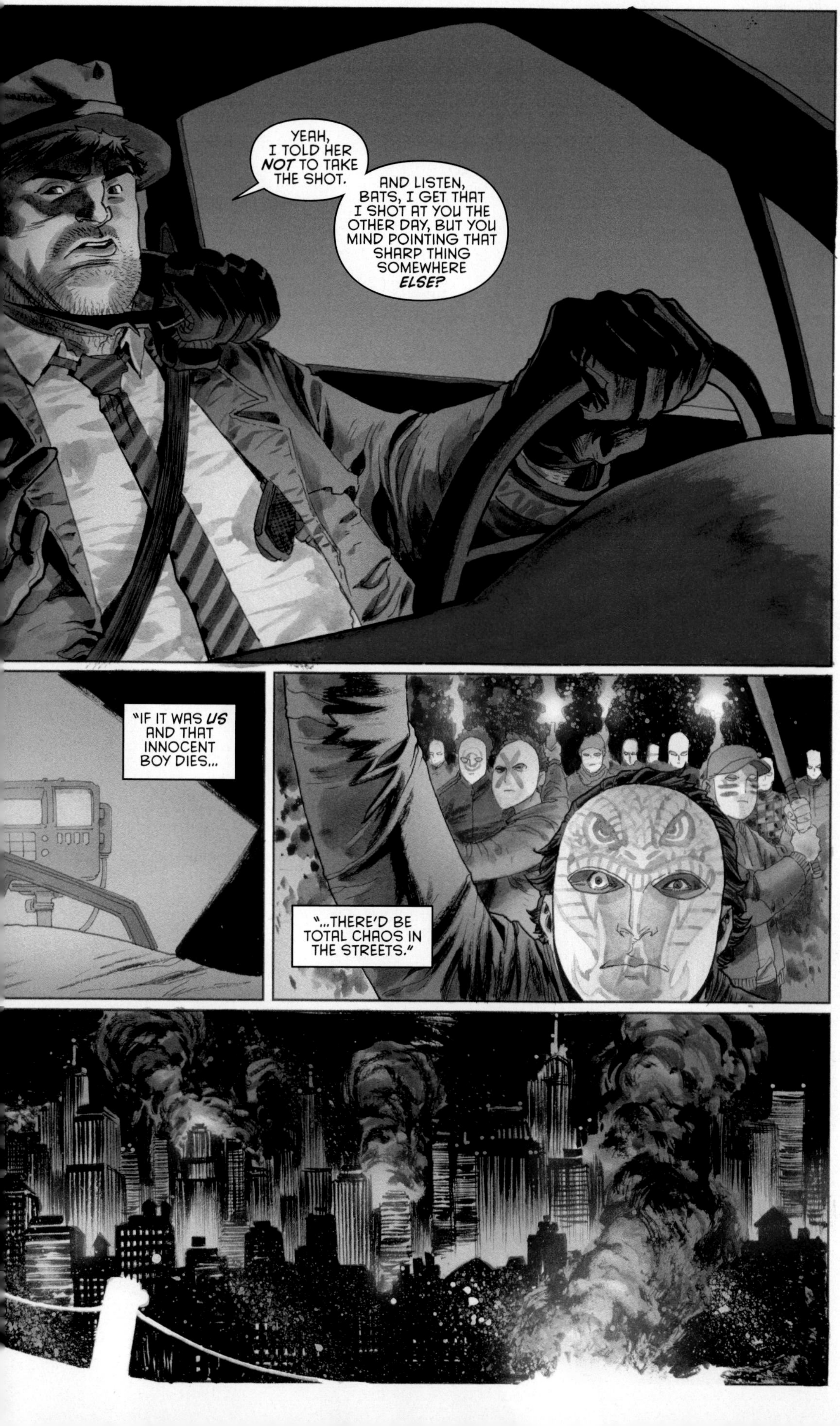
YEAH, I TOLD HER *NOT* TO TAKE THE SHOT.
AND LISTEN, BATS, I GET THAT I SHOT AT YOU THE OTHER DAY, BUT YOU MIND POINTING THAT SHARP THING SOMEWHERE *ELSE?*
"IF IT WAS *US* AND THAT INNOCENT BOY DIES...
"...THERE'D BE TOTAL CHAOS IN THE STREETS."

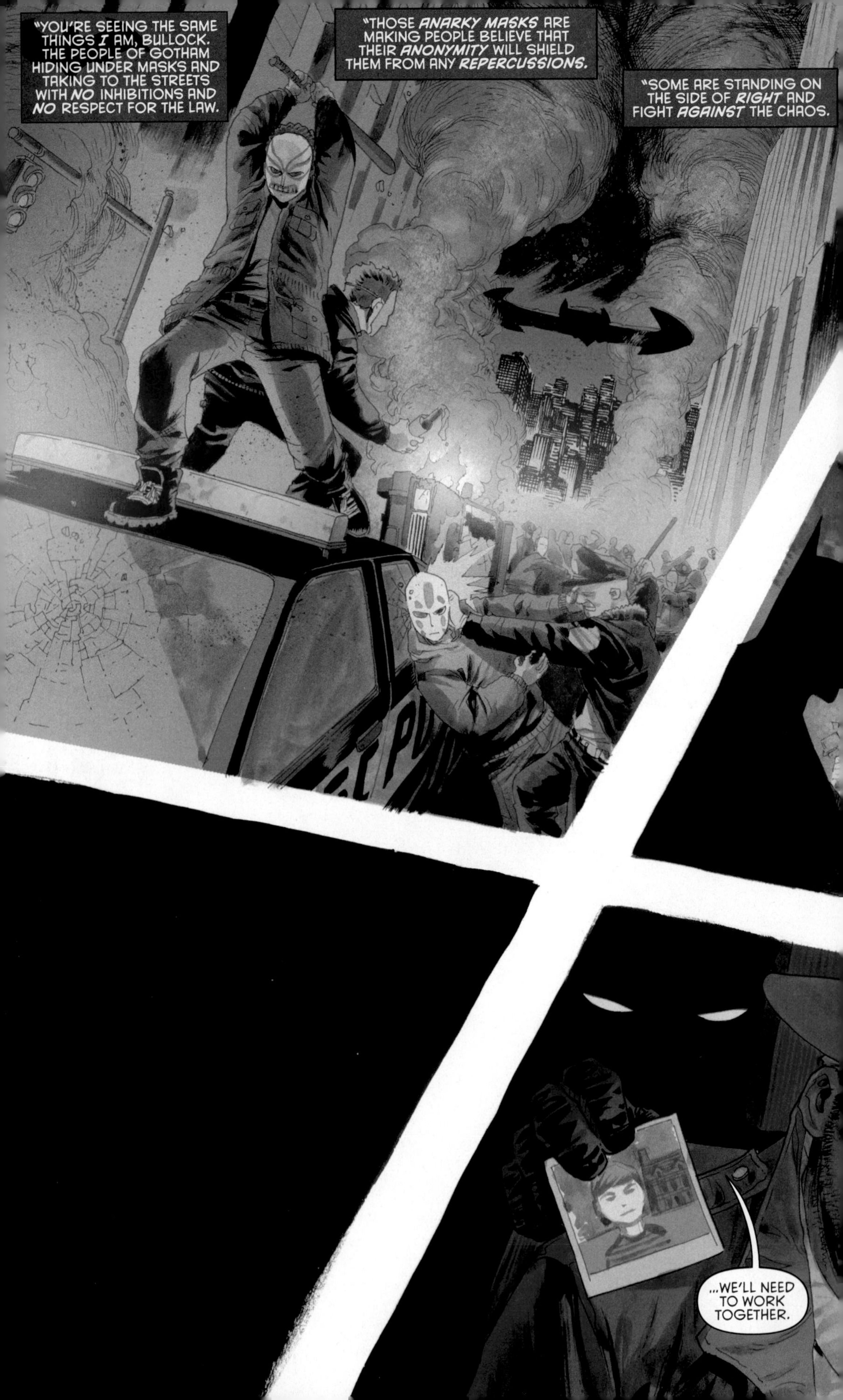

"YOU'RE SEEING THE SAME THINGS I AM, BULLOCK. THE PEOPLE OF GOTHAM HIDING UNDER MASKS AND TAKING TO THE STREETS WITH NO INHIBITIONS AND NO RESPECT FOR THE LAW.
"THOSE ANARKY MASKS ARE MAKING PEOPLE BELIEVE THAT THEIR ANONYMITY WILL SHIELD THEM FROM ANY REPERCUSSIONS.
"SOME ARE STANDING ON THE SIDE OF RIGHT AND FIGHT AGAINST THE CHAOS.
...WE'LL NEED TO WORK TOGETHER.

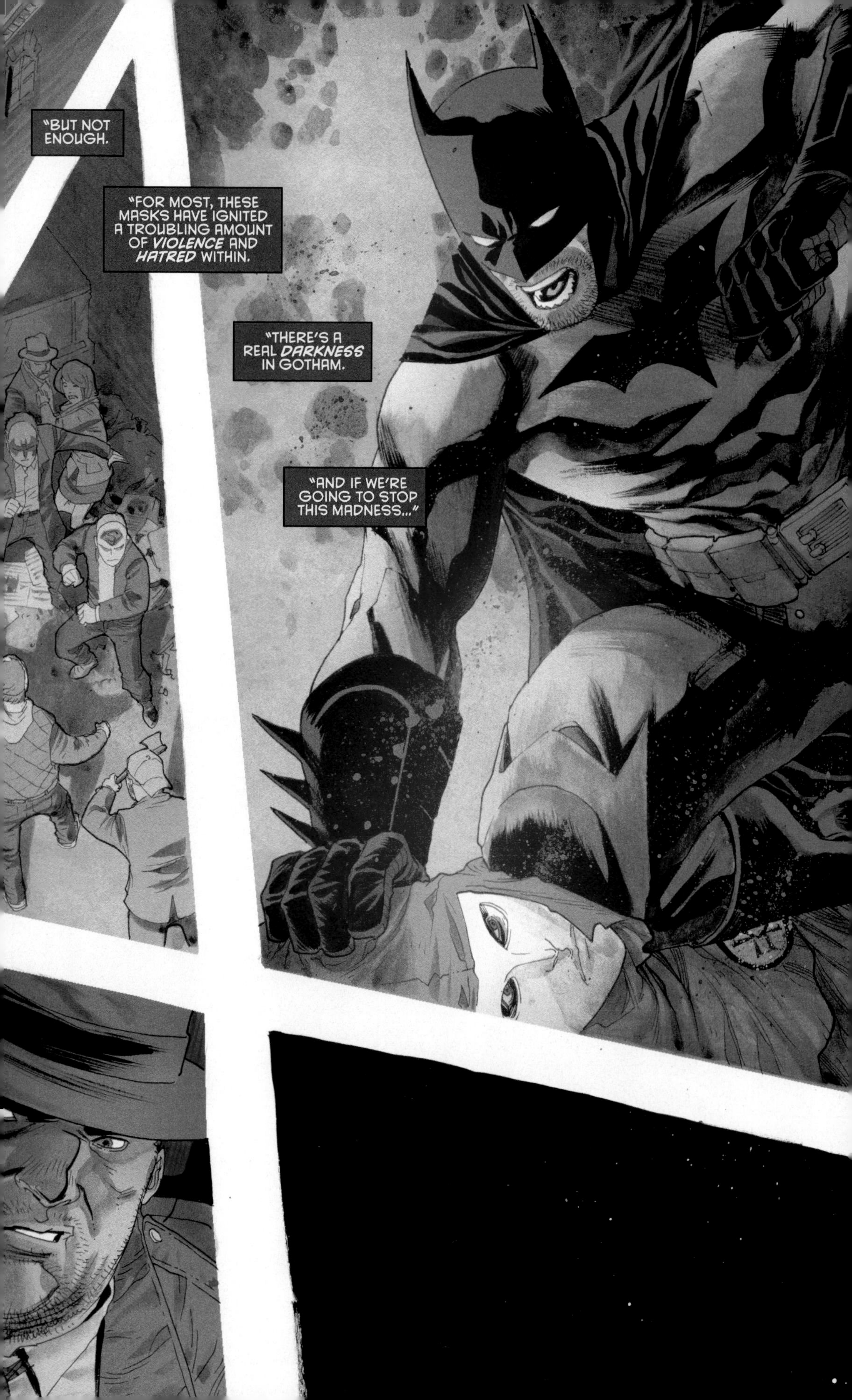
"BUT NOT ENOUGH.
"FOR MOST, THESE MASKS HAVE IGNITED A TROUBLING AMOUNT OF VIOLENCE AND HATRED WITHIN.
"THERE'S A REAL DARKNESS IN GOTHAM.
"AND IF WE'RE GOING TO STOP THIS MADNESS..."

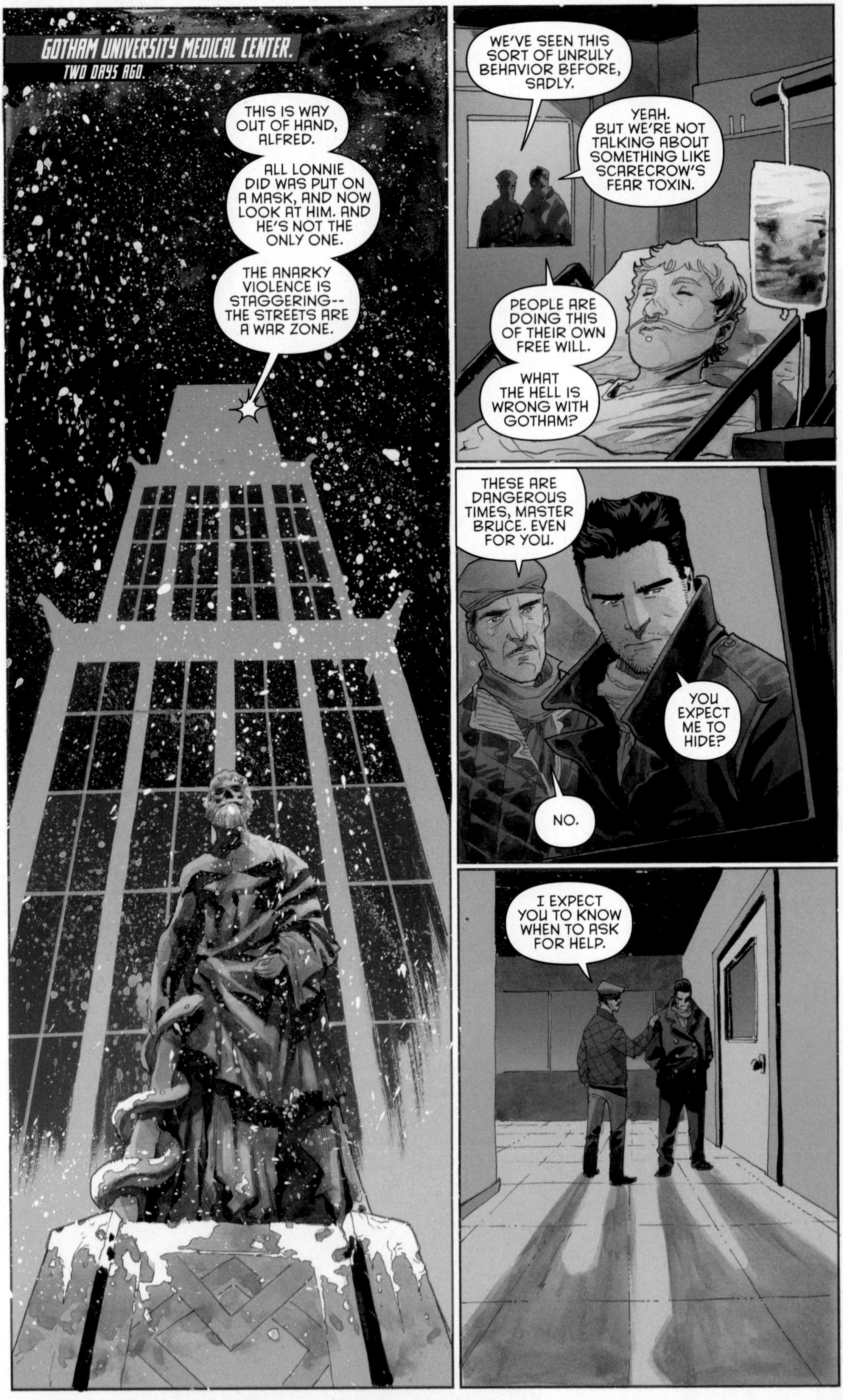
GOTHAM UNIVERSITY MEDICAL CENTER.
TWO DAYS AGO.
THIS IS WAY OUT OF HAND, ALFRED.
ALL LONNIE DID WAS PUT ON A MASK, AND NOW LOOK AT HIM. AND HE'S NOT THE ONLY ONE.
THE ANARKY VIOLENCE IS STAGGERING-- THE STREETS ARE A WAR ZONE.
WE'VE SEEN THIS SORT OF UNRULY BEHAVIOR BEFORE, SADLY.
YEAH. BUT WE'RE NOT TALKING ABOUT SOMETHING LIKE SCARECROW'S FEAR TOXIN.
PEOPLE ARE DOING THIS OF THEIR OWN FREE WILL.
WHAT THE HELL IS WRONG WITH GOTHAM?
THESE ARE DANGEROUS TIMES, MASTER BRUCE. EVEN FOR YOU.
YOU EXPECT ME TO HIDE?
NO.
I EXPECT YOU TO KNOW WHEN TO ASK FOR HELP.

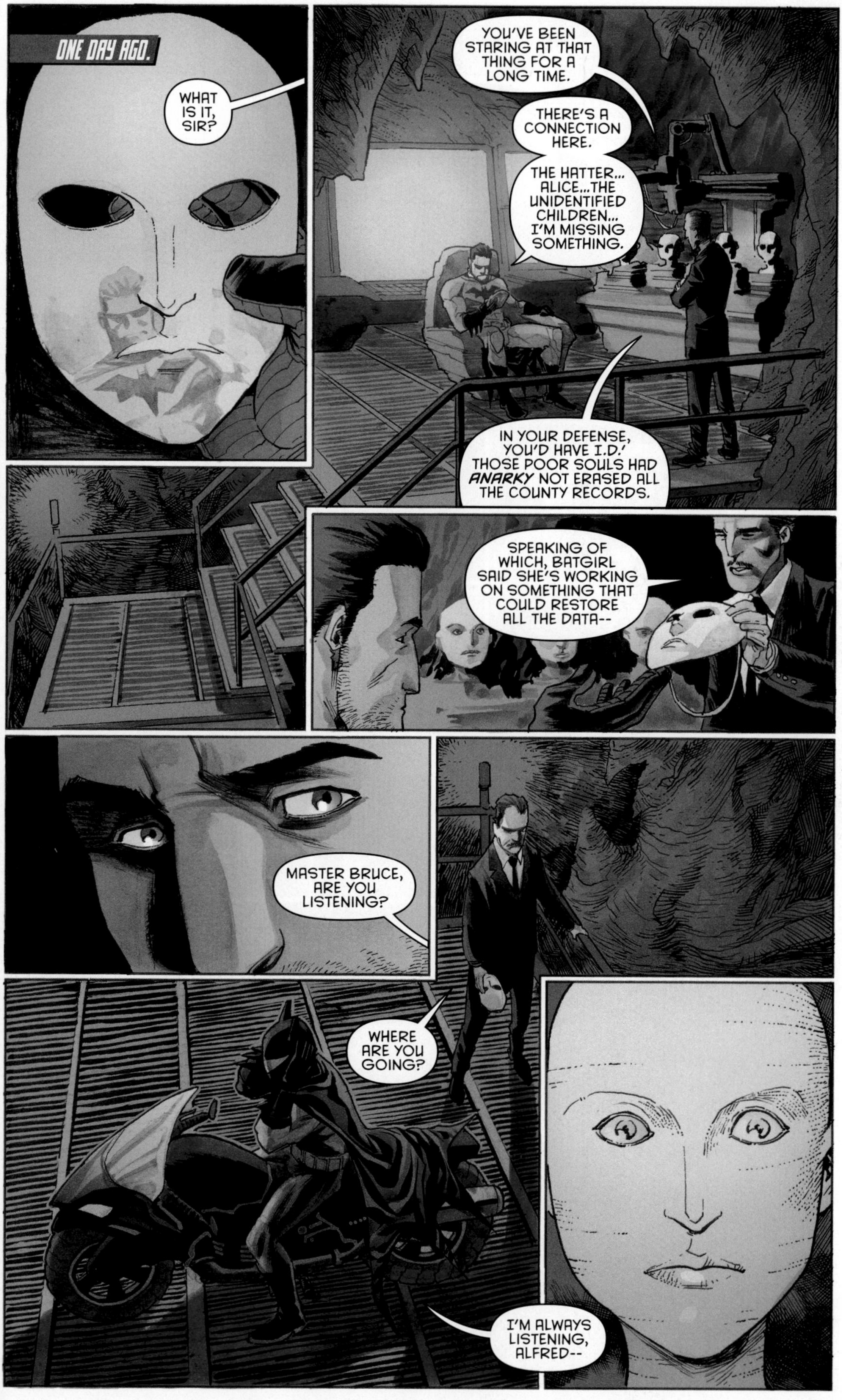
ONE DAY AGO.
WHAT IS IT, SIR?
YOU'VE BEEN STARING AT THAT THING FOR A LONG TIME.
THERE'S A CONNECTION HERE.
THE HATTER... ALICE...THE UNIDENTIFIED CHILDREN... I'M MISSING SOMETHING.
IN YOUR DEFENSE, YOU'D HAVE I.D.' THOSE POOR SOULS HAD ANARKY NOT ERASED ALL THE COUNTY RECORDS.
SPEAKING OF WHICH, BATGIRL SAID SHE'S WORKING ON SOMETHING THAT COULD RESTORE ALL THE DATA--
MASTER BRUCE, ARE YOU LISTENING?
WHERE ARE YOU GOING?
I'M ALWAYS LISTENING, ALFRED--

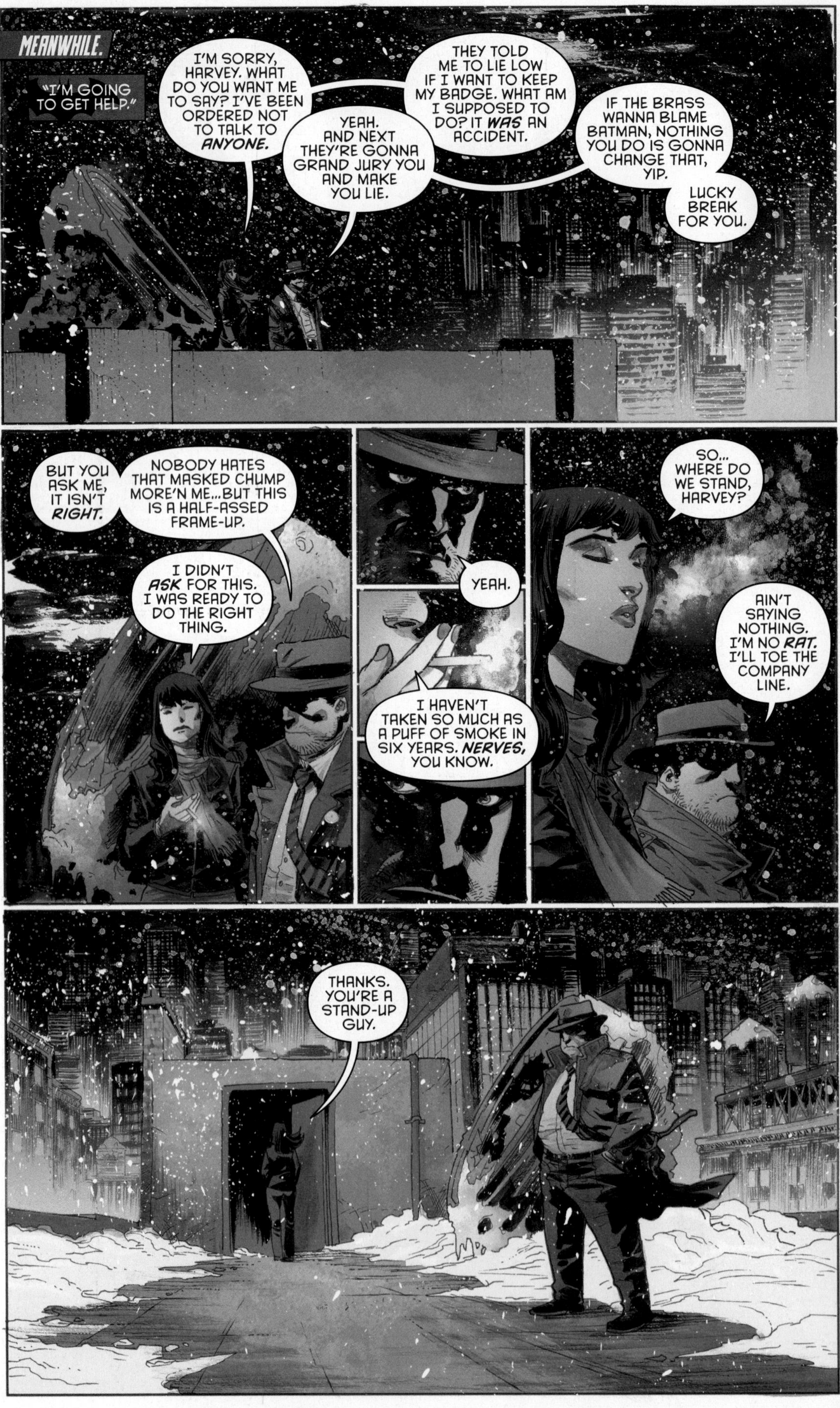
MEANWHILE.
"I'M GOING TO GET HELP."
I'M SORRY, HARVEY. WHAT DO YOU WANT ME TO SAY? I'VE BEEN ORDERED NOT TO TALK TO ANYONE.
YEAH. AND NEXT THEY'RE GONNA GRAND JURY YOU AND MAKE YOU LIE.
THEY TOLD ME TO LIE LOW IF I WANT TO KEEP MY BADGE. WHAT AM I SUPPOSED TO DO? IT WAS AN ACCIDENT.
IF THE BRASS WANNA BLAME BATMAN, NOTHING YOU DO IS GONNA CHANGE THAT, YIP.
LUCKY BREAK FOR YOU.
BUT YOU ASK ME, IT ISN'T RIGHT.
NOBODY HATES THAT MASKED CHUMP MORE'N ME...BUT THIS IS A HALF-ASSED FRAME-UP.
I DIDN'T ASK FOR THIS. I WAS READY TO DO THE RIGHT THING.
YEAH.
I HAVEN'T TAKEN SO MUCH AS A PUFF OF SMOKE IN SIX YEARS. NERVES, YOU KNOW.
SO... WHERE DO WE STAND, HARVEY?
AIN'T SAYING NOTHING. I'M NO RAT. I'LL TOE THE COMPANY LINE.
THANKS. YOU'RE A STAND-UP GUY.

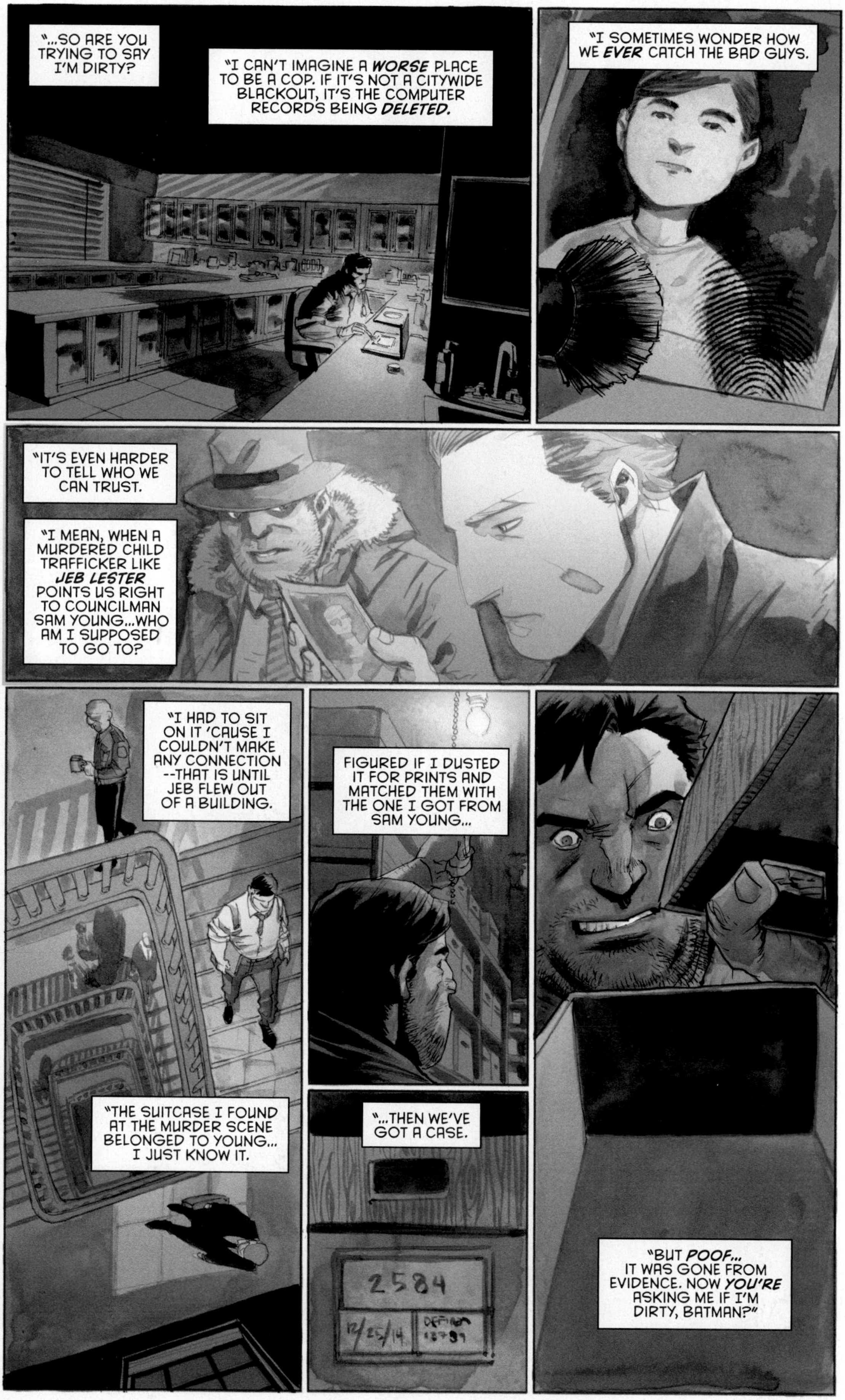
"...SO ARE YOU TRYING TO SAY I'M DIRTY?
"I CAN'T IMAGINE A **WORSE** PLACE TO BE A COP. IF IT'S NOT A CITYWIDE BLACKOUT, IT'S THE COMPUTER RECORDS BEING **DELETED.**
"I SOMETIMES WONDER HOW WE **EVER** CATCH THE BAD GUYS.
"IT'S EVEN HARDER TO TELL WHO WE CAN TRUST.
"I MEAN, WHEN A MURDERED CHILD TRAFFICKER LIKE **JEB LESTER** POINTS US RIGHT TO COUNCILMAN SAM YOUNG...WHO AM I SUPPOSED TO GO TO?
"I HAD TO SIT ON IT 'CAUSE I COULDN'T MAKE ANY CONNECTION --THAT IS UNTIL JEB FLEW OUT OF A BUILDING.
"THE SUITCASE I FOUND AT THE MURDER SCENE BELONGED TO YOUNG... I JUST KNOW IT.
FIGURED IF I DUSTED IT FOR PRINTS AND MATCHED THEM WITH THE ONE I GOT FROM SAM YOUNG...
"...THEN WE'VE GOT A CASE.
2584
12/25/14
"BUT **POOF...** IT WAS GONE FROM EVIDENCE. NOW **YOU'RE** ASKING ME IF I'M DIRTY, BATMAN?"

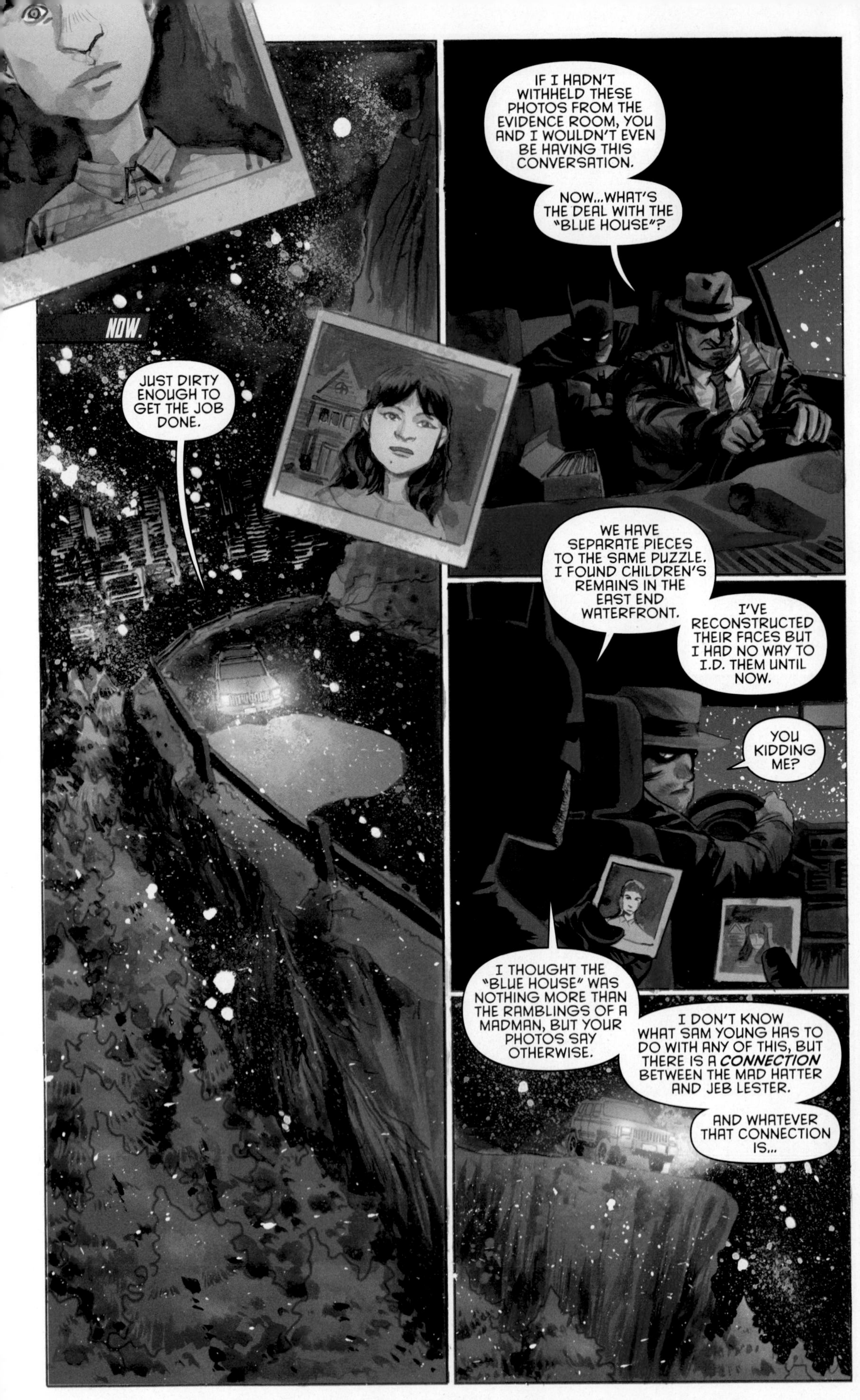
NOW.
JUST DIRTY ENOUGH TO GET THE JOB DONE.
IF I HADN'T WITHHELD THESE PHOTOS FROM THE EVIDENCE ROOM, YOU AND I WOULDN'T EVEN BE HAVING THIS CONVERSATION.
NOW...WHAT'S THE DEAL WITH THE "BLUE HOUSE"?
WE HAVE SEPARATE PIECES TO THE SAME PUZZLE. I FOUND CHILDREN'S REMAINS IN THE EAST END WATERFRONT.
I'VE RECONSTRUCTED THEIR FACES BUT I HAD NO WAY TO I.D. THEM UNTIL NOW.
YOU KIDDING ME?
I THOUGHT THE "BLUE HOUSE" WAS NOTHING MORE THAN THE RAMBLINGS OF A MADMAN, BUT YOUR PHOTOS SAY OTHERWISE.
I DON'T KNOW WHAT SAM YOUNG HAS TO DO WITH ANY OF THIS, BUT THERE IS A *CONNECTION* BETWEEN THE MAD HATTER AND JEB LESTER.
AND WHATEVER THAT CONNECTION IS...

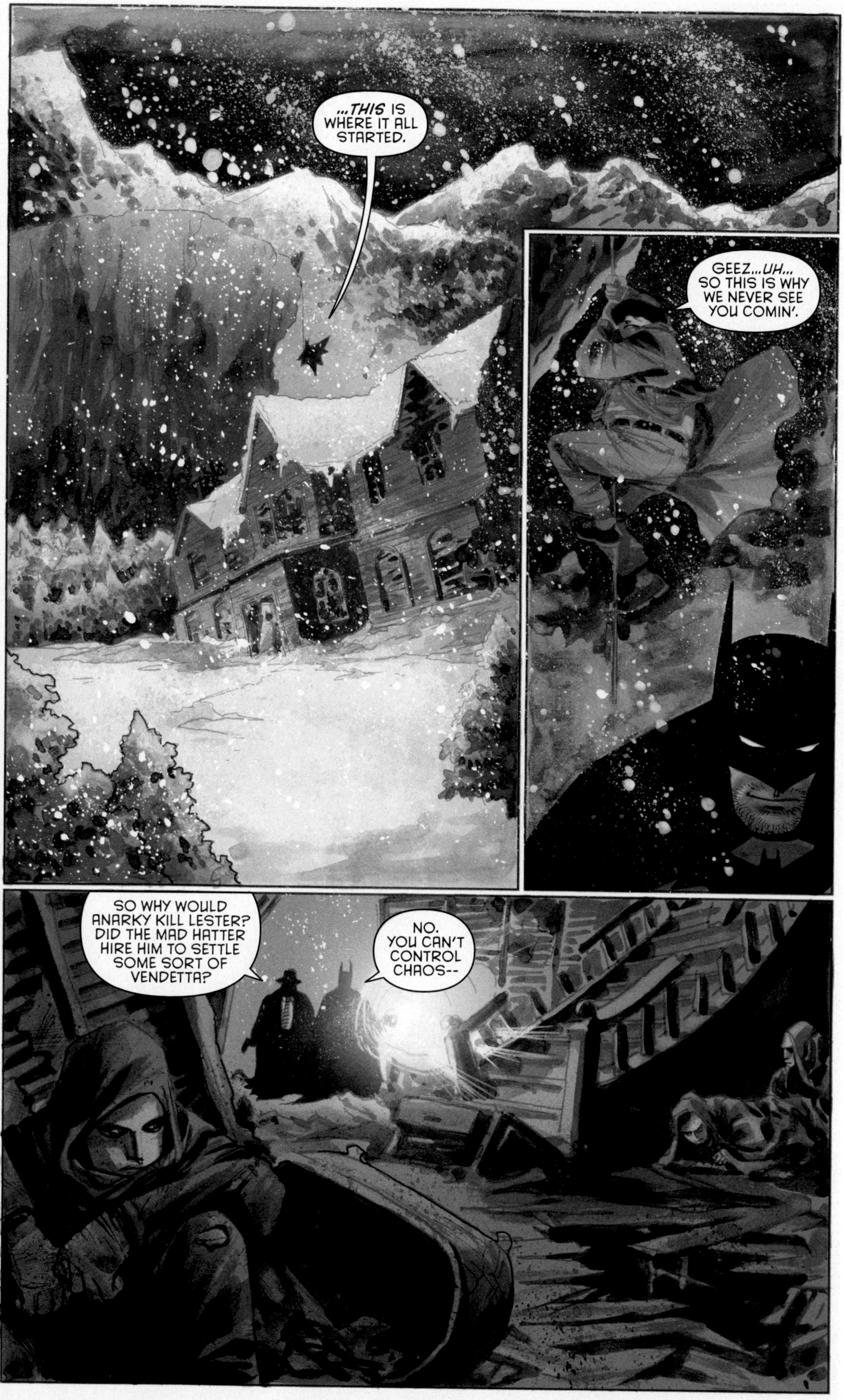
...THIS IS WHERE IT ALL STARTED.
GEEZ...UH... SO THIS IS WHY WE NEVER SEE YOU COMIN'.
SO WHY WOULD ANARKY KILL LESTER? DID THE MAD HATTER HIRE HIM TO SETTLE SOME SORT OF VENDETTA?
NO. YOU CAN'T CONTROL CHAOS--

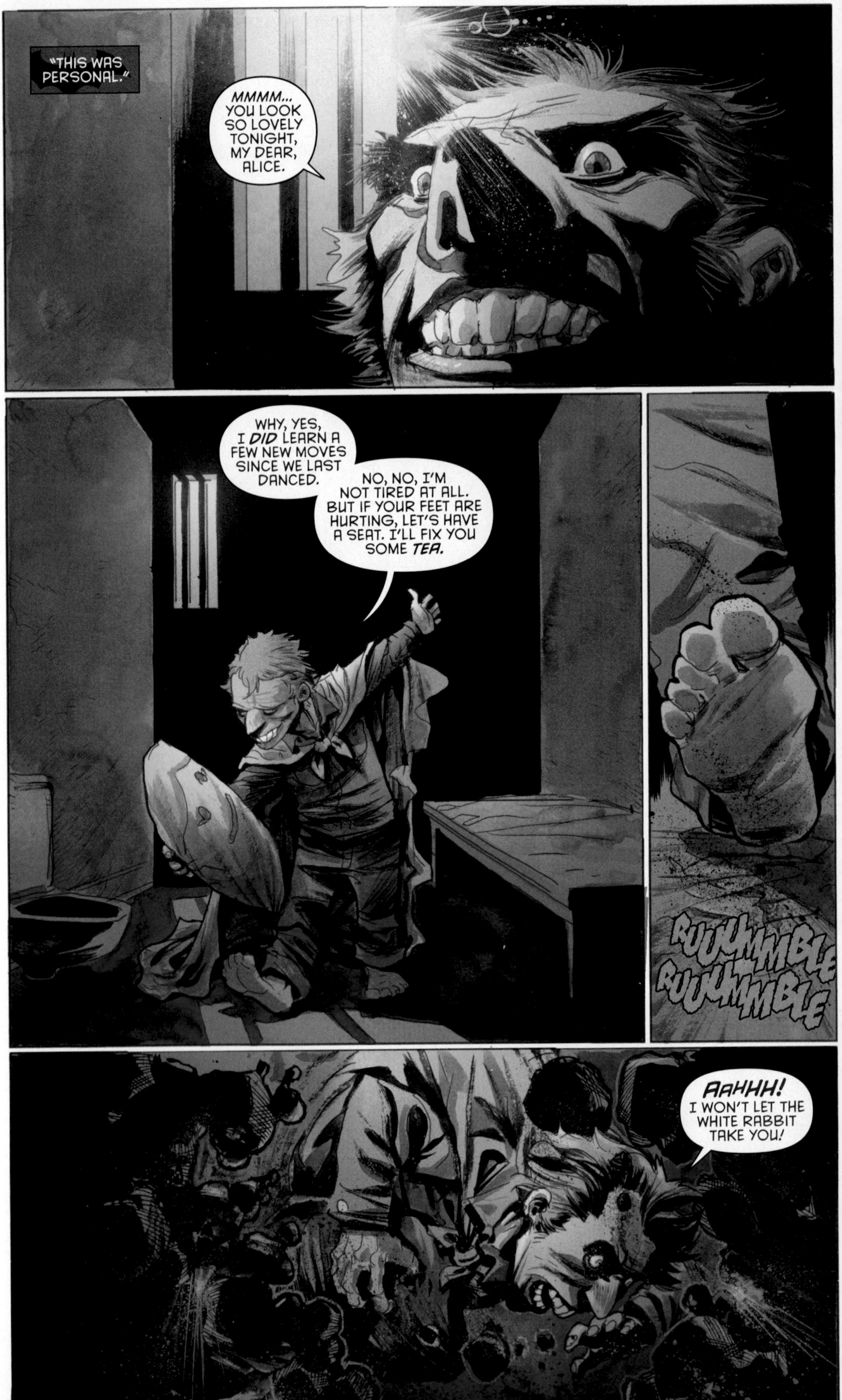
"THIS WAS PERSONAL."
MMMM... YOU LOOK SO LOVELY TONIGHT, MY DEAR, ALICE.
WHY, YES, I DID LEARN A FEW NEW MOVES SINCE WE LAST DANCED.
NO, NO, I'M NOT TIRED AT ALL. BUT IF YOUR FEET ARE HURTING, LET'S HAVE A SEAT. I'LL FIX YOU SOME TEA.
RUUMMBLE RUUMMBLE
AAHHH! I WON'T LET THE WHITE RABBIT TAKE YOU!

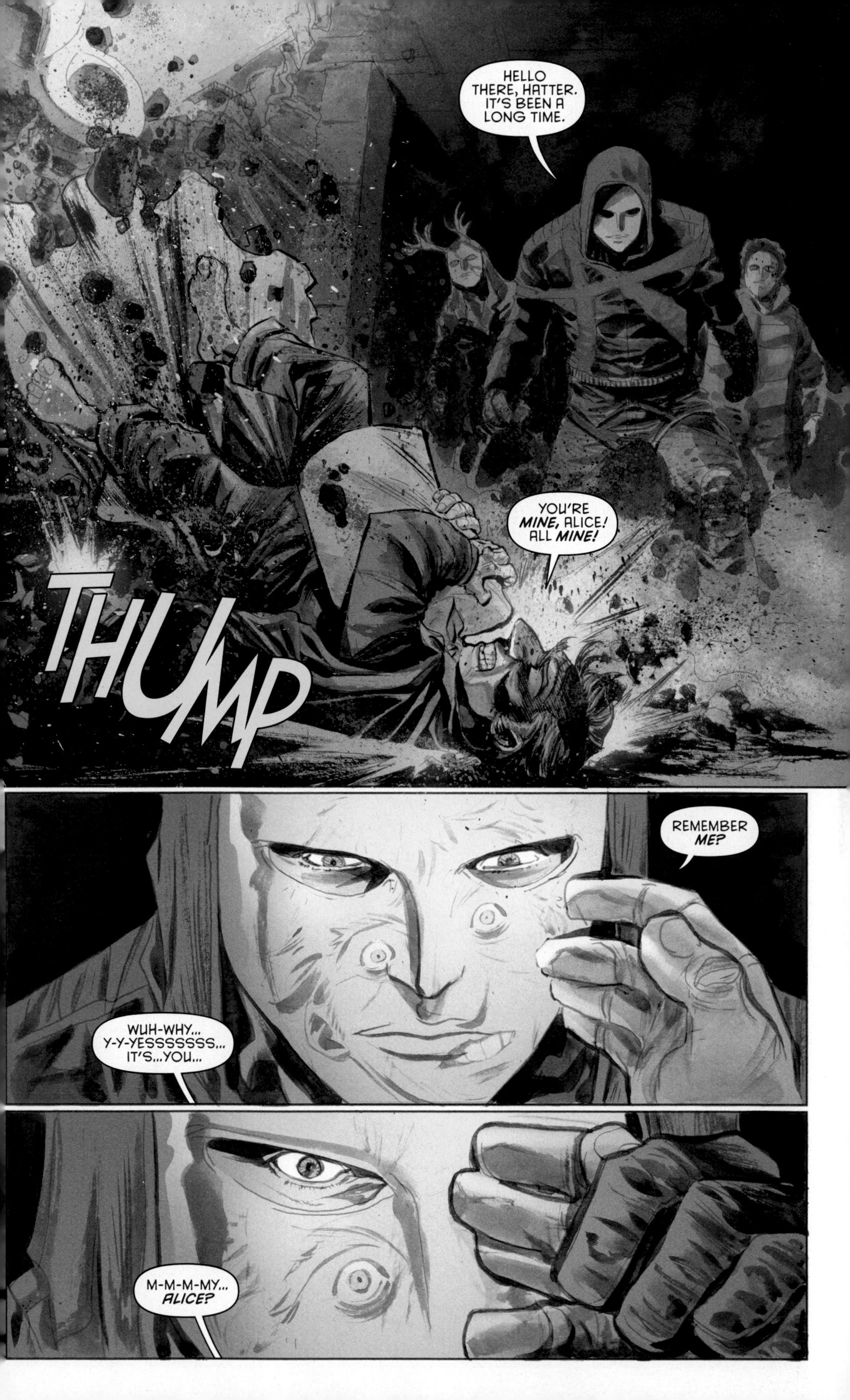
HELLO THERE, HATTER. IT'S BEEN A LONG TIME.
YOU'RE MINE, ALICE! ALL MINE!
THUMP
REMEMBER ME?
WUH-WHY... Y-Y-YESSSSSSS... IT'S...YOU...
M-M-M-MY... ALICE?

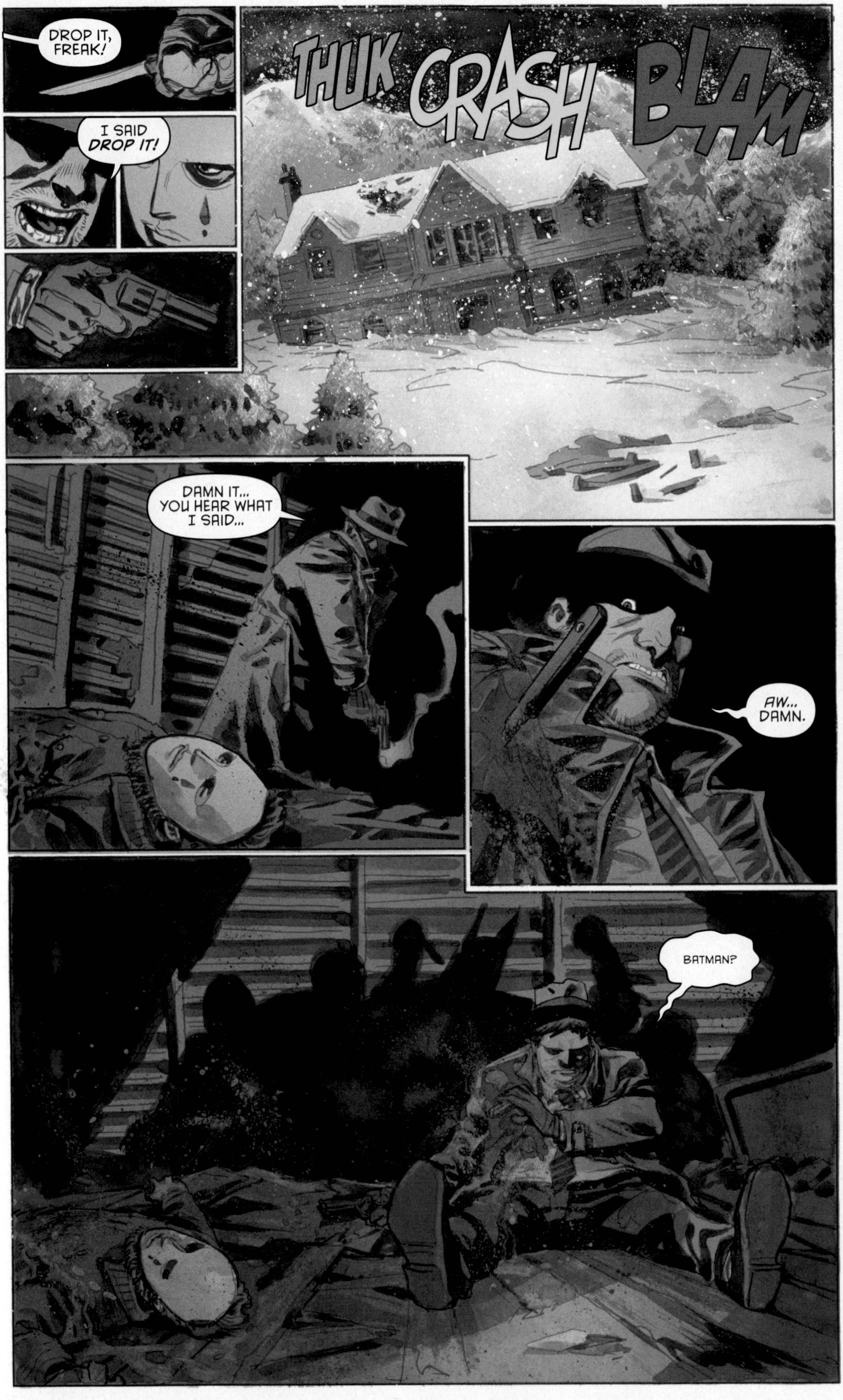
DROP IT, FREAK!
I SAID DROP IT!
THUK
CRASH
BLAM
DAMN IT... YOU HEAR WHAT I SAID...
AW... DAMN.
BATMAN?

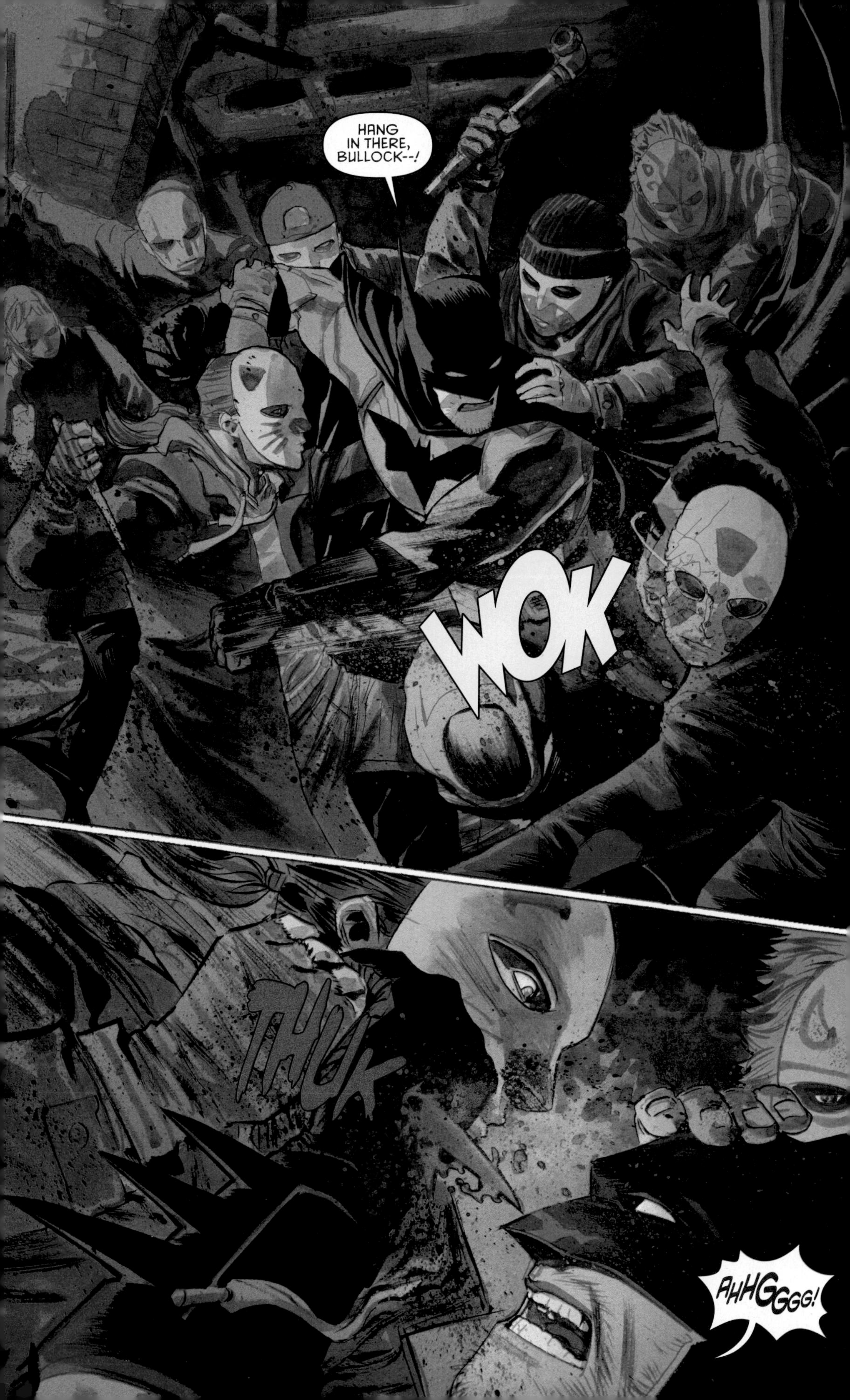
HANG IN THERE, BULLOCK--!
WOK
THUK
AHHGGGG!

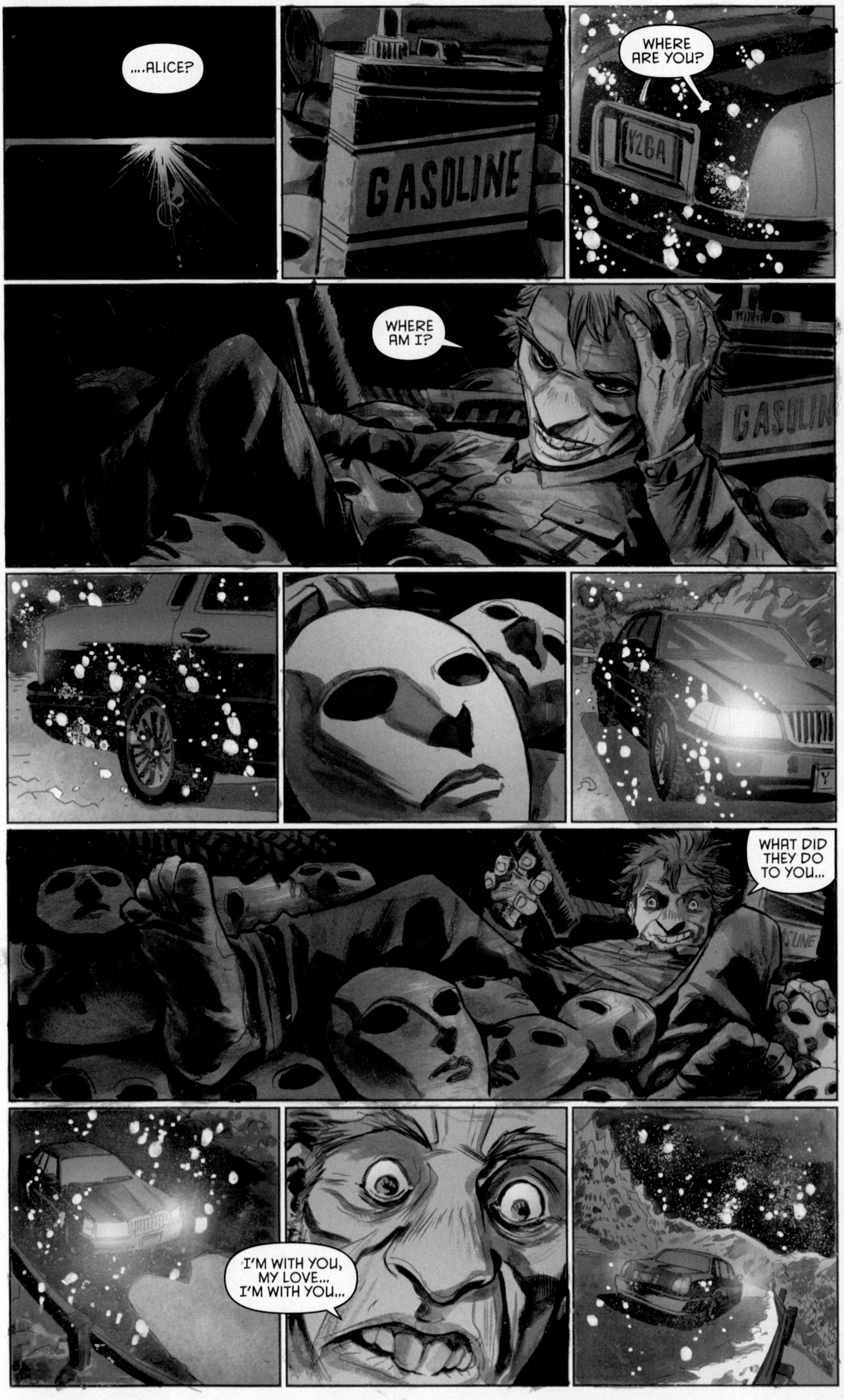
....ALICE?
GASOLINE
WHERE ARE YOU?
Y2BA
WHERE AM I?
GASOLINE
WHAT DID THEY DO TO YOU...
I'M WITH YOU, MY LOVE... I'M WITH YOU...

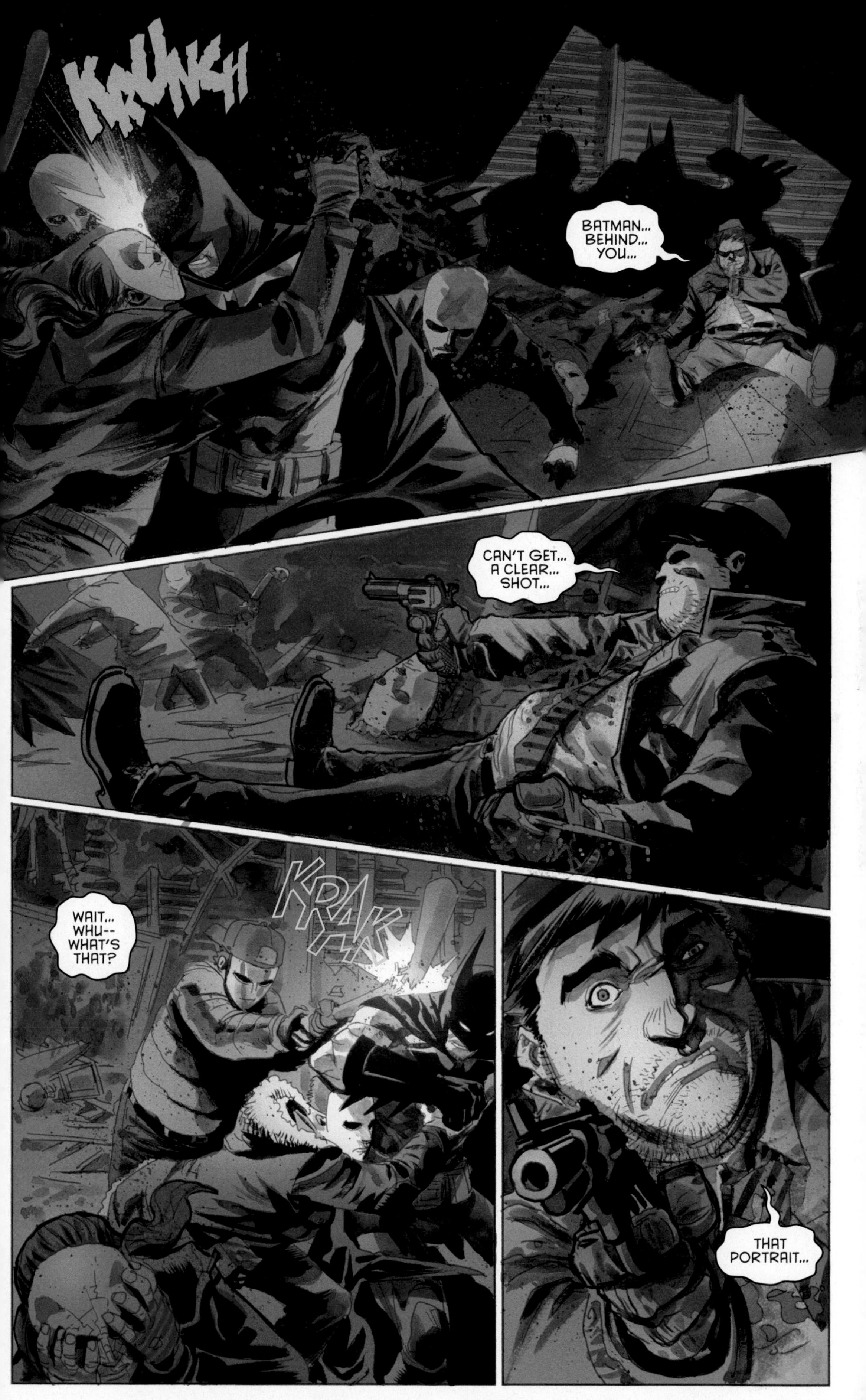
KRUNCH
BATMAN... BEHIND... YOU...
CAN'T GET... A CLEAR... SHOT...
WAIT... WHU-- WHAT'S THAT?
KRAK
THAT PORTRAIT...

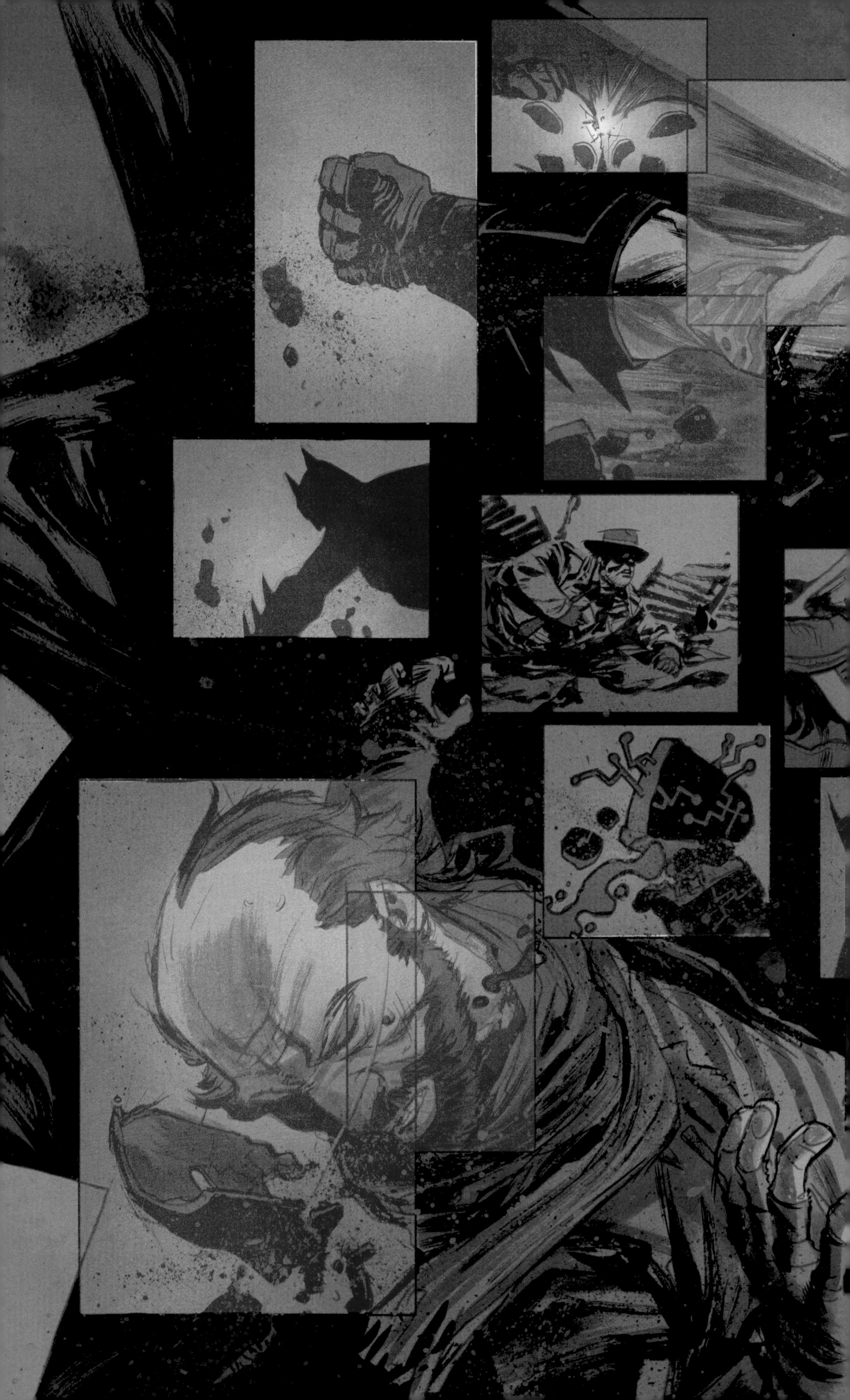

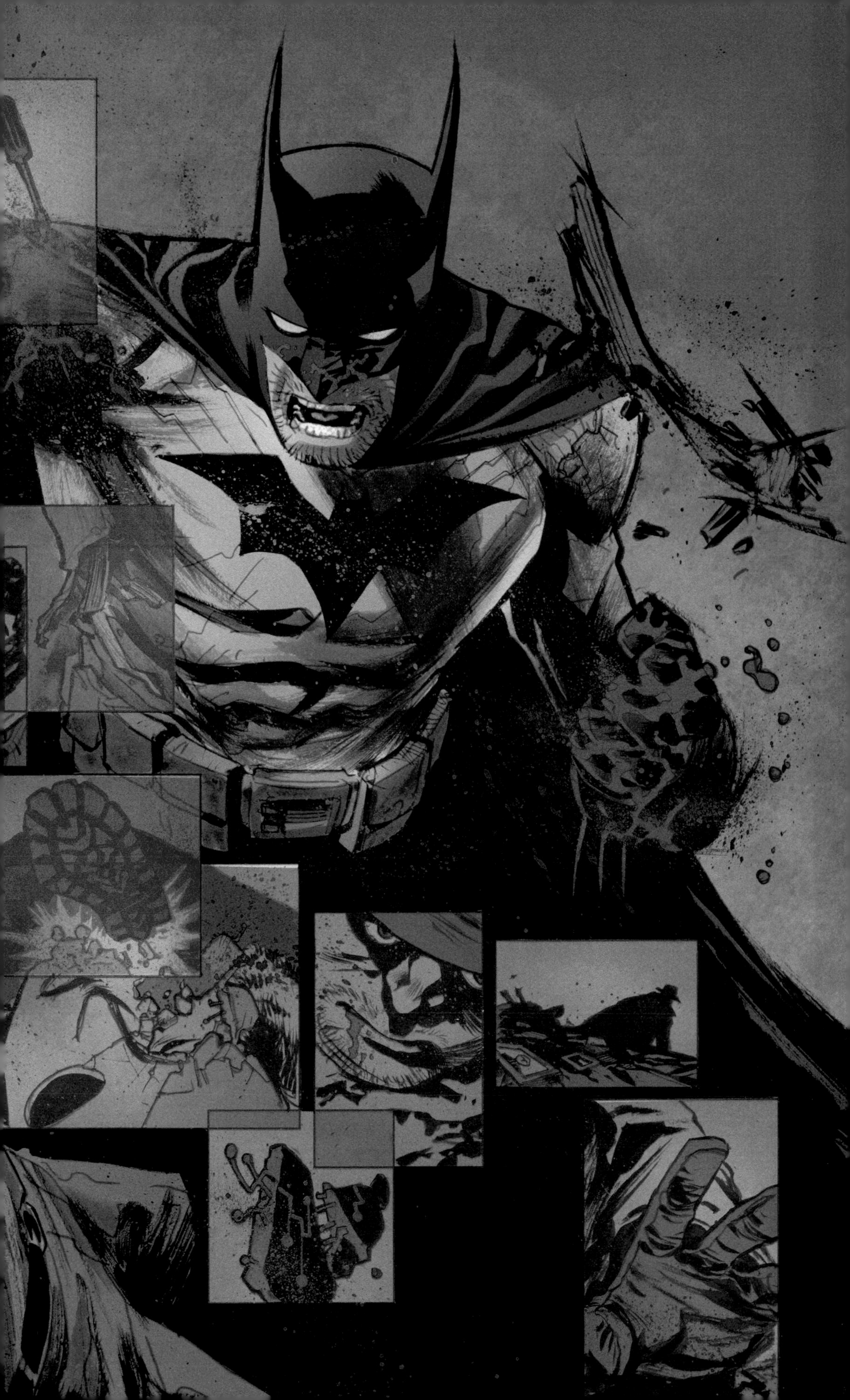

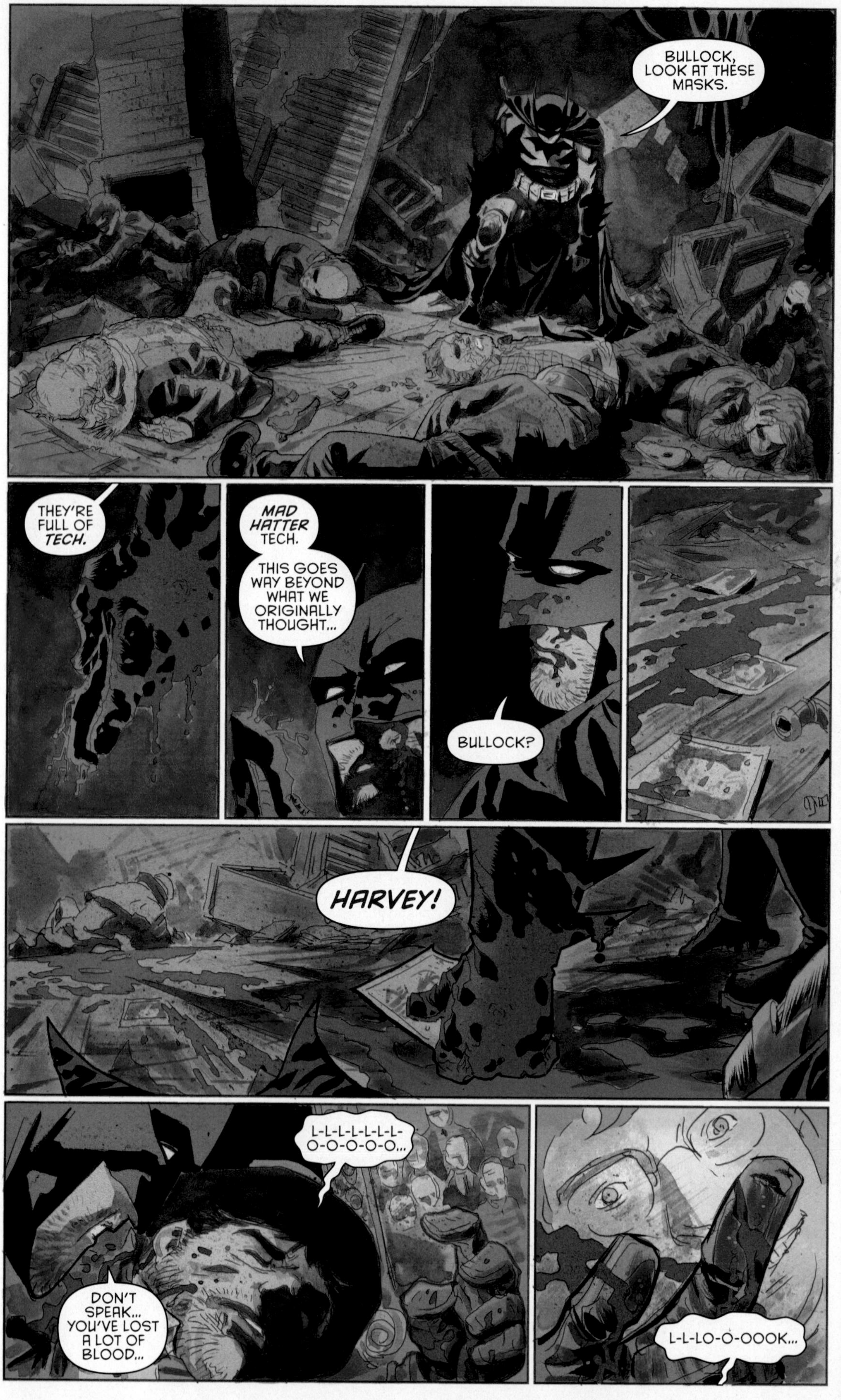
BULLOCK, LOOK AT THESE MASKS.
THEY'RE FULL OF *TECH.*
MAD HATTER TECH.
THIS GOES WAY BEYOND WHAT WE ORIGINALLY THOUGHT...
BULLOCK?
HARVEY!
L-L-L-L-L-L-L-O-O-O-O-O...
DON'T SPEAK... YOU'VE LOST A LOT OF BLOOD...
L-L-LO-O-OOOK...

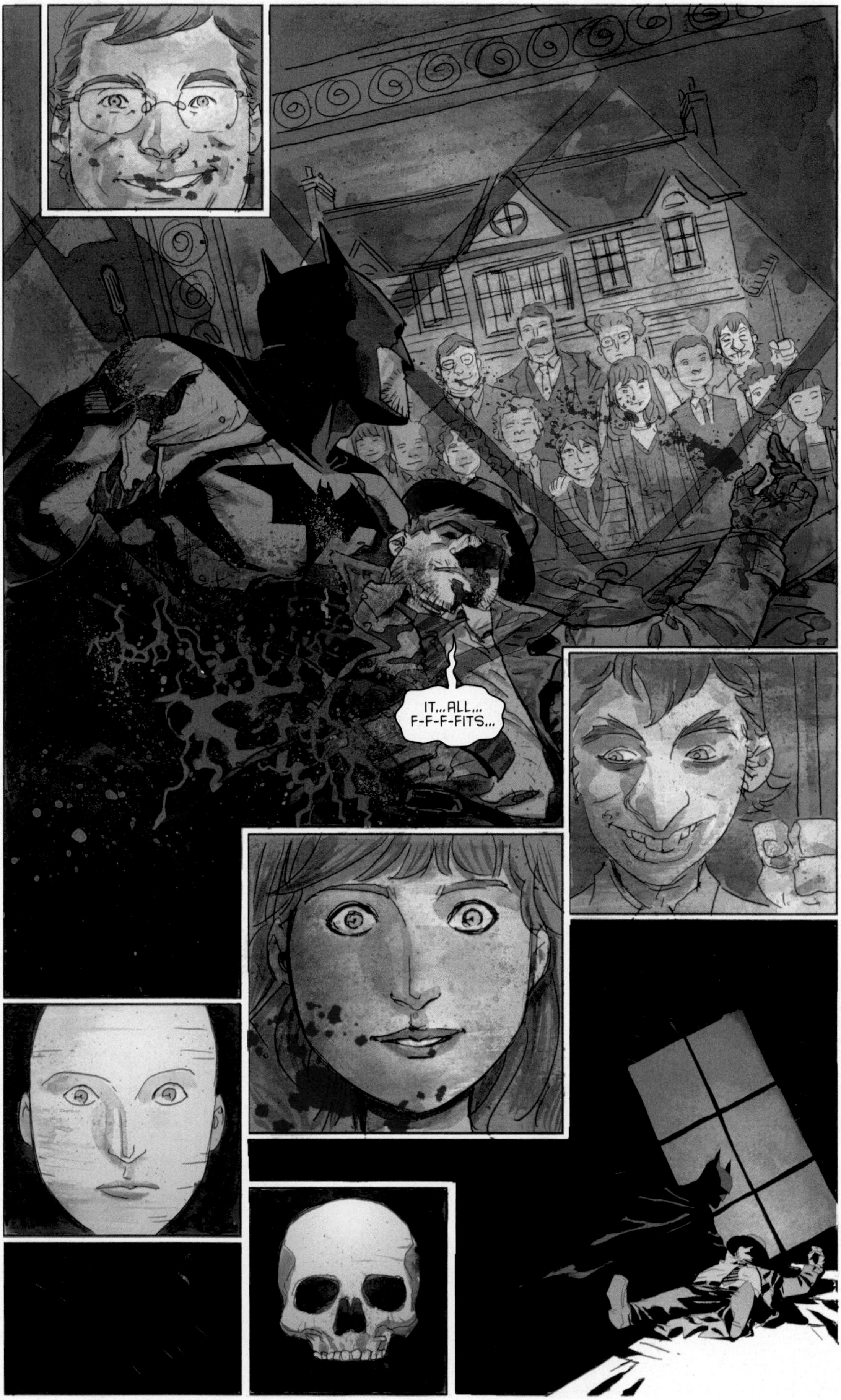
IT...ALL...
F-F-F-FITS...

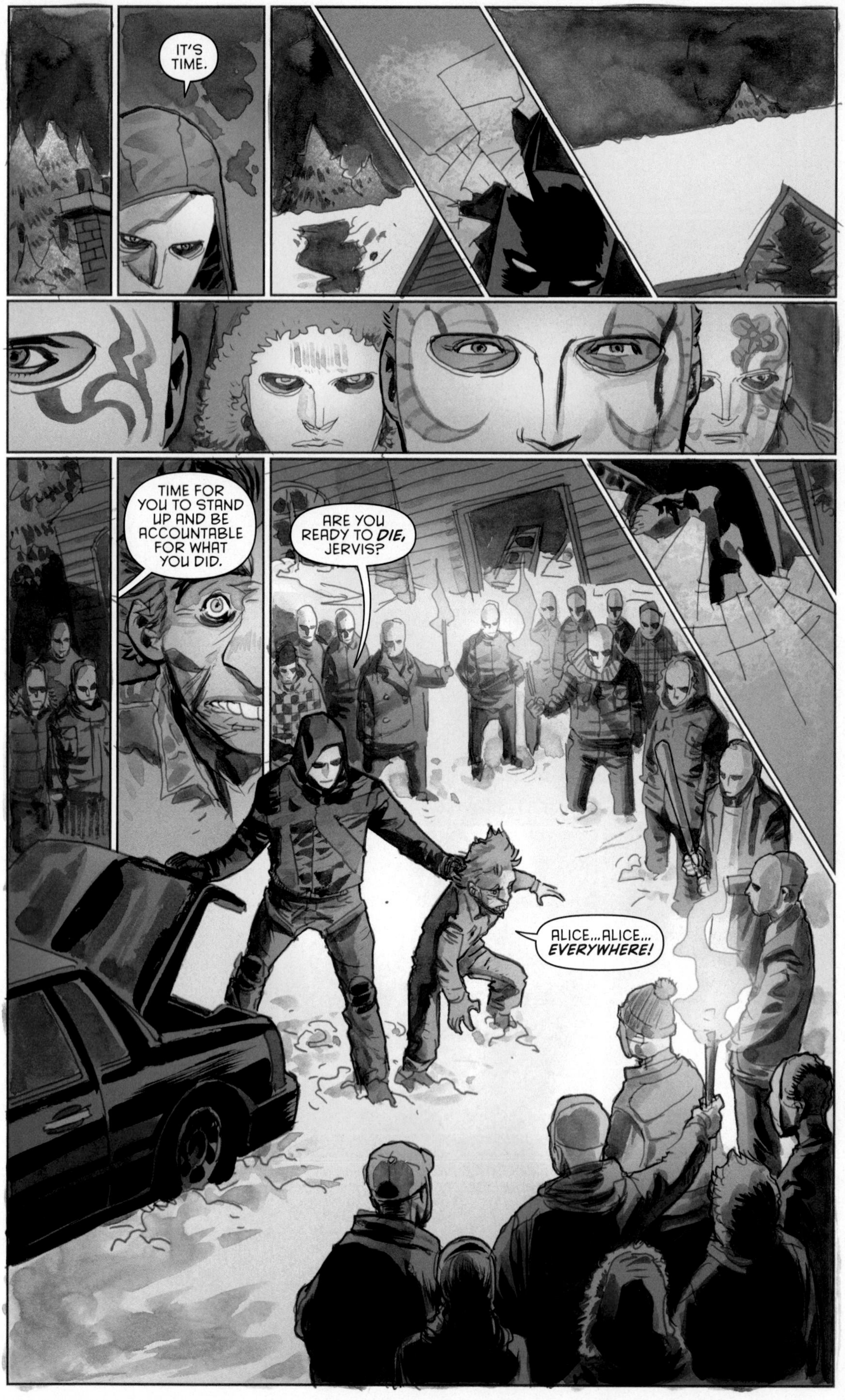
IT'S TIME.
TIME FOR YOU TO STAND UP AND BE ACCOUNTABLE FOR WHAT YOU DID.
ARE YOU READY TO *DIE,* JERVIS?
ALICE...ALICE... *EVERYWHERE!*

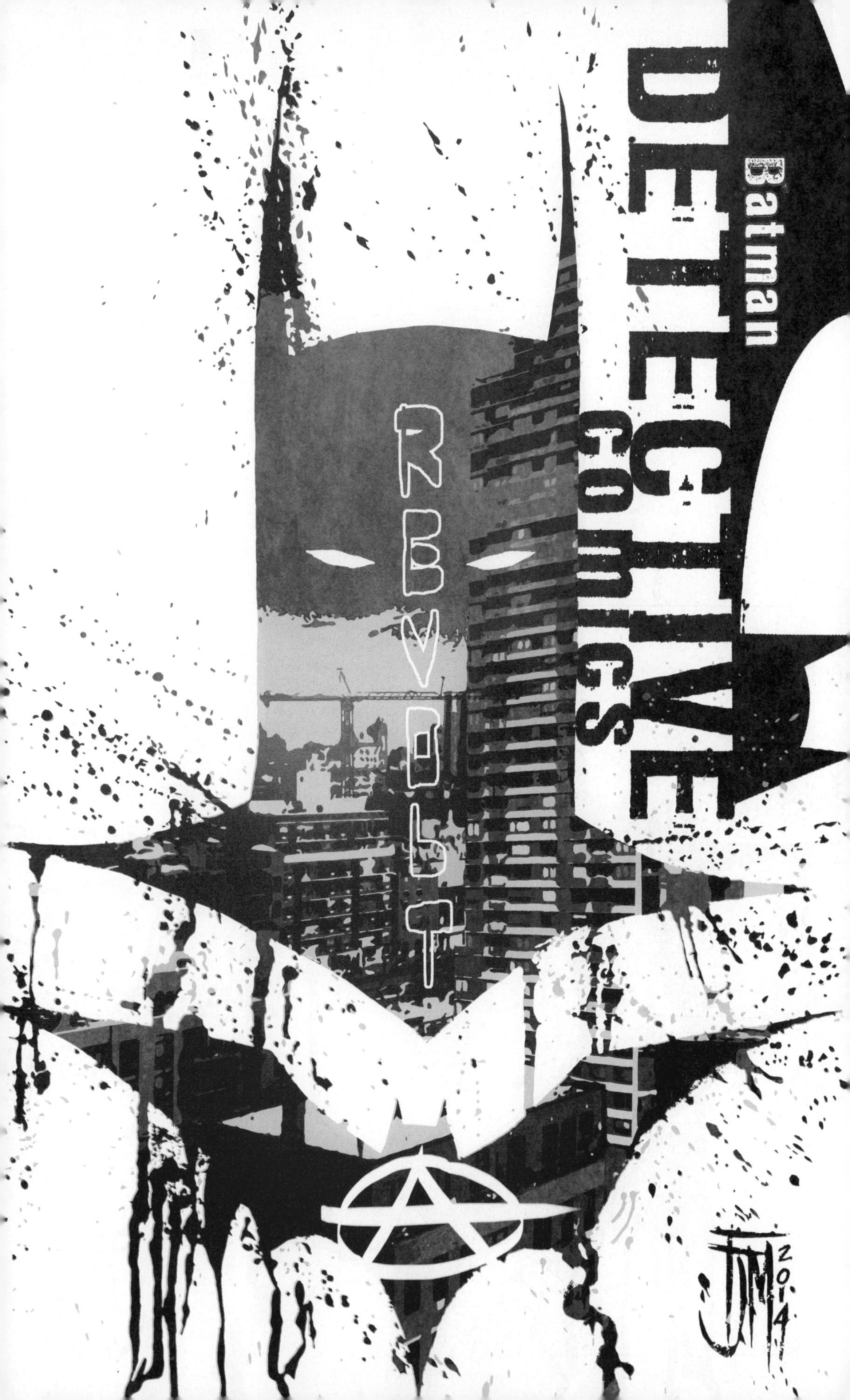
Batman
DETECTIVE COMICS
REVOLT
2014

ANARKY CONCLUSION

FRANCIS MANAPUL & BRIAN BUCCELLATO writers FRANCIS MANAPUL artist BRIAN BUCCELLATO colorist JARED K. FLETCHER letterer cover by FRANCIS MANAPUL

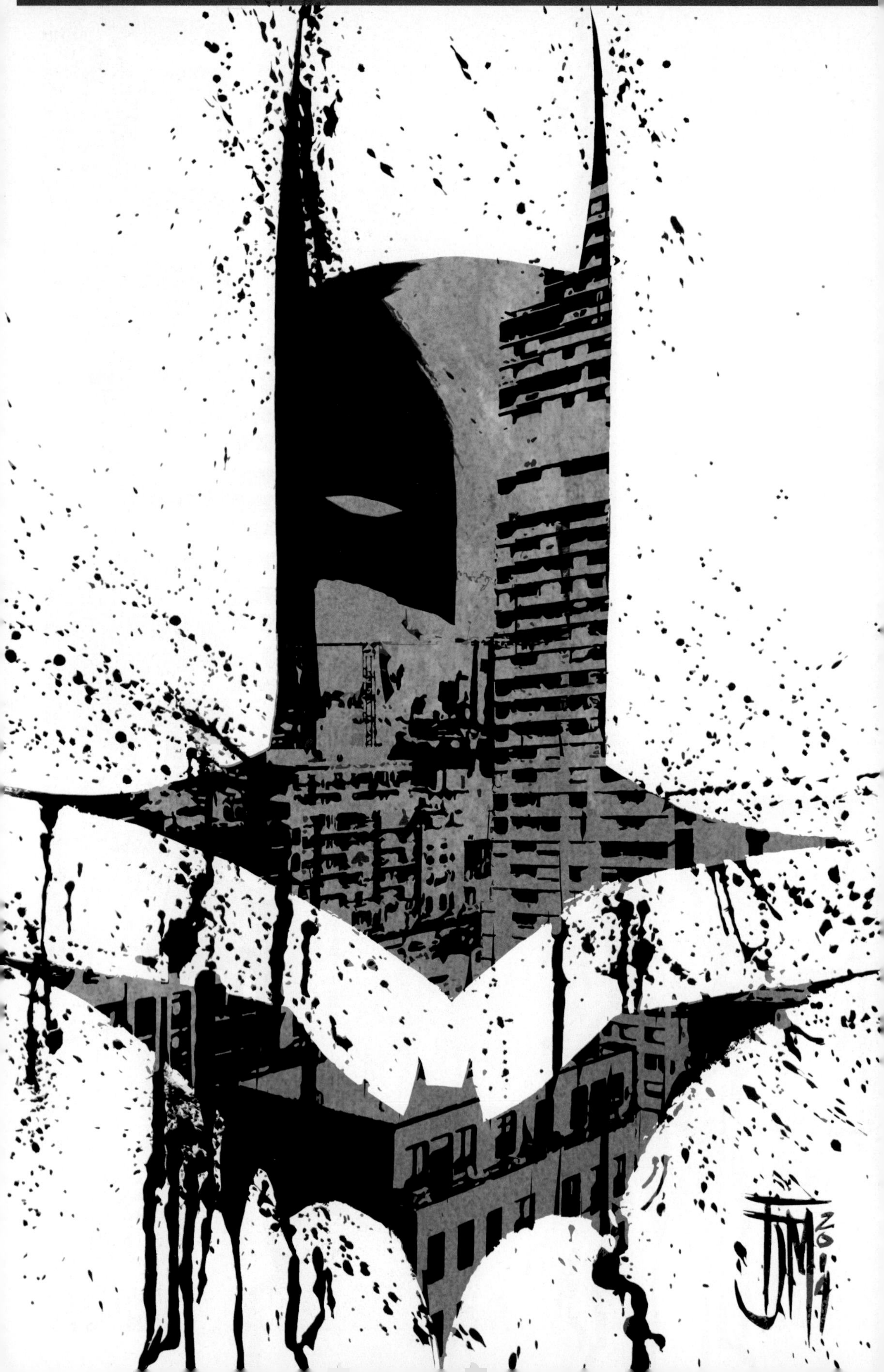

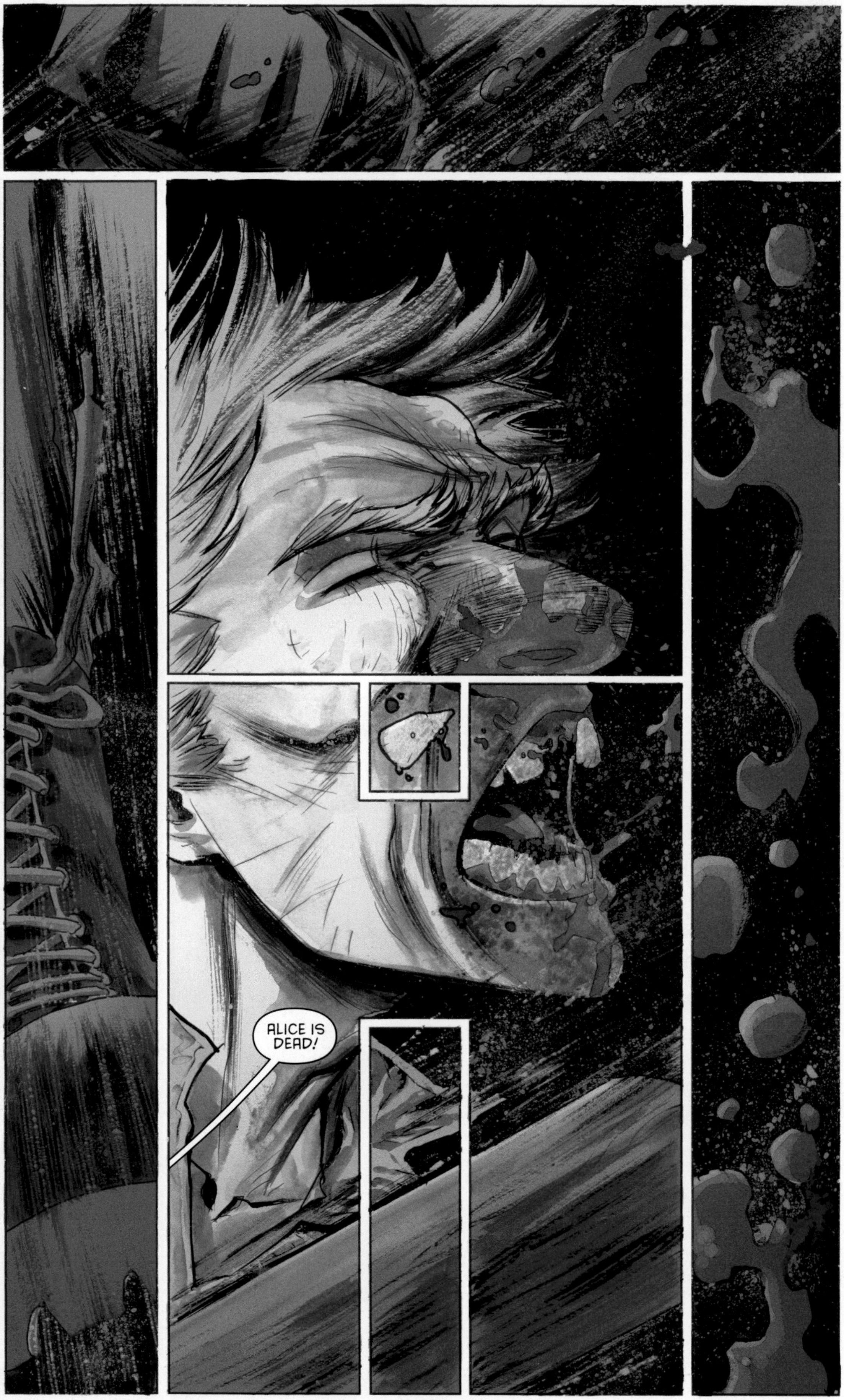
ALICE IS DEAD!

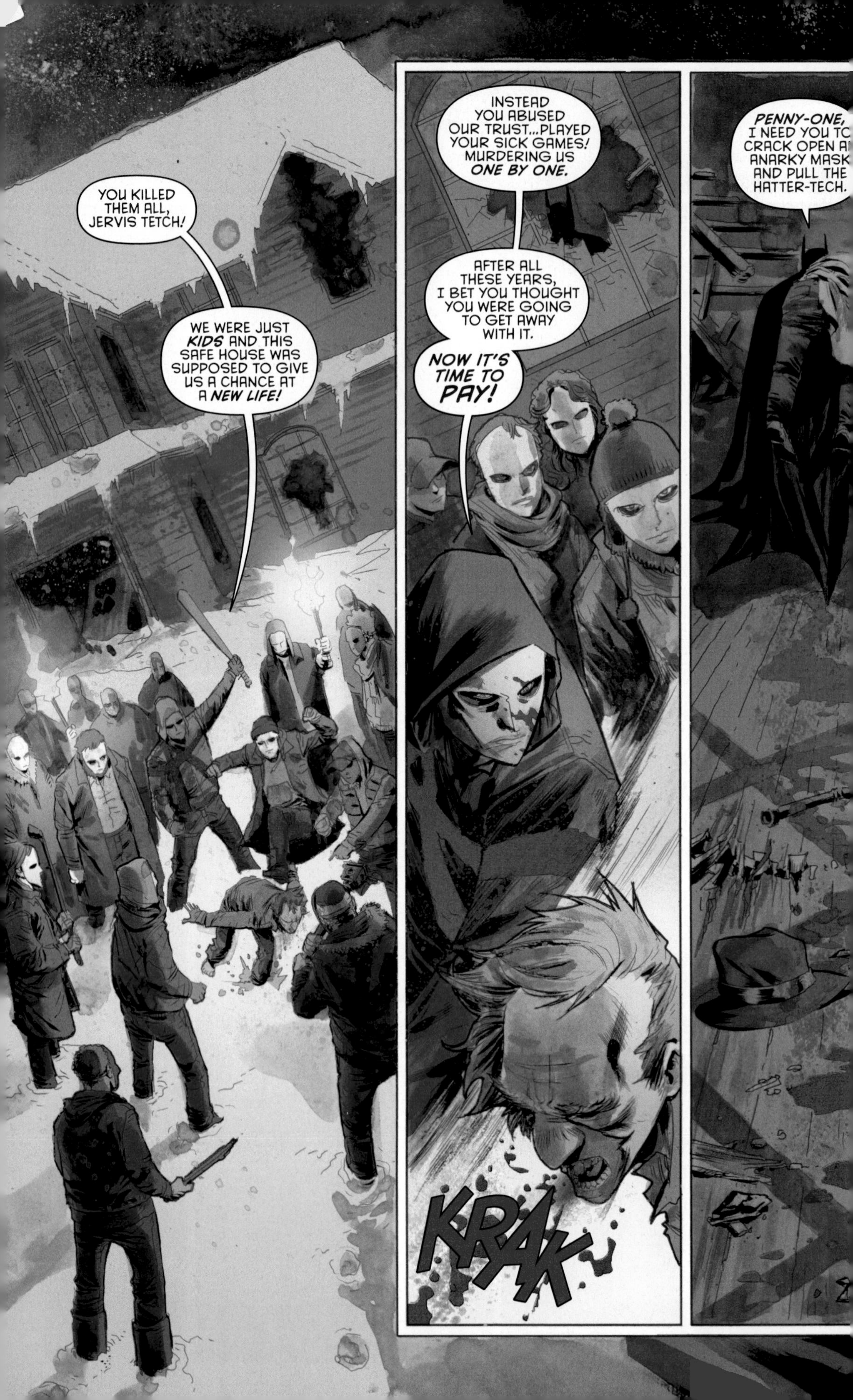
YOU KILLED THEM ALL, JERVIS TETCH!
WE WERE JUST KIDS AND THIS SAFE HOUSE WAS SUPPOSED TO GIVE US A CHANCE AT A NEW LIFE!
INSTEAD YOU ABUSED OUR TRUST...PLAYED YOUR SICK GAMES! MURDERING US ONE BY ONE.
AFTER ALL THESE YEARS, I BET YOU THOUGHT YOU WERE GOING TO GET AWAY WITH IT.
NOW IT'S TIME TO PAY!
KRAK
PENNY-ONE, I NEED YOU TO CRACK OPEN AN ANARKY MASK AND PULL THE HATTER-TECH.

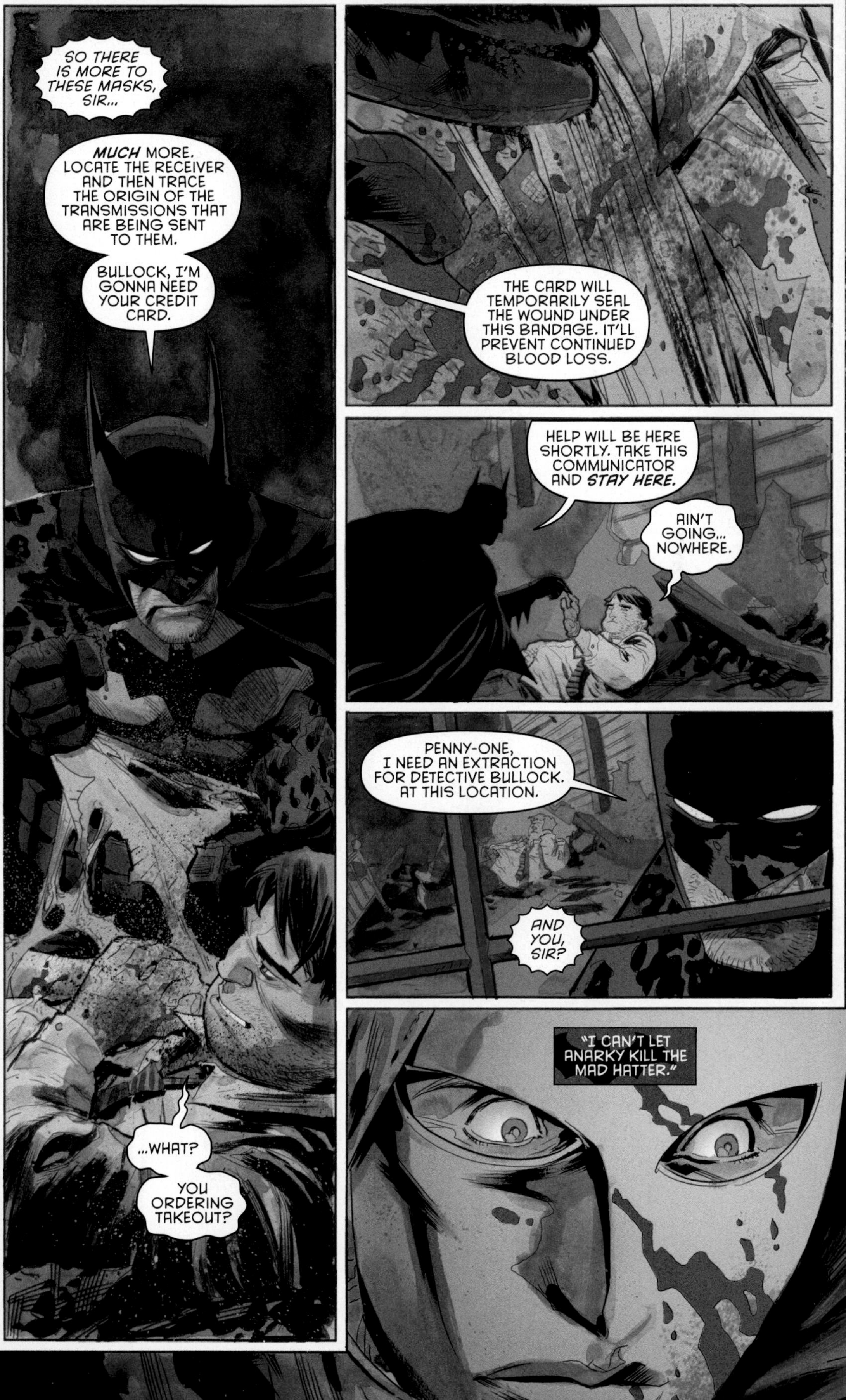
SO THERE IS MORE TO THESE MASKS, SIR...
MUCH MORE. LOCATE THE RECEIVER AND THEN TRACE THE ORIGIN OF THE TRANSMISSIONS THAT ARE BEING SENT TO THEM.
BULLOCK, I'M GONNA NEED YOUR CREDIT CARD.
...WHAT?
YOU ORDERING TAKEOUT?
THE CARD WILL TEMPORARILY SEAL THE WOUND UNDER THIS BANDAGE. IT'LL PREVENT CONTINUED BLOOD LOSS.
HELP WILL BE HERE SHORTLY. TAKE THIS COMMUNICATOR AND STAY HERE.
AIN'T GOING... NOWHERE.
PENNY-ONE, I NEED AN EXTRACTION FOR DETECTIVE BULLOCK. AT THIS LOCATION.
AND YOU, SIR?
"I CAN'T LET ANARKY KILL THE MAD HATTER."

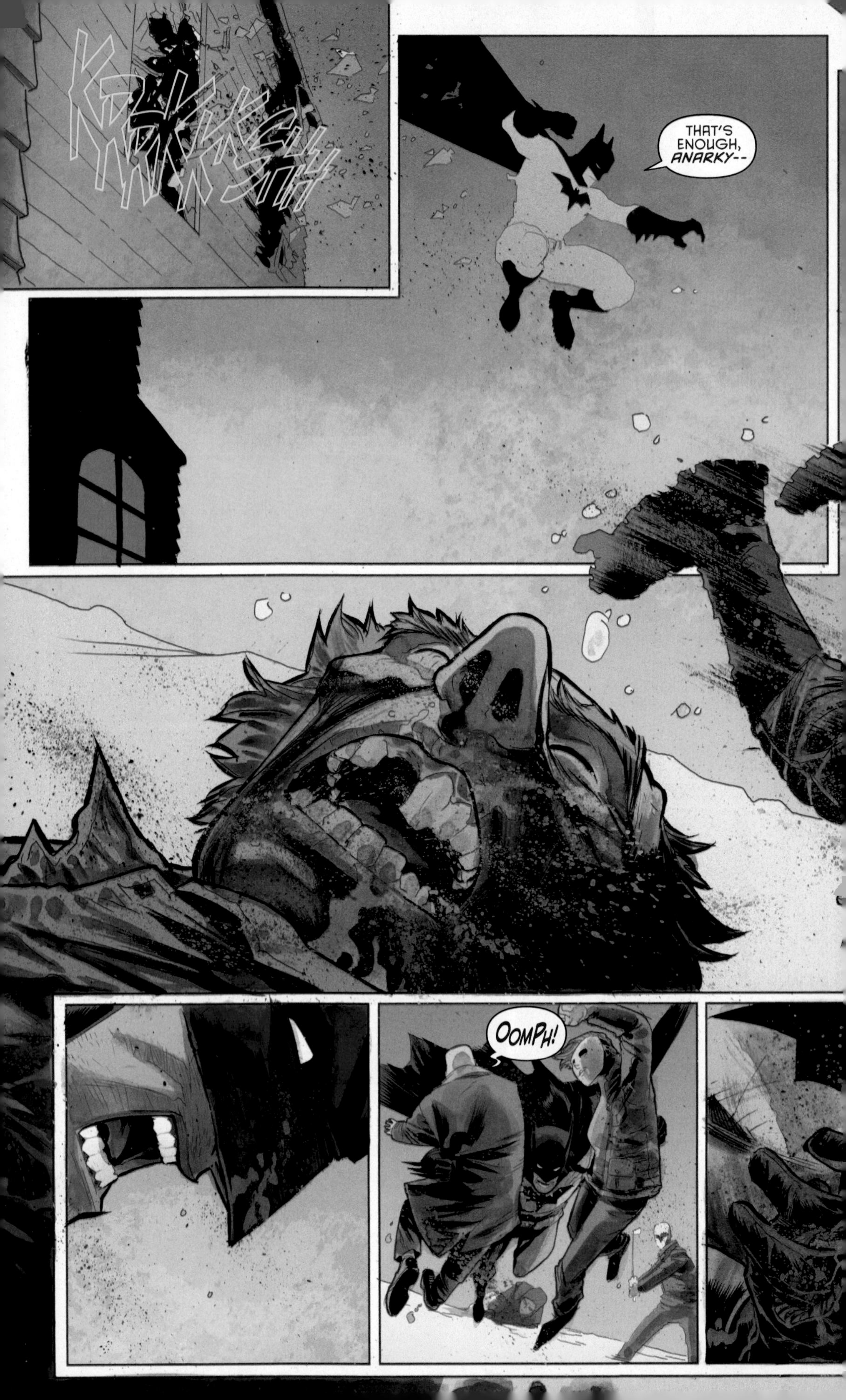
THAT'S ENOUGH, ANARKY--
OOMPH!

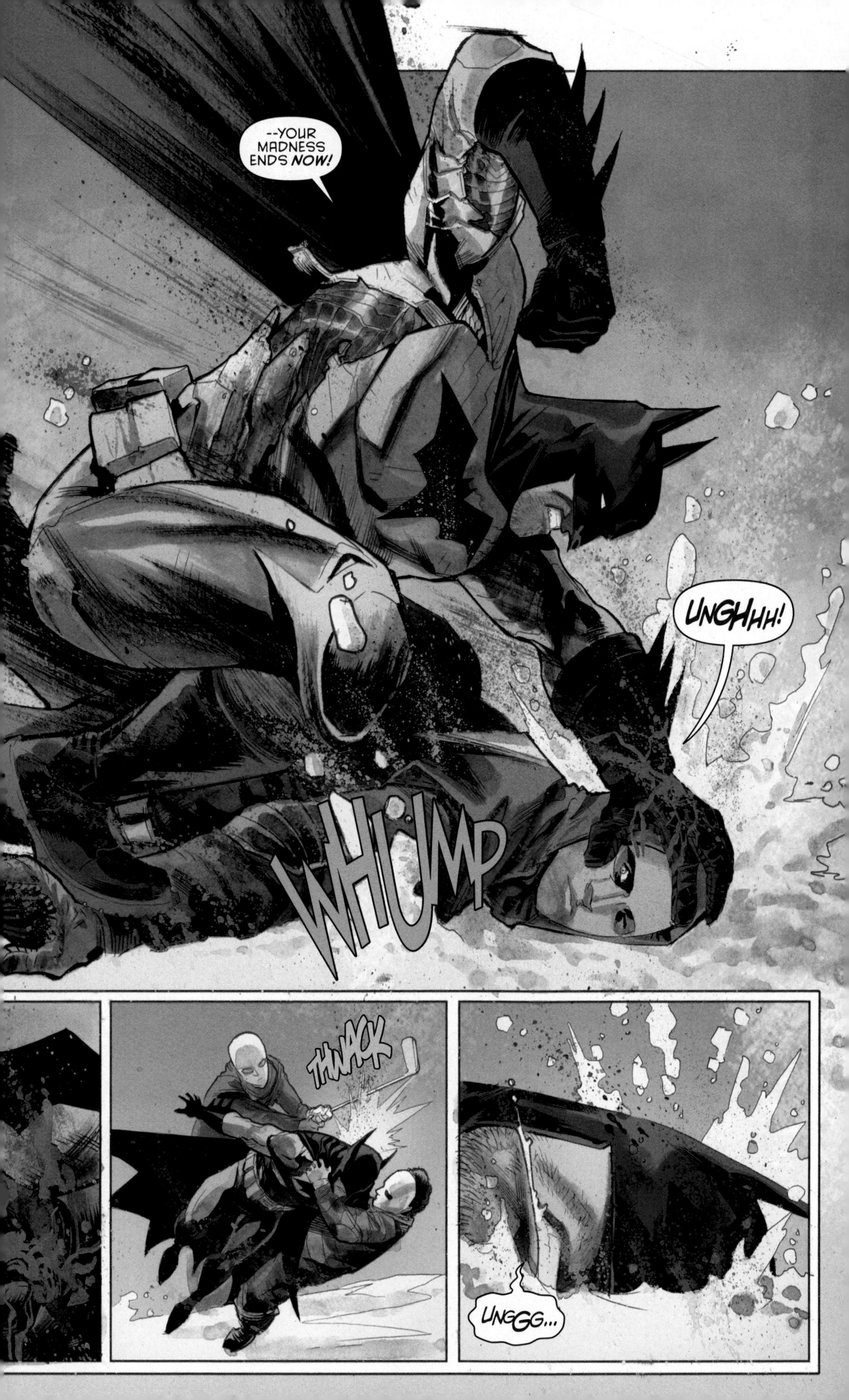
--YOUR MADNESS ENDS NOW!
UNGHHH!
WHUMP
THWACK
UNGGG...

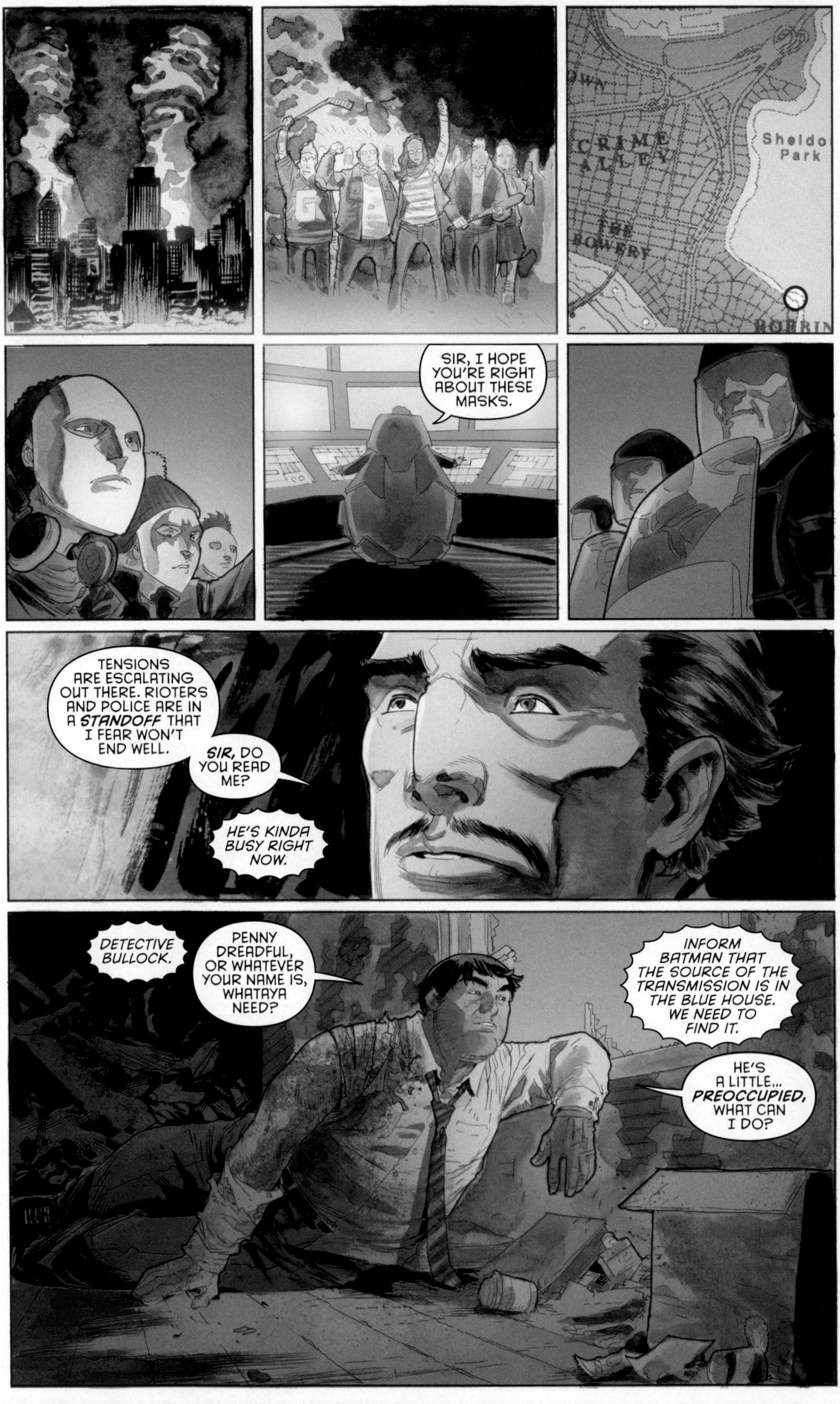
CRIME ALLEY
THE BOWERY
Park
SIR, I HOPE YOU'RE RIGHT ABOUT THESE MASKS.
TENSIONS ARE ESCALATING OUT THERE. RIOTERS AND POLICE ARE IN A *STANDOFF* THAT I FEAR WON'T END WELL.
SIR, DO YOU READ ME?
HE'S KINDA BUSY RIGHT NOW.
DETECTIVE BULLOCK.
PENNY DREADFUL, OR WHATEVER YOUR NAME IS, WHATAYA NEED?
INFORM BATMAN THAT THE SOURCE OF THE TRANSMISSION IS IN THE BLUE HOUSE. WE NEED TO FIND IT.
HE'S A LITTLE... *PREOCCUPIED,* WHAT CAN I DO?

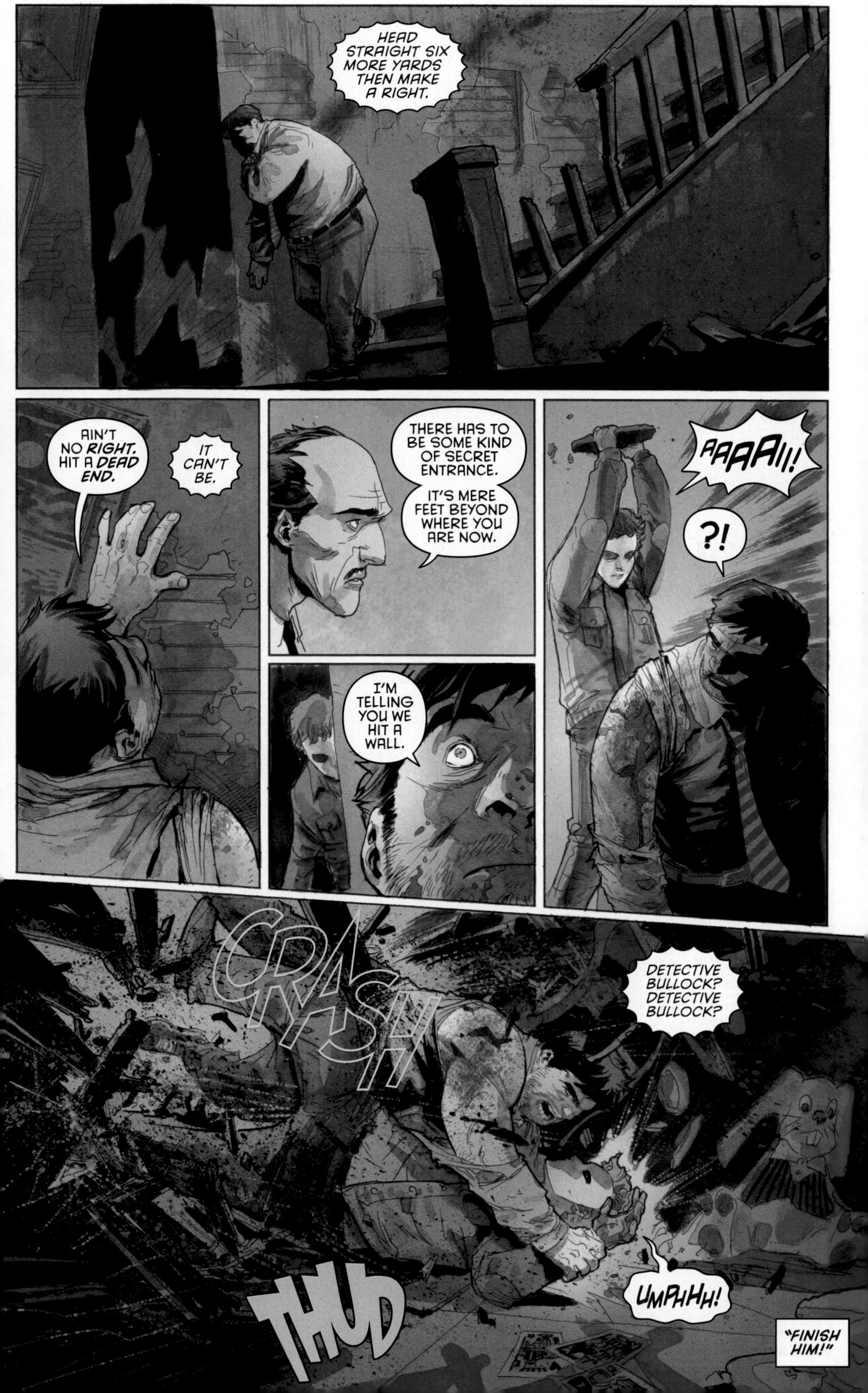
HEAD STRAIGHT SIX MORE YARDS THEN MAKE A RIGHT.
AIN'T NO RIGHT. HIT A DEAD END.
IT CAN'T BE.
THERE HAS TO BE SOME KIND OF SECRET ENTRANCE.
IT'S MERE FEET BEYOND WHERE YOU ARE NOW.
I'M TELLING YOU WE HIT A WALL.
AAAAII!
?!
CRASH
DETECTIVE BULLOCK? DETECTIVE BULLOCK?
THUD
UMPHHH!
"FINISH HIM!"

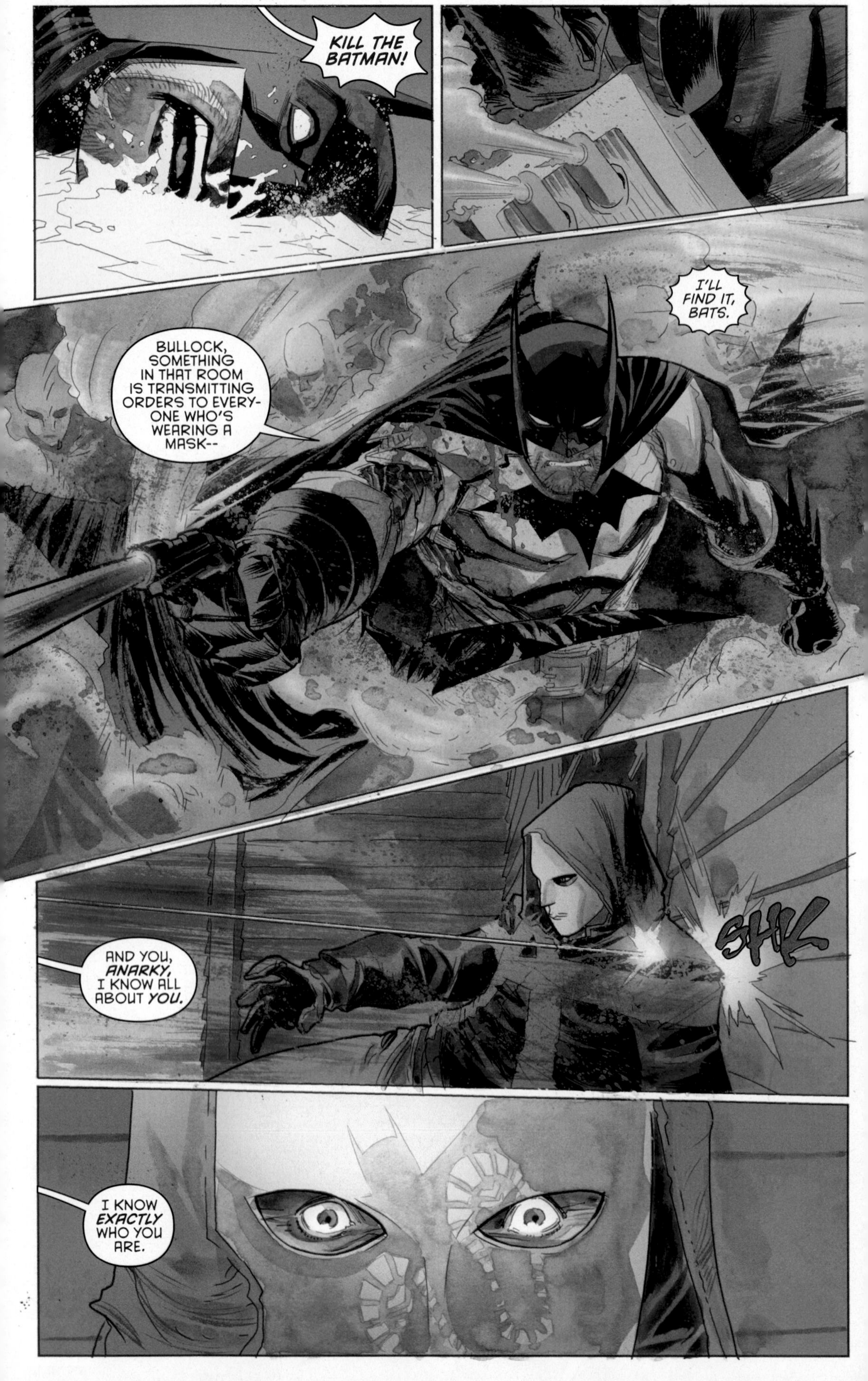
KILL THE BATMAN!
BULLOCK, SOMETHING IN THAT ROOM IS TRANSMITTING ORDERS TO EVERY-ONE WHO'S WEARING A MASK--
I'LL FIND IT, BATS.
SHK
AND YOU, ANARKY, I KNOW ALL ABOUT YOU.
I KNOW EXACTLY WHO YOU ARE.

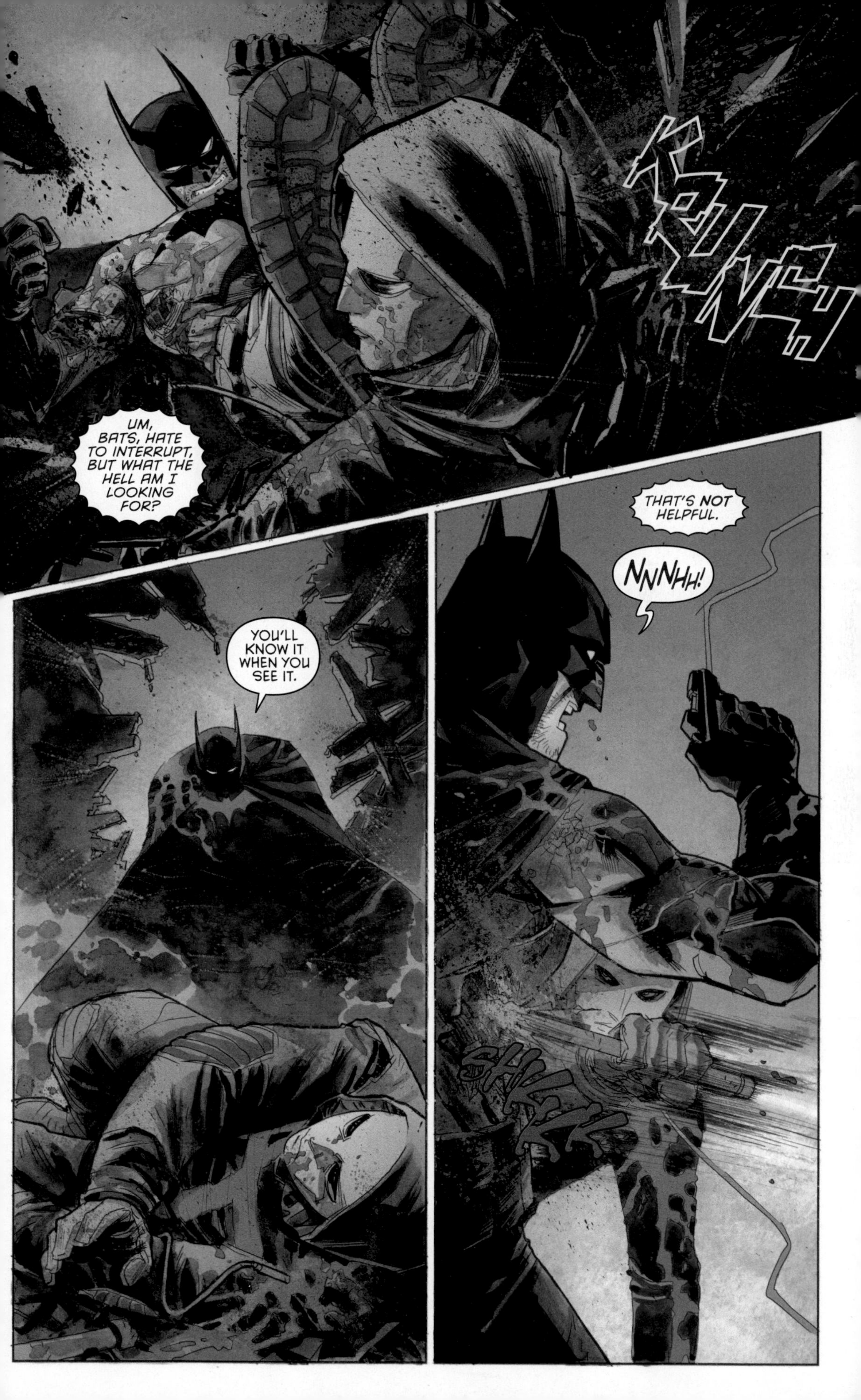
KRUNCH
UM, BATS, HATE TO INTERRUPT, BUT WHAT THE HELL AM I LOOKING FOR?
YOU'LL KNOW IT WHEN YOU SEE IT.
THAT'S NOT HELPFUL.
NNNHH!

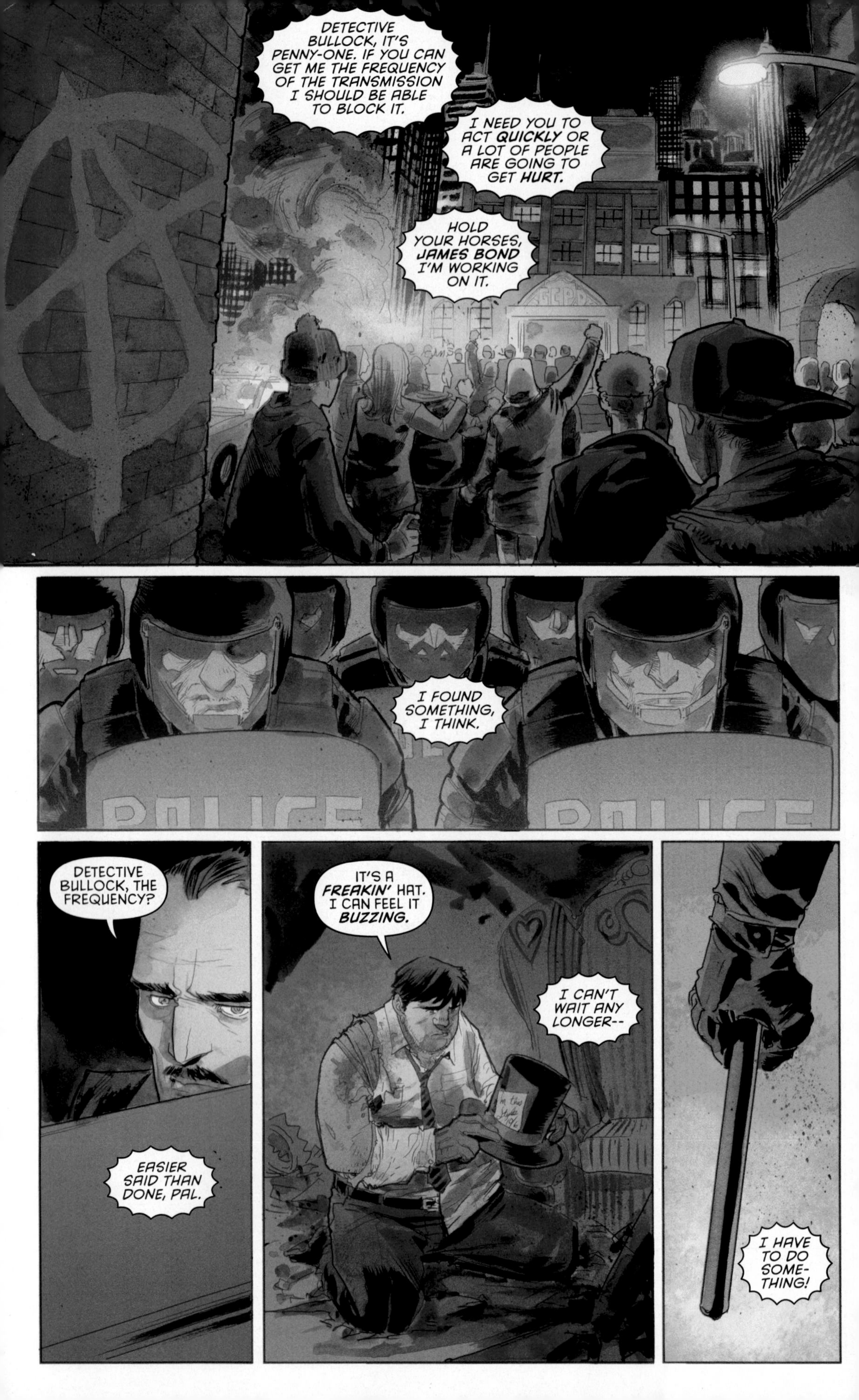
DETECTIVE BULLOCK, IT'S PENNY-ONE. IF YOU CAN GET ME THE FREQUENCY OF THE TRANSMISSION I SHOULD BE ABLE TO BLOCK IT.
I NEED YOU TO ACT QUICKLY OR A LOT OF PEOPLE ARE GOING TO GET HURT.
HOLD YOUR HORSES, JAMES BOND I'M WORKING ON IT.
GCPD
I FOUND SOMETHING, I THINK.
POLICE
POLICE
DETECTIVE BULLOCK, THE FREQUENCY?
EASIER SAID THAN DONE, PAL.
IT'S A FREAKIN' HAT. I CAN FEEL IT BUZZING.
I CAN'T WAIT ANY LONGER--
I HAVE TO DO SOME-THING!

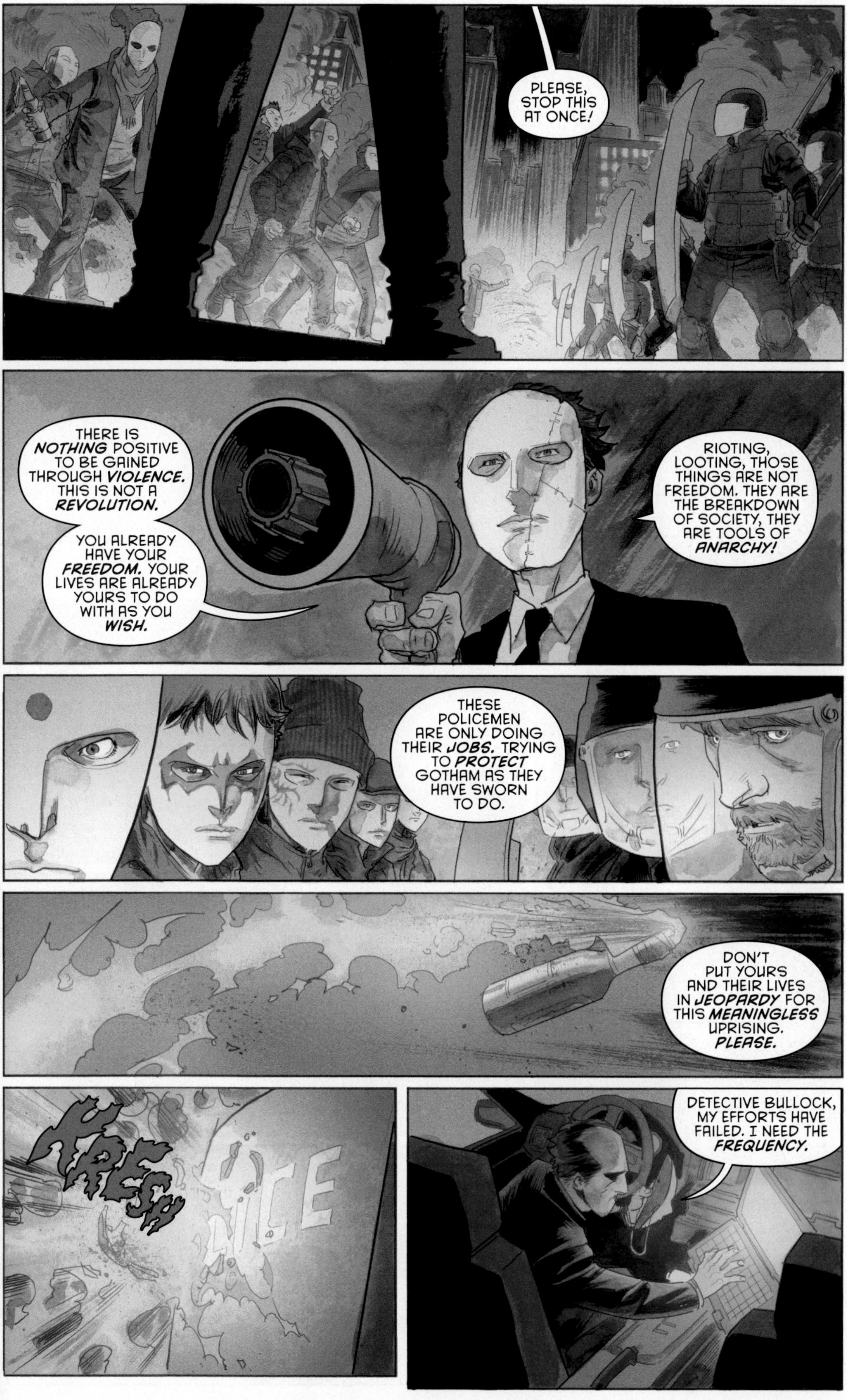
PLEASE, STOP THIS AT ONCE!
THERE IS NOTHING POSITIVE TO BE GAINED THROUGH VIOLENCE. THIS IS NOT A REVOLUTION.
YOU ALREADY HAVE YOUR FREEDOM. YOUR LIVES ARE ALREADY YOURS TO DO WITH AS YOU WISH.
RIOTING, LOOTING, THOSE THINGS ARE NOT FREEDOM. THEY ARE THE BREAKDOWN OF SOCIETY, THEY ARE TOOLS OF ANARCHY!
THESE POLICEMEN ARE ONLY DOING THEIR JOBS. TRYING TO PROTECT GOTHAM AS THEY HAVE SWORN TO DO.
DON'T PUT YOURS AND THEIR LIVES IN JEOPARDY FOR THIS MEANINGLESS UPRISING. PLEASE.
KRESH
DETECTIVE BULLOCK, MY EFFORTS HAVE FAILED. I NEED THE FREQUENCY.

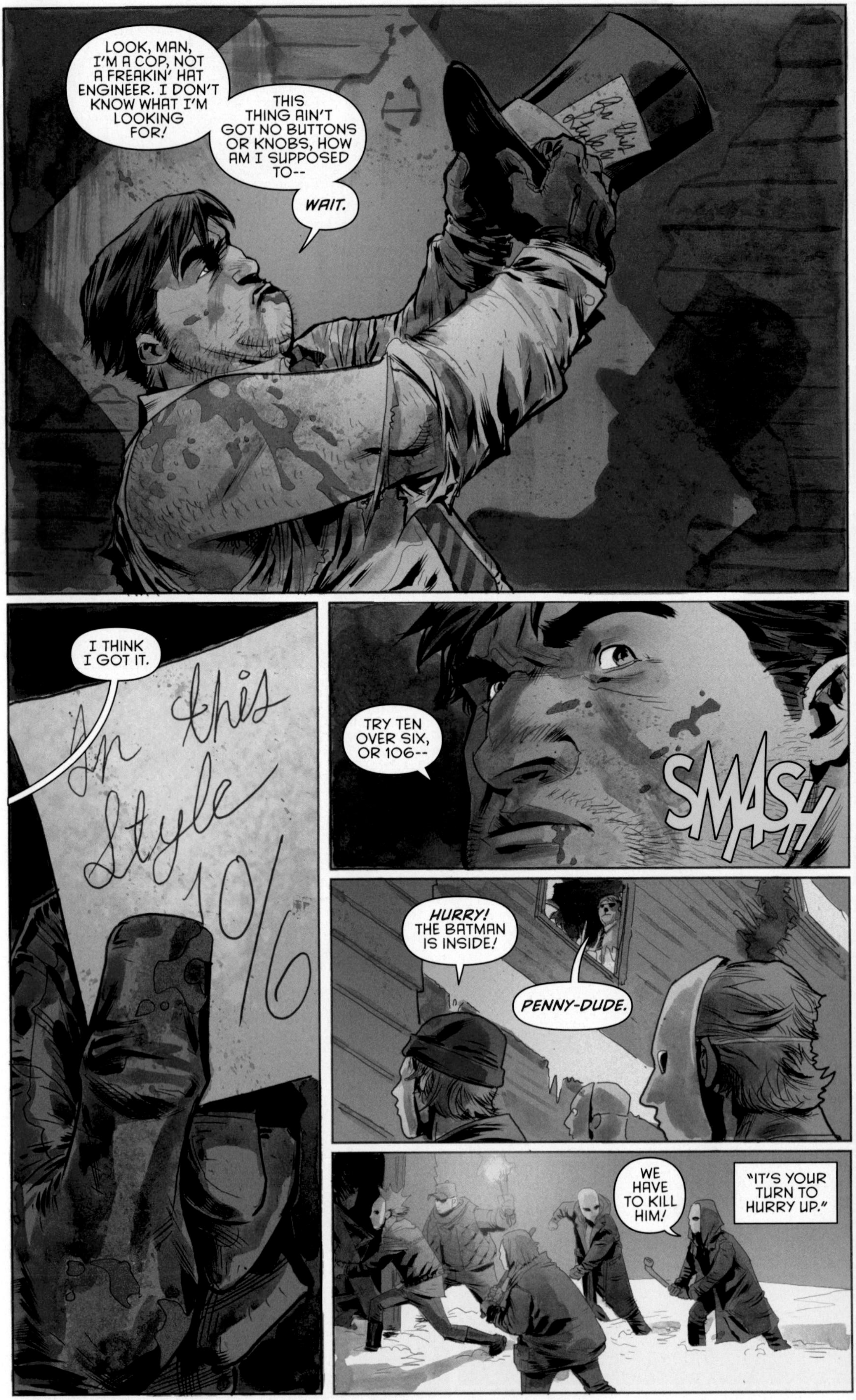

LOOK, MAN, I'M A COP, NOT A FREAKIN' HAT ENGINEER. I DON'T KNOW WHAT I'M LOOKING FOR!
THIS THING AIN'T GOT NO BUTTONS OR KNOBS, HOW AM I SUPPOSED TO--
WAIT.
I THINK I GOT IT.
In this Style 10/6
TRY TEN OVER SIX, OR 106--
SMASH
HURRY! THE BATMAN IS INSIDE!
PENNY-DUDE.
WE HAVE TO KILL HIM!
"IT'S YOUR TURN TO HURRY UP."

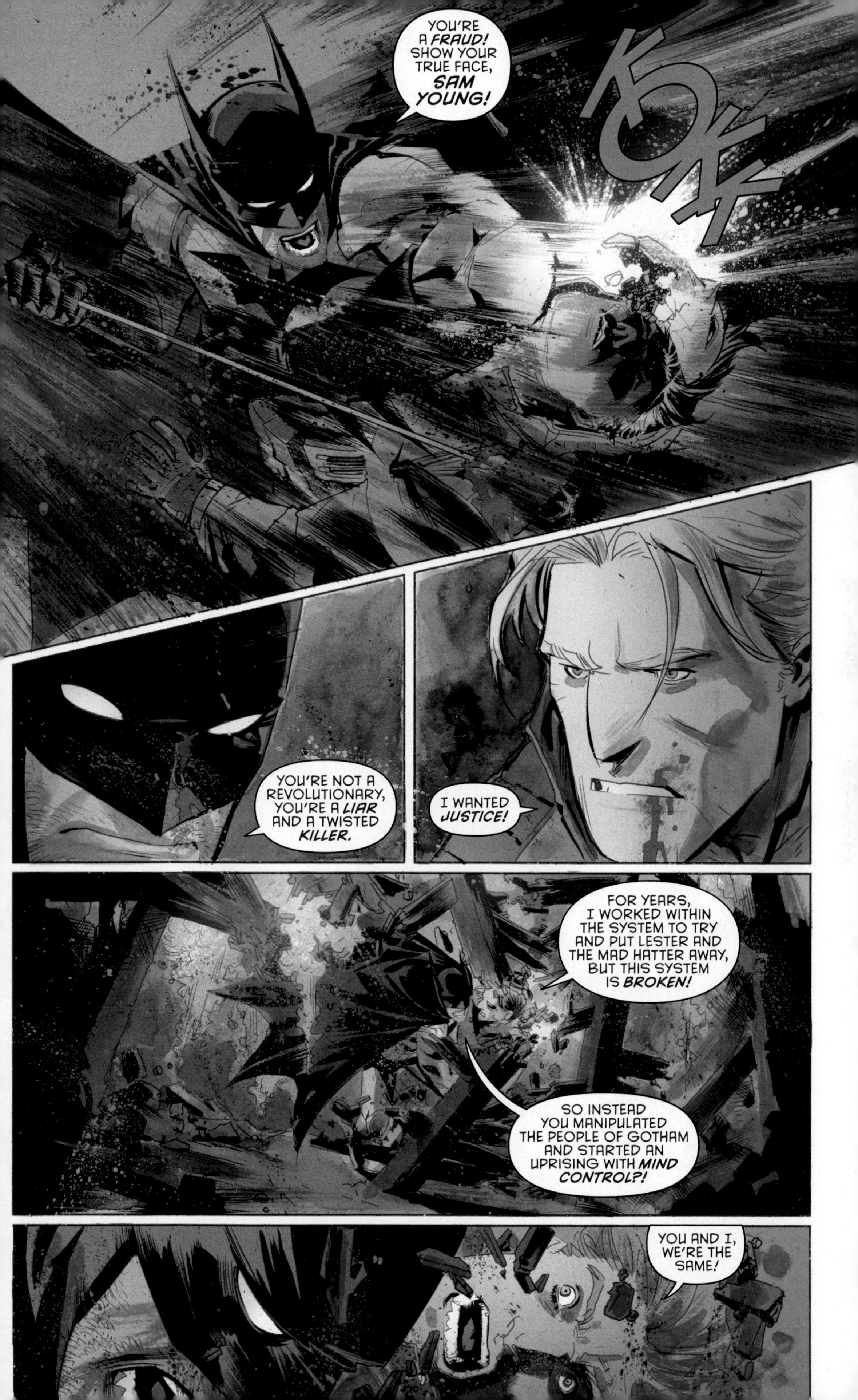
YOU'RE A FRAUD! SHOW YOUR TRUE FACE, SAM YOUNG!
KOKK
YOU'RE NOT A REVOLUTIONARY, YOU'RE A LIAR AND A TWISTED KILLER.
I WANTED JUSTICE!
FOR YEARS, I WORKED WITHIN THE SYSTEM TO TRY AND PUT LESTER AND THE MAD HATTER AWAY, BUT THIS SYSTEM IS BROKEN!
SO INSTEAD YOU MANIPULATED THE PEOPLE OF GOTHAM AND STARTED AN UPRISING WITH MIND CONTROL?!
YOU AND I, WE'RE THE SAME!

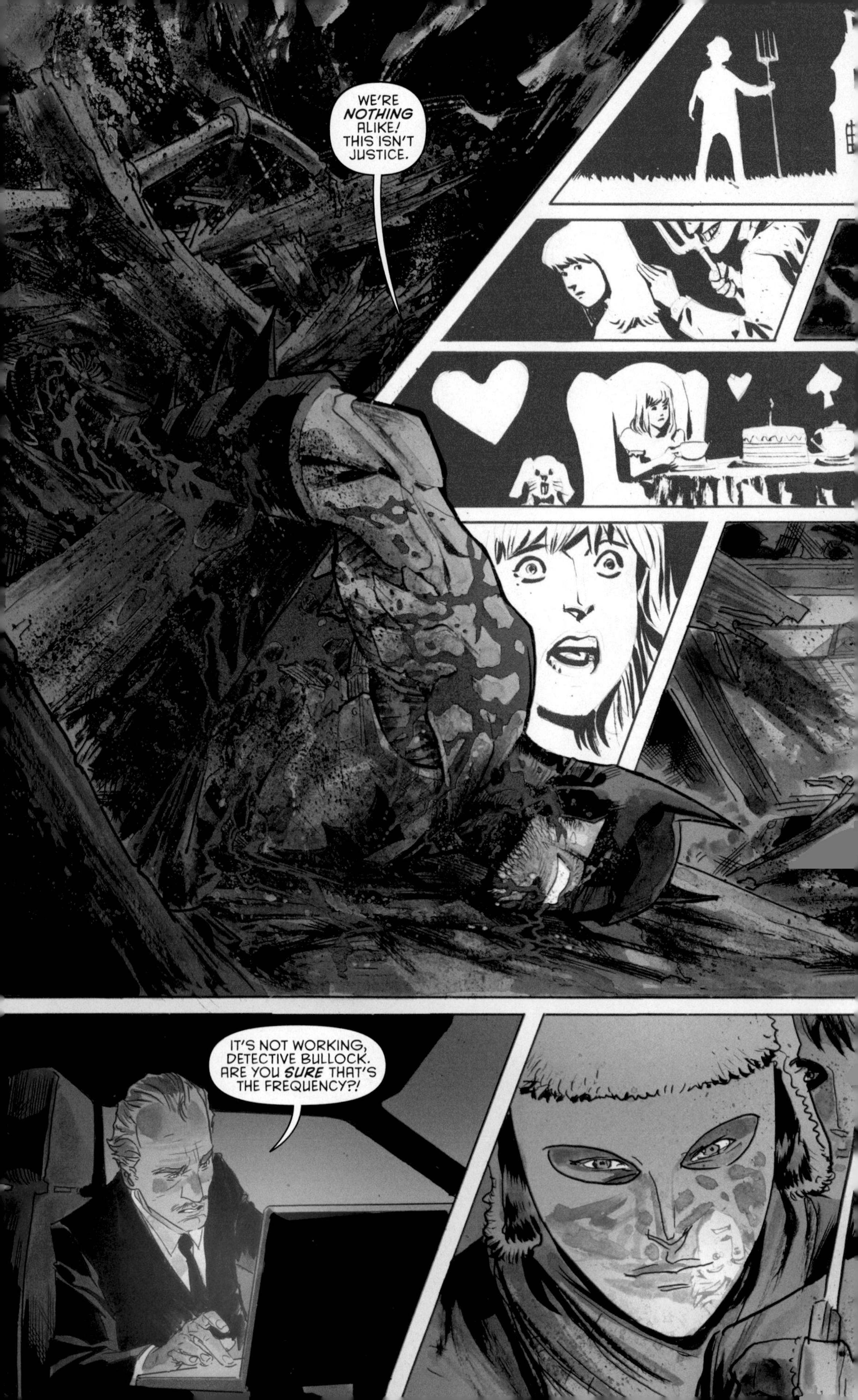
WE'RE *NOTHING* ALIKE! THIS ISN'T JUSTICE.
IT'S NOT WORKING, DETECTIVE BULLOCK. ARE YOU *SURE* THAT'S THE FREQUENCY?!

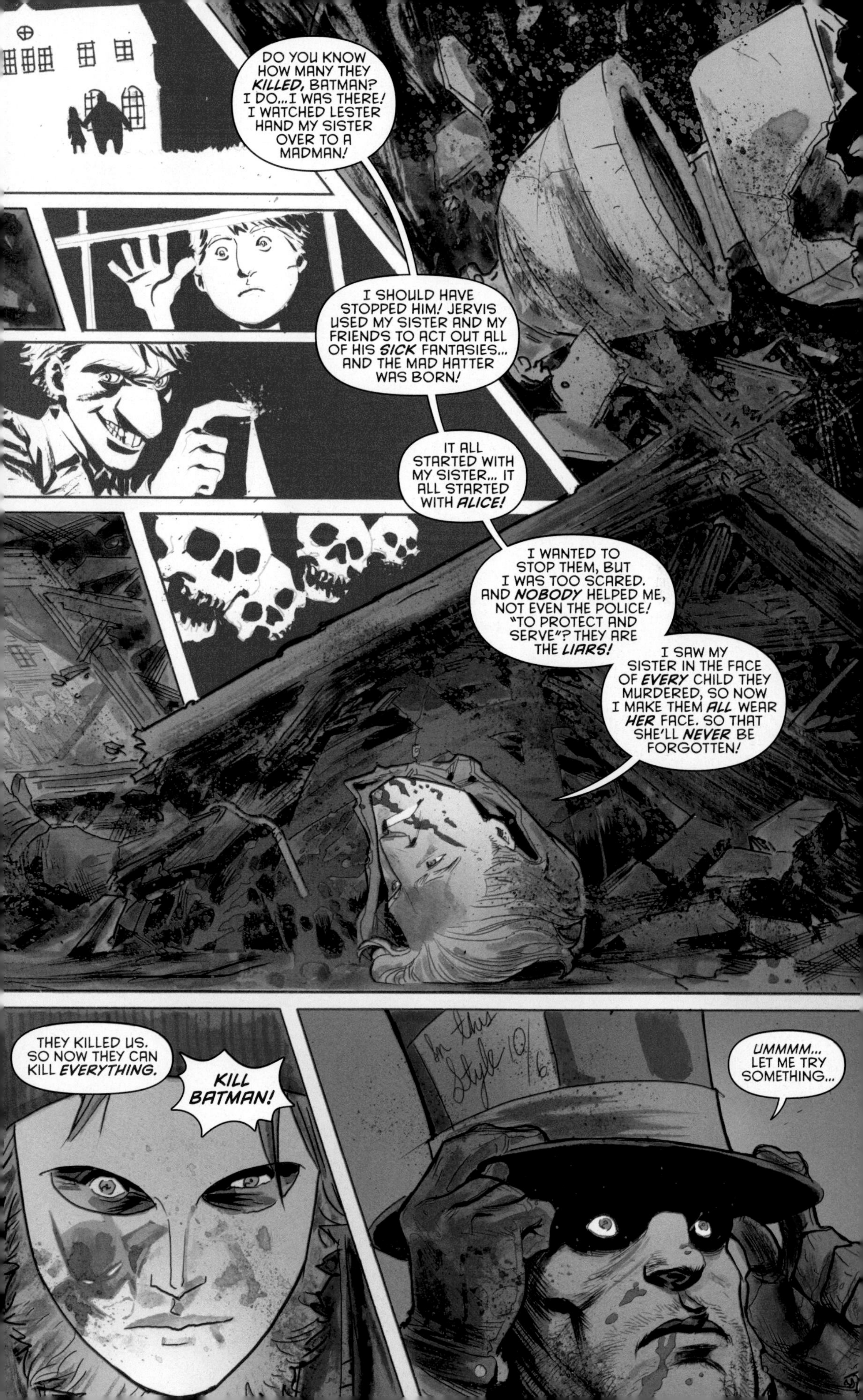
DO YOU KNOW HOW MANY THEY KILLED, BATMAN? I DO...I WAS THERE! I WATCHED LESTER HAND MY SISTER OVER TO A MADMAN!
I SHOULD HAVE STOPPED HIM! JERVIS USED MY SISTER AND MY FRIENDS TO ACT OUT ALL OF HIS SICK FANTASIES... AND THE MAD HATTER WAS BORN!
IT ALL STARTED WITH MY SISTER... IT ALL STARTED WITH ALICE!
I WANTED TO STOP THEM, BUT I WAS TOO SCARED. AND NOBODY HELPED ME, NOT EVEN THE POLICE! "TO PROTECT AND SERVE"? THEY ARE THE LIARS!
I SAW MY SISTER IN THE FACE OF EVERY CHILD THEY MURDERED, SO NOW I MAKE THEM ALL WEAR HER FACE. SO THAT SHE'LL NEVER BE FORGOTTEN!
THEY KILLED US. SO NOW THEY CAN KILL EVERYTHING.
KILL BATMAN!
In this Style 10/6
UMMMM... LET ME TRY SOMETHING...

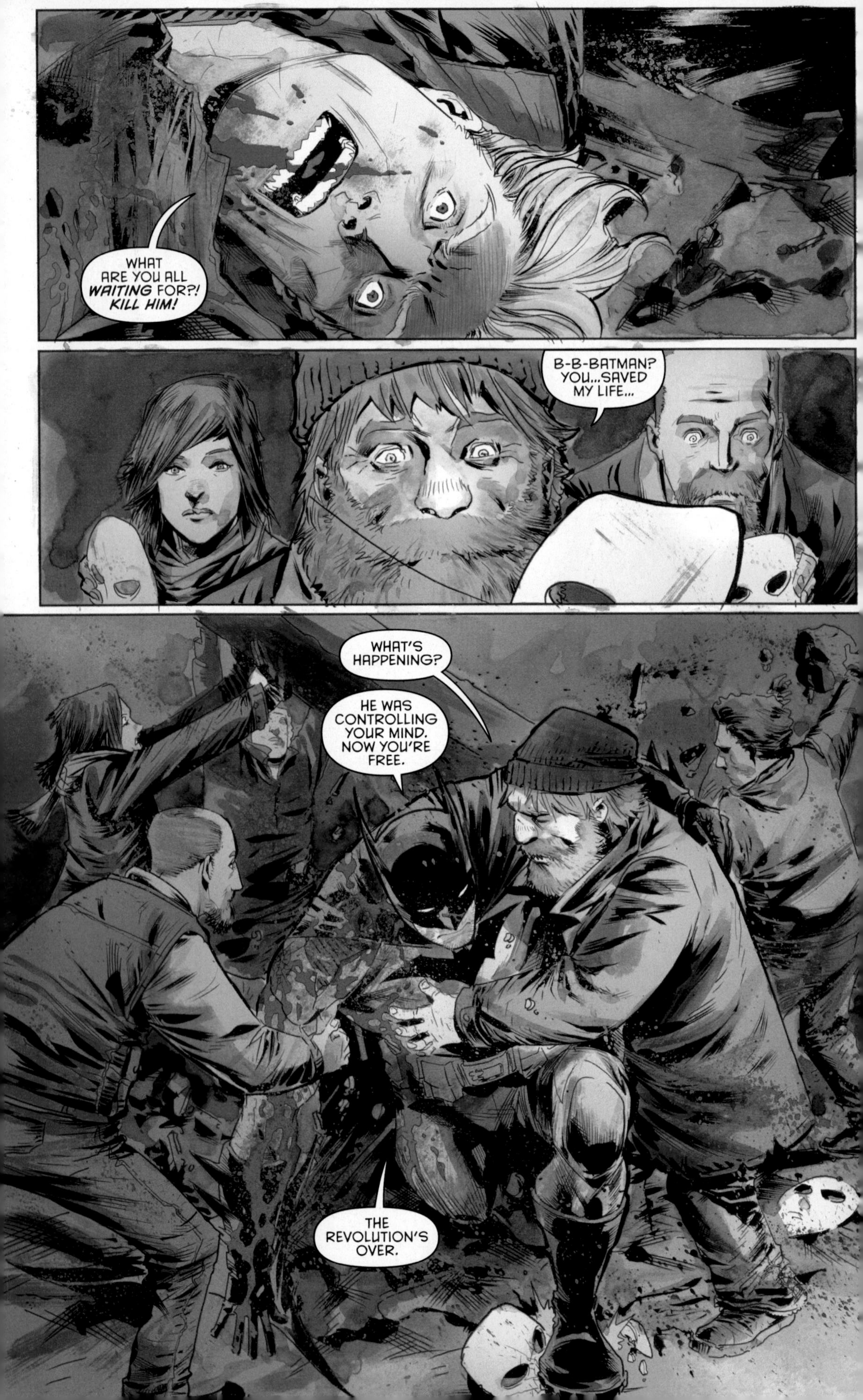
WHAT ARE YOU ALL WAITING FOR?! KILL HIM!
B-B-BATMAN? YOU...SAVED MY LIFE...
WHAT'S HAPPENING?
HE WAS CONTROLLING YOUR MIND. NOW YOU'RE FREE.
THE REVOLUTION'S OVER.

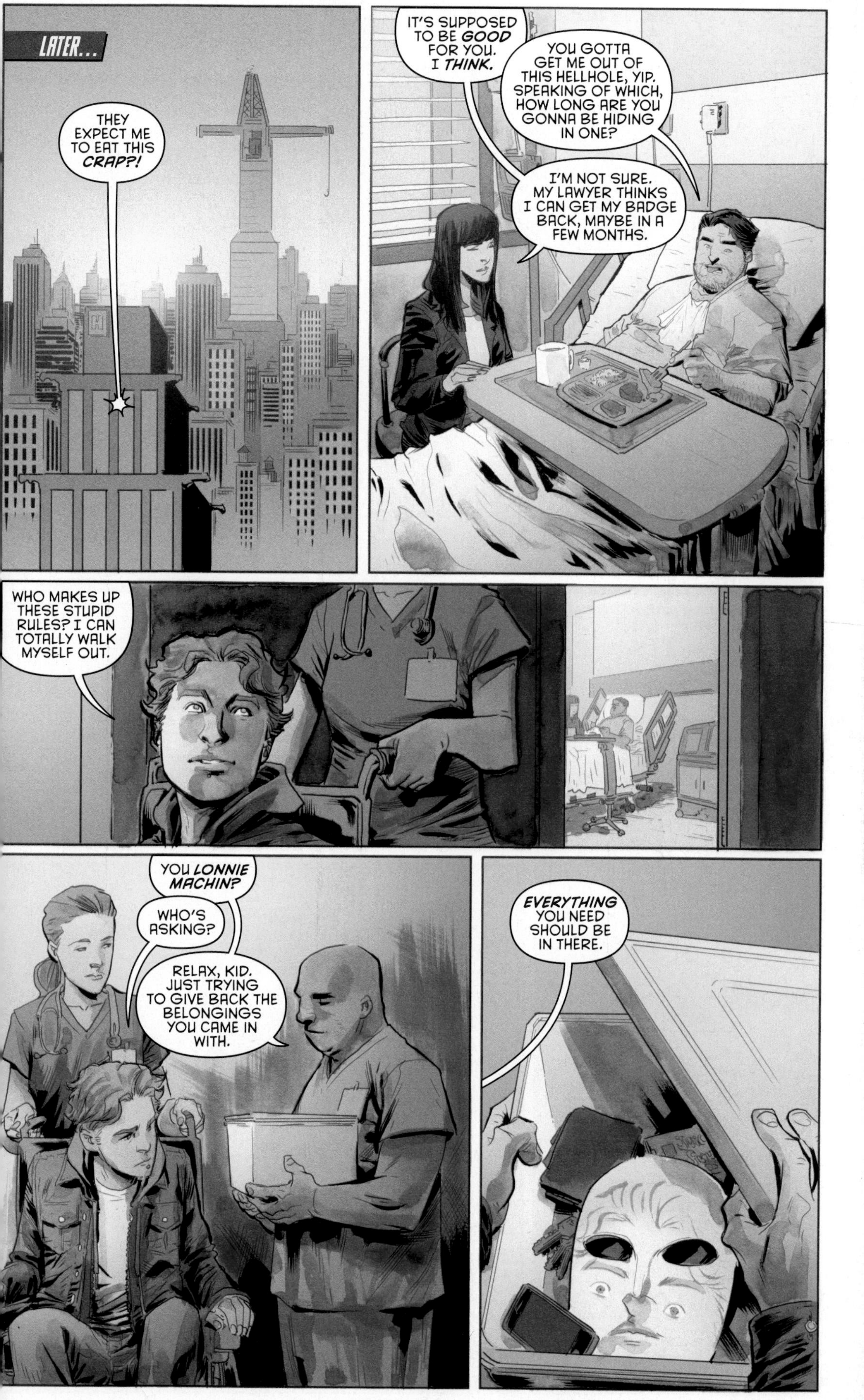
LATER...
THEY EXPECT ME TO EAT THIS CRAP?!
IT'S SUPPOSED TO BE GOOD FOR YOU. I THINK.
YOU GOTTA GET ME OUT OF THIS HELLHOLE, YIP. SPEAKING OF WHICH, HOW LONG ARE YOU GONNA BE HIDING IN ONE?
I'M NOT SURE. MY LAWYER THINKS I CAN GET MY BADGE BACK, MAYBE IN A FEW MONTHS.
WHO MAKES UP THESE STUPID RULES? I CAN TOTALLY WALK MYSELF OUT.
YOU LONNIE MACHIN?
WHO'S ASKING?
RELAX, KID. JUST TRYING TO GIVE BACK THE BELONGINGS YOU CAME IN WITH.
EVERYTHING YOU NEED SHOULD BE IN THERE.

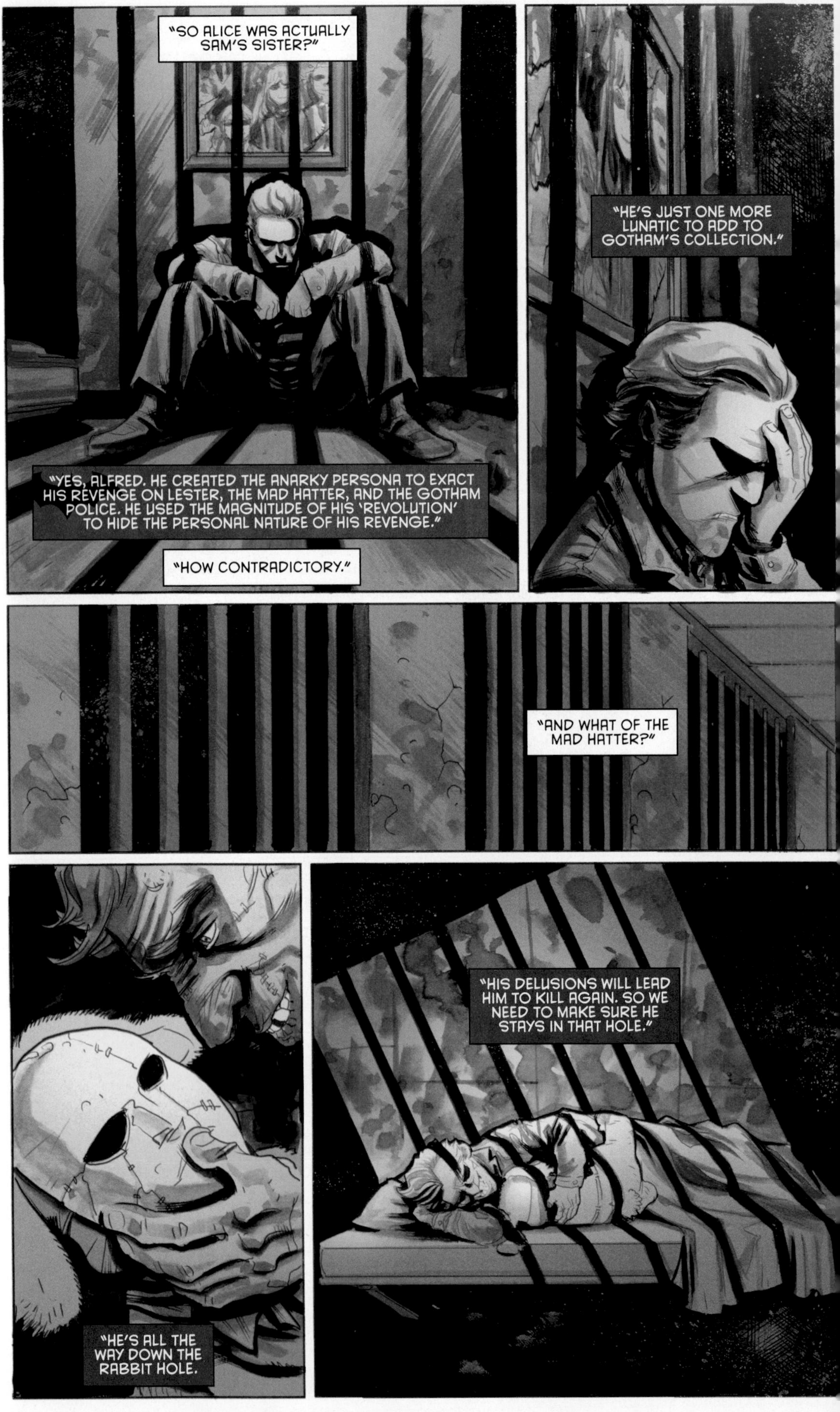

"SO ALICE WAS ACTUALLY SAM'S SISTER?"
"YES, ALFRED. HE CREATED THE ANARKY PERSONA TO EXACT HIS REVENGE ON LESTER, THE MAD HATTER, AND THE GOTHAM POLICE. HE USED THE MAGNITUDE OF HIS 'REVOLUTION' TO HIDE THE PERSONAL NATURE OF HIS REVENGE."
"HOW CONTRADICTORY."
"HE'S JUST ONE MORE LUNATIC TO ADD TO GOTHAM'S COLLECTION."
"AND WHAT OF THE MAD HATTER?"
"HE'S ALL THE WAY DOWN THE RABBIT HOLE.
"HIS DELUSIONS WILL LEAD HIM TO KILL AGAIN. SO WE NEED TO MAKE SURE HE STAYS IN THAT HOLE."

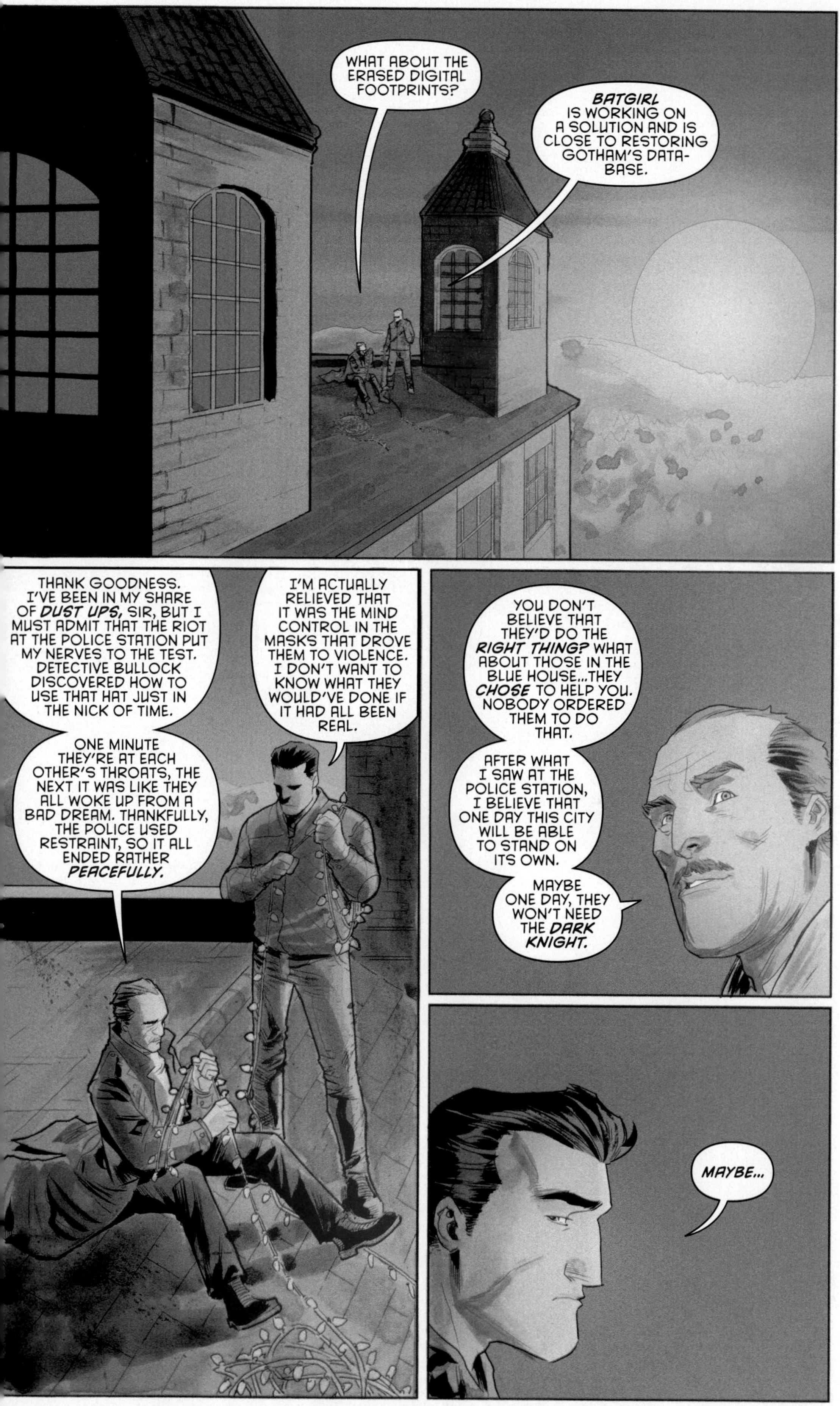

WHAT ABOUT THE ERASED DIGITAL FOOTPRINTS?
BATGIRL IS WORKING ON A SOLUTION AND IS CLOSE TO RESTORING GOTHAM'S DATA-BASE.
THANK GOODNESS. I'VE BEEN IN MY SHARE OF DUST UPS, SIR, BUT I MUST ADMIT THAT THE RIOT AT THE POLICE STATION PUT MY NERVES TO THE TEST. DETECTIVE BULLOCK DISCOVERED HOW TO USE THAT HAT JUST IN THE NICK OF TIME.
ONE MINUTE THEY'RE AT EACH OTHER'S THROATS, THE NEXT IT WAS LIKE THEY ALL WOKE UP FROM A BAD DREAM. THANKFULLY, THE POLICE USED RESTRAINT, SO IT ALL ENDED RATHER PEACEFULLY.
I'M ACTUALLY RELIEVED THAT IT WAS THE MIND CONTROL IN THE MASKS THAT DROVE THEM TO VIOLENCE. I DON'T WANT TO KNOW WHAT THEY WOULD'VE DONE IF IT HAD ALL BEEN REAL.
YOU DON'T BELIEVE THAT THEY'D DO THE RIGHT THING? WHAT ABOUT THOSE IN THE BLUE HOUSE...THEY CHOSE TO HELP YOU. NOBODY ORDERED THEM TO DO THAT.
AFTER WHAT I SAW AT THE POLICE STATION, I BELIEVE THAT ONE DAY THIS CITY WILL BE ABLE TO STAND ON ITS OWN.
MAYBE ONE DAY, THEY WON'T NEED THE DARK KNIGHT.
MAYBE...

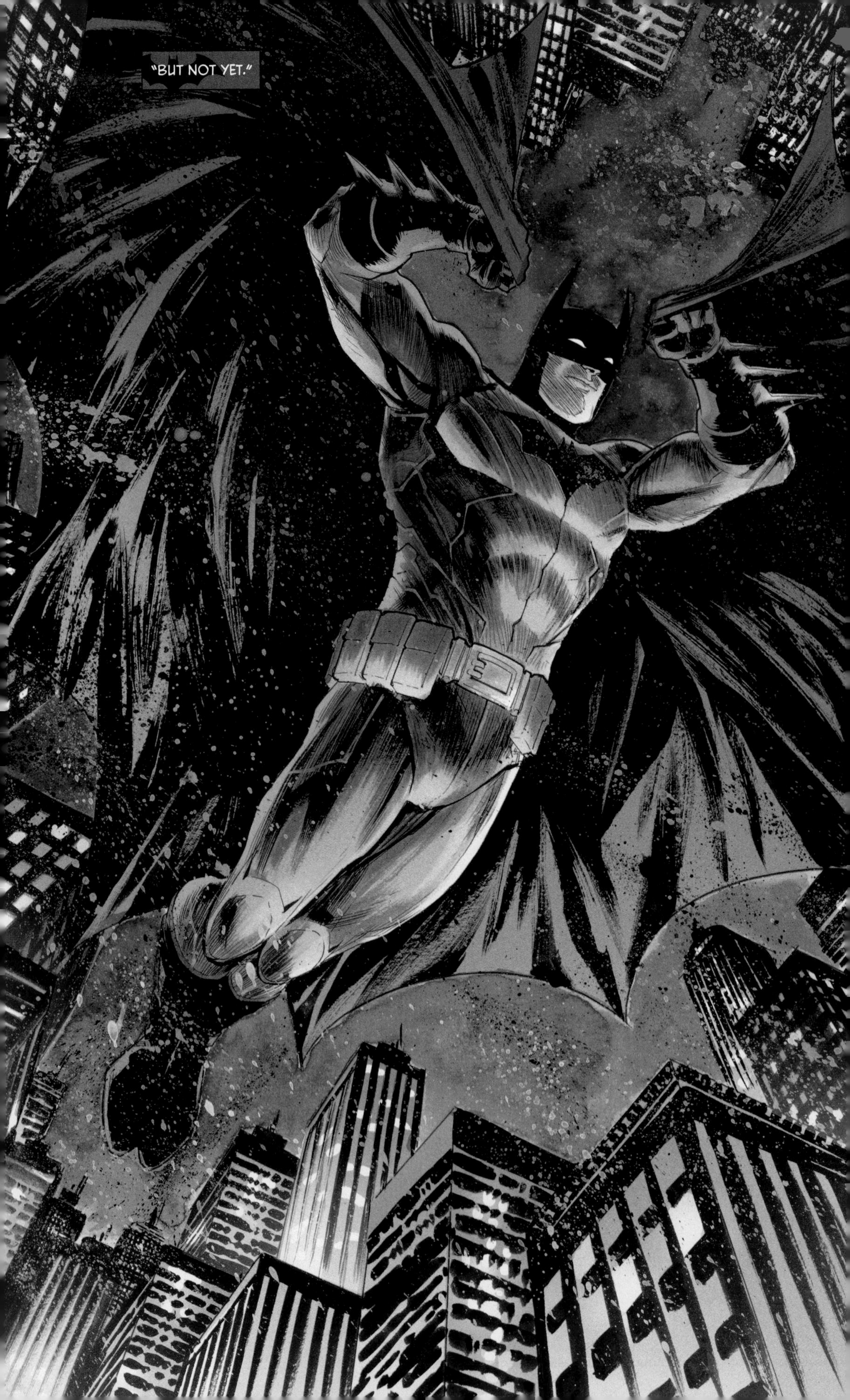
"BUT NOT YET."

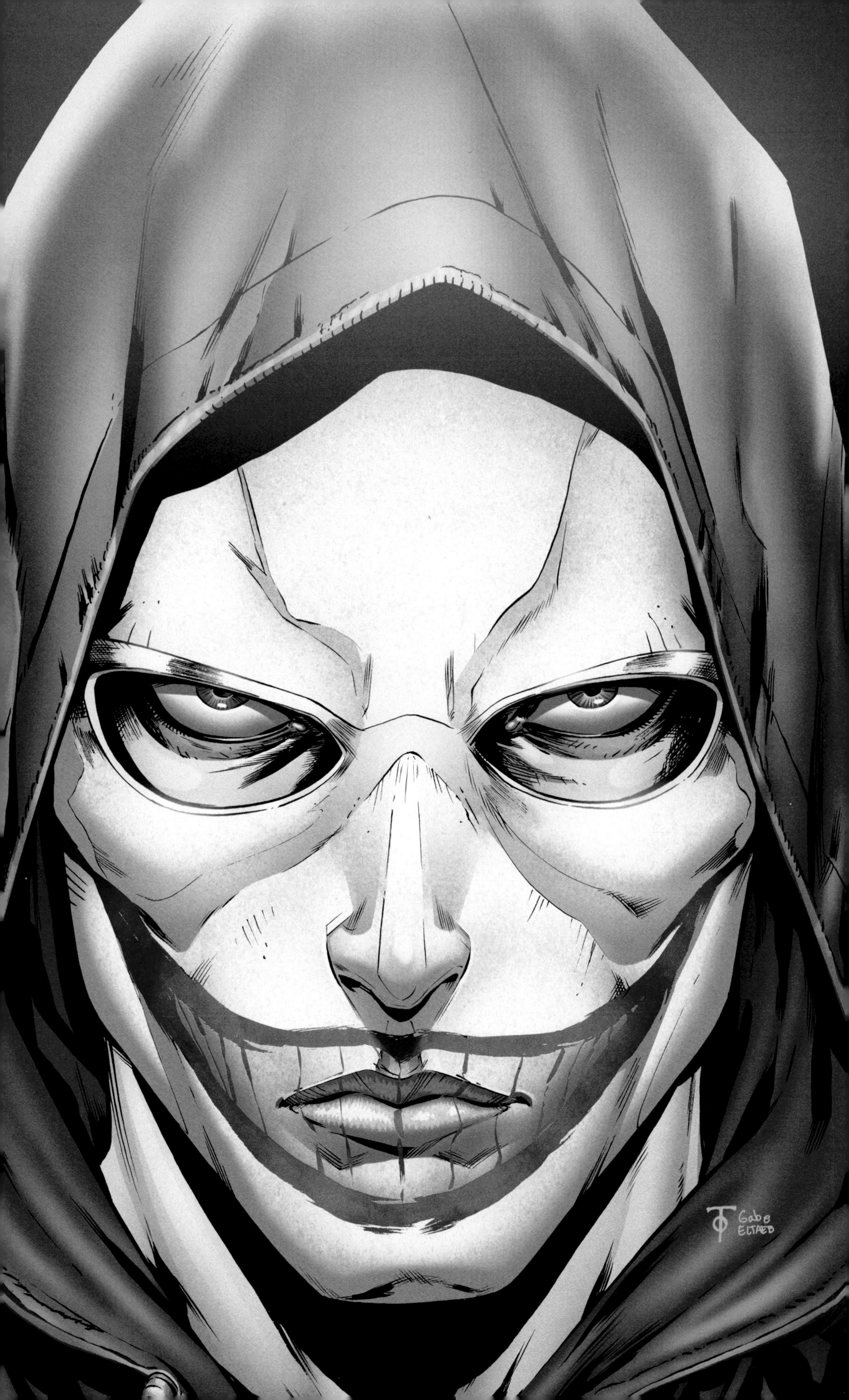
Gabe
ELTAEB

ENDGAME

BRIAN BUCCELLATO writer ROGE ANTONIO & RONAN CLIQUET artists NICK FILARDI colorist DAVE SHARPE letterer cover by MARCUS TO & GABE ELTAEB

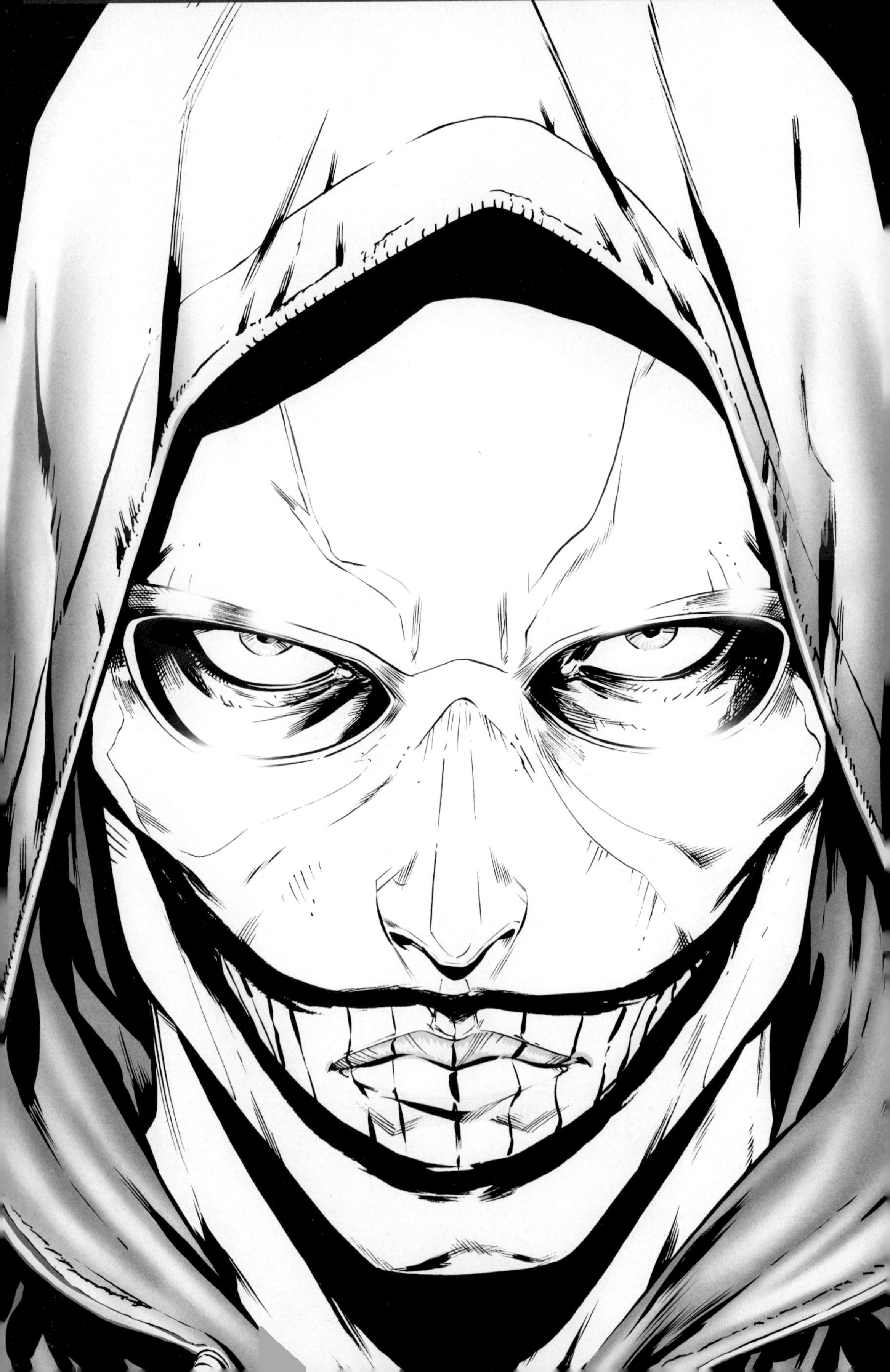

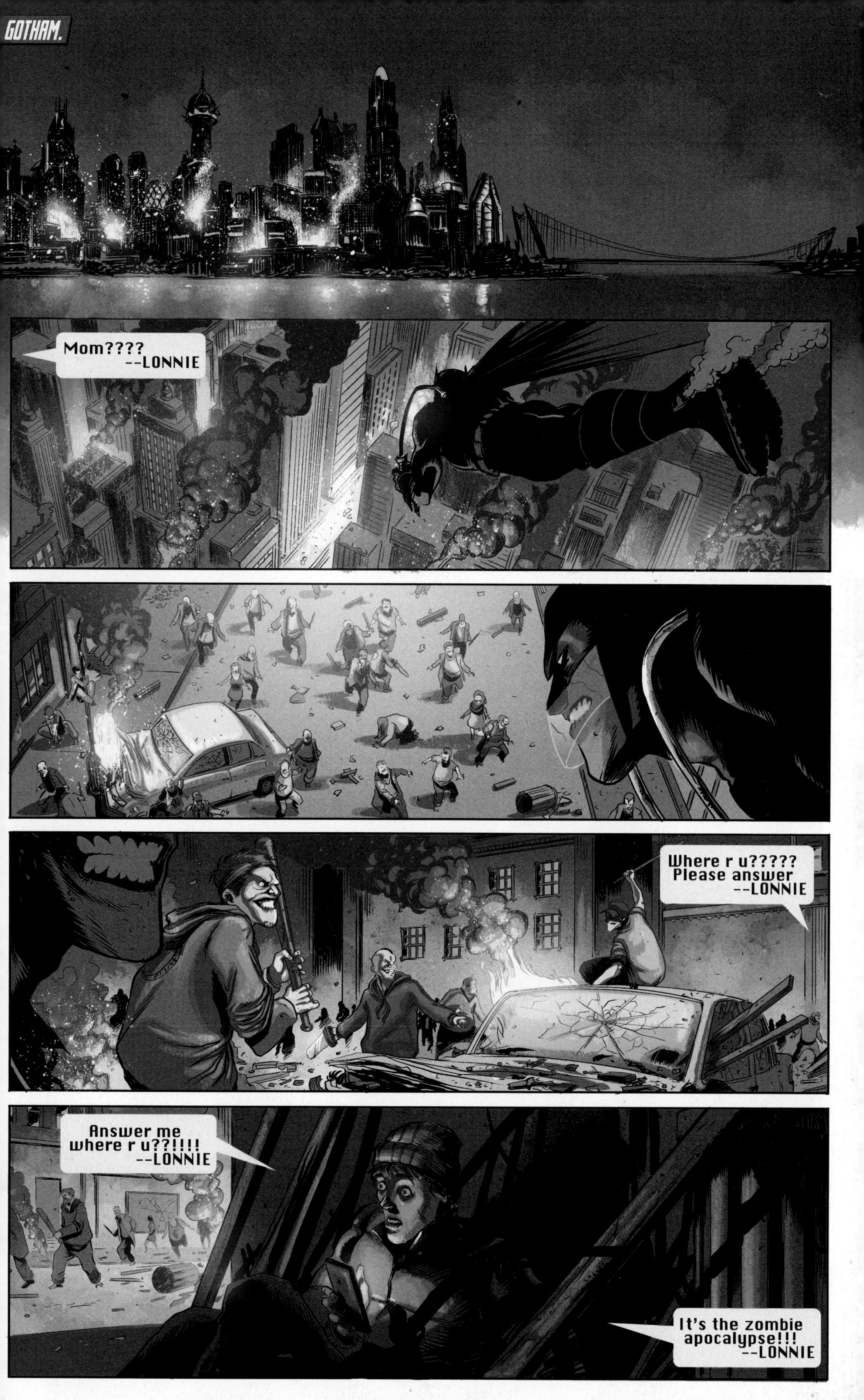
GOTHAM.
Mom????
--LONNIE
Where r u?????
Please answer
--LONNIE
Answer me
where r u??!!!!
--LONNIE
It's the zombie
apocalypse!!!
--LONNIE

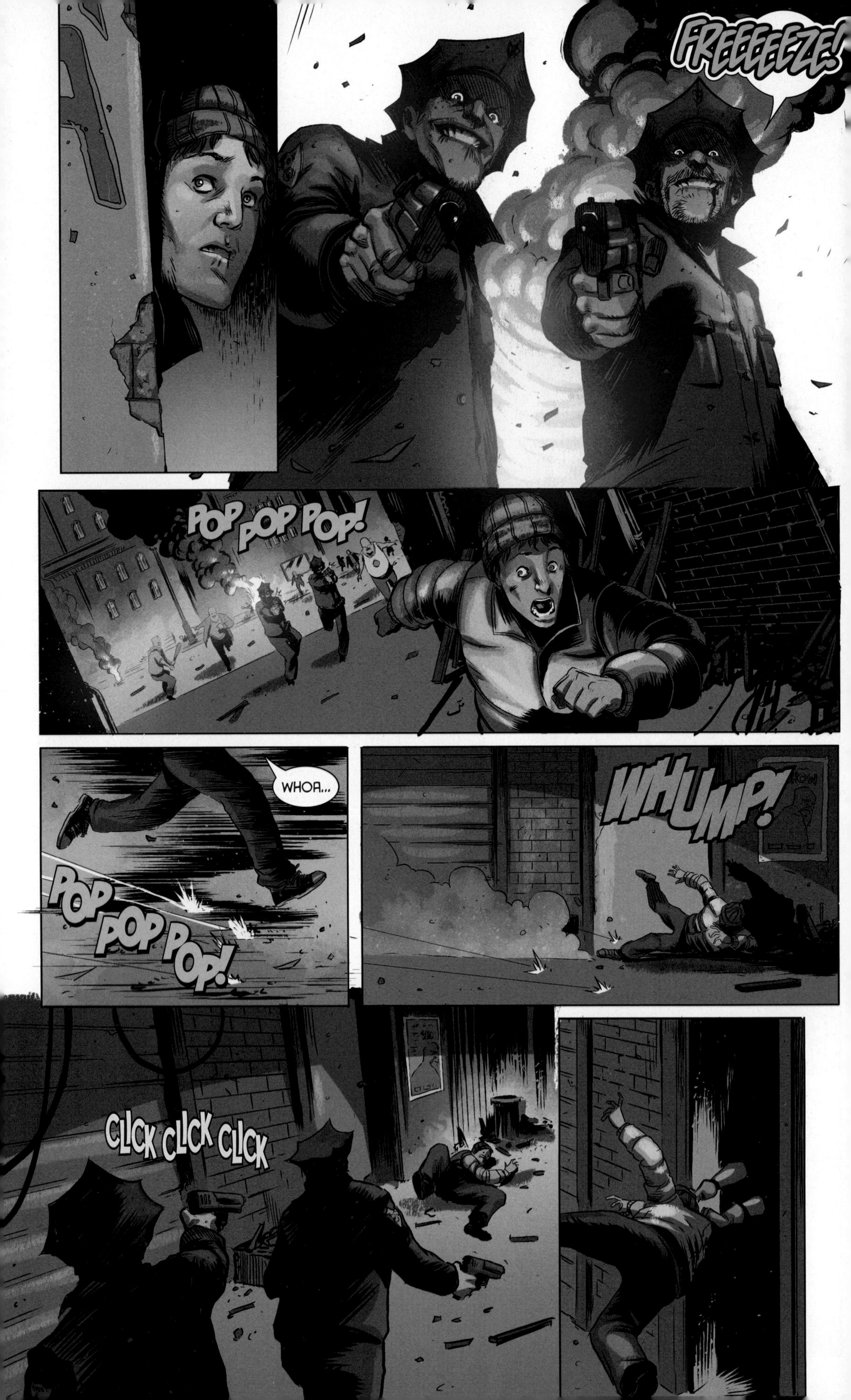
FREEEEEEZE!
POP POP POP!
WHOA...
POP POP POP!
WHUMP!
CLICK CLICK CLICK

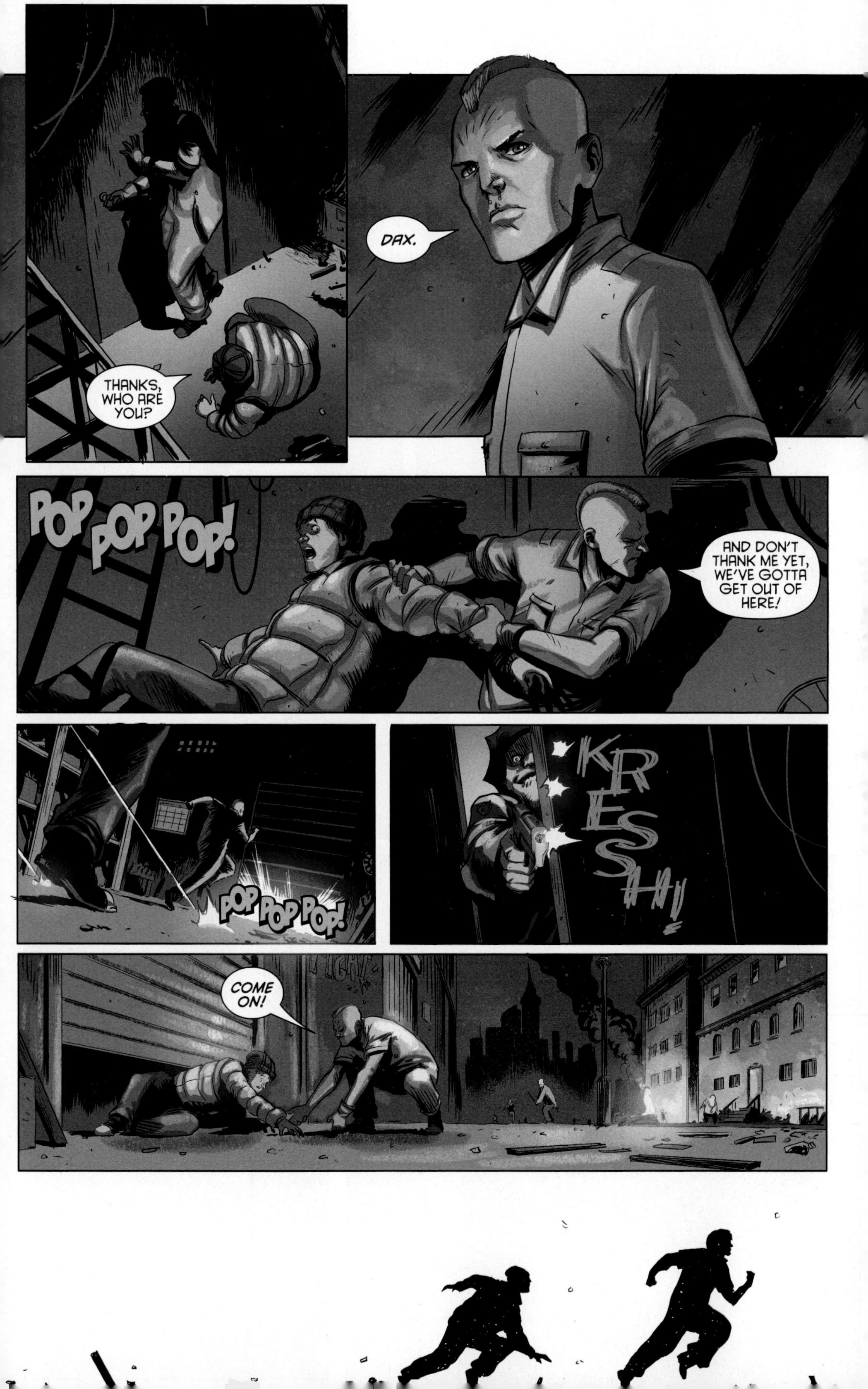
THANKS, WHO ARE YOU?
DAX.
POP POP POP!
AND DON'T THANK ME YET, WE'VE GOTTA GET OUT OF HERE!
POP POP POP!
KRESSH!
COME ON!

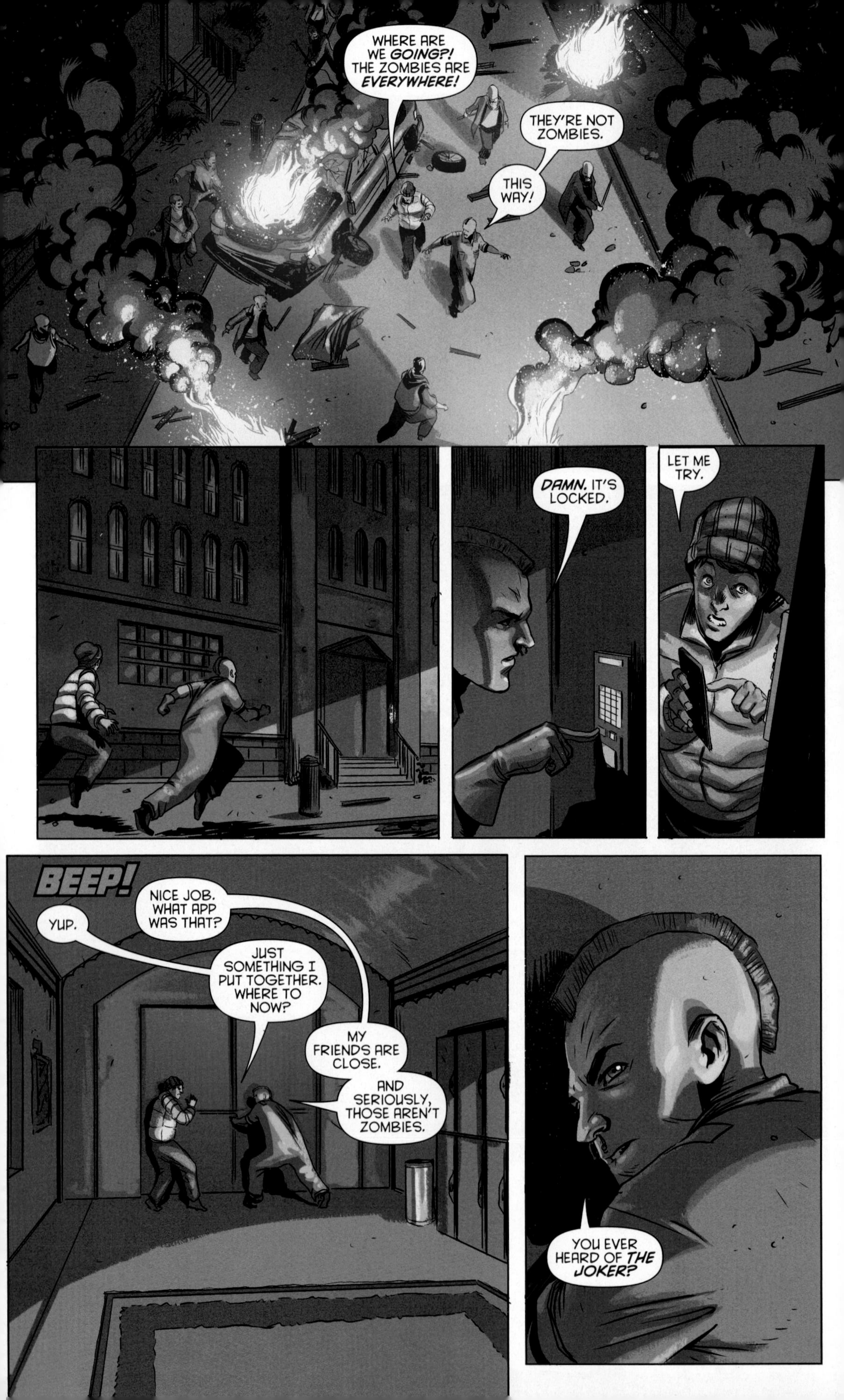
WHERE ARE WE GOING?! THE ZOMBIES ARE EVERYWHERE!
THEY'RE NOT ZOMBIES.
THIS WAY!
DAMN. IT'S LOCKED.
LET ME TRY.
BEEP!
NICE JOB. WHAT APP WAS THAT?
YUP.
JUST SOMETHING I PUT TOGETHER. WHERE TO NOW?
MY FRIENDS ARE CLOSE.
AND SERIOUSLY, THOSE AREN'T ZOMBIES.
YOU EVER HEARD OF THE JOKER?

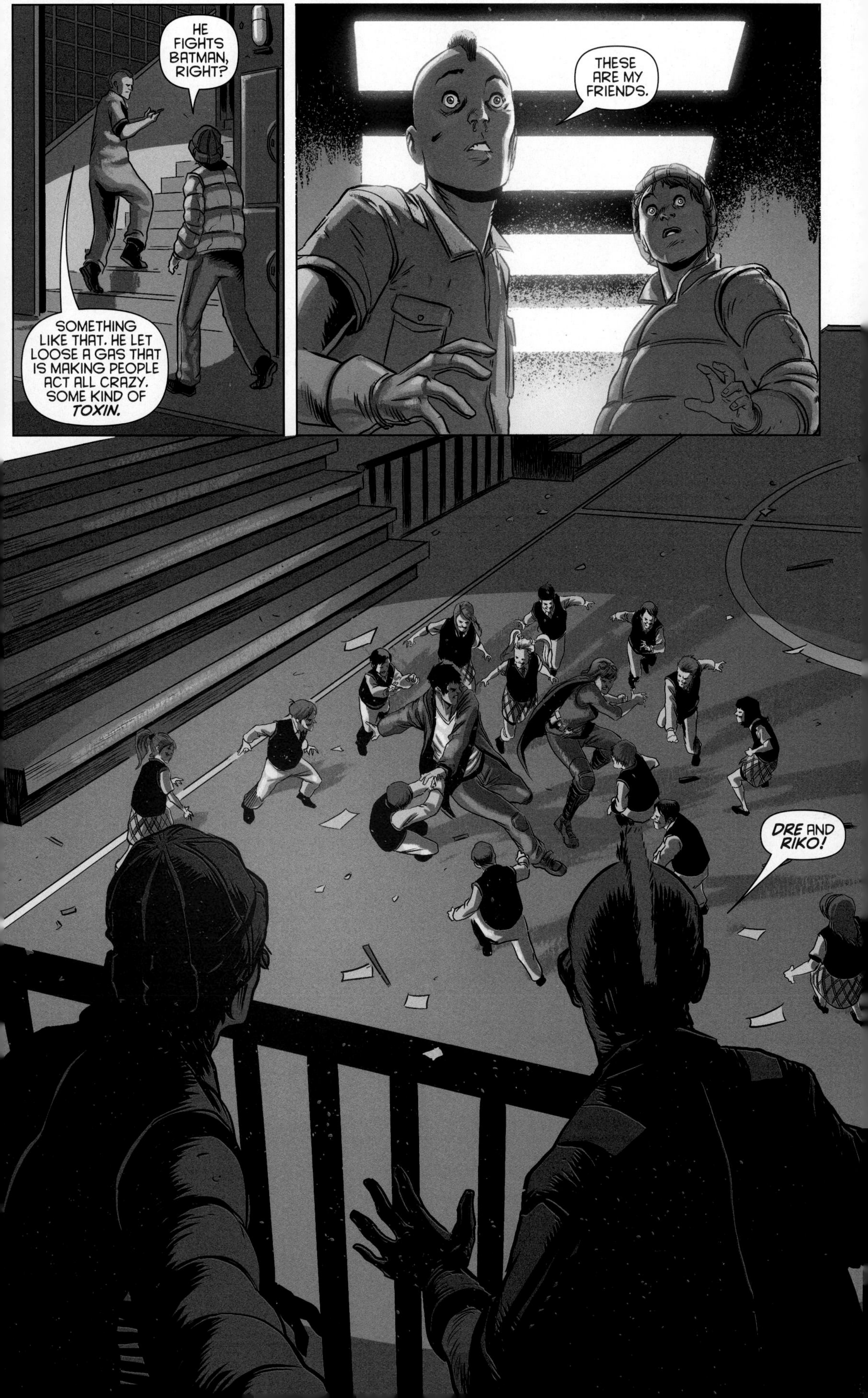
HE FIGHTS BATMAN, RIGHT?
SOMETHING LIKE THAT. HE LET LOOSE A GAS THAT IS MAKING PEOPLE ACT ALL CRAZY. SOME KIND OF *TOXIN.*
THESE ARE MY FRIENDS.
DRE AND *RIKO!*

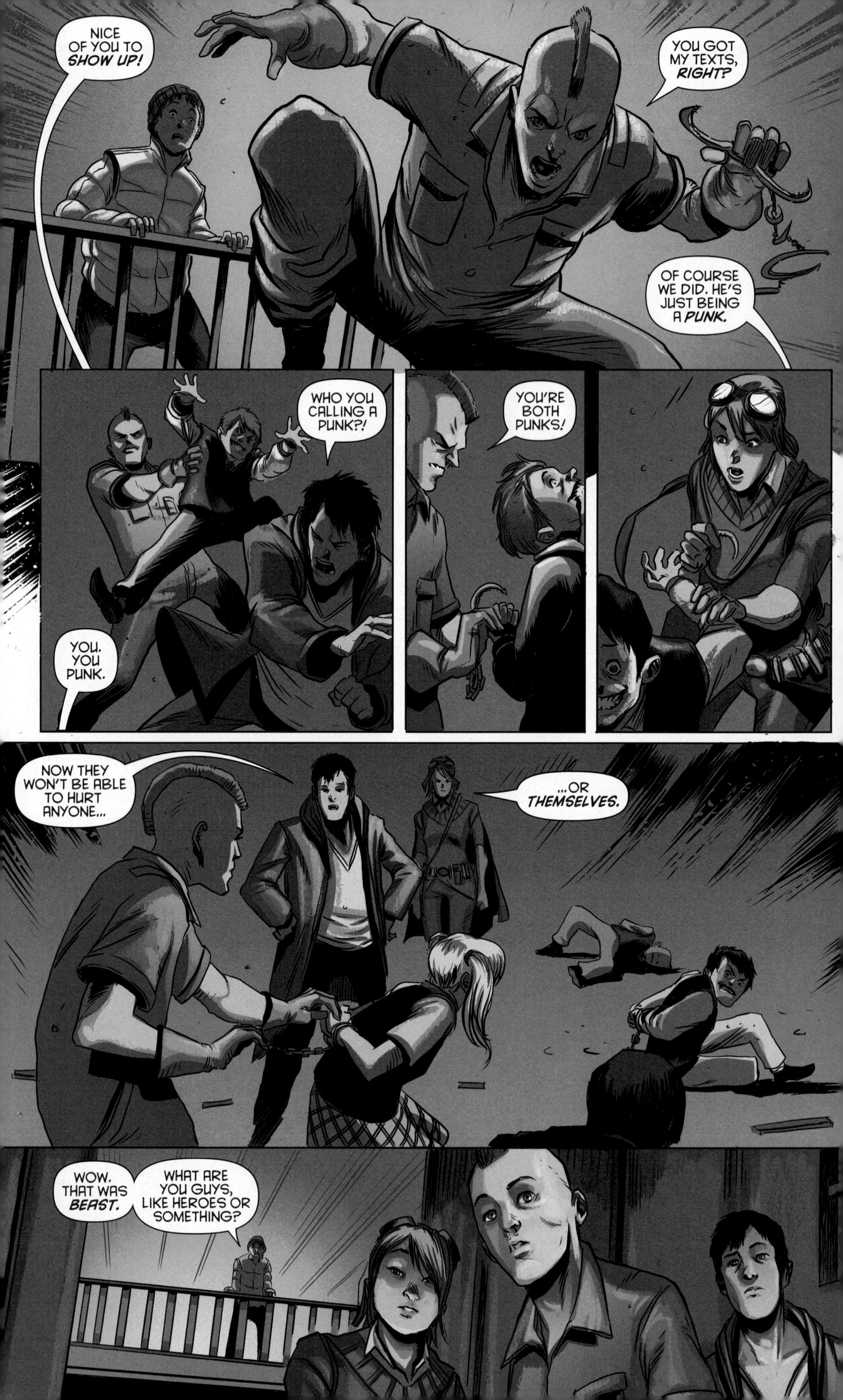
NICE OF YOU TO SHOW UP!
YOU GOT MY TEXTS, RIGHT?
OF COURSE WE DID. HE'S JUST BEING A PUNK.
WHO YOU CALLING A PUNK?!
YOU. YOU PUNK.
YOU'RE BOTH PUNKS!
NOW THEY WON'T BE ABLE TO HURT ANYONE...
...OR THEMSELVES.
WOW. THAT WAS BEAST.
WHAT ARE YOU GUYS, LIKE HEROES OR SOMETHING?

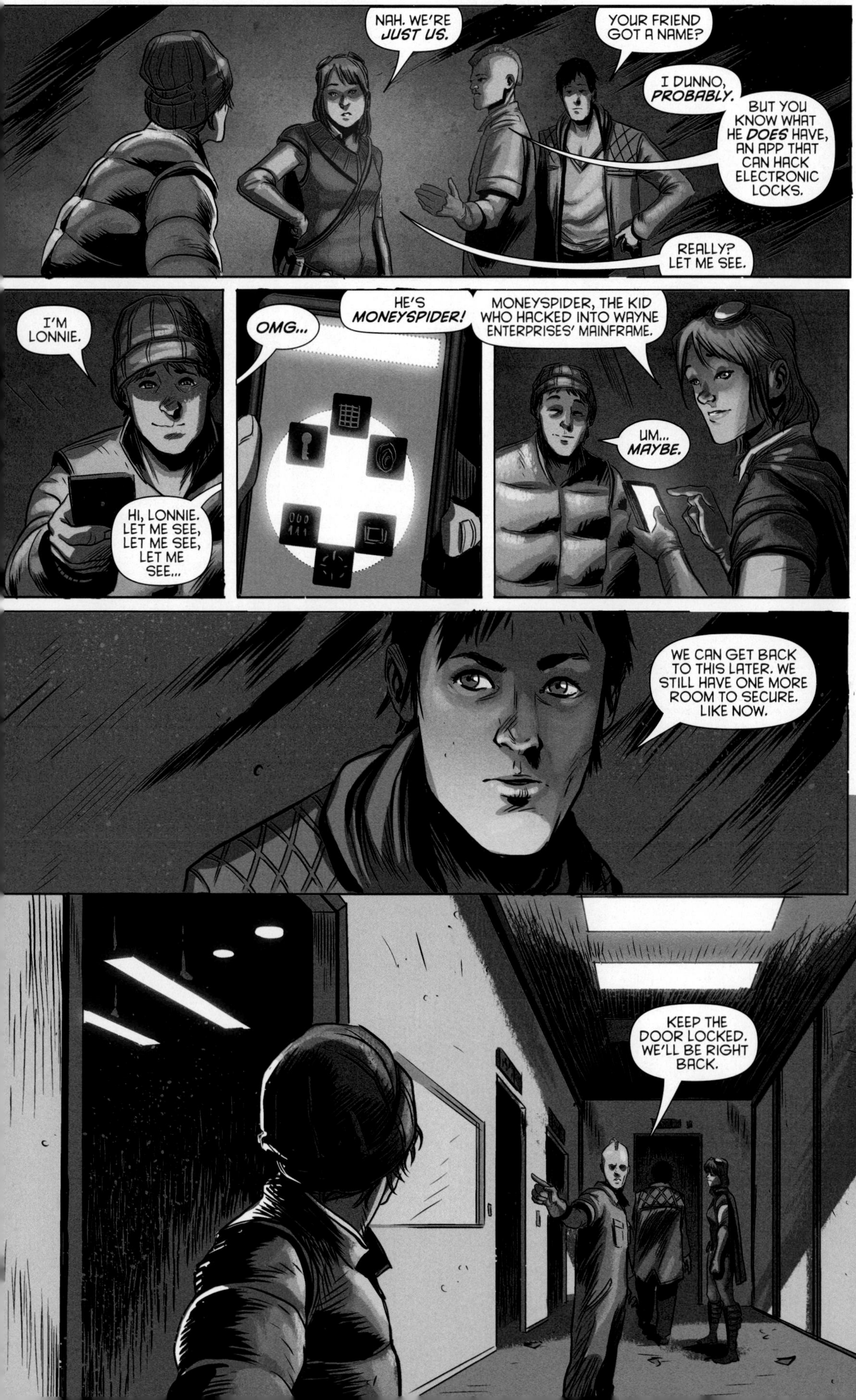
NAH. WE'RE *JUST US.*
YOUR FRIEND GOT A NAME?
I DUNNO, ***PROBABLY.***
BUT YOU KNOW WHAT HE ***DOES*** HAVE, AN APP THAT CAN HACK ELECTRONIC LOCKS.
REALLY? LET ME SEE.
I'M LONNIE.
HI, LONNIE. LET ME SEE, LET ME SEE, LET ME SEE...
OMG...
HE'S ***MONEYSPIDER!***
MONEYSPIDER, THE KID WHO HACKED INTO WAYNE ENTERPRISES' MAINFRAME.
UM... ***MAYBE.***
WE CAN GET BACK TO THIS LATER. WE STILL HAVE ONE MORE ROOM TO SECURE. LIKE NOW.
KEEP THE DOOR LOCKED. WE'LL BE RIGHT BACK.

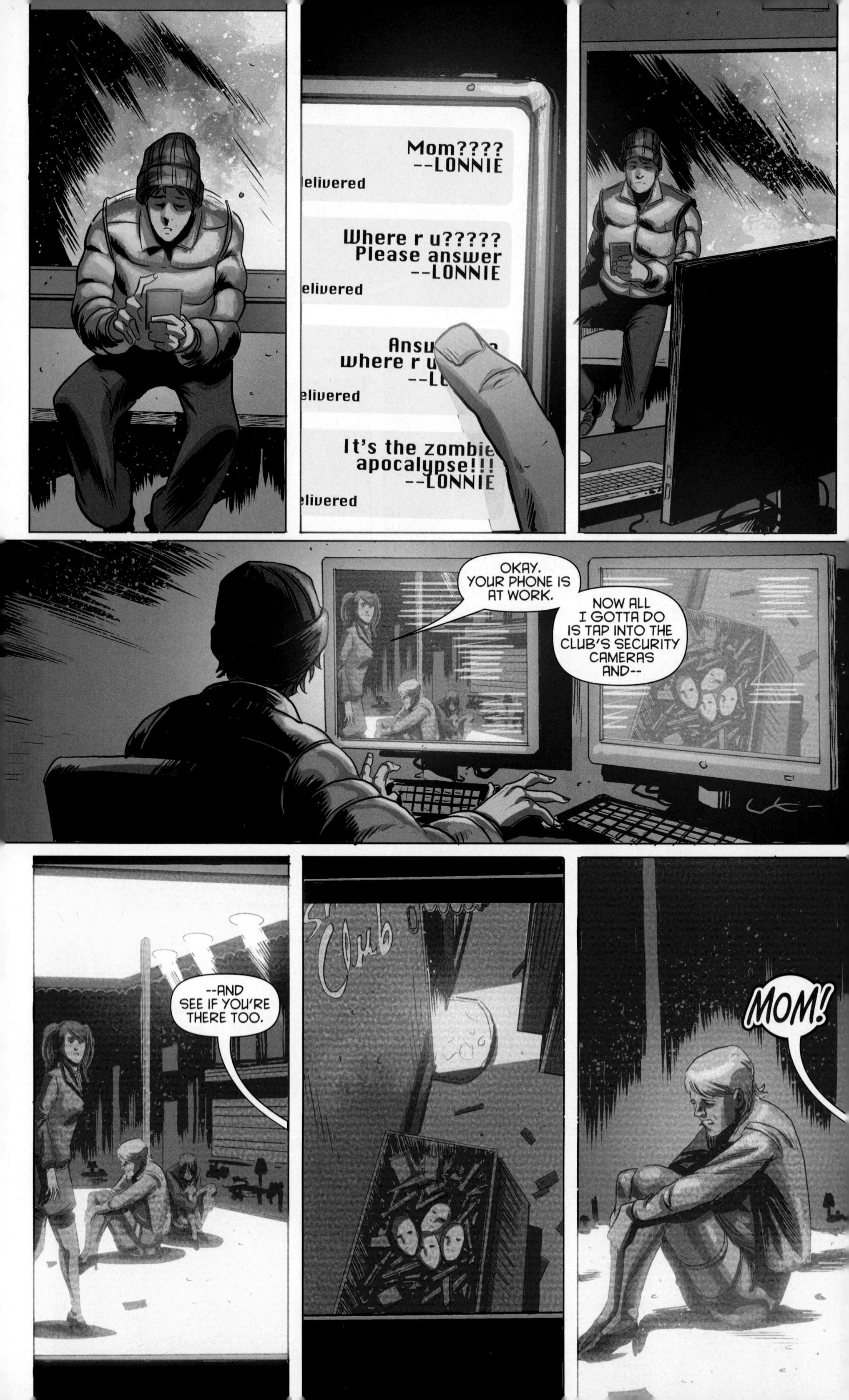
Mom????
--LONNIE
elivered
Where r u?????
Please answer
--LONNIE
elivered
Ansu
where r u
--L
elivered
It's the zombie
apocalypse!!!
--LONNIE
elivered
OKAY. YOUR PHONE IS AT WORK.
NOW ALL I GOTTA DO IS TAP INTO THE CLUB'S SECURITY CAMERAS AND--
--AND SEE IF YOU'RE THERE TOO.
Club
MOM!

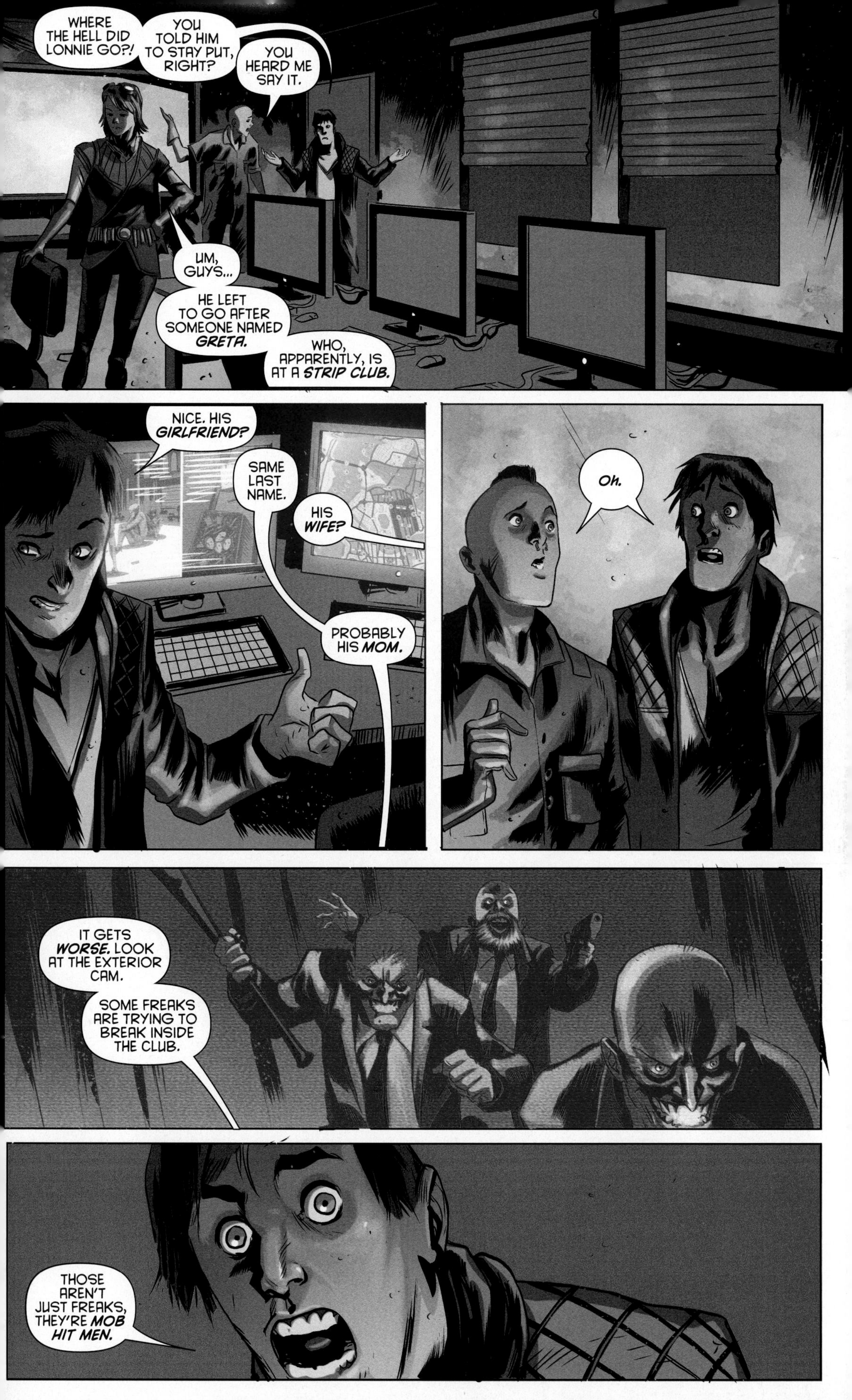

WHERE THE HELL DID LONNIE GO?!
YOU TOLD HIM TO STAY PUT, RIGHT?
YOU HEARD ME SAY IT.
UM, GUYS...
HE LEFT TO GO AFTER SOMEONE NAMED GRETA.
WHO, APPARENTLY, IS AT A STRIP CLUB.
NICE. HIS GIRLFRIEND?
SAME LAST NAME.
HIS WIFE?
PROBABLY HIS MOM.
Oh.
IT GETS WORSE. LOOK AT THE EXTERIOR CAM.
SOME FREAKS ARE TRYING TO BREAK INSIDE THE CLUB.
THOSE AREN'T JUST FREAKS, THEY'RE MOB HIT MEN.

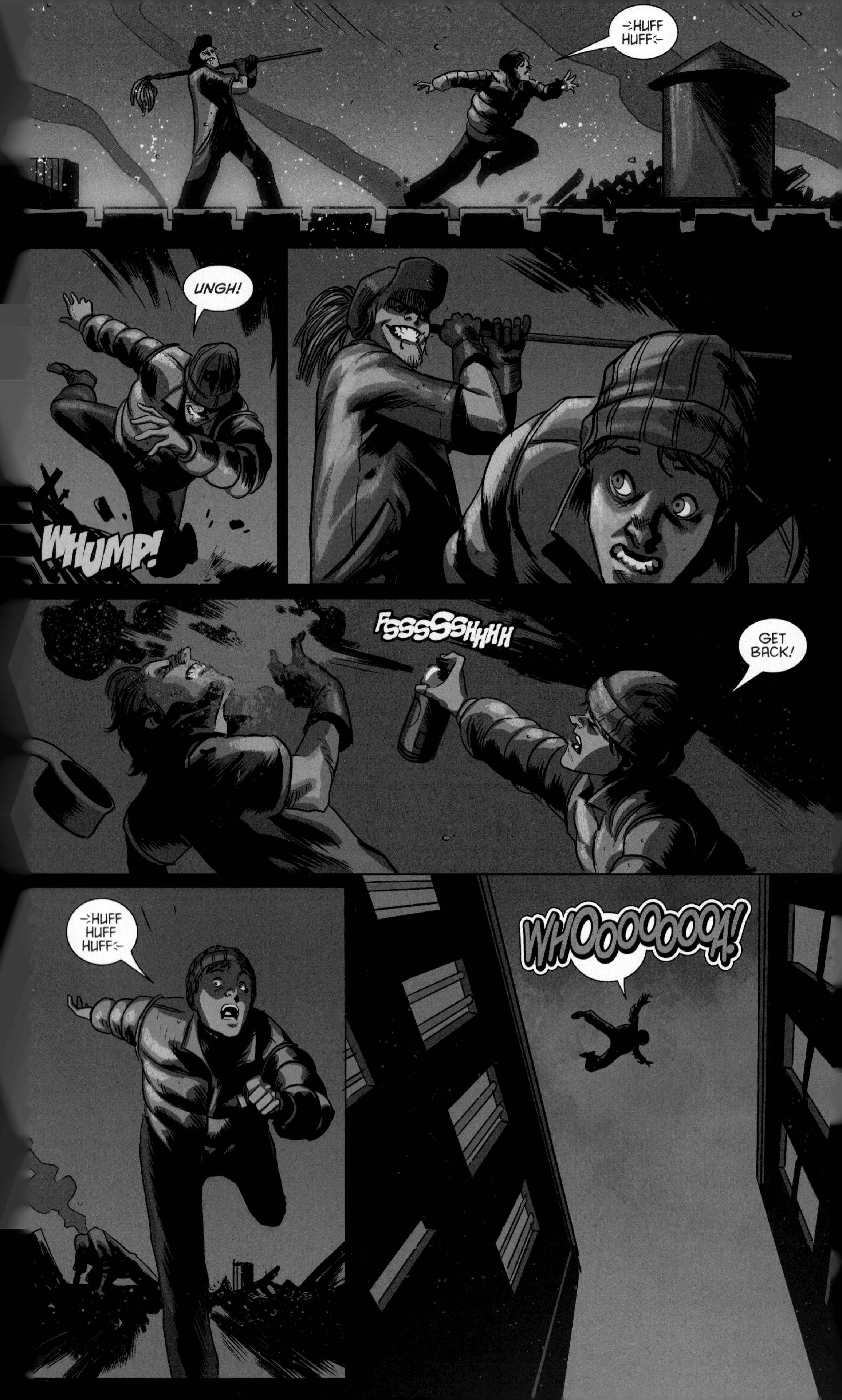

HUFF HUFF
UNGH!
WHUMP!
FSSSSSHHHH
GET BACK!
HUFF HUFF HUFF
WHOOOOOOOA!

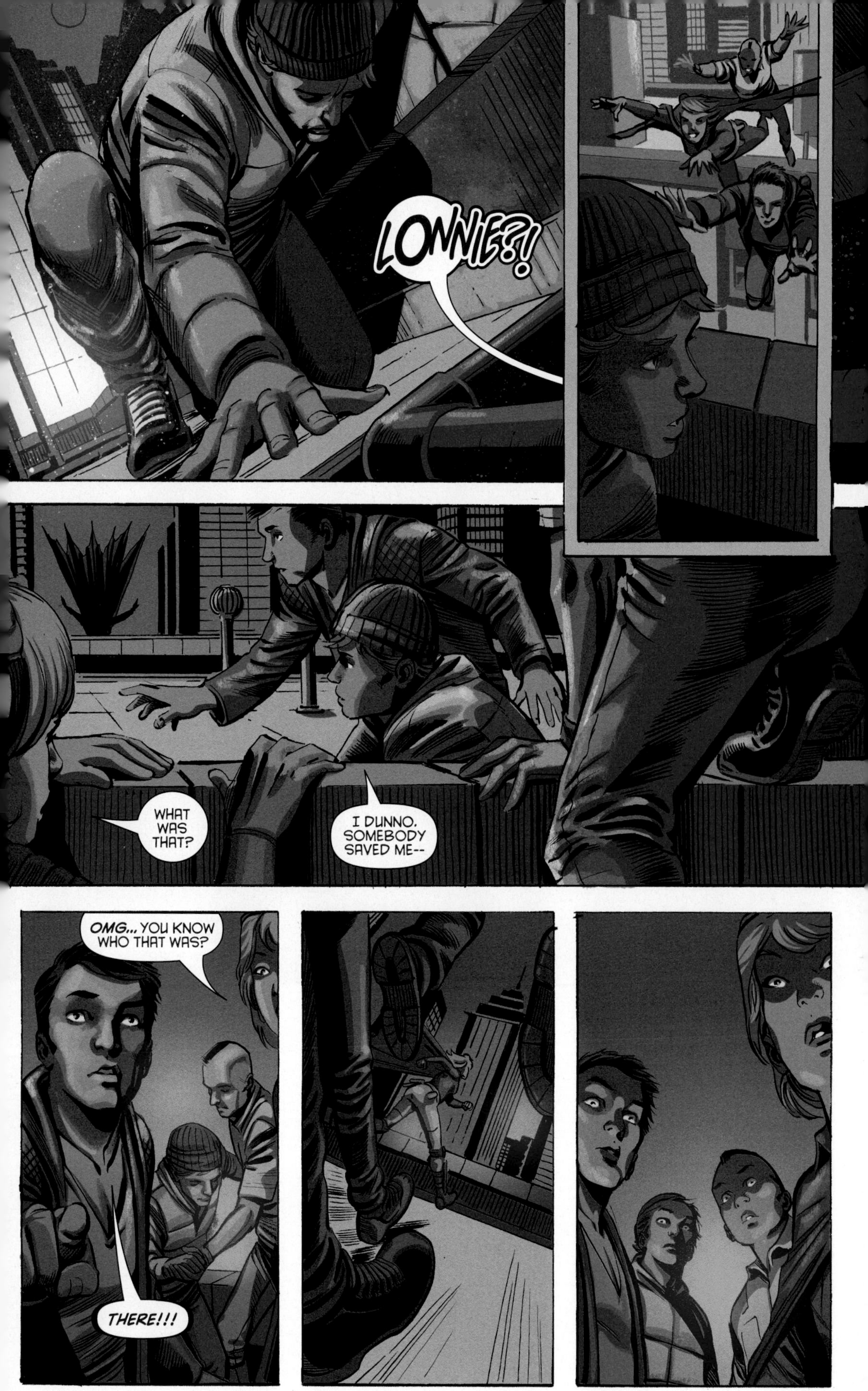
LONNIE?!
WHAT WAS THAT?
I DUNNO. SOMEBODY SAVED ME--
OMG... YOU KNOW WHO THAT WAS?
THERE!!!

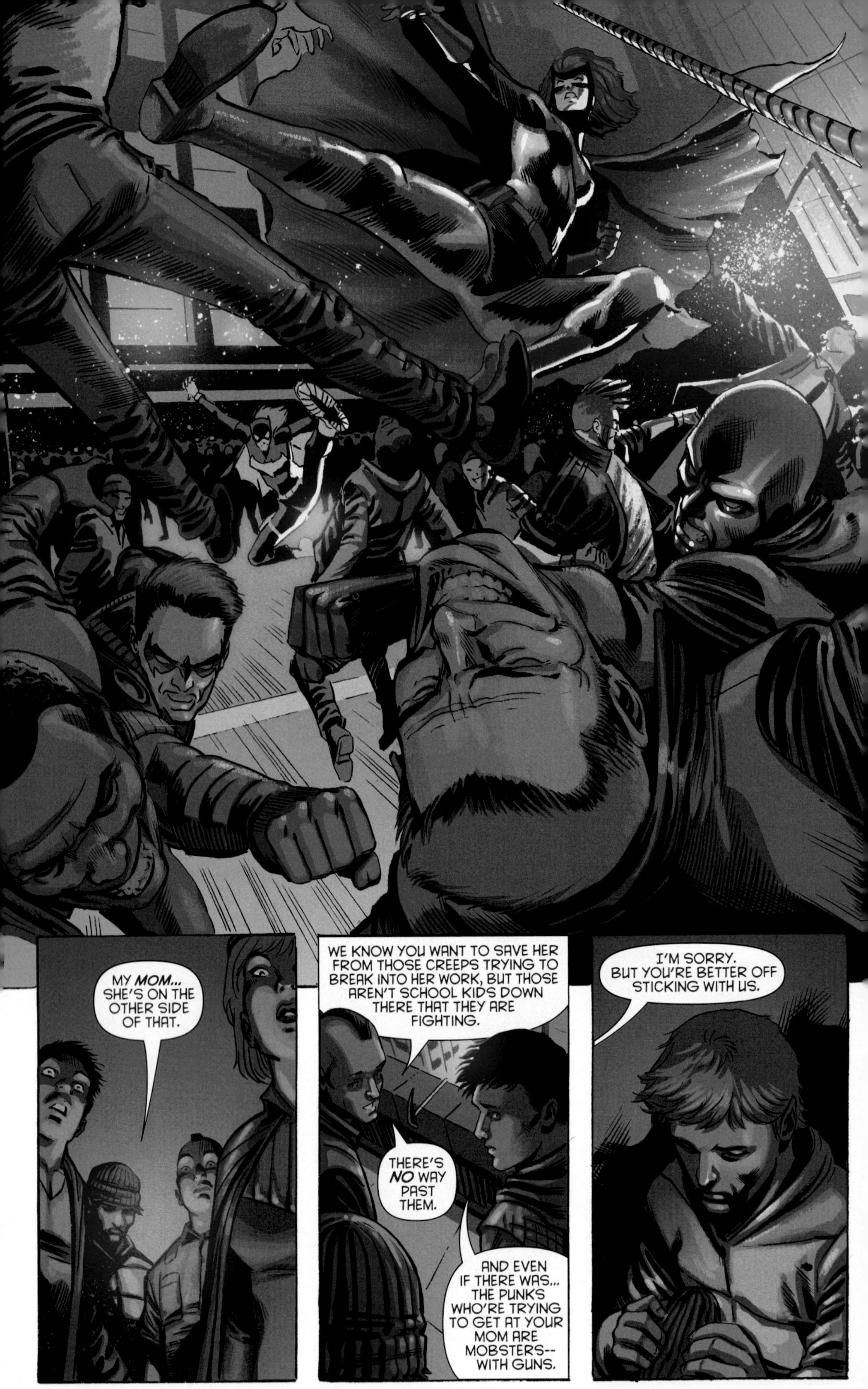

MY MOM... SHE'S ON THE OTHER SIDE OF THAT.
WE KNOW YOU WANT TO SAVE HER FROM THOSE CREEPS TRYING TO BREAK INTO HER WORK, BUT THOSE AREN'T SCHOOL KIDS DOWN THERE THAT THEY ARE FIGHTING.
THERE'S NO WAY PAST THEM.
AND EVEN IF THERE WAS... THE PUNKS WHO'RE TRYING TO GET AT YOUR MOM ARE MOBSTERS-- WITH GUNS.
I'M SORRY. BUT YOU'RE BETTER OFF STICKING WITH US.

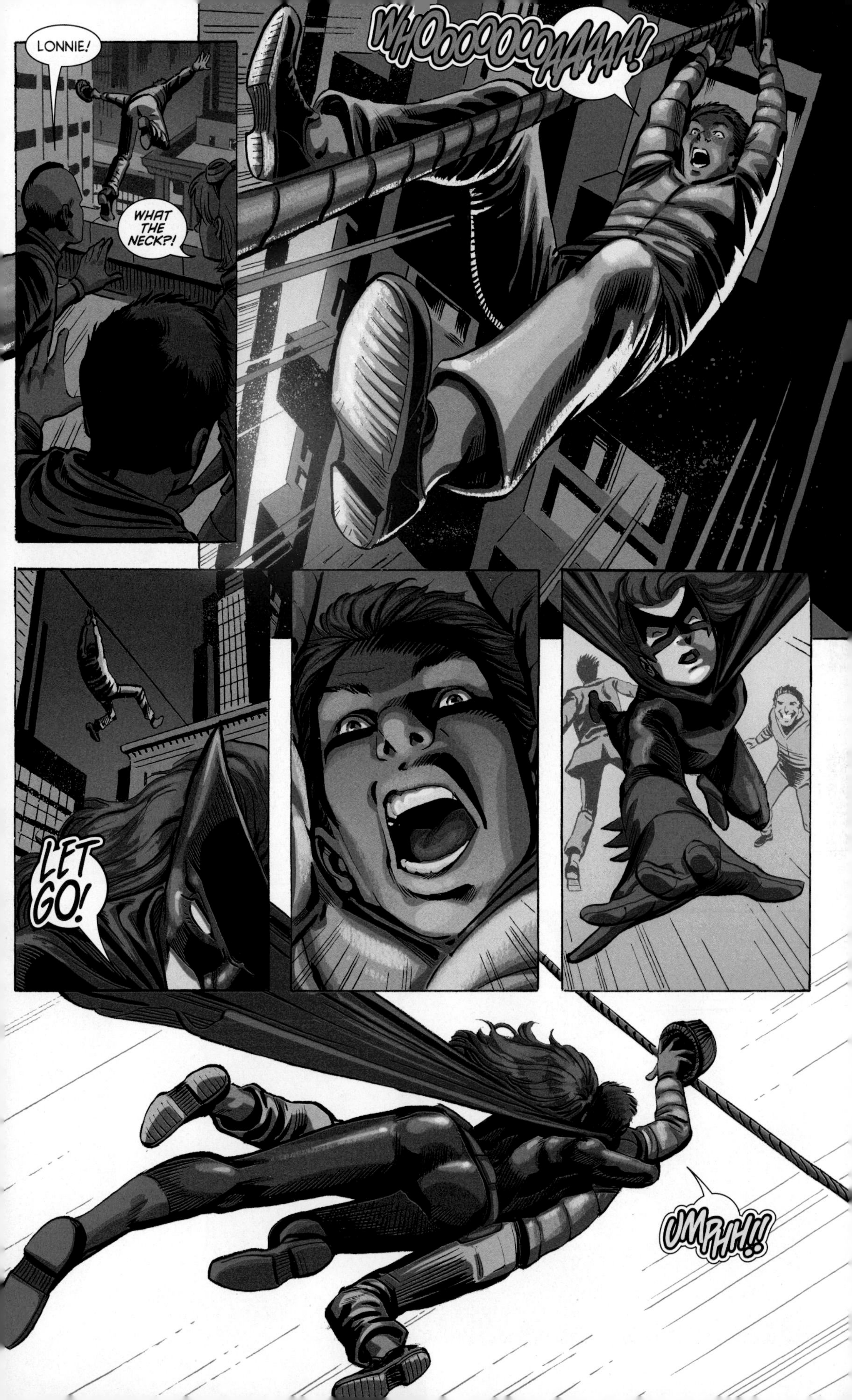
LONNIE!
WHOOOOOOOAAAAA!
WHAT THE NECK?!
LET GO!
UMPHH!!

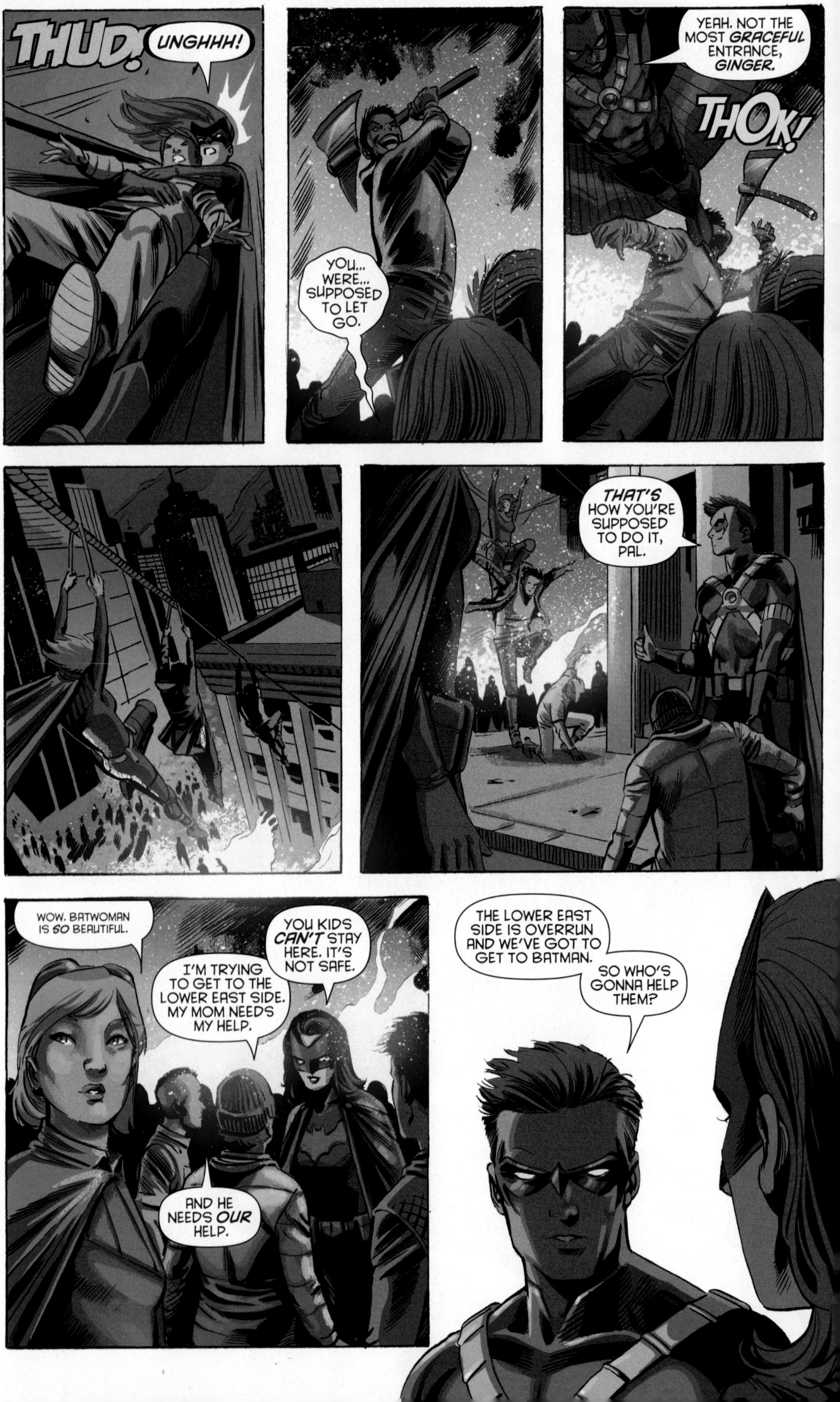
THUD!
UNGHHH!
YOU... WERE... SUPPOSED TO LET GO.
YEAH. NOT THE MOST GRACEFUL ENTRANCE, GINGER.
THOK!
THAT'S HOW YOU'RE SUPPOSED TO DO IT, PAL.
WOW. BATWOMAN IS SO BEAUTIFUL.
I'M TRYING TO GET TO THE LOWER EAST SIDE. MY MOM NEEDS MY HELP.
YOU KIDS CAN'T STAY HERE. IT'S NOT SAFE.
AND HE NEEDS OUR HELP.
THE LOWER EAST SIDE IS OVERRUN AND WE'VE GOT TO GET TO BATMAN.
SO WHO'S GONNA HELP THEM?

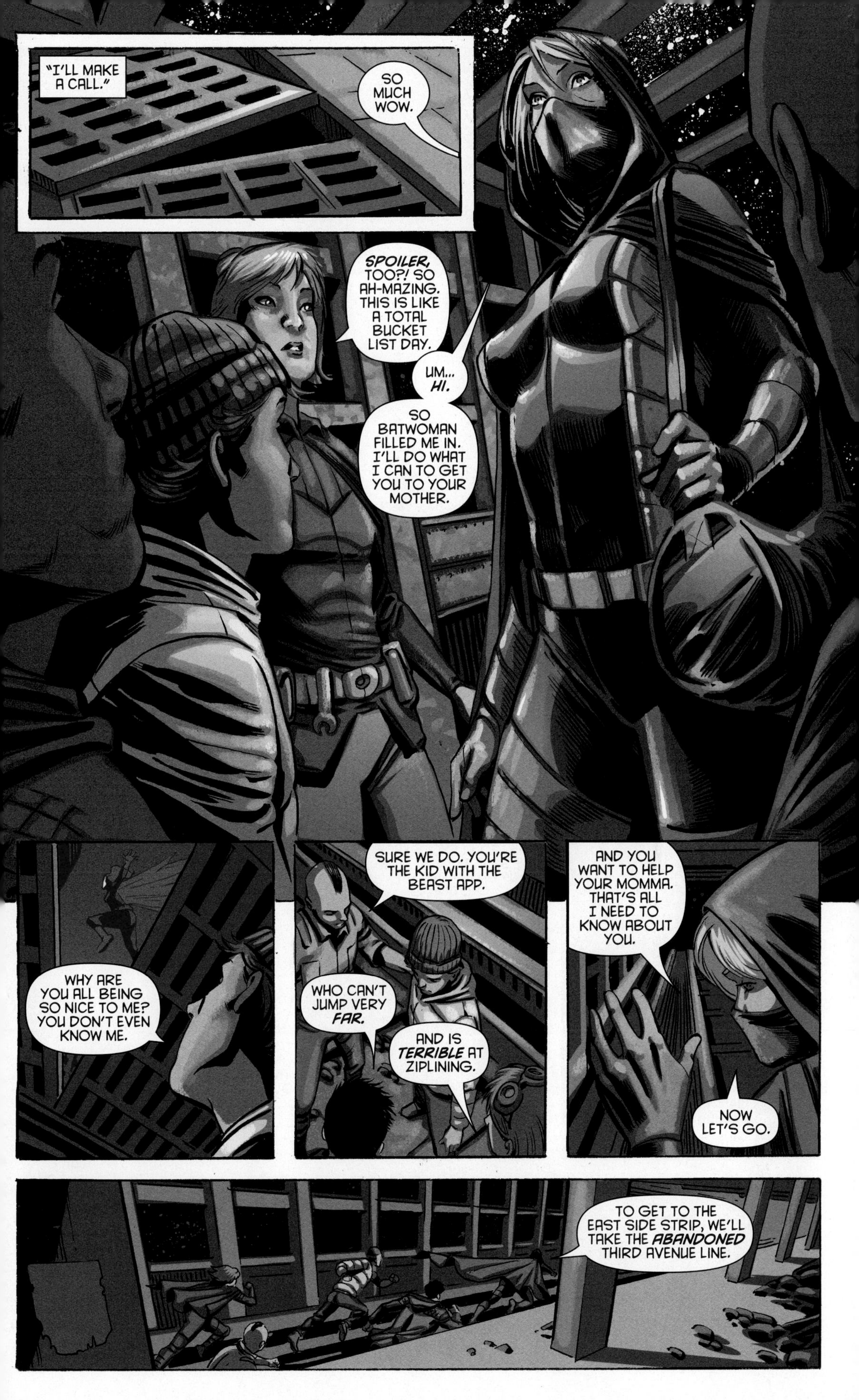
"I'LL MAKE A CALL."
SO MUCH WOW.
SPOILER, TOO?! SO AH-MAZING. THIS IS LIKE A TOTAL BUCKET LIST DAY.
UM... HI.
SO BATWOMAN FILLED ME IN. I'LL DO WHAT I CAN TO GET YOU TO YOUR MOTHER.
WHY ARE YOU ALL BEING SO NICE TO ME? YOU DON'T EVEN KNOW ME.
SURE WE DO. YOU'RE THE KID WITH THE BEAST APP.
WHO CAN'T JUMP VERY FAR.
AND IS TERRIBLE AT ZIPLINING.
AND YOU WANT TO HELP YOUR MOMMA. THAT'S ALL I NEED TO KNOW ABOUT YOU.
NOW LET'S GO.
TO GET TO THE EAST SIDE STRIP, WE'LL TAKE THE ABANDONED THIRD AVENUE LINE.

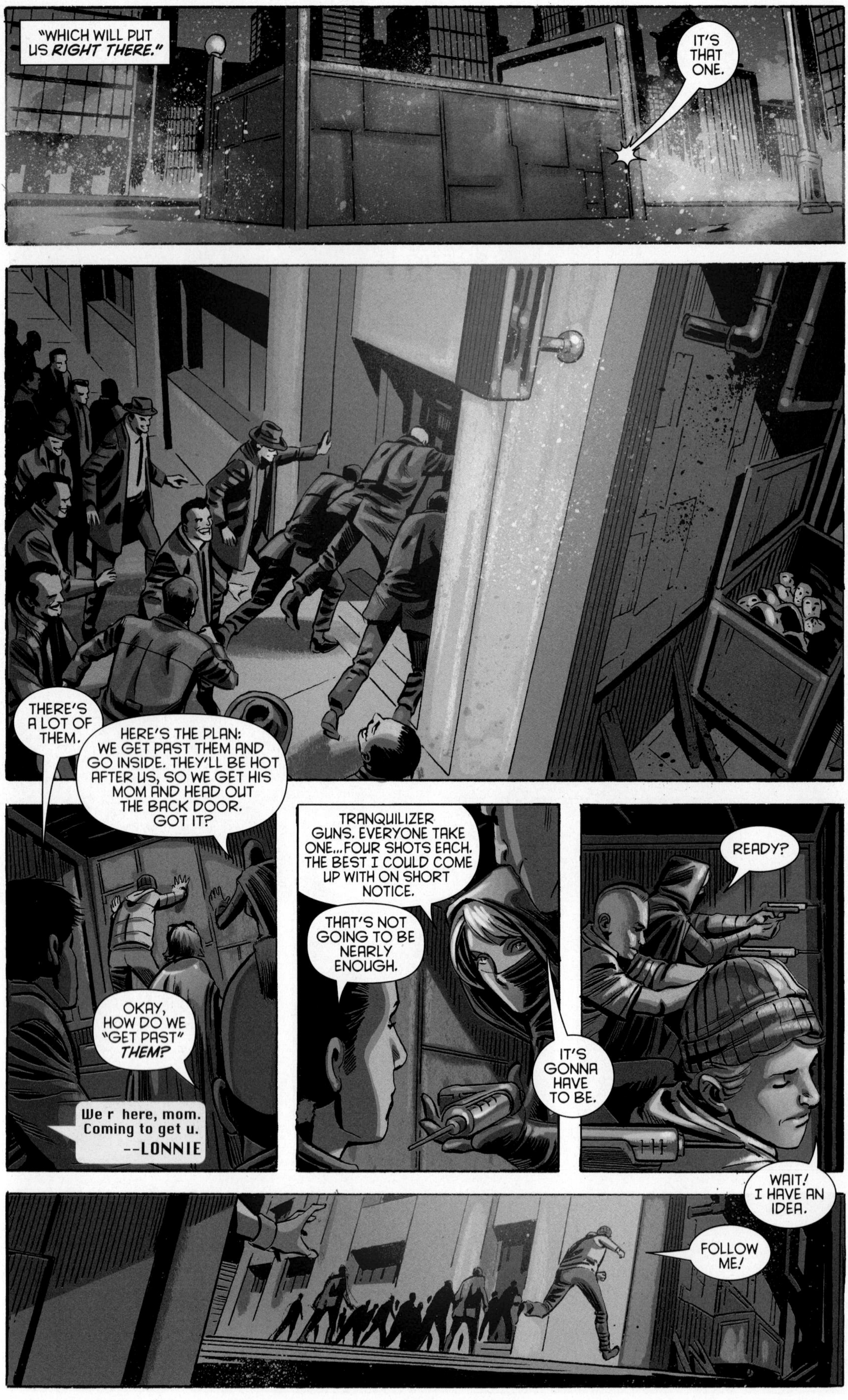
"WHICH WILL PUT US *RIGHT THERE.*"
IT'S THAT ONE.
THERE'S A LOT OF THEM.
HERE'S THE PLAN: WE GET PAST THEM AND GO INSIDE. THEY'LL BE HOT AFTER US, SO WE GET HIS MOM AND HEAD OUT THE BACK DOOR. GOT IT?
OKAY, HOW DO WE "GET PAST" *THEM?*
We r here, mom. Coming to get u. --LONNIE
TRANQUILIZER GUNS. EVERYONE TAKE ONE...FOUR SHOTS EACH. THE BEST I COULD COME UP WITH ON SHORT NOTICE.
THAT'S NOT GOING TO BE NEARLY ENOUGH.
IT'S GONNA HAVE TO BE.
READY?
WAIT! I HAVE AN IDEA.
FOLLOW ME!

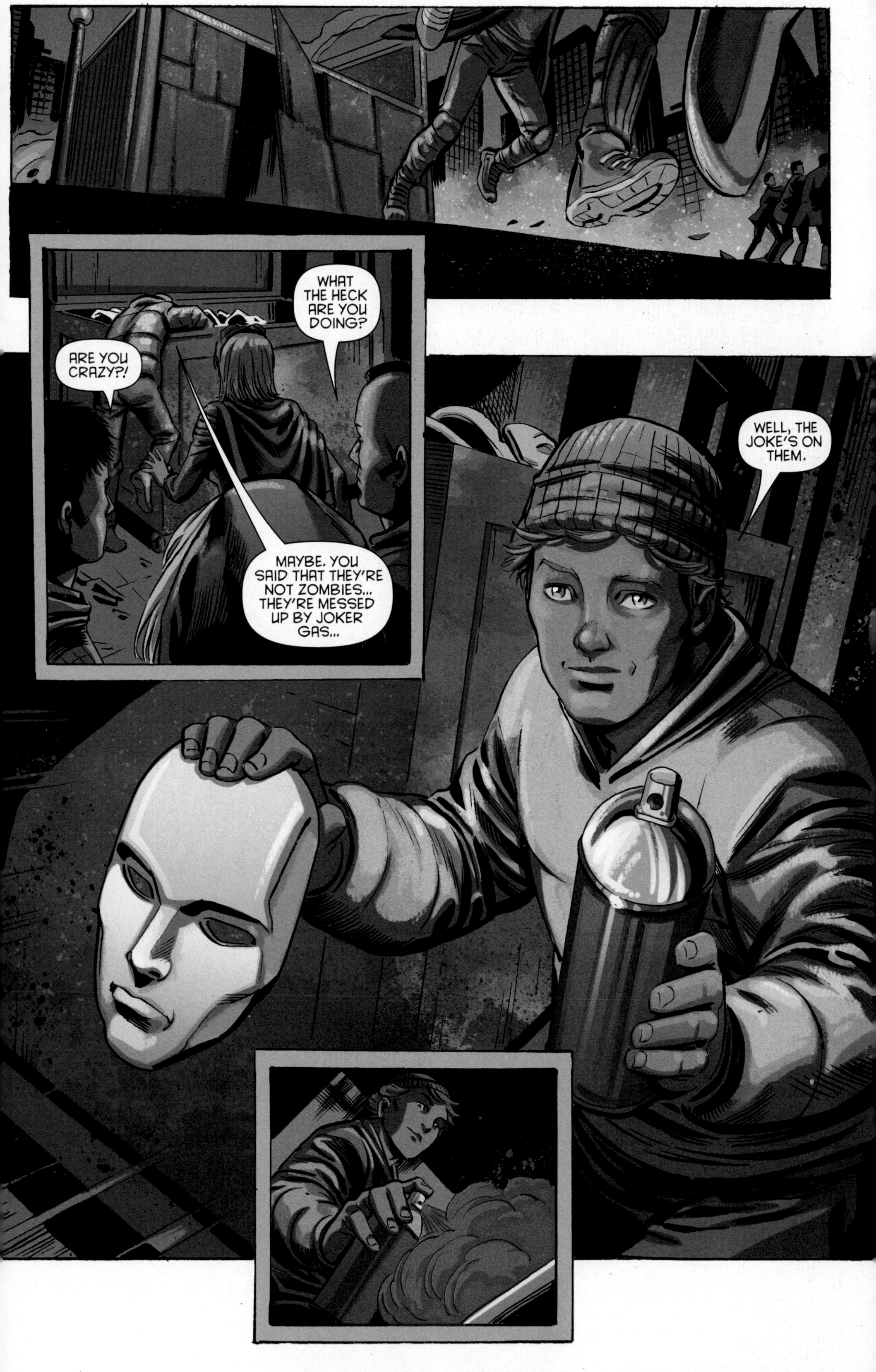
WHAT THE HECK ARE YOU DOING?
ARE YOU CRAZY?!
MAYBE. YOU SAID THAT THEY'RE NOT ZOMBIES... THEY'RE MESSED UP BY JOKER GAS...
WELL, THE JOKE'S ON THEM.

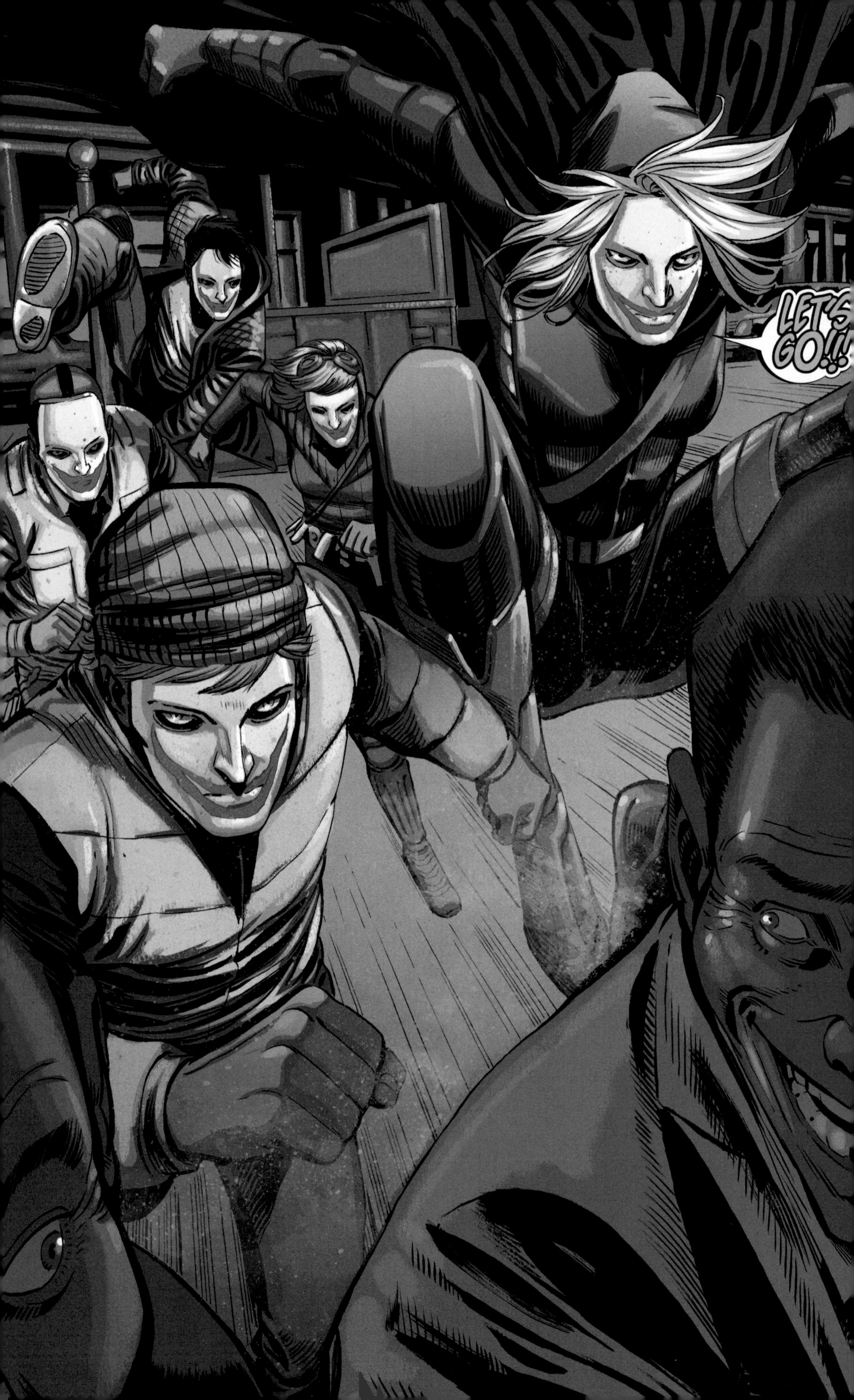
LET'S GO!!!

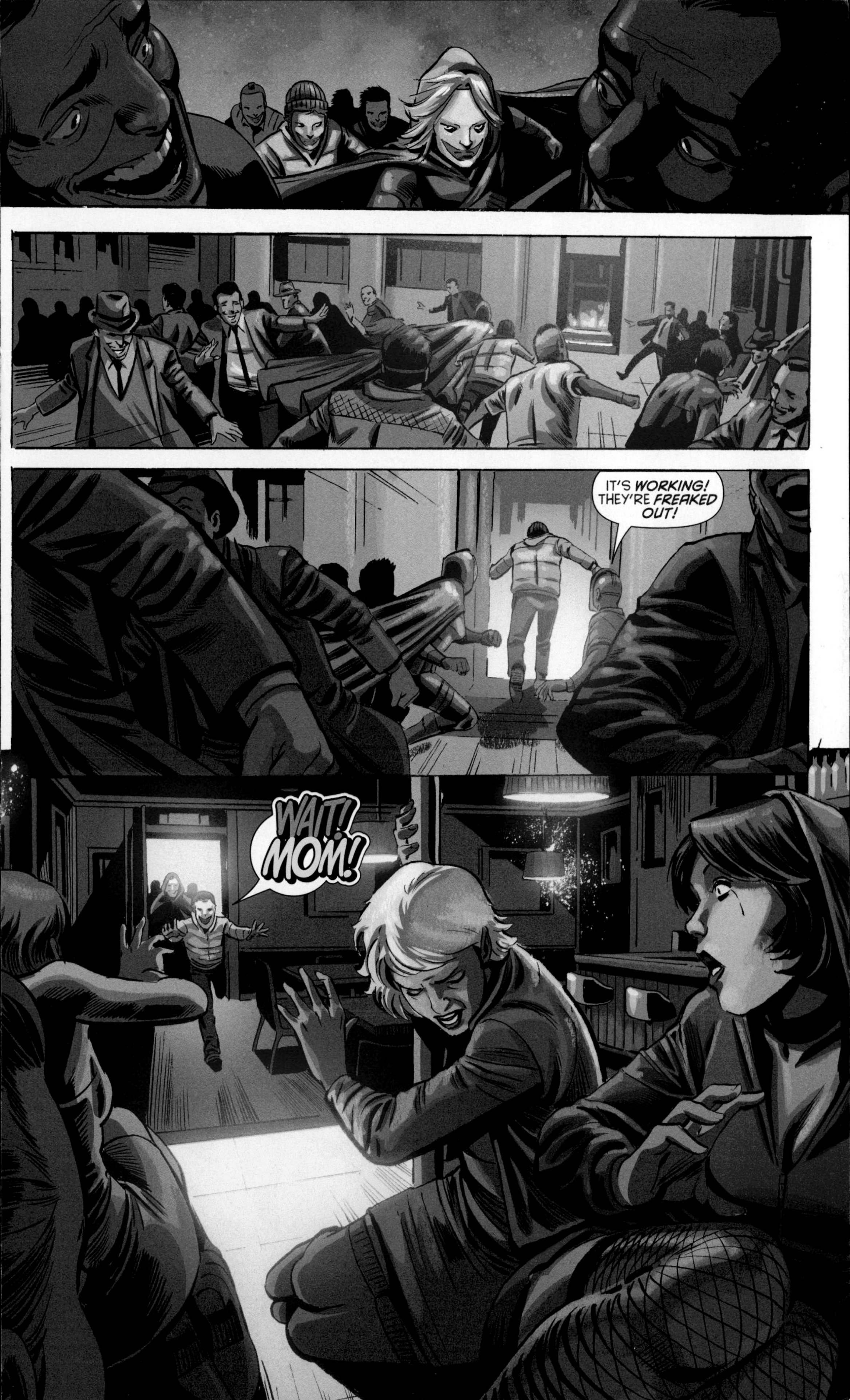
IT'S WORKING! THEY'RE FREAKED OUT!
WAIT! MOM!

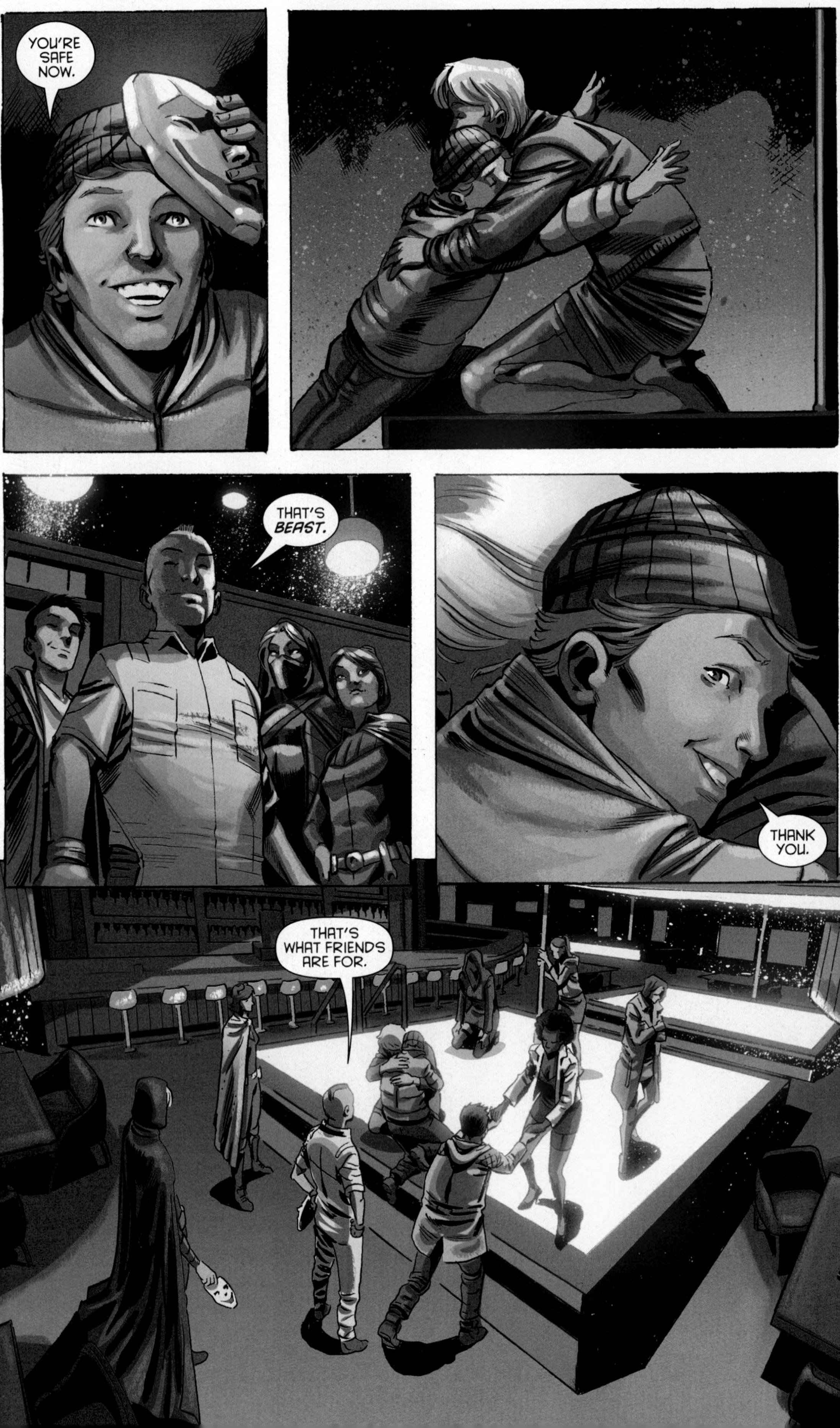
YOU'RE SAFE NOW.
THAT'S BEAST.
THANK YOU.
THAT'S WHAT FRIENDS ARE FOR.

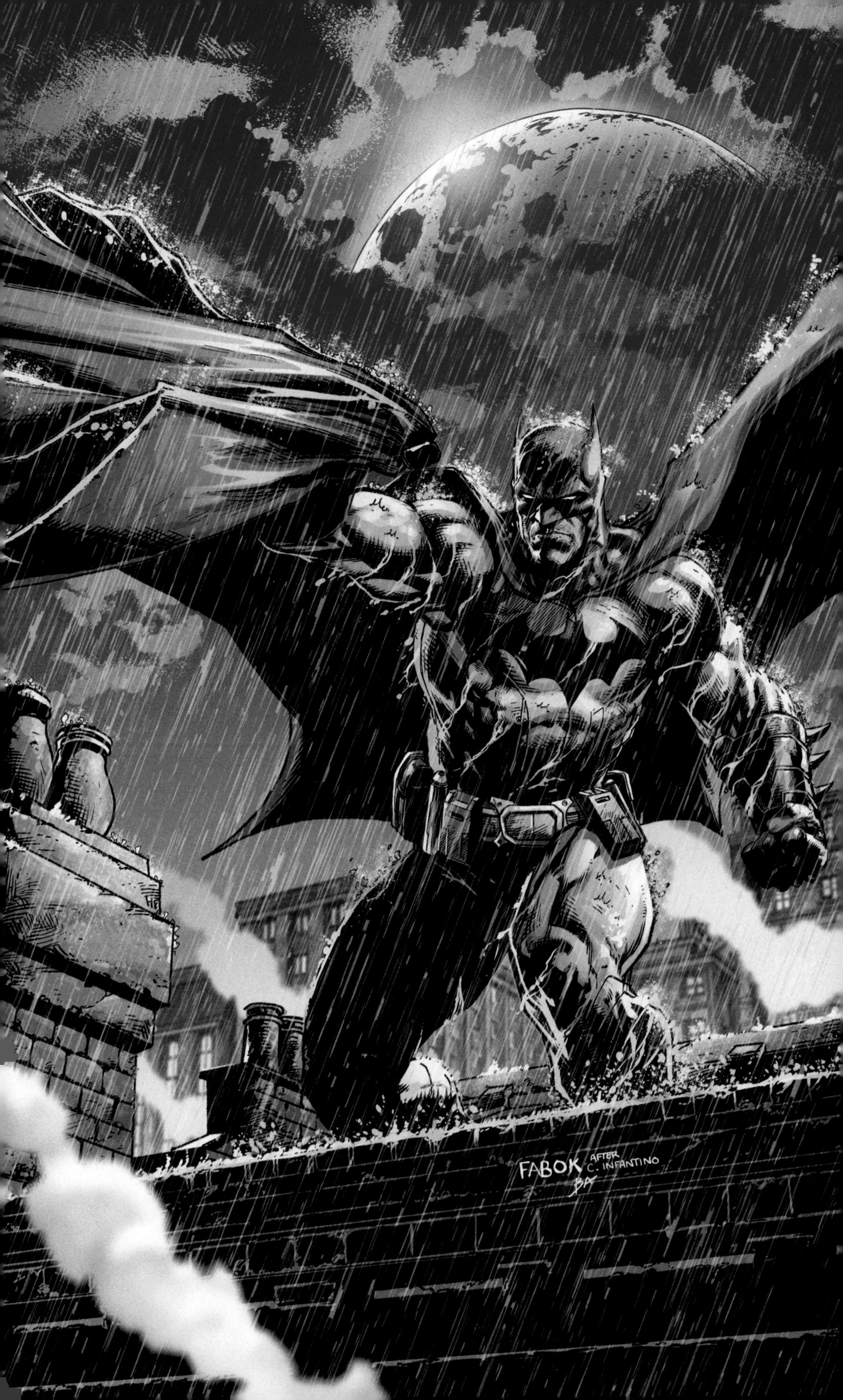
FABOK AFTER C. INFANTINO
BA

BRIAN BUCCELLATO writer SCOTT HEPBURN, CLIFF RICHARDS & FABRIZIO FIORENTINO artists BRIAN BUCCELLATO & LEE LOUGHRIDGE colorists DEZI SIENTY letterer
cover by JASON FABOK & BRAD ANDERSON

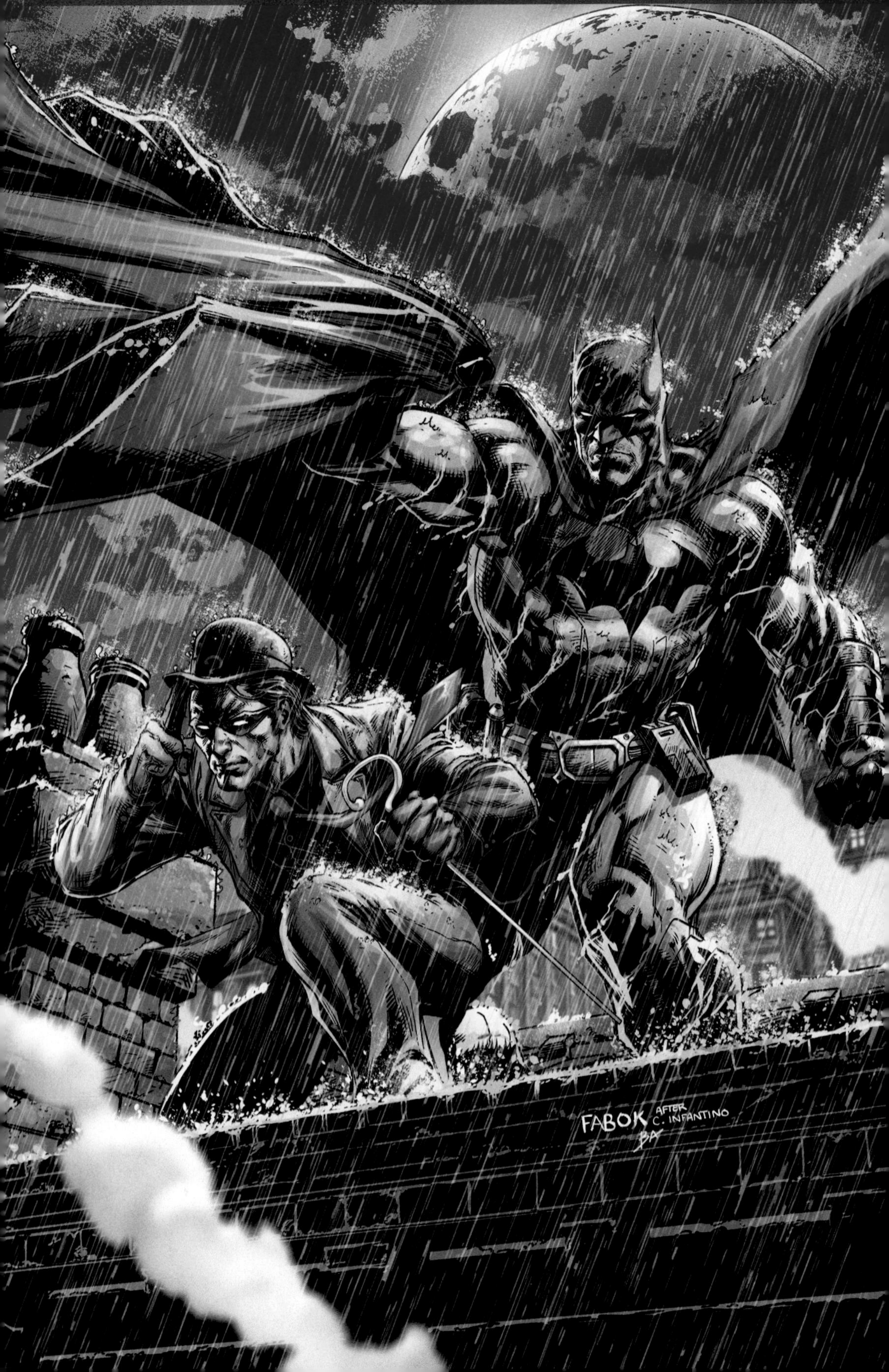
FABOK AFTER C. INFANTINO
BA

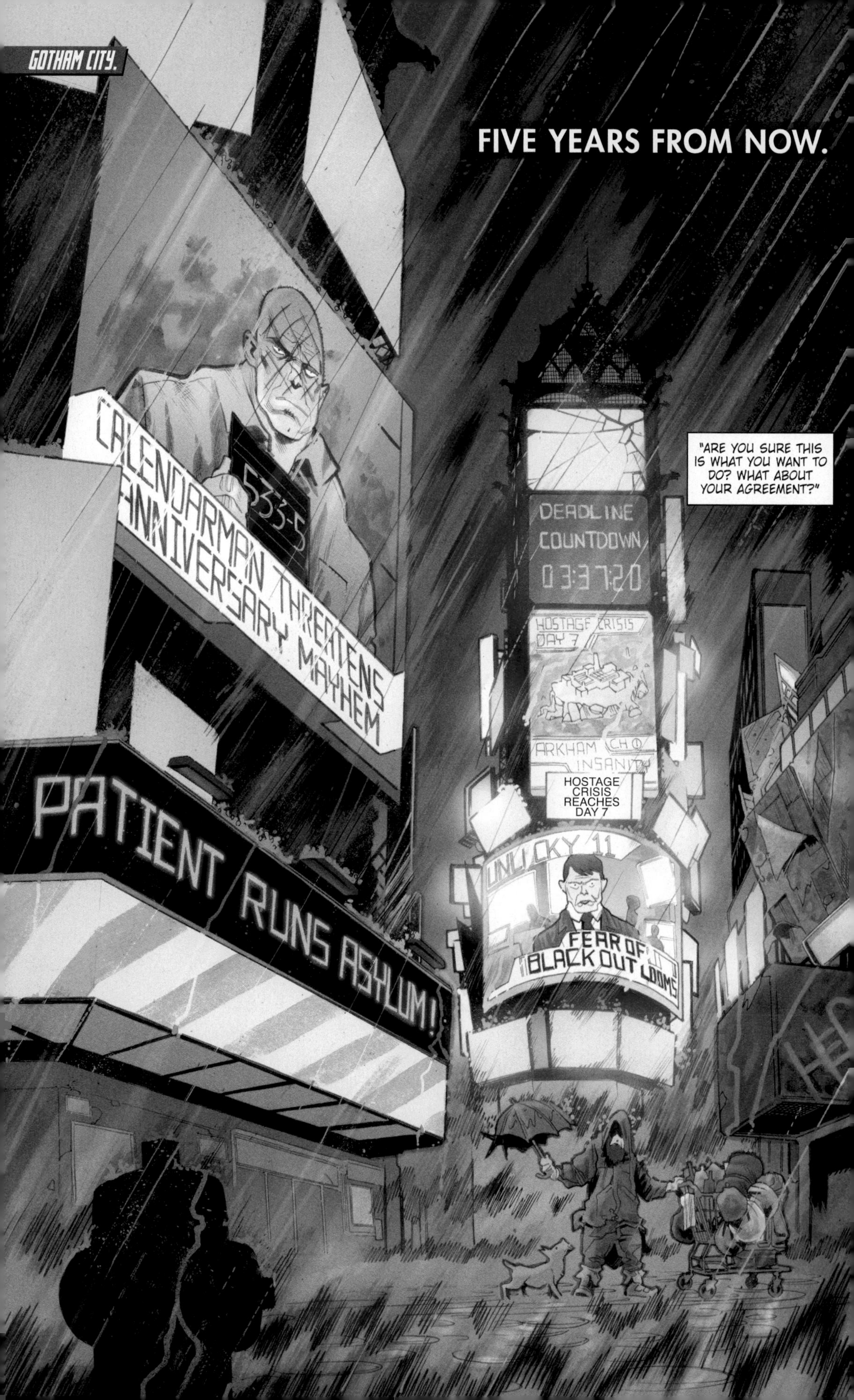
GOTHAM CITY.
FIVE YEARS FROM NOW.
CALENDARMAN THREATENS ANNIVERSARY MAYHEM
DEADLINE COUNTDOWN 03:37:20
"ARE YOU SURE THIS IS WHAT YOU WANT TO DO? WHAT ABOUT YOUR AGREEMENT?"
HOSTAGE CRISIS DAY 7
ARKHAM INSANITY
HOSTAGE CRISIS REACHES DAY 7
PATIENT RUNS ASYLUM!
FEAR OF BLACK OUT LOOMS

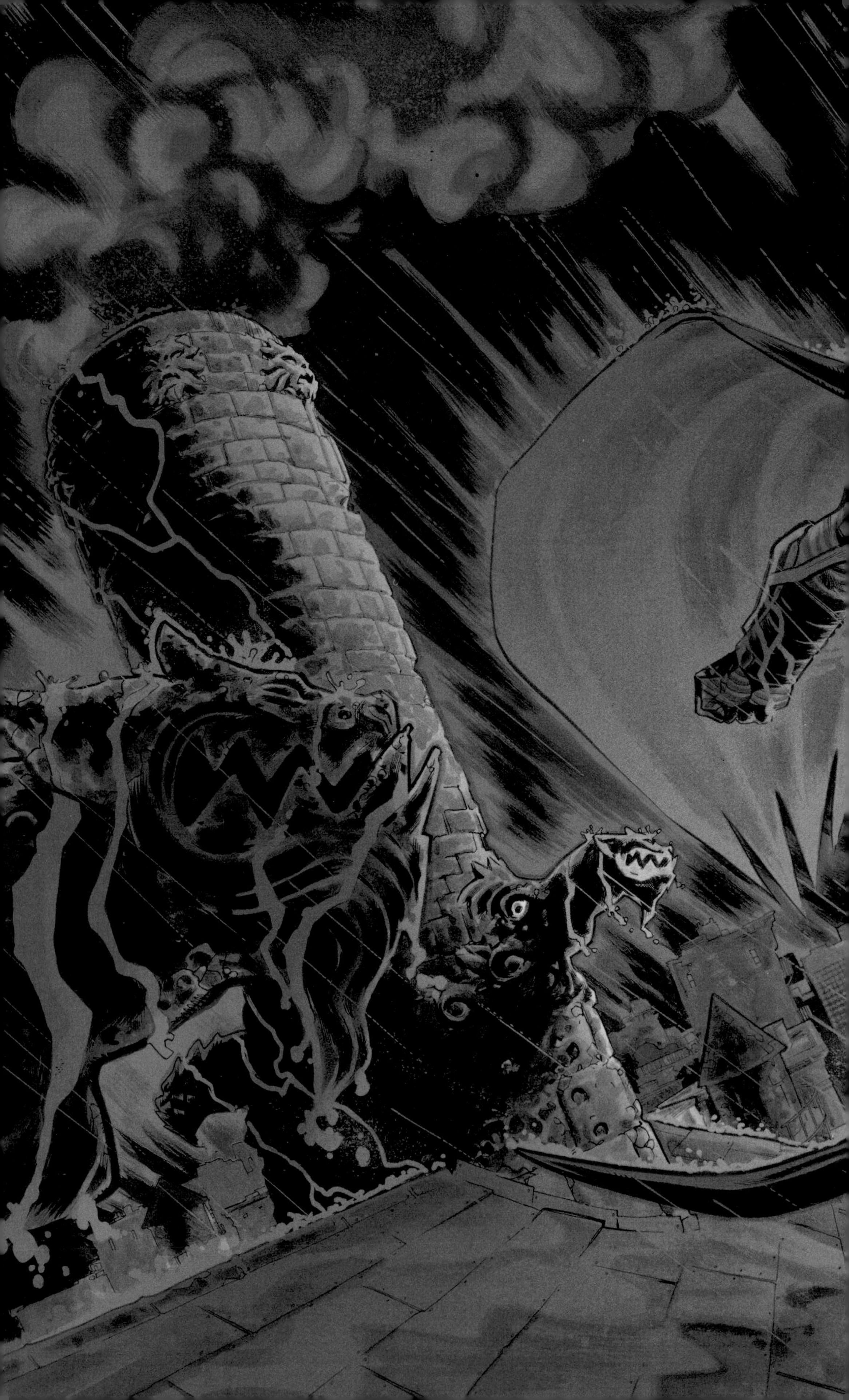

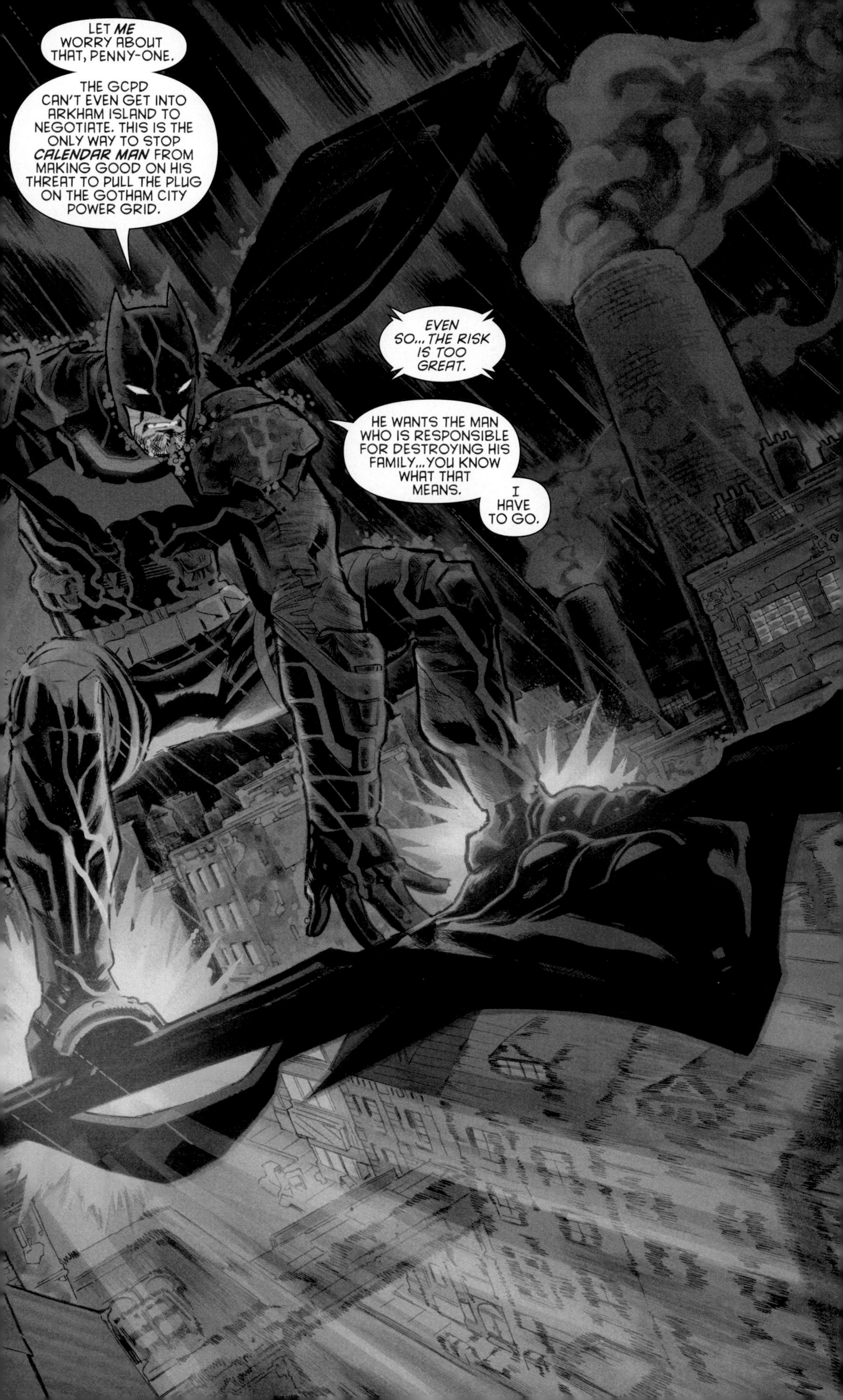
LET *ME* WORRY ABOUT THAT, PENNY-ONE.
THE GCPD CAN'T EVEN GET INTO ARKHAM ISLAND TO NEGOTIATE. THIS IS THE ONLY WAY TO STOP *CALENDAR MAN* FROM MAKING GOOD ON HIS THREAT TO PULL THE PLUG ON THE GOTHAM CITY POWER GRID.
EVEN SO...THE RISK IS TOO GREAT.
HE WANTS THE MAN WHO IS RESPONSIBLE FOR DESTROYING HIS FAMILY...YOU KNOW WHAT THAT MEANS.
I HAVE TO GO.

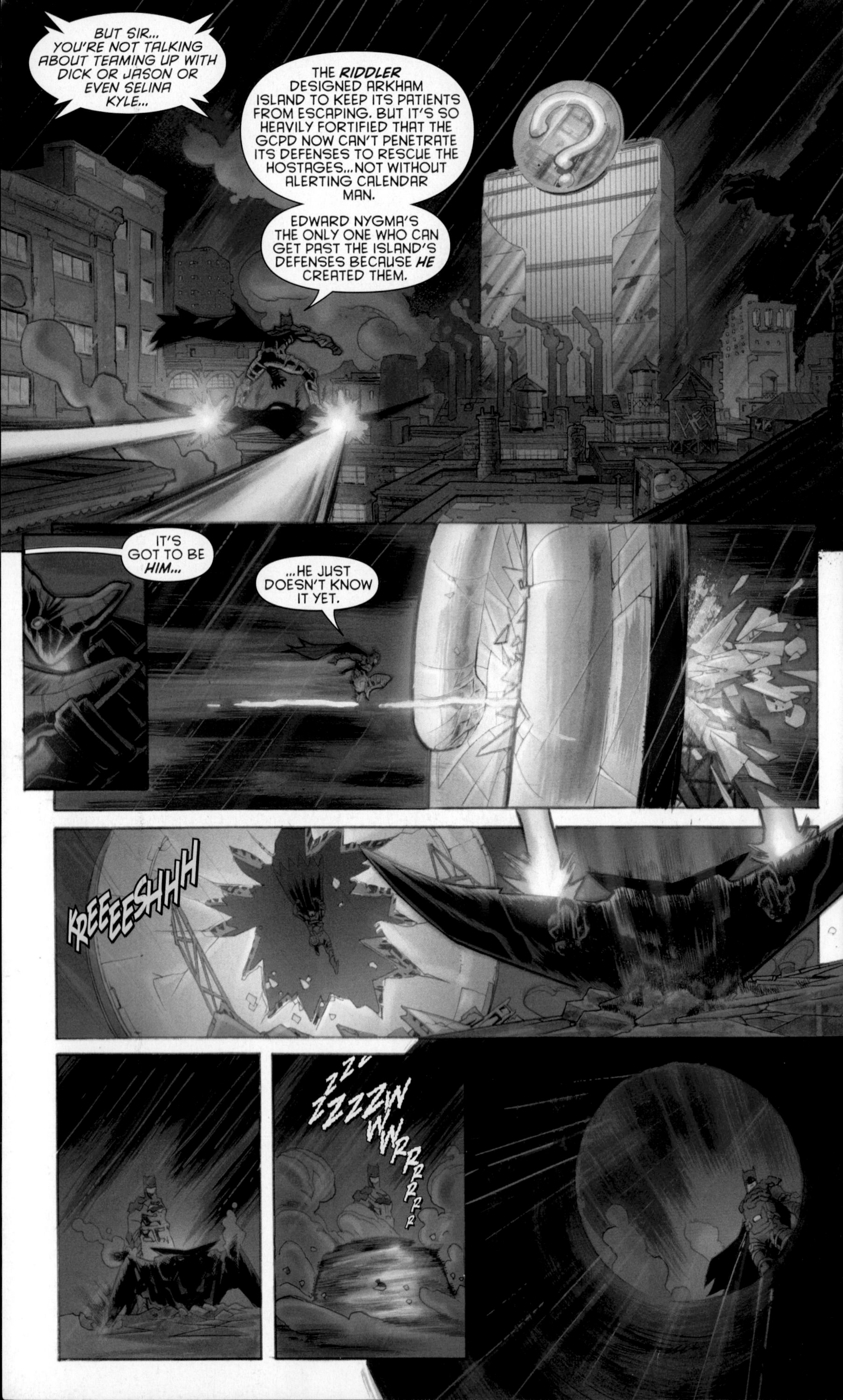

BUT SIR... YOU'RE NOT TALKING ABOUT TEAMING UP WITH DICK OR JASON OR EVEN SELINA KYLE...
THE RIDDLER DESIGNED ARKHAM ISLAND TO KEEP ITS PATIENTS FROM ESCAPING. BUT IT'S SO HEAVILY FORTIFIED THAT THE GCPD NOW CAN'T PENETRATE ITS DEFENSES TO RESCUE THE HOSTAGES...NOT WITHOUT ALERTING CALENDAR MAN.
EDWARD NYGMA'S THE ONLY ONE WHO CAN GET PAST THE ISLAND'S DEFENSES BECAUSE HE CREATED THEM.
IT'S GOT TO BE HIM...
...HE JUST DOESN'T KNOW IT YET.
KREEEESHHH
ZZZZZW WWRRRRRRRR

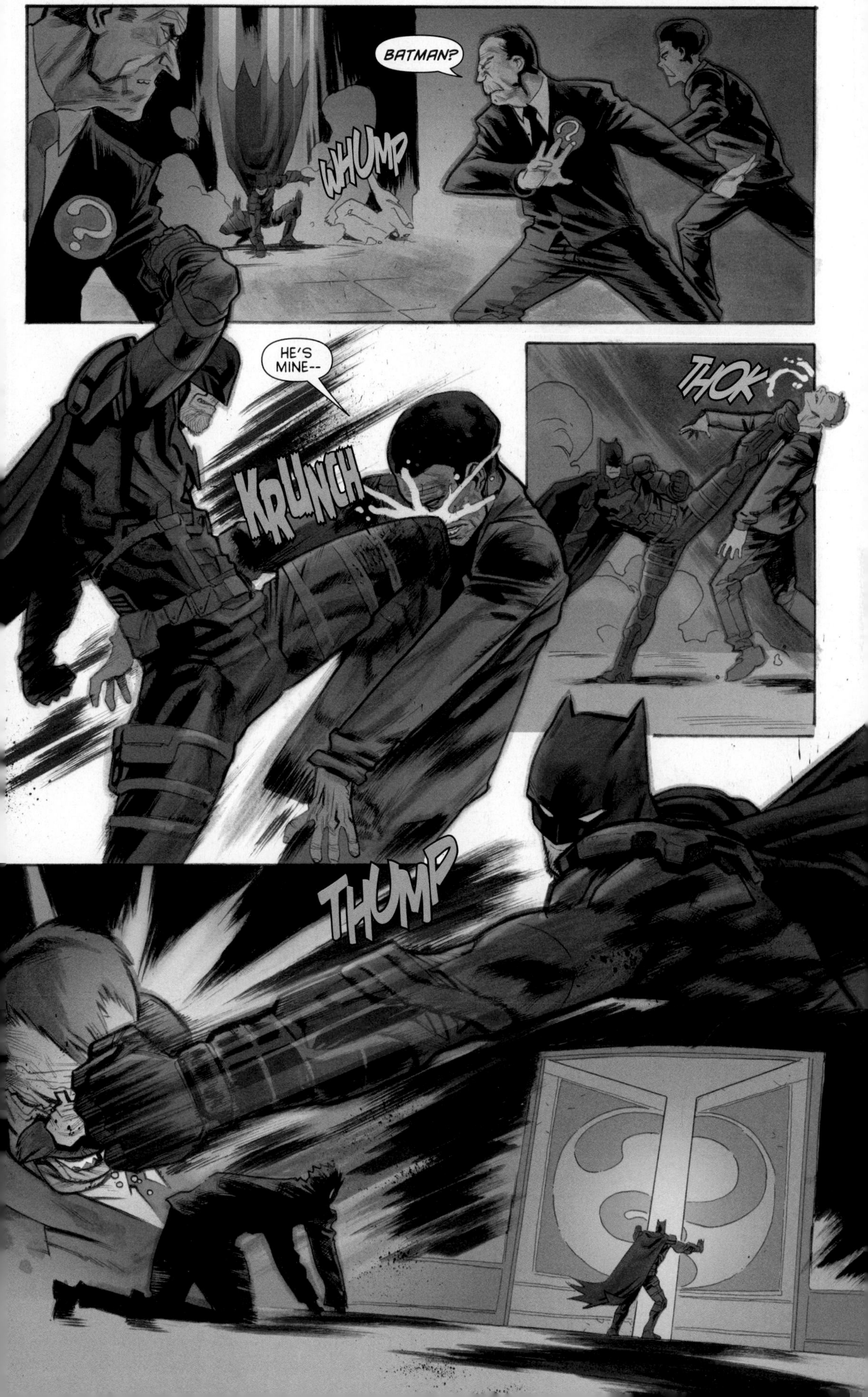
BATMAN?
WHUMP
HE'S MINE--
KRUNCH
THOK
THUMP

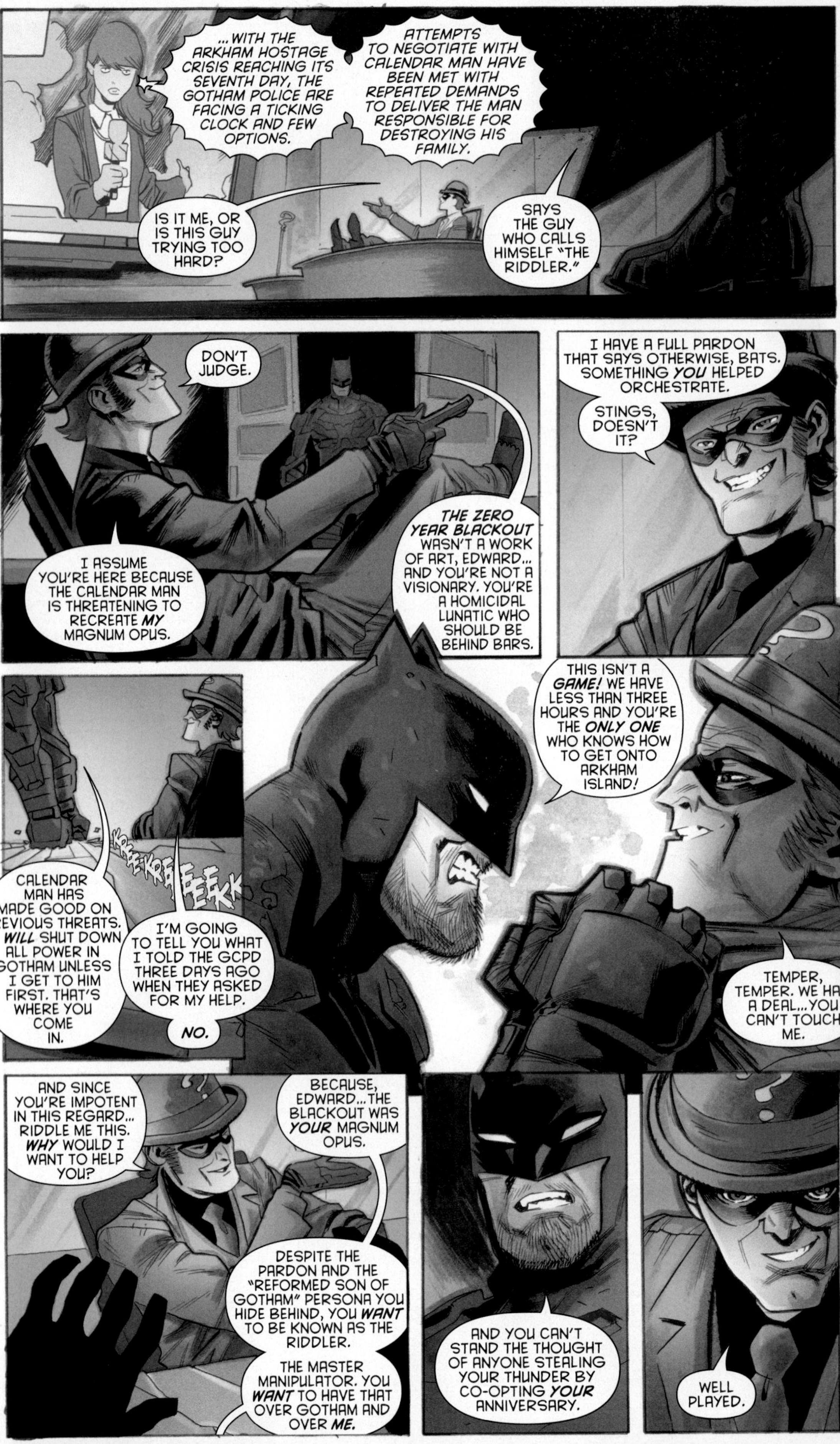
...WITH THE ARKHAM HOSTAGE CRISIS REACHING ITS SEVENTH DAY, THE GOTHAM POLICE ARE FACING A TICKING CLOCK AND FEW OPTIONS.
ATTEMPTS TO NEGOTIATE WITH CALENDAR MAN HAVE BEEN MET WITH REPEATED DEMANDS TO DELIVER THE MAN RESPONSIBLE FOR DESTROYING HIS FAMILY.
IS IT ME, OR IS THIS GUY TRYING TOO HARD?
SAYS THE GUY WHO CALLS HIMSELF "THE RIDDLER."
DON'T JUDGE.
I ASSUME YOU'RE HERE BECAUSE THE CALENDAR MAN IS THREATENING TO RECREATE *MY* MAGNUM OPUS.
THE ZERO YEAR BLACKOUT WASN'T A WORK OF ART, EDWARD... AND YOU'RE NOT A VISIONARY. YOU'RE A HOMICIDAL LUNATIC WHO SHOULD BE BEHIND BARS.
I HAVE A FULL PARDON THAT SAYS OTHERWISE, BATS. SOMETHING *YOU* HELPED ORCHESTRATE.
STINGS, DOESN'T IT?
CALENDAR MAN HAS MADE GOOD ON PREVIOUS THREATS. HE *WILL* SHUT DOWN ALL POWER IN GOTHAM UNLESS I GET TO HIM FIRST. THAT'S WHERE YOU COME IN.
KREEE-KREEEEEKK
I'M GOING TO TELL YOU WHAT I TOLD THE GCPD THREE DAYS AGO WHEN THEY ASKED FOR MY HELP.
NO.
THIS ISN'T A *GAME!* WE HAVE LESS THAN THREE HOURS AND YOU'RE THE *ONLY ONE* WHO KNOWS HOW TO GET ONTO ARKHAM ISLAND!
TEMPER, TEMPER. WE HA[D] A DEAL...YOU CAN'T TOUCH ME.
AND SINCE YOU'RE IMPOTENT IN THIS REGARD... RIDDLE ME THIS. *WHY* WOULD I WANT TO HELP YOU?
BECAUSE, EDWARD... THE BLACKOUT WAS *YOUR* MAGNUM OPUS.
DESPITE THE PARDON AND THE "REFORMED SON OF GOTHAM" PERSONA YOU HIDE BEHIND, YOU *WANT* TO BE KNOWN AS THE RIDDLER.
THE MASTER MANIPULATOR. YOU *WANT* TO HAVE THAT OVER GOTHAM AND OVER *ME.*
AND YOU CAN'T STAND THE THOUGHT OF ANYONE STEALING YOUR THUNDER BY CO-OPTING *YOUR* ANNIVERSARY.
WELL PLAYED.

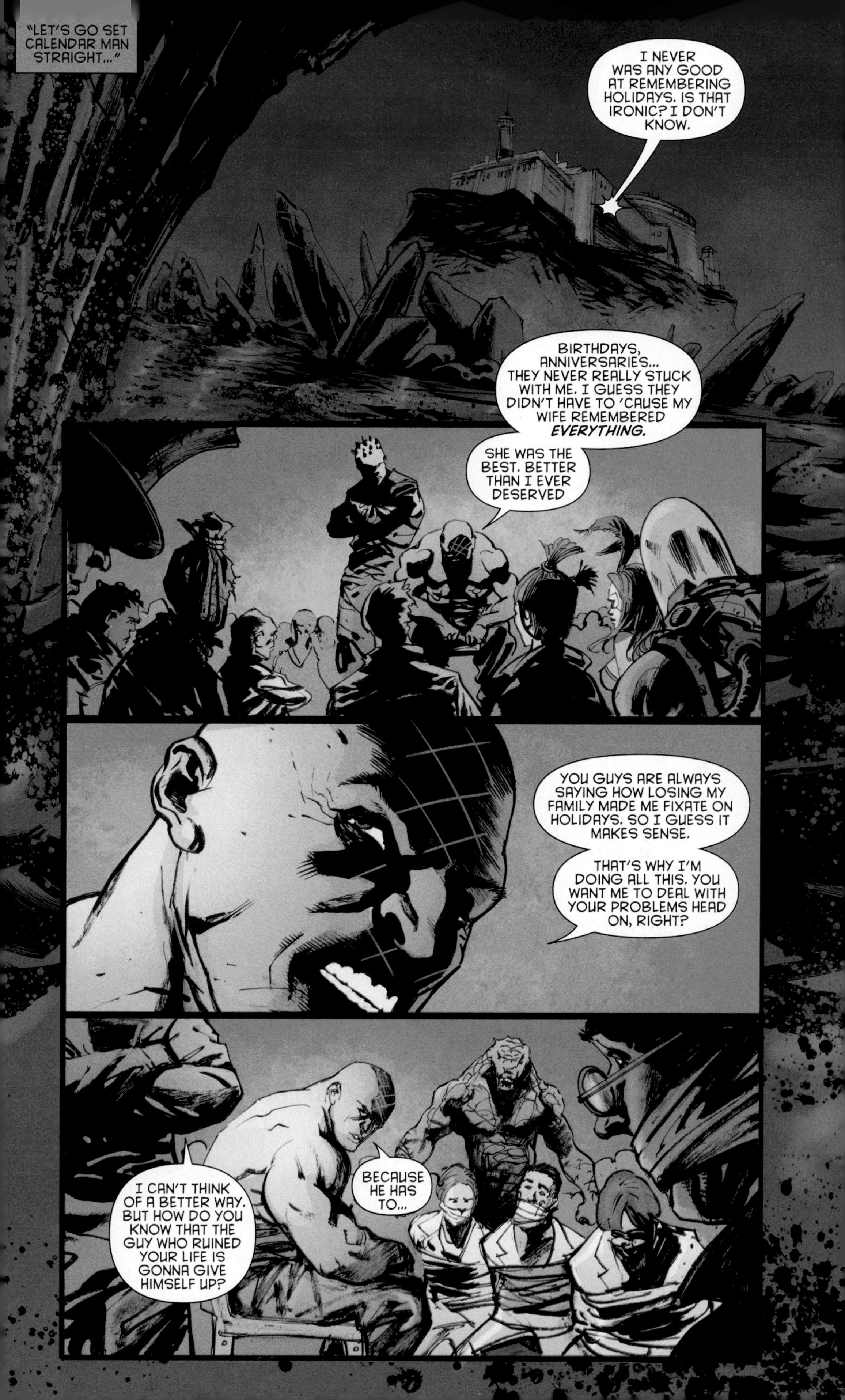
"LET'S GO SET CALENDAR MAN STRAIGHT..."
I NEVER WAS ANY GOOD AT REMEMBERING HOLIDAYS. IS THAT IRONIC? I DON'T KNOW.
BIRTHDAYS, ANNIVERSARIES... THEY NEVER REALLY STUCK WITH ME. I GUESS THEY DIDN'T HAVE TO 'CAUSE MY WIFE REMEMBERED *EVERYTHING.*
SHE WAS THE BEST. BETTER THAN I EVER DESERVED
YOU GUYS ARE ALWAYS SAYING HOW LOSING MY FAMILY MADE ME FIXATE ON HOLIDAYS. SO I GUESS IT MAKES SENSE.
THAT'S WHY I'M DOING ALL THIS. YOU WANT ME TO DEAL WITH YOUR PROBLEMS HEAD ON, RIGHT?
I CAN'T THINK OF A BETTER WAY. BUT HOW DO YOU KNOW THAT THE GUY WHO RUINED YOUR LIFE IS GONNA GIVE HIMSELF UP?
BECAUSE HE HAS TO...

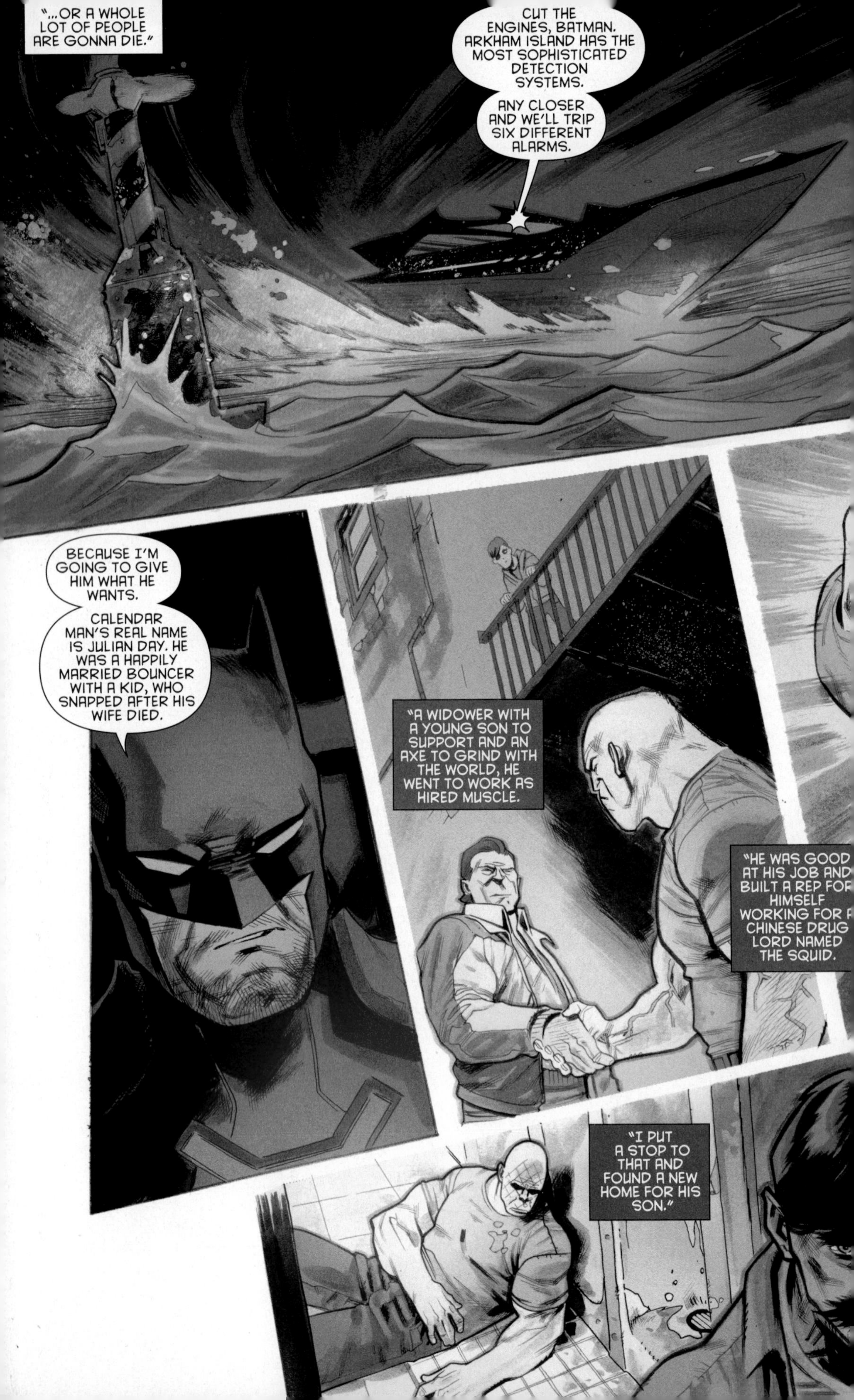
"...OR A WHOLE LOT OF PEOPLE ARE GONNA DIE."
CUT THE ENGINES, BATMAN. ARKHAM ISLAND HAS THE MOST SOPHISTICATED DETECTION SYSTEMS.
ANY CLOSER AND WE'LL TRIP SIX DIFFERENT ALARMS.
BECAUSE I'M GOING TO GIVE HIM WHAT HE WANTS.
CALENDAR MAN'S REAL NAME IS JULIAN DAY. HE WAS A HAPPILY MARRIED BOUNCER WITH A KID, WHO SNAPPED AFTER HIS WIFE DIED.
"A WIDOWER WITH A YOUNG SON TO SUPPORT AND AN AXE TO GRIND WITH THE WORLD, HE WENT TO WORK AS HIRED MUSCLE.
"HE WAS GOOD AT HIS JOB AND BUILT A REP FOR HIMSELF WORKING FOR A CHINESE DRUG LORD NAMED THE SQUID.
"I PUT A STOP TO THAT AND FOUND A NEW HOME FOR HIS SON."

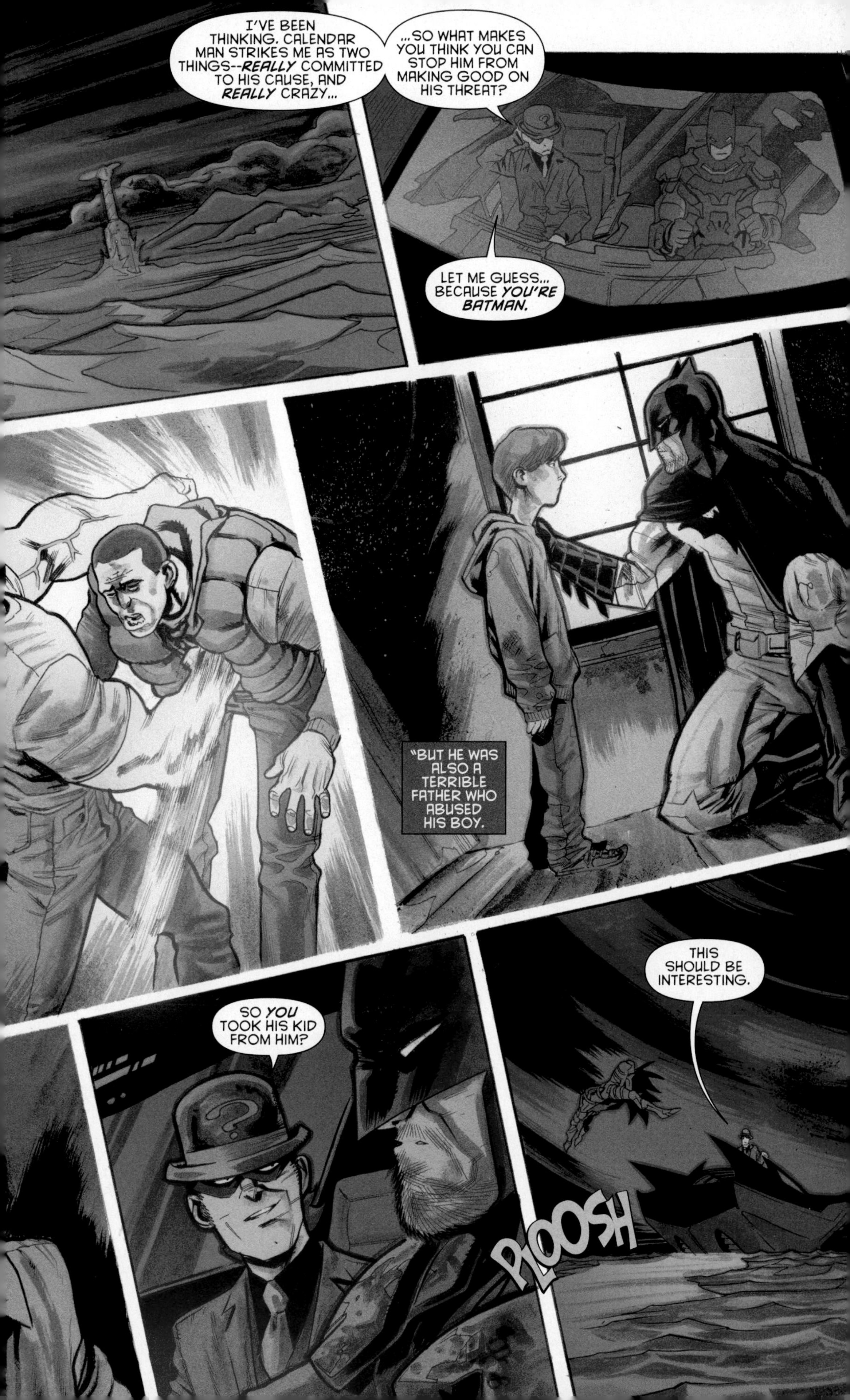
I'VE BEEN THINKING. CALENDAR MAN STRIKES ME AS TWO THINGS--REALLY COMMITTED TO HIS CAUSE, AND REALLY CRAZY...
...SO WHAT MAKES YOU THINK YOU CAN STOP HIM FROM MAKING GOOD ON HIS THREAT?
LET ME GUESS... BECAUSE YOU'RE BATMAN.
"BUT HE WAS ALSO A TERRIBLE FATHER WHO ABUSED HIS BOY.
SO YOU TOOK HIS KID FROM HIM?
THIS SHOULD BE INTERESTING.
PLOOSH

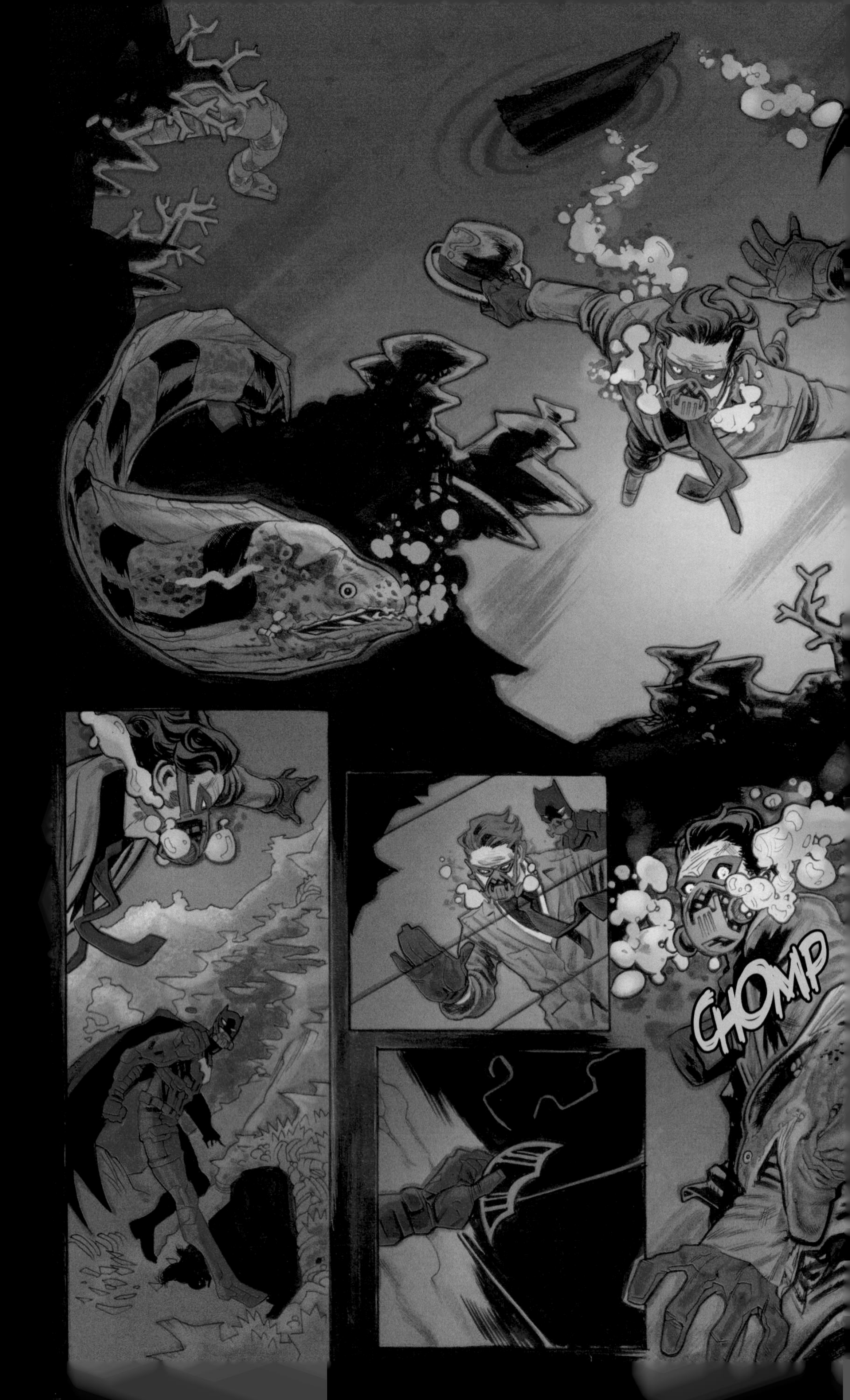
CHOMP

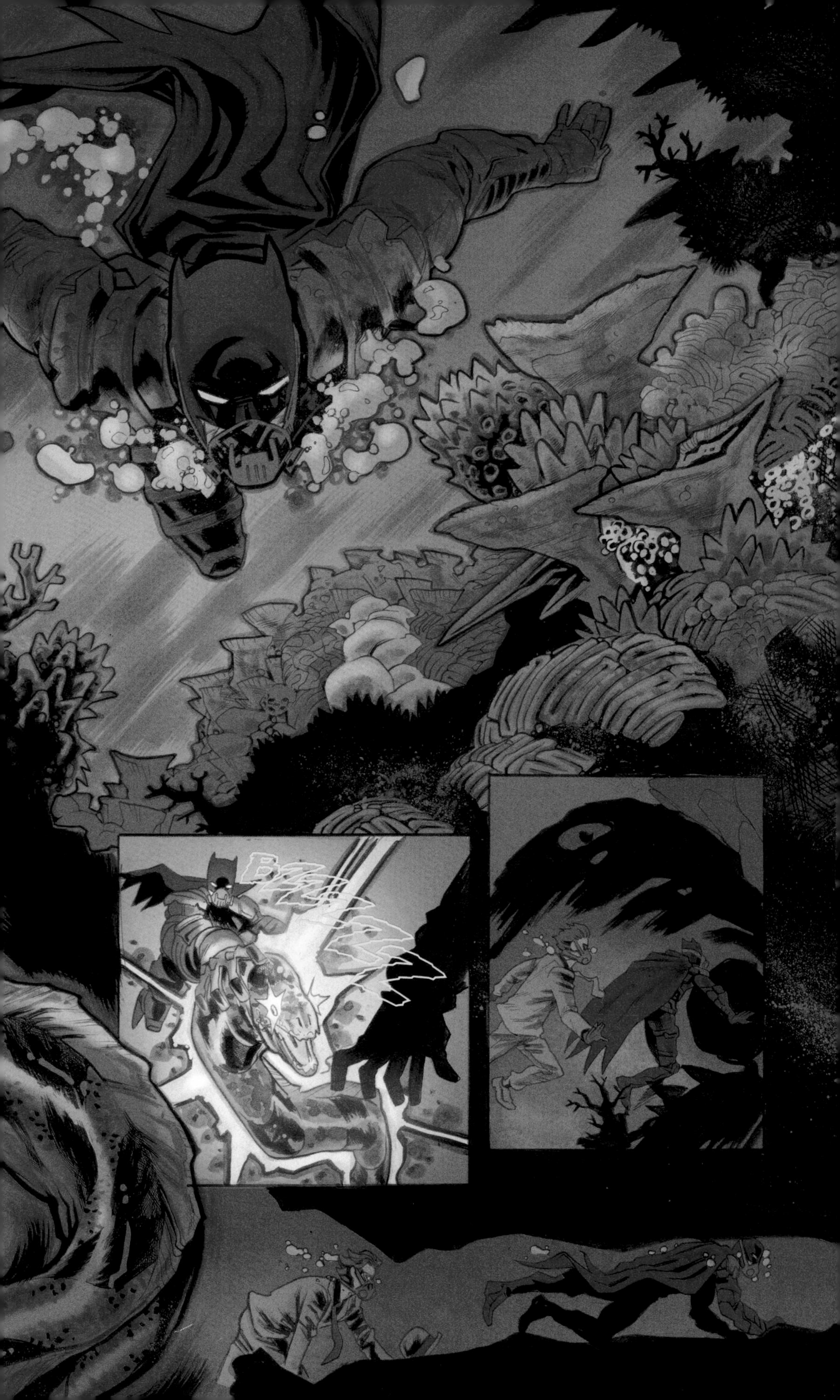

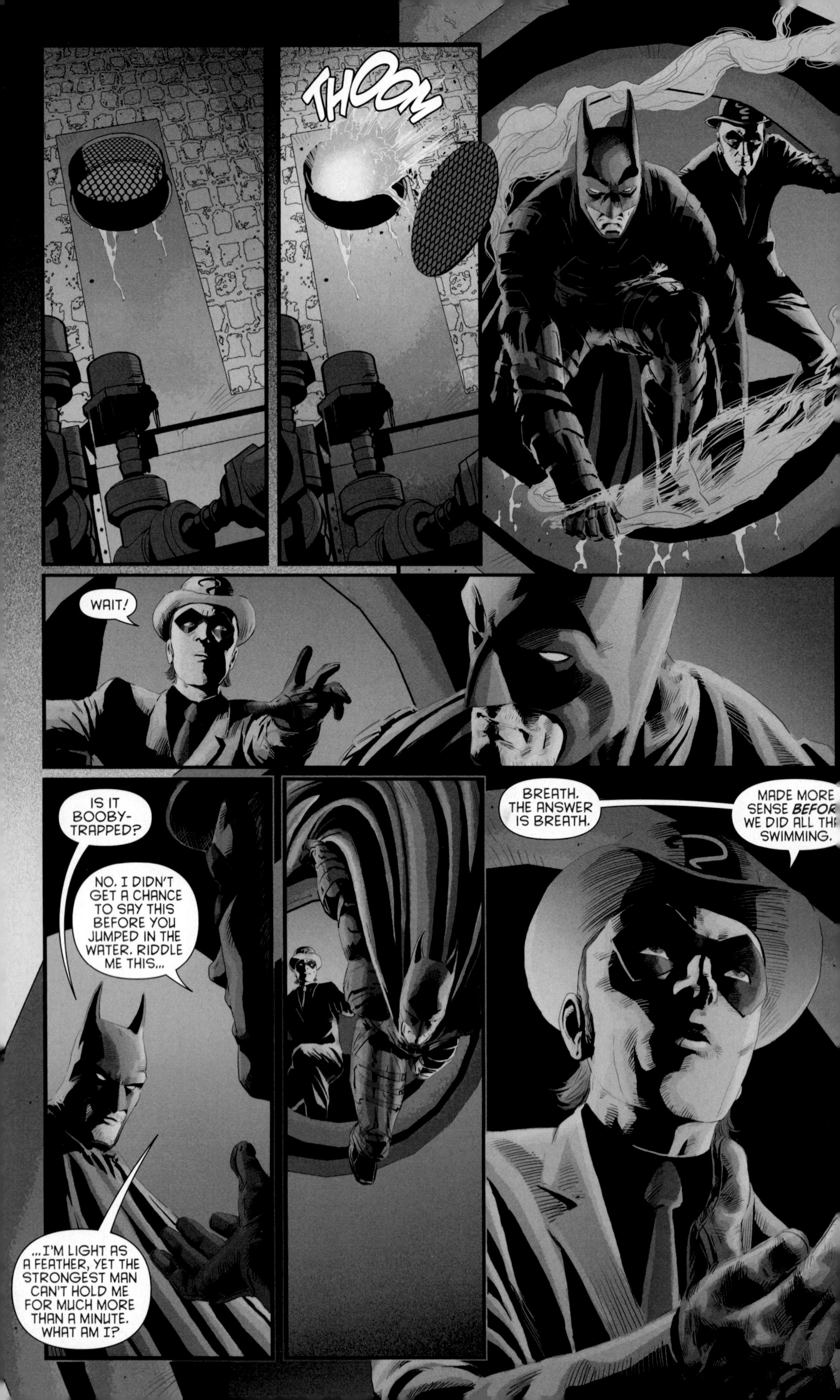

THOOM
WAIT!
IS IT BOOBY-TRAPPED?
NO. I DIDN'T GET A CHANCE TO SAY THIS BEFORE YOU JUMPED IN THE WATER. RIDDLE ME THIS...
...I'M LIGHT AS A FEATHER, YET THE STRONGEST MAN CAN'T HOLD ME FOR MUCH MORE THAN A MINUTE. WHAT AM I?
BREATH. THE ANSWER IS BREATH.
MADE MORE SENSE BEFOR
WE DID ALL TH
SWIMMING.

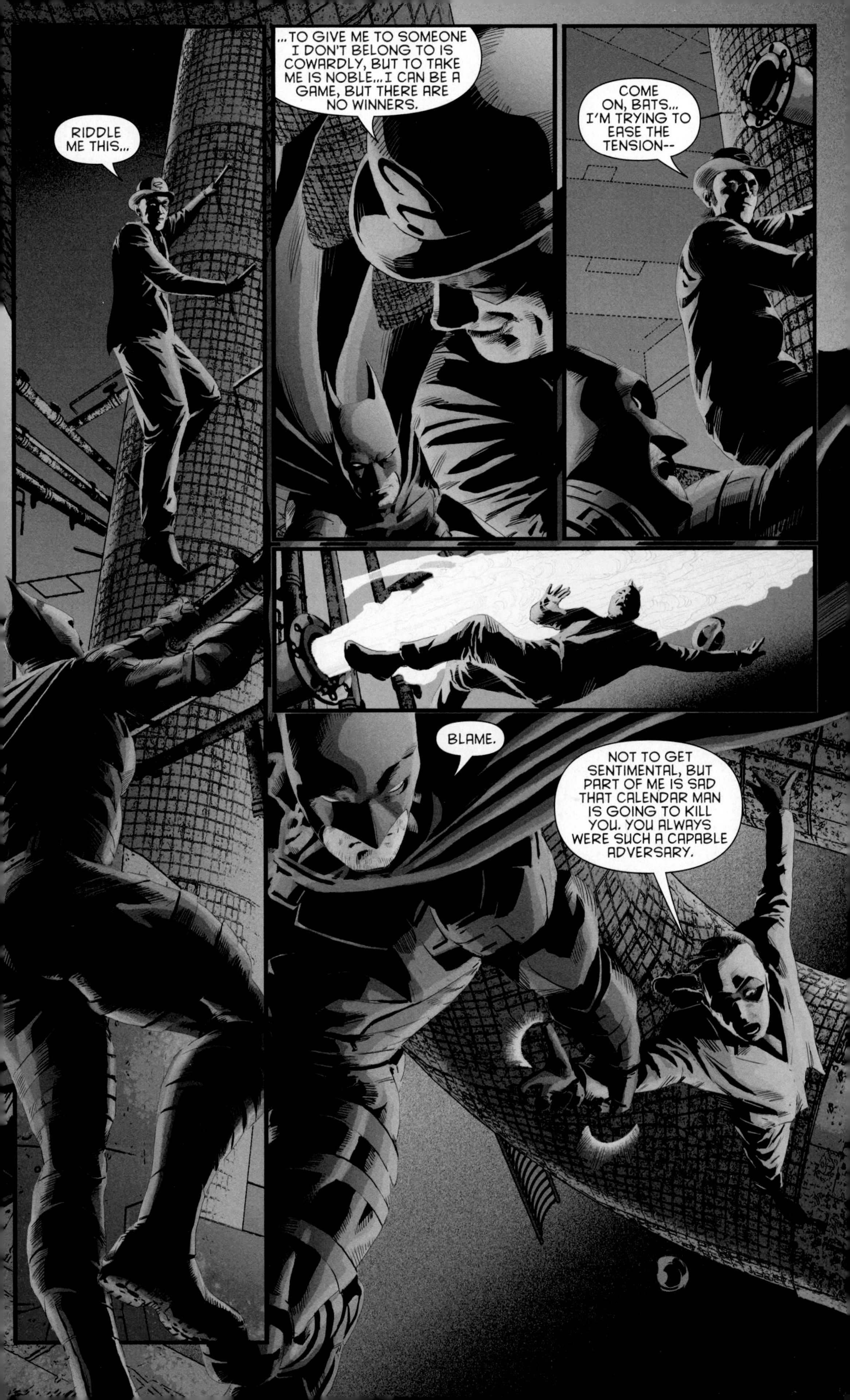
RIDDLE ME THIS...
...TO GIVE ME TO SOMEONE I DON'T BELONG TO IS COWARDLY, BUT TO TAKE ME IS NOBLE... I CAN BE A GAME, BUT THERE ARE NO WINNERS.
COME ON, BATS... I'M TRYING TO EASE THE TENSION--
BLAME.
NOT TO GET SENTIMENTAL, BUT PART OF ME IS SAD THAT CALENDAR MAN IS GOING TO KILL YOU. YOU ALWAYS WERE SUCH A CAPABLE ADVERSARY.

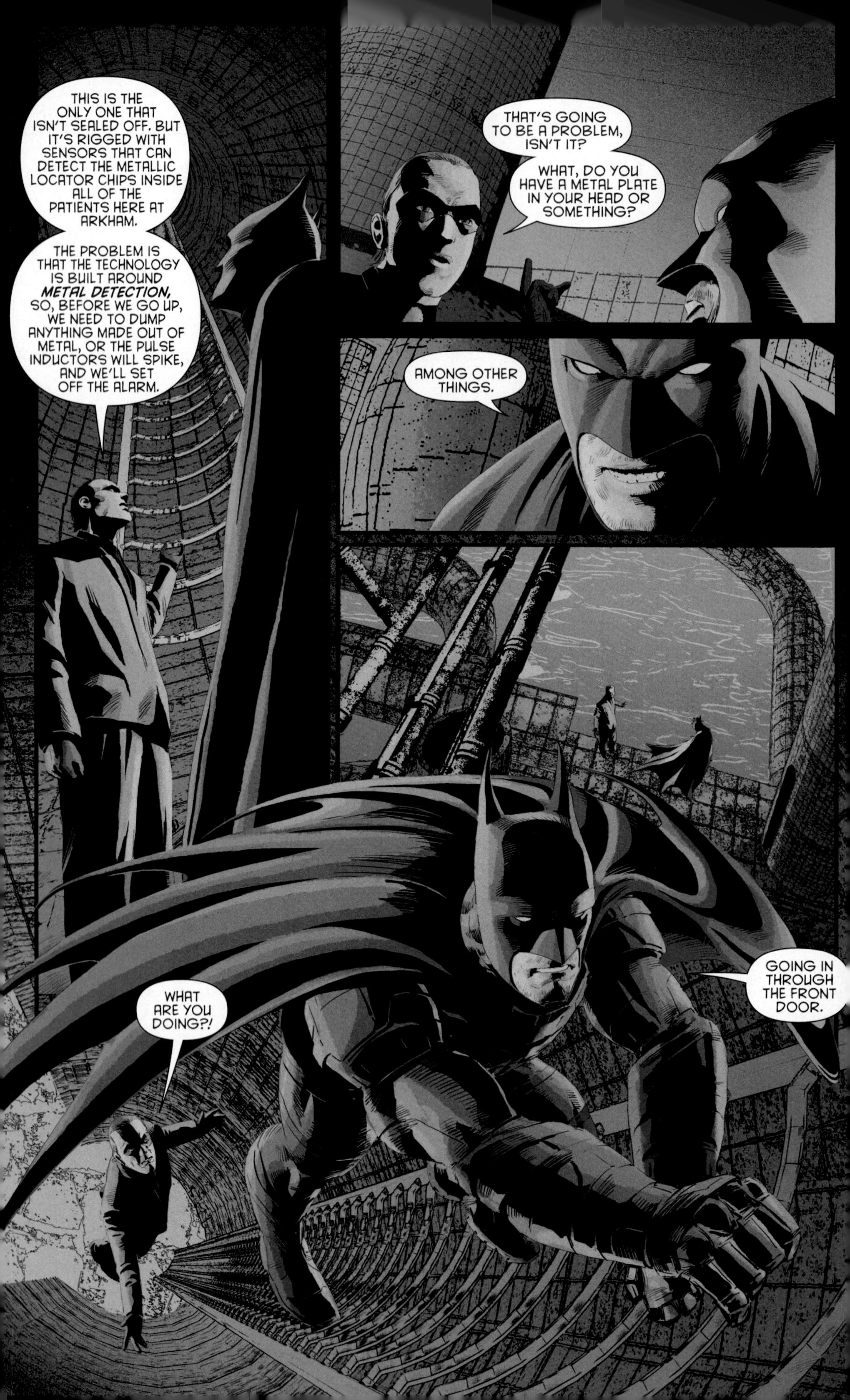
THIS IS THE ONLY ONE THAT ISN'T SEALED OFF. BUT IT'S RIGGED WITH SENSORS THAT CAN DETECT THE METALLIC LOCATOR CHIPS INSIDE ALL OF THE PATIENTS HERE AT ARKHAM.
THE PROBLEM IS THAT THE TECHNOLOGY IS BUILT AROUND *METAL DETECTION,* SO, BEFORE WE GO UP, WE NEED TO DUMP ANYTHING MADE OUT OF METAL, OR THE PULSE INDUCTORS WILL SPIKE, AND WE'LL SET OFF THE ALARM.
THAT'S GOING TO BE A PROBLEM, ISN'T IT?
WHAT, DO YOU HAVE A METAL PLATE IN YOUR HEAD OR SOMETHING?
AMONG OTHER THINGS.
GOING IN THROUGH THE FRONT DOOR.
WHAT ARE YOU DOING?!

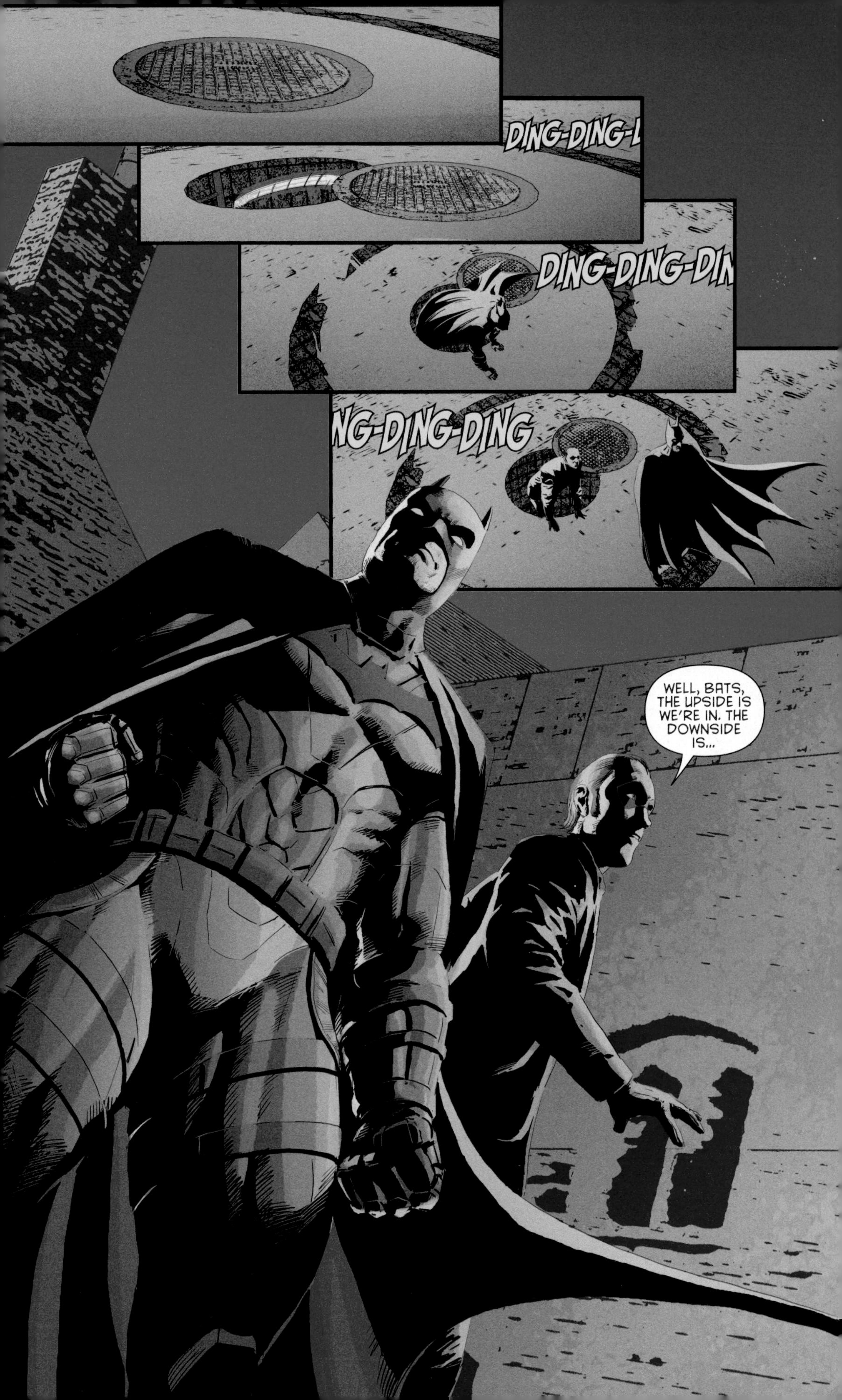
DING-DING-D
DING-DING-DIN
NG-DING-DING
WELL, BATS, THE UPSIDE IS WE'RE IN. THE DOWNSIDE IS...

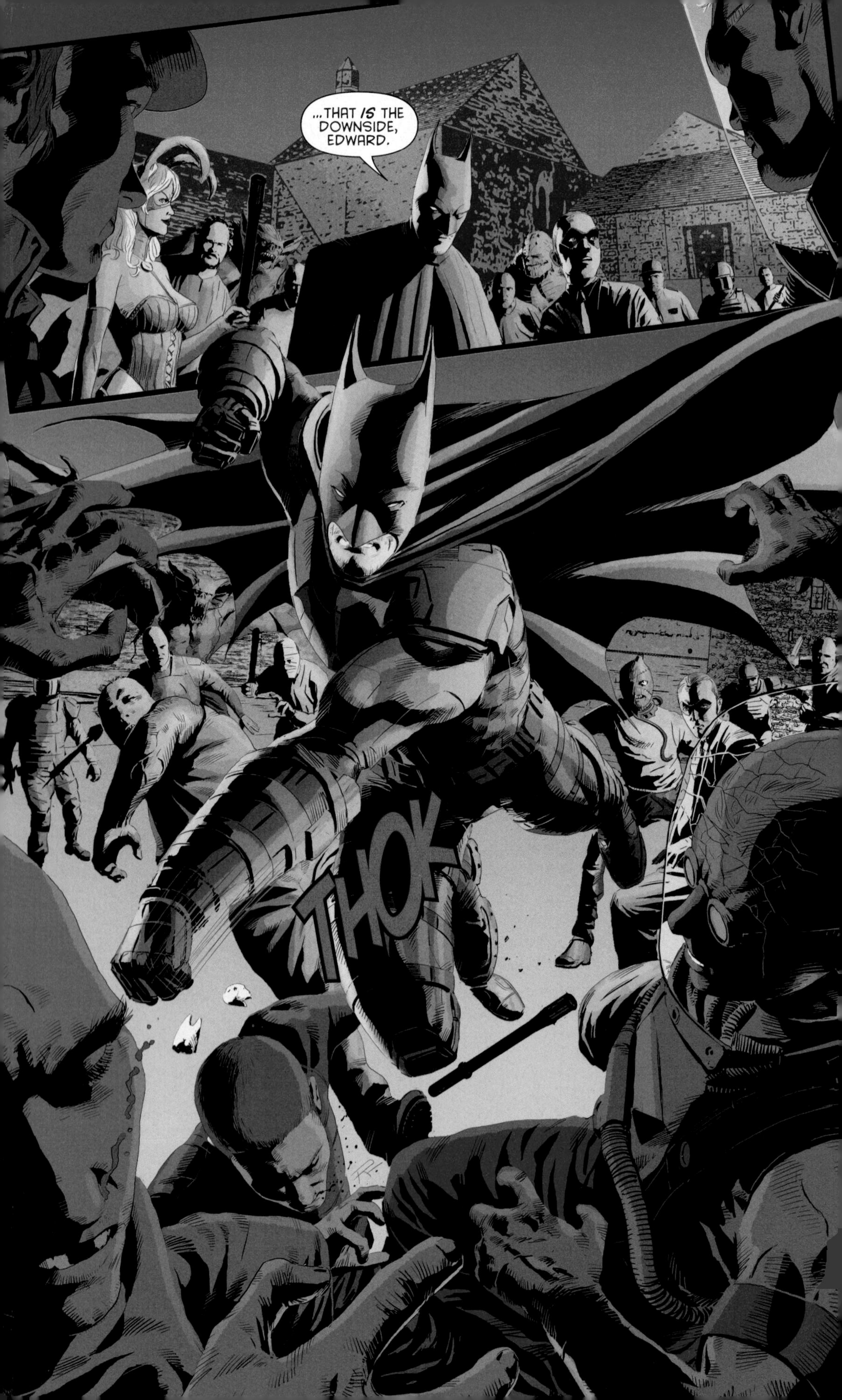
...THAT IS THE DOWNSIDE, EDWARD.
THOK

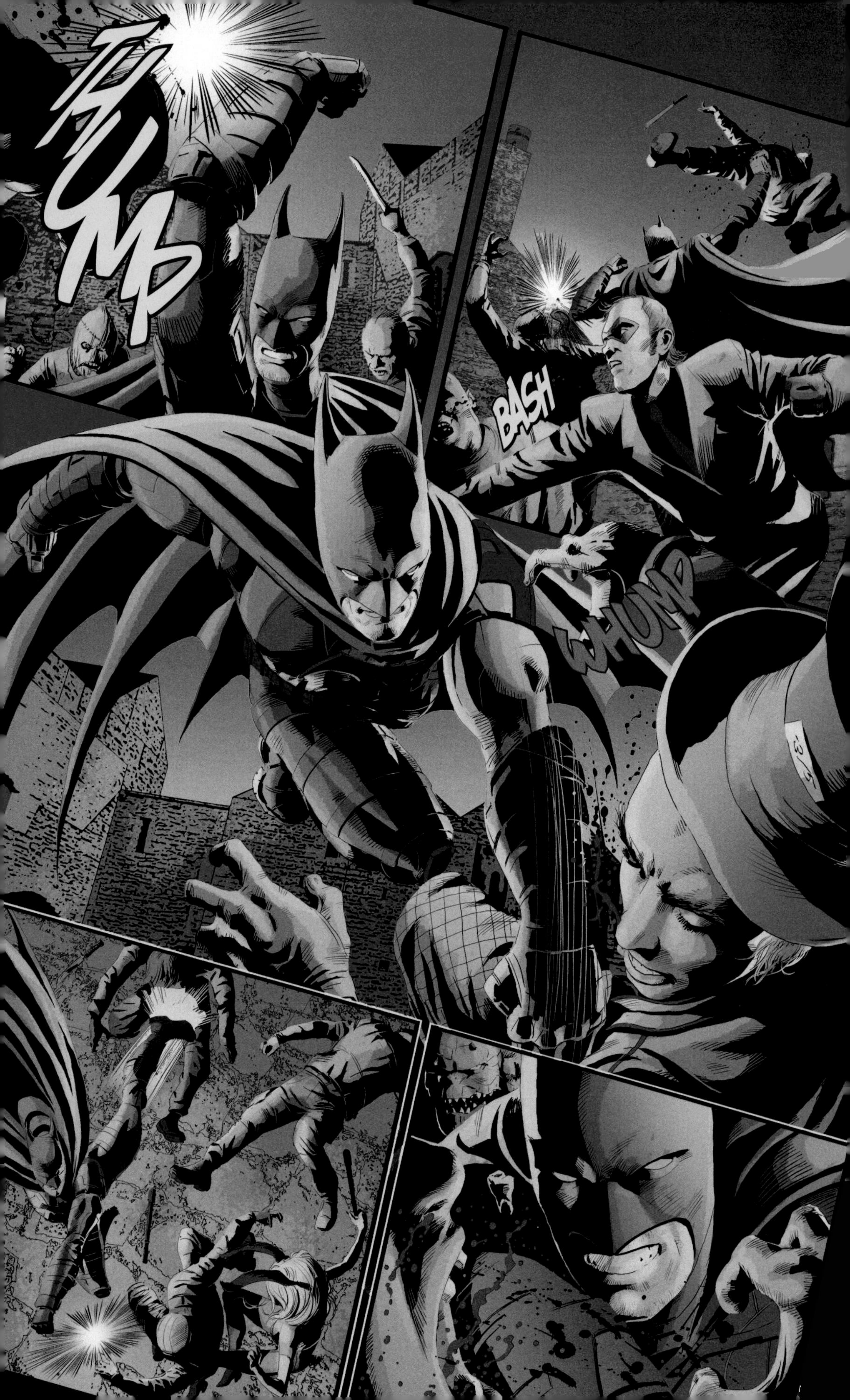
THUMP
BASH
WHUMP
3/5

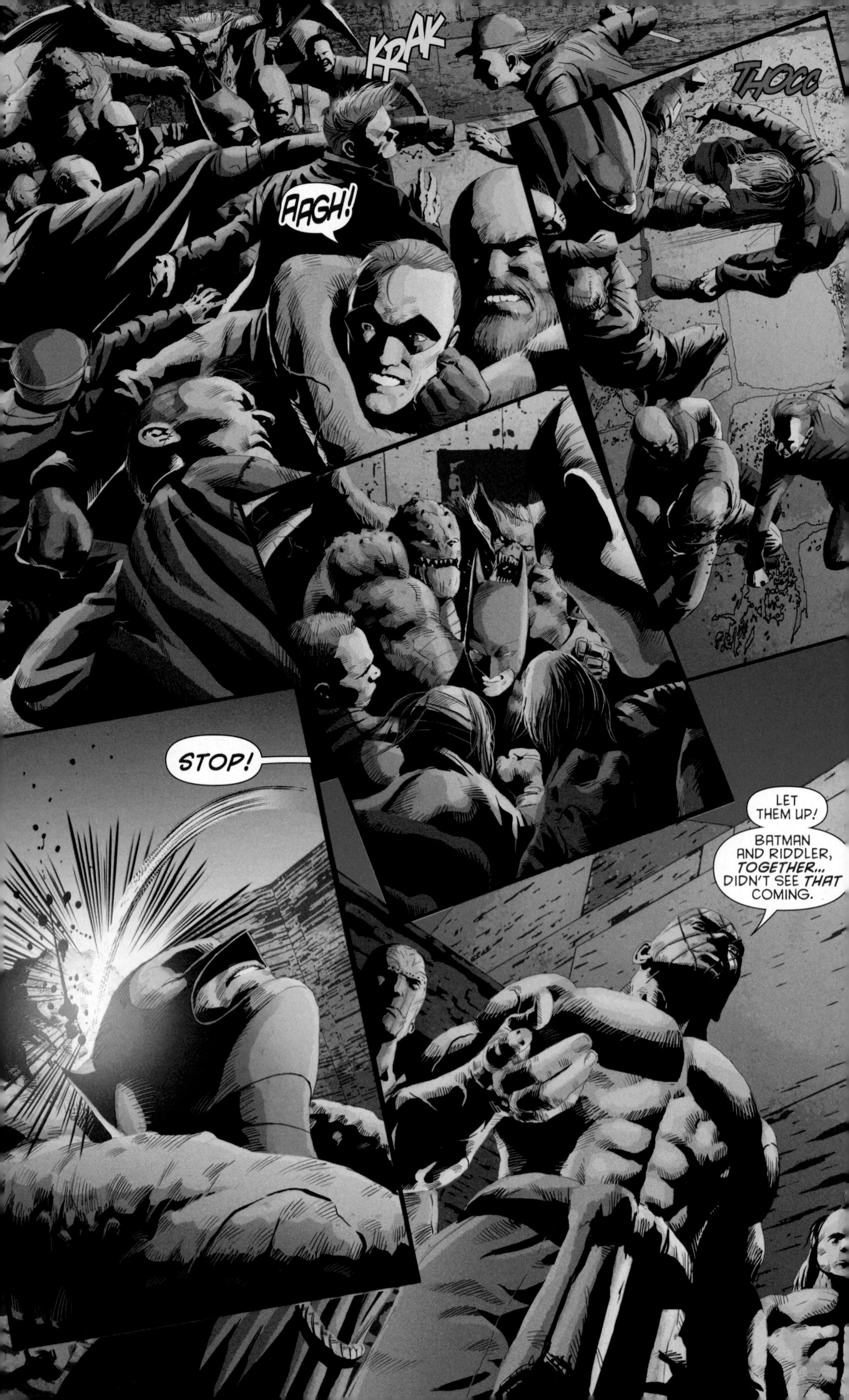
KRAK
THOCC
AAGH!
STOP!
LET THEM UP!
BATMAN AND RIDDLER, *TOGETHER*... DIDN'T SEE *THAT* COMING.

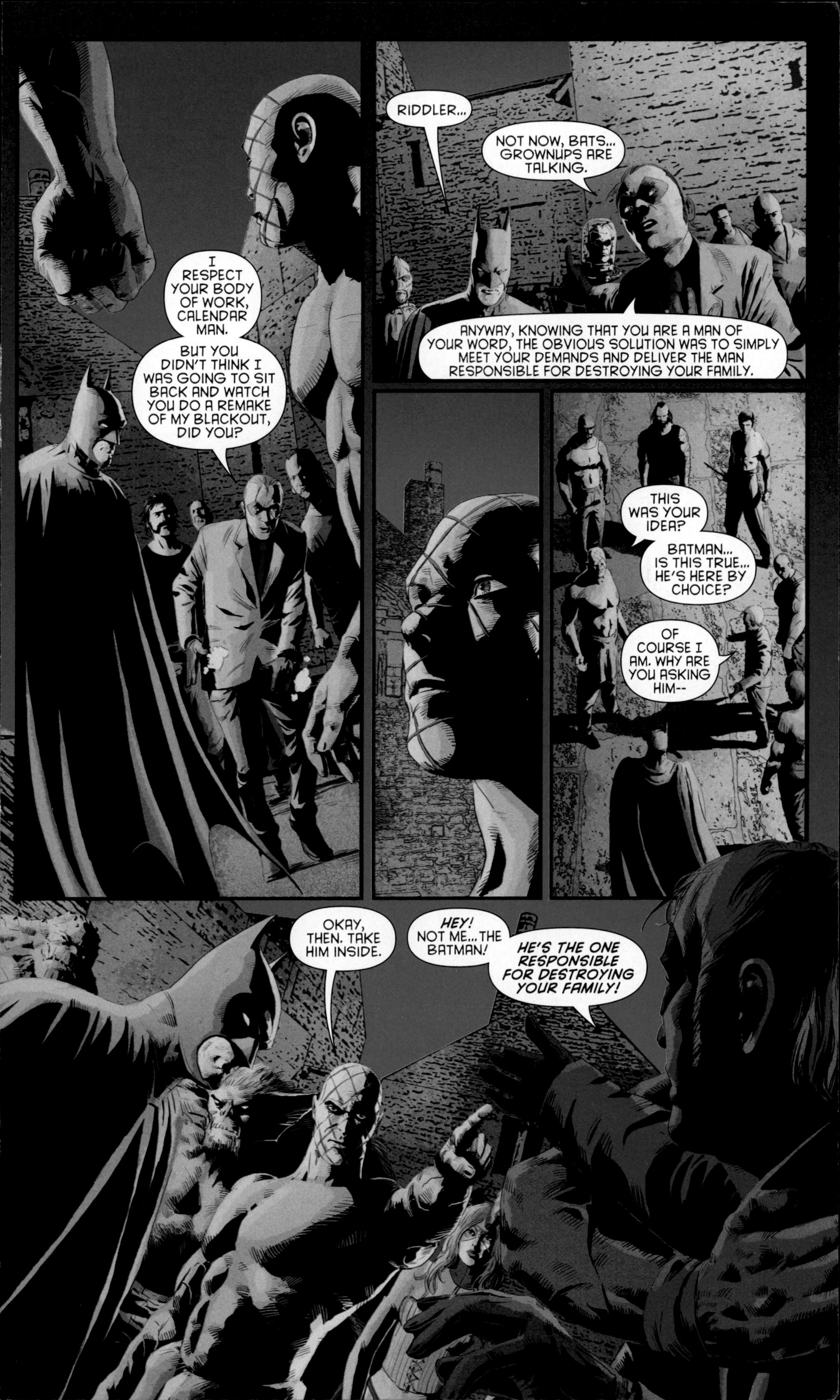
I RESPECT YOUR BODY OF WORK, CALENDAR MAN.
BUT YOU DIDN'T THINK I WAS GOING TO SIT BACK AND WATCH YOU DO A REMAKE OF MY BLACKOUT, DID YOU?
RIDDLER...
NOT NOW, BATS... GROWNUPS ARE TALKING.
ANYWAY, KNOWING THAT YOU ARE A MAN OF YOUR WORD, THE OBVIOUS SOLUTION WAS TO SIMPLY MEET YOUR DEMANDS AND DELIVER THE MAN RESPONSIBLE FOR DESTROYING YOUR FAMILY.
THIS WAS YOUR IDEA?
BATMAN... IS THIS TRUE... HE'S HERE BY CHOICE?
OF COURSE I AM. WHY ARE YOU ASKING HIM--
OKAY, THEN. TAKE HIM INSIDE.
HEY! NOT ME... THE BATMAN!
HE'S THE ONE RESPONSIBLE FOR DESTROYING YOUR FAMILY!

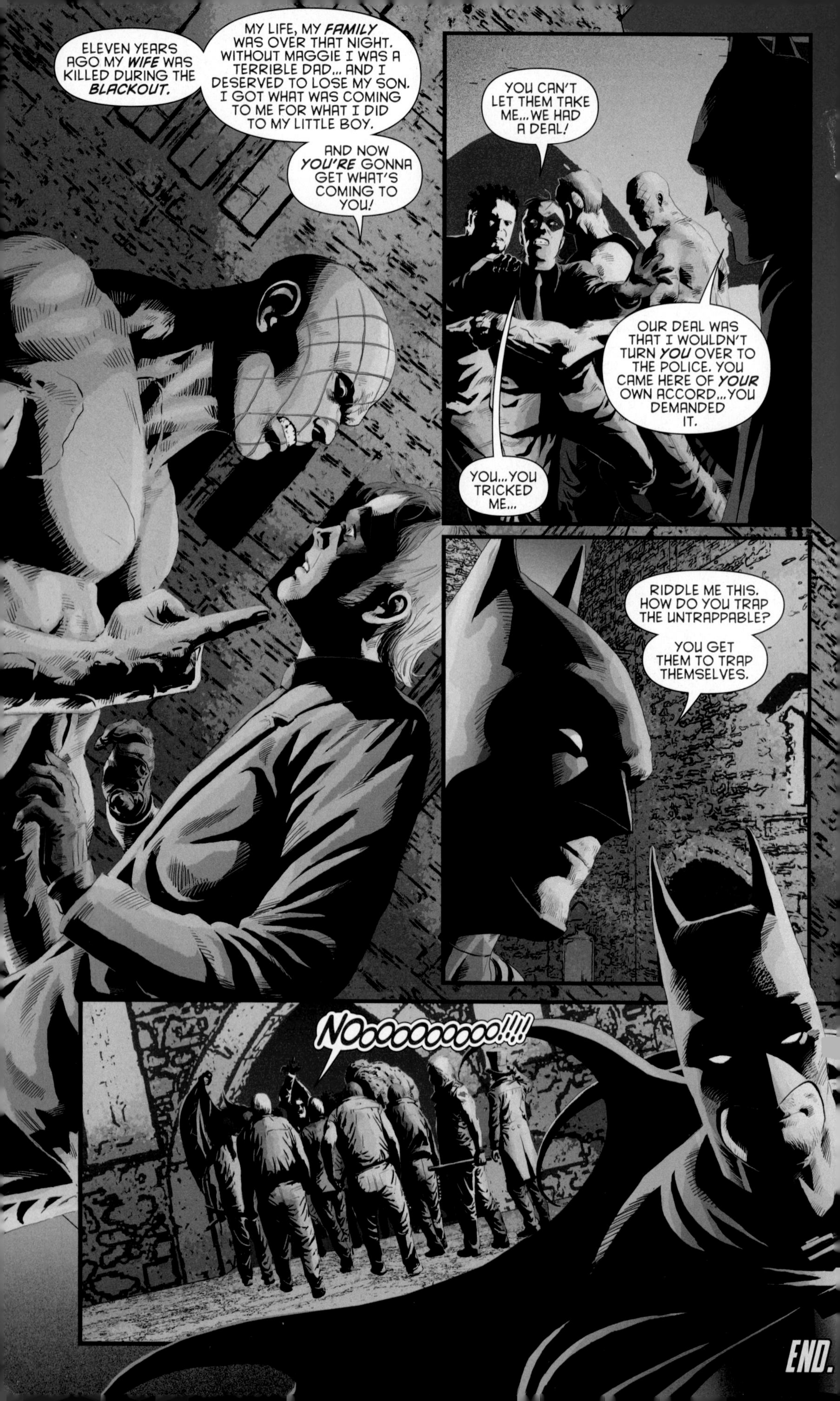
ELEVEN YEARS AGO MY *WIFE* WAS KILLED DURING THE *BLACKOUT.*
MY LIFE, MY *FAMILY* WAS OVER THAT NIGHT. WITHOUT MAGGIE I WAS A TERRIBLE DAD... AND I DESERVED TO LOSE MY SON. I GOT WHAT WAS COMING TO ME FOR WHAT I DID TO MY LITTLE BOY.
AND NOW *YOU'RE* GONNA GET WHAT'S COMING TO YOU!
YOU CAN'T LET THEM TAKE ME...WE HAD A DEAL!
OUR DEAL WAS THAT I WOULDN'T TURN *YOU* OVER TO THE POLICE. YOU CAME HERE OF *YOUR* OWN ACCORD...YOU DEMANDED IT.
YOU...YOU TRICKED ME...
RIDDLE ME THIS. HOW DO YOU TRAP THE UNTRAPPABLE?
YOU GET THEM TO TRAP THEMSELVES.
NOOOOOOOOOOO!!!!
END.

"This is your go-to book."—ENTERTAINMENT WEEKLY

"DETECTIVE COMICS is head-spinningly spectacular from top to bottom."—MTV GEEK

START AT THE BEGINNING!

BATMAN: DETECTIVE COMICS VOLUME 1: FACES OF DEATH

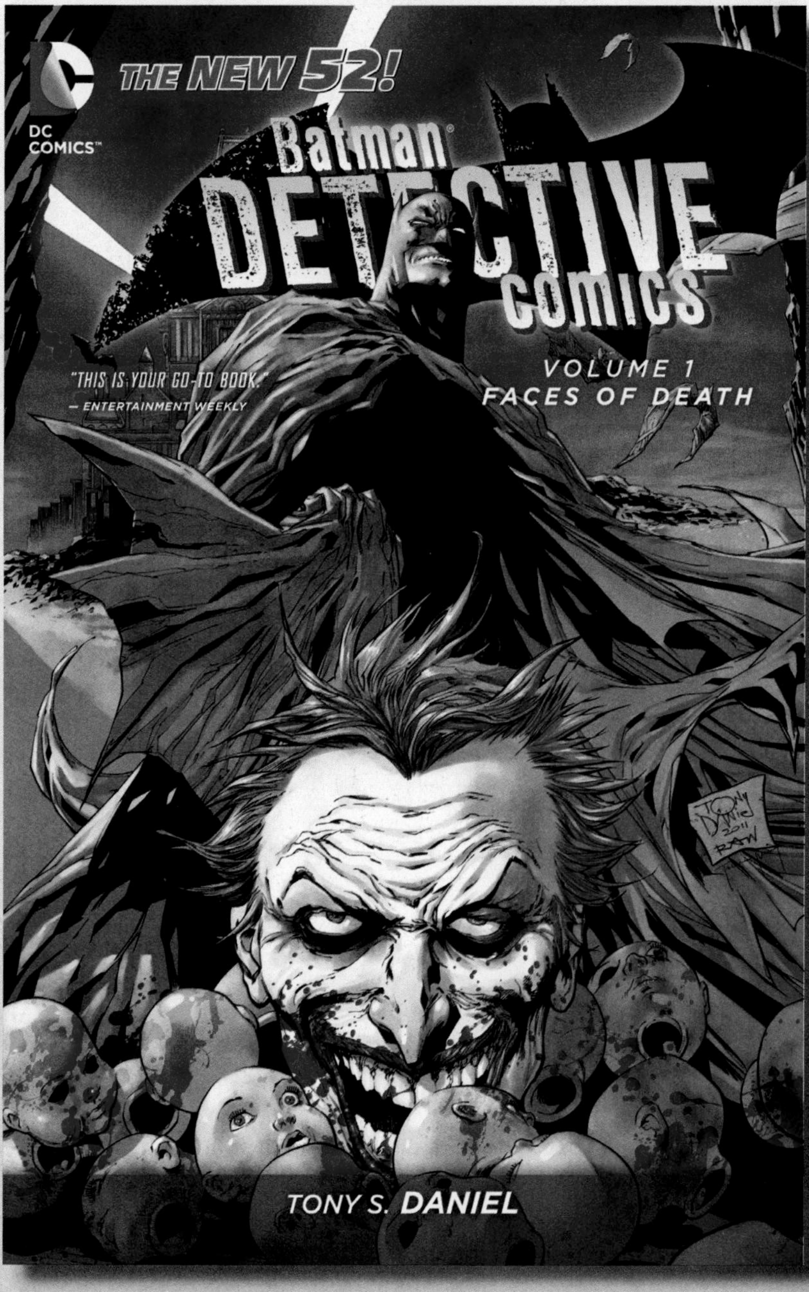
THE NEW 52!
DC COMICS
Batman
DETECTIVE
COMICS
"THIS IS YOUR GO-TO BOOK."
— ENTERTAINMENT WEEKLY
VOLUME 1
FACES OF DEATH
TONY S. DANIEL

BATMAN: DETECTIVE COMICS VOL. 2: SCARE TACTICS

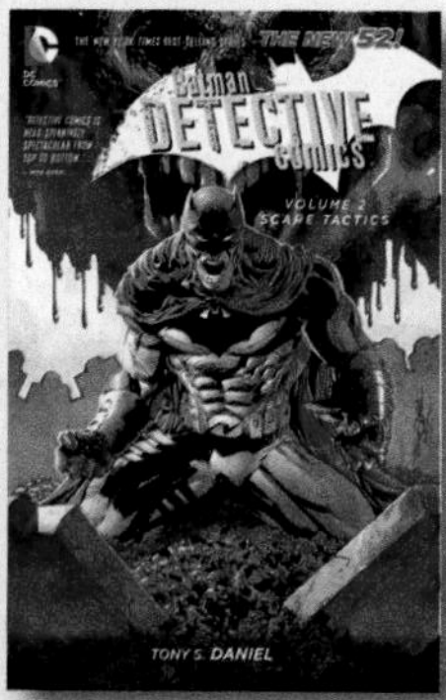
THE NEW 52!
Batman
DETECTIVE
COMICS
TONY S. DANIEL

BATMAN: DETECTIVE COMICS VOL. 3: EMPEROR PENGUIN

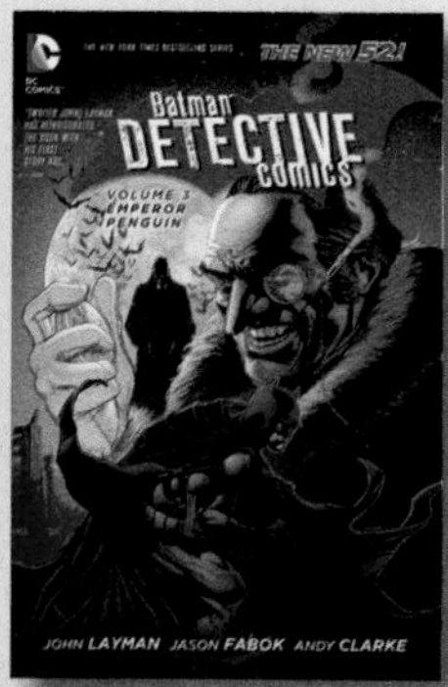
THE NEW 52!
Batman
DETECTIVE
COMICS
JOHN LAYMAN JASON FABOK ANDY CLARKE

THE JOKER: DEATH OF THE FAMILY

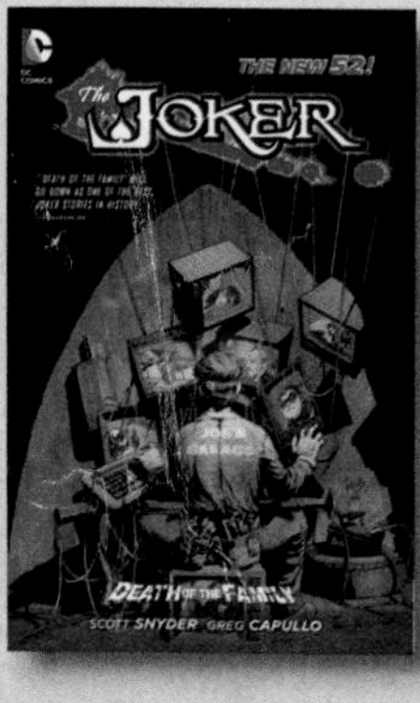
THE NEW 52!
The JOKER
DEATH OF THE FAMILY
SCOTT SNYDER GREG CAPULLO

"Compelling drama. A great example of the literary and artistic maturity of the graphic novel format."
—SCHOOL LIBRARY JOURNAL

FROM THE *NEW YORK TIMES* BEST-SELLING WRITERS

ED BRUBAKER & GREG RUCKA

with MICHAEL LARK

GOTHAM CENTRAL
BOOK TWO:
JOKERS AND MADMEN

GOTHAM CENTRAL
BOOK THREE:
ON THE FREAK BEAT

GOTHAM CENTRAL
BOOK FOUR:
CORRIGAN

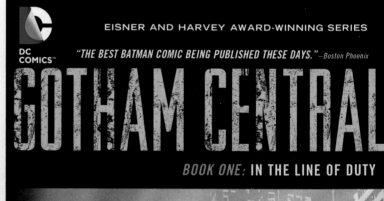

EISNER AND HARVEY AWARD-WINNING SERIES

"THE BEST BATMAN COMIC BEING PUBLISHED THESE DAYS." —Boston Phoenix

GOTHAM CENTRAL

BOOK ONE: IN THE LINE OF DUTY

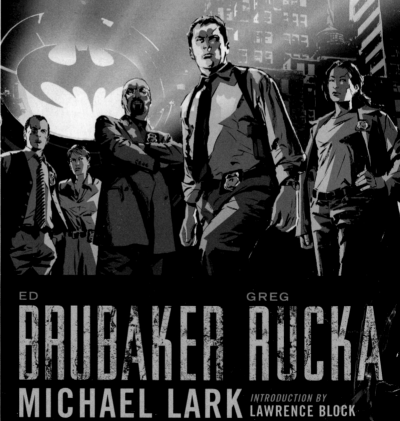

ED BRUBAKER GREG RUCKA

MICHAEL LARK INTRODUCTION BY LAWRENCE BLOCK